THE FATHERS
OF THE CHURCH

A NEW TRANSLATION

VOLUME 82

THE FATHERS
OF THE CHURCH

A NEW TRANSLATION

SAINT
JOHN CHRYSOSTOM

HOMILIES ON GENESIS
18–45

Translated by

ROBERT C. HILL
School of Divinity
The University of Sydney

THE CATHOLIC UNIVERSITY OF AMERICA PRESS
Washington, D.C.

Copyright © 1990
THE CATHOLIC UNIVERSITY OF AMERICA PRESS, INC.
All rights reserved

LIBRARY OF CONGRESS CATALOGING-IN-PUBLICATION DATA

(Revised for volume 2)
John Chrysostom, Saint, d. 407.
    Homilies on Genesis.

    (The Fathers of the Church ; vv. 74, 82)
    Translation of: Homiliai eis ten Genesin.
    Bibliography: p. vii–viii.
    Contents: v. 1. Homilies 1–17—v. 2. 18–45.
        1. Bible. O.T.—Genesis—Sermons.   2. Sermons,
English—Translations from Greek.   3. Sermons, Greek—
Translations into English.   I. Title.   II. Series:
Fathers of the church ; v. 74, etc.
    ~~BR60.F3 JO 16 BS1235~~   270 s 222′.1106   85–27988
    ISBN 0–8132–0074–1 (vol. 1)
    ISBN 0–8132–082–2 (vol. 2)

To my wife Marie

CONTENTS

viiiCONTENTS

ABBREVIATIONS

"Akribeia"	Hill, Robert C., *"Akribeia*: a principle of Chrysostom's exegesis," *Colloquium* 14 (October, 1981), pp. 32–36.
CCG	*Corpus Christianorum. Series graeca.* Turnhout: Brepols, 1976–.
CPG	*Clavis Patrum Graecorum*, Vol. II. ed. M. Geerard. Turnhout: Brepols, 1974.
DBS	*Dictionnaire de la Bible. Supplément*, ed. L. Pirot. Paris, 1928– .
FOTC	The Fathers of the Church. New York and Washington, D.C., 1947–.
"horses"	Hill, Robert C., "On giving up horses for Lent," *Clergy Review* 68 (March, 1983), pp. 105–106.
"Incarnation"	Hill, Robert C., "Saint John Chrysostom and the Incarnation of the Word in Scripture," *Compass Theology Review* 14 (1980), pp. 34–38.
Inspiration	Hill, Robert C., *Saint John Chrysostom's Teaching on Inspiration in his Old Testament Homilies.* Sydney, 1981.
JThS	*The Journal of Theological Studies.* London, 1899–.
ODCC	*The Oxford Dictionary of the Christian Church.* 2d ed. ed. F. L. Cross and E. A. Livingstone. Oxford, 1984.
PG	*Patrologiae cursus completus: Series graeca*, 161 volumes. ed. J. P. Migne. Paris, 1857–1866.
SC	*Sources Chrétiennes*, ed. H. de Lubac and J. Daniélou. Paris, 1942–.
SP	*Studia Patristica.* International Conference on Patristic Studies at Oxford. (Berlin, and elsewhere)
"sunkatabasis"	Hill, Robert C., "On looking again at *sunkatabasis*," *Prudentia* 13 (1981), pp. 3–11.
"terminology"	Hill, Robert C., "Chrysostom's terminology for the inspired Word," *Estudios Biblicos* 41 (1983), pp. 367–373.
TRE	*Theologische Realenzyklopädie*

Abbreviations of Classical and Patristic texts follow OCD and ODCC.

HOMILIES
18–45

*Homilies 1–17 of Saint John Chrysostom are in
Volume 74 of* The Fathers of the Church *series.*

HOMILY 18

"Adam gave his wife the name Zoe, because she was the mother of all the living. The Lord God made garments of skin for Adam and his wife and clad them in them. God said, 'Lo, Adam has become like one of us.'"[1]

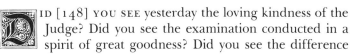ID [148] YOU SEE yesterday the loving kindness of the Judge? Did you see the examination conducted in a spirit of great goodness? Did you see the difference in the kinds of punishment—how the one who caused their downfall by means of deceit was punished, on the one hand, and how, on the other hand, the punishment inflicted on the fallen demonstrates God's great love? Did you see of how much benefit this proved to be the occasion for us, to be present in court and see how the examination proceeded? After all, they realized, Adam and Eve both, the degree and significance of the good things they had deprived themselves of through transgression of the command given them, stripped as they were of that ineffable glory and of the life that was scarcely inferior to the angels'. We saw the Lord's longsuffering, we learnt the gravity of indifference and how it renders us bereft of goods already in our possession and leaves us desolate, covering us in deep confusion.

(2) Hence, I beseech you, let us remain alert: may their lapses become an antidote for us, and their indifference prove to be a motive for caution on our part, especially as the punishment for those erring in the same way in the future will

---

1. Gen 3.20–22. In adopting Zoe as the woman's name, the LXX is translating the Hebrew *ḥavah* rather than simply transliterating it as *(H)eva*, so as the better to reproduce the balance between name and function in the original; perhaps likewise the best English version of the name would be "Life," to balance "living." When at Tob 8.6 such balance is not required, the LXX is content with *Eva*. Chrysostom, however, in his commentary on the text settles at once for the latter, preferring tradition to philology.

be the greater, the more they have been reluctant to profit
from their example. You see, people who after these events
sin in the same respect will not have the same sentence meted
out to them, something we can briefly learn from the world's
wise teacher—I mean [149] blessed Paul—when he says, "As
many as sinned without the Law will perish without the Law,
whereas as many as sinned with the Law in force will be
judged by the Law."[2] What he means is this: those prior to
the Law will not receive the same sentence as those after the
Law; instead, those sinning after the giving of the Law will
undergo heavier penalties. "As many as sinned without the
Law will perish without the Law," that is to say, the fact of
having no instruction or assistance from the Law makes the
penalty milder for them. "Whereas as many as sinned with
the Law in force will be judged by the Law"; these on the
other hand, he is saying, having the Law as teacher and being
so much the wiser yet sinning in the same way as the others,
will receive the heavier penalty.

(3) But let us listen to what was read today also. "Adam
called his wife Eve, which means life, because she was the
mother of all the living." See the precision of Sacred Scripture, how it didn't pass over even this detail, but taught us
that Adam named his wife as well. "He called his wife Eve,
which means life," the text says, you see, "because she was the
mother of all the living"—that is to say, she is the source of
all those who will come from her, the root and foundation of
the future race. Then, after teaching us the naming of the
woman, it further shows us God's goodness, how he does not
overlook them in their depth of shame and nakedness after
being created by him. "The Lord God made garments of skin
for Adam and his wife," the text says, "and clad them in
them." In other words, take the case of a kindly father with
a son of his own who was brought up with every care, who
enjoyed every indulgence, had the run of a fine house, was
clad in a silken tunic, and had free access to his father's substance and wealth; later, when he saw him tumble headlong

2. Rom 2.12.

from this great indulgence into an abyss of wickedness, he stripped him of all those assets, subjected him to his own authority and, divesting him of his clothes, clad him in a lowly garment usually worn by slaves lest he be completely naked and indecent. Well, in just the same way the loving God, when they rendered themselves unworthy of that gleaming and resplendent vesture in which they were adorned and which ensured they were prepared against bodily needs, stripped them of all that glory and the enjoyment they were partakers of before suffering that terrible fall. He showed them great pity and had mercy on their fall: seeing them covered in confusion and ignorant of what to do to avoid being naked and feeling ashamed, he makes garments of skin for them and clothes them in them.

(4) What I mean is that the machinations of the devil are quite different: when he finds people ready to do his will, he proves their undoing through some slight enjoyment, then drags them down to the very depths of wickedness and covers them in utter shame and degradation, leaving them prostrate, a piteous spectacle for all to see—whereas the Guardian of our souls, seeing them in utter helplessness, doesn't allow himself to ignore their condition but devises a covering for them, while indicating to them through the frugality of the garment the sort of garments they have caused themselves to deserve. [150] "The Lord God made garments of skin for Adam and his wife, and clad them in them." See the extent of the considerateness of Sacred Scripture. Still, what I've often said I say again now: let us understand everything in a sense befitting God. Let us understand "made" in the sense of "gave directions for": he ordered that they be clad in garments of skin as a constant reminder of their disobedience.

(5) Let the affluent pay heed, those who pamper themselves with cloth from the silkworm and are clad in silk, and let them learn how at the beginning from the outset the loving Lord instructed the human race: when the firstformed man became liable to the punishment of death through the Fall and the Lord had to clothe him in a garment to hide his shame, he made them garments of skin, to teach us to shun

the soft and dissolute life, and not to pine for one that is lazy and characterized by inactivity, but rather strive for an austere life. Perhaps, however, the wealthy will react badly to our words and will say, What reason is there in that? do you bid us wear garments of skin? No, I'm not saying that; after all, not even Adam and Eve wore those garments all the time, the loving Lord always adding further kindnesses to his previous ones, you see. I mean, when he rendered them liable to bodily necessities for the future, stripping them of the angelic way of life and its freedom from suffering, he later arranged for clothes for human beings out of sheep's fleece for no other reason than that they should have covering and that this rational creature should not live his life in nakedness and ugliness just like brute beasts. Accordingly, let the wearing of clothes be a constant reminder to us of the loss of advantages and instruction about the punishment which the race of human beings received on account of disobedience. Accordingly, let those people who make use of such paraphernalia that they are no longer familiar with garments of sheep's wool, but are clad in silk and have been carried to such extremes that they even drape gold with covering, the female sex particularly demonstrating this kind of luxury—let them, I say, tell us: Why do you dress up the body with these things and delight in clothing of that kind, not understanding that this covering was devised as severe punishment for the Fall? I mean, why do you not heed Paul's words, "We will be content to have food and clothing"[3]? Do you see that it is necessary to be concerned with one thing only, that the body not be naked, and to have an eye only to this, that no further worry be had about variety of dress?

(6) Let us, however, move to what follows. "God said, 'Lo, Adam has become like one of us in knowing good and ill. Now there is a risk that at some time he may put out his hand and pick fruit from the tree of life, eat it and live forever.' The Lord God sent him out of the garden of delight to till the soil from which he was taken."[4] See again God's consid-

3. 1 Tim 6.8.   4. Gen 3.22–23.

erateness. "The Lord God said," the text says, "'Lo, Adam has become like one of us in knowing good and ill.'" Do you see how remarkable is the ordinariness of the expression? Let us, however, take it all in a sense befitting God.[5] You see, the intention at this point is to remind us through these words of the deception practiced on them by the devil through the instrumentality of the serpent. I mean, that was when that creature said, "'If you eat, you will be [151] like gods,'" and they presumed to taste it in the hope of achieving this equality. Hence also God wanted again to make them ashamed, to bring them to a sense of their sins and to show them the gravity of their disobedience and the excess of the deception, said, "'Lo, Adam has become like one of us.'" Great is the reproach in this sentence, capable of touching the heart of the transgressor. Was this your reason, he is saying, for despising my command, that you had notions of equality? Lo, you have become what you expected—or rather, not what you expected but what you deserved to become. "'Lo,'" he says, "'Adam has become like one of us in knowing good and evil.'" This, in fact, is what the guileful devil said to them through the serpent, that "'your eyes will be opened, and you will be like gods, knowing good and ill.'"

(7) "'Now there is a risk that at some time he may put out his hand and pick fruit from the tree of life, eat it and live forever.'" See here, I ask you, the Lord's loving kindness. I mean, we must study the saying precisely so that nothing concealed under the surface can escape us. When God gave Adam the command, he bade him abstain from nothing, with the single exception of that tree, and when he presumed to taste it he received the sentence of death; he made this clear to him in giving him the command in case he should break it, though he had given him no express instructions about the

---

5. As remarked at many points in Vol. I (FOTC 74) and explained at length in Introduction (20), *synkatabasis*, "considerateness" (not "condescension"), is for Chrysostom characteristic of the divine Author of the Scriptures. Hence, the need in the commentator and reader/listener to respond by acknowledging both the "ordinariness," *tapeinōsis*, of the language so considerately used, especially in the case of anthropormorphisms like the present, and divine transcendence, not to be put at risk.

tree of life. I mean, since he created him immortal, as I see it and you can understand, it would have been possible for Adam, if he had wanted, to partake of that tree along with the others, a tree that was able to provide him with endless life—hence he was given no instruction about it.

(8) If, however, someone of a meddling nature should enquire why it was called the tree of life, let him learn that it was not possible for human beings to discern all God's works precisely by following their own reasoning. The Lord, you see, decided that the human being created by him should have some practice in disobedience and obedience while living in the garden, and decided to provide examples there of these two trees, one of life, the other of death (so to say) in the sense that tasting it and breaking the command brought death on him. So when by partaking of this tree he became liable to death and subject in the future to the needs of the body, and the entry of sin had its beginnings as the result of which death also was fittingly provided for by the Lord, no longer did he allow Adam in the garden but bade him leave there, showing us that his sole motive in doing this was his love for him.

(9) To learn this precisely, we must read again the words of Sacred Scripture. "'Now there is a risk that at some time he may put out his hand and pick fruit from the tree, eat it and live forever.'" In other words, since he had given signs of considerable intemperance through the command already given him (he is saying) and had become subject to death, lest he presume further to lay hold of this tree which offers endless life and go on sinning forever, it would be better for him to be driven from here. And so the expulsion from the garden was a mark of care rather than necessity. Our Lord, you see, is like this: he reveals his care for us in punishing no less than in blessing, and even his punishment is inflicted for the sake of admonition. Because if in fact he knew that we would not get worse by sinning and escaping, he would not have punished us; but to check our decline into greater evil and to stem the tide of wickedness, he applies punishment out of fidelity to his own loving kindness—[152] which is exactly

what he did in this case: in his care for the firstformed human being he bade him be driven out of the garden. "The Lord God sent him out of the garden of delight to till the soil from which he was taken." See here once again, I ask you, the precision of Sacred Scripture: "The Lord God sent him out of the garden of delight," the text says, "to till the soil from which he was taken." See, he puts the sentence into effect, driving him out of the garden of delight and obliging him to till the soil from which he was taken. It was not without purpose that he said, "from which he was taken." It was that he might in this work have a constant reminder of his humiliation, and be in a position to know that his subsistence derived from that source, and the composition of his body originally came from the soil—hence, he says, till the soil from which he himself was composed. He had said as much also in the sentence, "'In the sweat of your brow may you eat your bread.'" Accordingly at this point also he says the same thing in the phrase, "'to till the soil from which he was taken.'"

(10) Then, so that we may learn how great was the distance he moved him from the garden, Sacred Scripture teaches us this further fact in the words, "The Lord God drove Adam out and situated him opposite the garden of delight."[6] Notice how each of the events proved an occasion of loving kindness on the part of the common Lord of all, and each example of punishment abounds with goodness. I mean, the expulsion was not the sole mark of love and goodness: there was also his location opposite the garden so that he might have unending anguish in recollecting from what heights he had fallen and cast himself into such depths. Yet even if the sight of it was the cause of unbearable pain, it was nevertheless an occasion of no little benefit: the constant sight proved to be an encouragement for this grieving man to carefulness in the future lest he fall into the same sin again. Such, after all, is the habit of human nature by and large: since, while we are in a position to enjoy good things, we don't know how to use

6. Gen 3.24a in the LXX version, which by supplying the pronoun "him" has slightly altered the sense of the whole verse.

them as we ought, we come to our senses with the loss of these
things by learning through experience and gaining a sense of
our own indifference. In this way we are taught by the change
of fortunes from what heights we have fallen and with what
troubles we have tortured ourselves. And so the instruction
that the one who had lost his place there should dwell nearby
and opposite the garden was a sign of deep concern in order
that he might have the constant reminder from the sight of
it and feel a sense of loss from it and never presume to eat
from the tree through lusting after life while finding himself
outside. Thus, you see, Sacred Scripture describes everything
to us in a manner that shows considerateness for our limitations.

(11) "He set the Cherubim and the flailing sword of fire to
guard the approach to the tree of life."[7] Their indifference,
which they had already demonstrated in regard to the command given them, proved the cause of the approach being
barred against them with such precautions. Consider, I ask
you, that the loving God was not content with their dwelling
opposite the garden: he placed these powers, the Cherubim
and the flailing sword of fire, to guard the way leading there.
It was not without purpose that "flailing" was added: the reason was to teach us that every way was barred to him since
[153] that sword was turning around and blocking every way
leading there, sufficient to provide him with a reminder and
fill him with constant fear.

(12) "Now, Adam had intercourse with his wife Eve."[8] Consider when this happened. After their disobedience, after
their loss of the garden, then it was that the practice of intercourse had its beginning. You see, before their disobedience
they followed a life like that of the angels, and there was no
mention of intercourse. How could there be, when they were
not subject to the needs of the body? So, at the outset and
from the beginning the practice of virginity was in force; but
when through their indifference disobedience came on the
scene and the ways of sin were opened, virginity took its leave

7. Gen 3.24b in the LXX version.   8. Gen 4.1.

for the reason that they had proved unworthy of such a degree of good things, and in its place the practice of intercourse took over for the future. Accordingly, consider, I ask you, dearly beloved, how great the esteem of virginity, how elevated and important a thing it is, surpassing human nature and requiring assistance from on high. I mean, for proof that those who practice virginity with enthusiasm demonstrate in the body the characteristics of incorporeal powers, listen to the words of Christ to the Sadducees: when they were discussing the question of resurrection and wanted to learn his view, they asked, "Master, there were seven brothers of our acquaintance. The eldest married and died without children, leaving his wife to his brother. The second died, and having no offspring left his wife to his brother; likewise with the third, fourth, fifth, sixth and seventh. So at the resurrection to which of the seven will the wife belong? After all, she belonged to them all." So what reply did Christ make to them? "You are mistaken, not understanding the Scriptures nor the power of God: at the resurrection, far from marrying or being given in marriage, they will be like angels."[9] Do you see how those who have followed the vocation to virginity for the love of Christ imitate the life of angels through treading the earth and being clad in a body? I mean, the greater and more elevated the task, so much and even greater the laurels, the rewards and the good things promised to those who give evidence of the practice of good works along with this vocation.

(13) "Now, Adam had intercourse with his wife Eve," the text says, "and she conceived and gave birth to Cain." Since sin had come on the scene through the act of disobedience, and the sentence had the effect of making them liable to death, for the future God in his inventiveness arranged for the continuance of the human race according to his wisdom by allowing for the propagation of the race through intercourse.

(14) "She said, 'I have gained a human being, thanks to

<hr/>

9. A paraphrase of Matt 22.24–30, which has parallels in Mark 12.19–25 and Luke 20.28–36.

God.'" See how the imposition of the punishment brought the woman to her senses? She attributes the child she bore not to a natural process but to God, and displays her own gratitude. Do you see how the punishment proved an occasion of admonition to them? The text says, remember, "'I have gained a human being, thanks to God.'" It was not nature, she is saying, that presented me with the child; [154] instead, grace from above has given him to me.

(15) "She proceeded to give birth to his brother Abel."[10] Since she proved to be grateful for the birth of the first child and acknowledged the former kindness, she enjoyed the good fortune of the second. Our Lord is like this, you see: when we display gratitude for previous good deeds and acknowledge the benefactor, he lavishes his gifts upon us more generously. Accordingly, because she attributed the birth to God, for that reason she receives another child. You see, the generation of children was the greatest consolation from then on, once mortality had come on the scene. For this reason, of course, the loving God at once and from the beginning reduced the severity of their punishment and stripped away the fearsome visage of death by favoring them with the propagation of children, foreshadowing, as it were, in this event an image of resurrection and ensuring that others would rise up in place of the fallen.

(16) "Abel was a shepherd, whereas Cain was a tiller of the soil." Sacred Scripture taught us the occupations of each of the children and the fact that while one preferred tending flocks, the other tilled the soil. "In the course of time Cain brought an offering of the fruits of the earth to the Lord."[11] Consider how the Lord of nature added knowledge to conscience. After all, who brought this to our understanding? It was none other than knowledge associated with conscience. The text says, "He brought an offering of the fruits of the earth to the Lord." He knew and understood that he should offer from his own possessions some produce to God as to his master, not because God needs them, but for the purpose

10. Gen 4.2.   11. Gen 4.3.

of demonstrating his gratitude as being himself a beneficiary of such kindness. God, you see, is proof against need, and depends on nothing we have to offer; but in his ineffable love he shows considerateness for us, and for the sake of our salvation he allows these things to happen so that knowledge of the Lord may be for the human race a school of virtue.

(17) "Abel also for his part brought an offering of the first-born of his flock."[12] It was not idly or in vain that in beginning this sermon we taught your good selves that our Lord does not recognize differences in appearance but takes account of intentions and rewards the will. Here, too, to be sure, notice this happening. Accordingly, let us attend with precision, dearly beloved, to the text and see what Scripture says about Cain on the one hand and Abel on the other, and let us not pass it by heedlessly.[13] I mean, Sacred Scripture says nothing idly or by chance; instead, even if it happens to be a syllable or a single jot, it has some treasure concealed in it. Such, after all, is the nature of all things spiritual. So what does the text say? "In the course of time Cain brought an offering of the fruits of the earth to the Lord, and Abel also for his part brought an offering of the firstborn of his flock, and in fact the fattest of them." The meaning of the verse is clear even from the reading to those already capable of following more closely. But since we should exercise our concern in general for everyone (spiritual teaching, after all, recognizes no distinction), come now, let us expose the meaning of the words more clearly and rehearse these same words again. "Cain," the text says, "brought an offering of the fruits of the earth to the Lord"; then, wanting to teach us about Abel as well, Sacred Scripture says that he for his part also brought his offering [155] from his occupation and his shepherding. "He, for his part, also brought an offering," the text says,

---

12. Gen 4.4.

13. Over and over again Chrysostom reminds his readers of the "precision," *akribeia*, of the text of Scripture—a gift of divine considerateness—and of the corresponding obligation to precision in the commentator/reader. Hence the respect shown at Antioch for the literal sense of the sacred text. See Introduction (21) (FOTC 74) and my article, *"Akribeia."*

remember, "of the firstborn of his flock, and in fact the fattest of them." Notice how it hints to us of the piety of this man's attitude, and the fact that he did not casually offer any one of his sheep, but "one of the firstborn," that is, from the valuable and special ones. In Cain's case, on the contrary, nothing of the kind is suggested; rather, the fact that he brought "an offering of the fruits of the earth," as if to say, whatever came to hand, without any display of zeal or precise care.

(18) I repeat, and I shall not cease to make the point: God accepts our offerings not because he needs what we have to offer but because he wants our gratitude to be demonstrated through them as well. In other words, the person who makes an offering to God and offers him something of his own, and who calls to mind the difference in nature and the fact that a human being has been granted such a great honor, should give as good an account of himself as possible and offer the choicest gifts. But notice in this case, I ask you, dearly beloved: here you have the opportunity to contemplate what behooves you, namely, that the person who through indifference betrayed his own welfare duly pays the penalty. I mean, it wasn't a case of one man having a teacher and the other having a counsellor and adviser: each had instructions from his own conscience, and being moved by the intelligence supplied to the human race from above he proceeded to make his offering, such as it was; but the difference in attitude that emerged and the mediocrity of choice caused one man's offering to be acceptable and the other's to be spurned.

(19) "God took notice of Abel and his gifts." See how in this case is fulfilled the saying in the gospel that the first will be last and the last first.[14] I mean, see how the one who enjoyed priority belonging to the firstborn and consequently made his offering first was shown to be inferior to his brother since he made it unworthily: as both presented their offerings, Sacred Scripture says, "God took notice of Abel and his gifts." What does that mean, "He took notice"? He accepted, he approved of the attitude, he rewarded the choice, he was

14. Cf. Mark 10.32; Matt 19.30; Luke 13.30.

satisfied (so to say) with what was done. You see, we speak about God and presume to open our mouth about that pure nature, yet being human we would have no choice but to understand these things through language. Notice, however, this remarkable feature: "God took notice of Abel and his gifts," the text says; it calls the offering of sheep gifts on account of the importance, the choice quality, the untainted appearance of what was offered. Accordingly, God took notice of him for the reason that he had made the offering with a pure intention, and of his gifts for the reason not only that they were free of imperfection but that they were in every respect clearly precious, both from the viewpoint of the offerer's intention and from the fact of their being the firstborn and in fact specially selected from them, among the fattest of them and the very prize ones.

(20) "God took notice of Abel and his gifts," the text says, "whereas to Cain and his offerings he paid no heed." Since Abel made his offering with a proper attitude and pure intention, "God took notice," the text says—that is, he accepted, he was satisfied, he approved of them; but it called the offerings gifts, by this means dignifying the attitude of the offerer. "Whereas to Cain and his offerings he paid no heed." Notice [156] the precision of Sacred Scripture: by the phrase "he paid no heed" it shows us the rejection of what was offered, and by calling what was offered from the soil offerings he teaches us something else again. I mean, see how he shows us through the very events and terms that the Lord wants all these things to be done by us so that the kind of intention we have should be made clear through the actions we take, and so that we may be in a position to know that we are subject to a Lord and Creator who brought us from nothing to being. In other words, in naming the sheep gifts and calling the things from the earth offerings, Sacred Scripture teaches us that neither the herding of sheep nor the collection of fruits of the earth is what is looked for by the Lord but simply the disposition of one's attitude. Hence in this case, too, one man proved acceptable with his gift on this score, whereas the other was rejected along with his gift on that account. The

verse, "God took notice of Abel and his gifts, whereas to Cain and his offering he paid no heed," let us take in a sense befitting God. I mean, the intention in the words is that he communicated to them the awareness that while he was satisfied with one man's choice, he took umbrage at the other's attitude.

(21) Such, however, is the way God does things; let us now see what follows. "This annoyed Cain very much and his face fell."[15] What is the meaning of the words, "This annoyed Cain very much"? There were two reasons for his annoyance, not just that he alone had been rejected, but also that his brother's gift had been accepted. "This annoyed Cain," the text says, "and his face fell." What was it that annoyed him? Both things annoyed him, the Lord's ignoring his offering and his brother's gift being welcomed. So it was necessary that he recognize his guilt and adjust the error of his ways. After all, our Lord is loving, and when we err he does not turn away from us because of our error as if we continued in the error; on the contrary, he keeps no record of it. In order that you may learn this with precision and see the indescribable magnitude of the loving kindness, consider in these present events the exceeding degree of his goodness and the extent of his longsuffering. I mean, when he saw Cain annoyed unreasonably and, so to say, at the point of drowning in the waves of his annoyance, he did not ignore him; instead, that love which he had shown for his father in giving him the opportunity for excuse and opening the way to renewed confidence in the words, "Where are you?" despite that damaging fall—the very same love he now demonstrates towards the man who had proved so ungrateful, and stretches out his hand to this person who was at the point of tumbling down the cliff, as you might say, desirous as he was of offering him the opportunity to adjust the error of his ways. So he says to him, " 'For what reason are you so annoyed? For what reason has your face fallen? Is it not true that, even if you make your offering correctly but fail to choose the offering correctly, you commit

15. Gen 4.5.

sin? Be at peace, then: his movement is towards you, and you will be superior to him.' "[16]

(22) Consider, I ask you, dearly beloved, the ineffable considerateness in his care when he saw Cain under assault, so to speak, from the passion of envy, see how out of fidelity to his own goodness he applied various remedies to him so that he might be quickly plucked from the water and not be drowned. "'For what reason are you annoyed? For what reason has your face fallen?'" Why on earth, he is saying, are you overcome with such resentment as to show the extent of your displeasure on your face? "'For what reason has your face fallen?'" Why has this event so affected you? Why have you not considered what your obligation was? [157] You weren't making your offering to a human being, capable of being deceived, were you? Did you not realize that I wasn't looking for some offering or other of yours, but for the pure intention of the offerer? "'For what reason are you annoyed? For what reason has your face fallen? Is it not true that, even if you make your offering correctly but fail to choose the offering correctly, you commit sin?'" That is to say, while your having the idea of making an offering was commendable, still your not choosing the offering correctly led to the rejection of the offering. The one who makes an offering to God, you know, must show great care in the choice, and the greater the difference between the recipient and the offerer, the greater the distinction you should lend to your choice. You, however, gave no thought to these matters but simply offered whatever came to hand; hence they in turn could not be judged acceptable. You see, just as your intention in making the offering did not make allowance for the difference in status, and so caused the offering presented by you to be rejected; in like manner, your brother's intention, which happened to be correct and revealed great care in the choice, caused his gifts to be ac-

16. Gen 4.6–7, a text that has always puzzled interpreters; Speiser observes that this LXX rendering almost perfectly adheres to the letters of the Hebrew text but divides words differently, yielding a different sense in the way Chrysostom takes the words here. Actually, Chrysostom allows for a still further interpretation when he opens the matter again in Homily 19.

ceptable. Still, I am not demanding a penalty for the error but merely highlighting the sin and offering you advice, provided you want to take it, mend your ways and not involve yourself in worse evils.

(23) So what is the upshot? You have sinned, and sinned grievously, but I am not imposing punishment for the sin; after all, I am loving, and "I do not want the death of the sinner, rather that he be converted and live."[17] Since, then, you have sinned, be at peace, lend calm to your thinking and rid yourself of the onset of the waves crashing around your mind, settle the storm lest you add to the previous sin another more grievous one and set your mind on something beyond repair. Don't give yourself into the clutches of the wicked demon. "'You have sinned, be at peace.'" He knew right from the outset that the future attack against his brother would take place, and by these words he checks it beforehand. You see, since he was God and knew the unspoken intentions of Cain's mind, he was aware of the movements of his heart; so with this earnest exhortation and the considerateness of his words he applies the appropriate remedy to him, doing everything in his power in case this man should reject the medication and fall headlong into the abyss of fratricide. "'You have sinned, be at peace.'" Don't think, he says, even if I have turned away from your offering owing to your incorrect attitude and have welcomed your brother's gift because of his sound choice, that I have stripped you of your pride of place and removed you from the distinction of firstborn. "'Be at peace,'" even if he has been deemed worthy of my regard and his gifts have proved acceptable, nevertheless "'his movement is towards you, and you will be superior to him.'" And so even after this sin I permit you to have the privilege of being firstborn, and I bid him be subject to your authority and your control.

(24) See the Lord's loving kindness, how he wishes to defuse the wild frenzy and remove the anger by means of his words. You see, he observed the stages of his thinking and

17. Ezek 18.23.

realized the savagery of his deadly intention; so he intends at this early stage to sedate his thinking and bring repose to his mind by placing his brother subject to him and not undermining his authority. But even despite such great concern and such potent remedies, [158] Cain gained nothing from the experience. Such was the degree of difference in their attitudes and the excess of evil intent.

(25) Lest, however, we prolong the sermon unduly and thus seem to tax the patience of your good selves, and lest our homily bore you to tears and be considered an ordeal to you, let us bring the talking to a halt at this stage. Let us commend this point to your warm attention, to avoid imitating conduct of that kind, bid good riddance to evil, and devote yourself to the Lord's command with great attention and with your whole heart, especially in the wake of such examples and others like them. I mean, in future none of us will be able to take refuge in ignorance. After all, if that man—I mean Cain—was not in a position to find anyone living before his time who did anything of that kind, and still was subjected to that severe and unbearable punishment, as you will later discover, what is it likely that we will suffer—we who have committed those sins and even worse ones despite such a generous measure of grace? Will it not assuredly be everlasting fire, the worm that does not die, gnashing of teeth, exterior darkness, a fiery hell and all those other ineluctable punishments awaiting us? I mean, there will be no grounds for excuse left for us, since we have been so much disposed to sloth and so remiss. Surely, after all, we are all aware of what is to be done, and the sorts of things that should not be done? and that those who practice the former will enjoy the choicest of rewards, while those who fall victim to the latter will undergo condemnation to the most extreme of penalties?

(26) Hence I beseech, entreat and implore you not to let our assembling here prove to be of no avail; instead, let attention to our words be followed by deeds, so that having the certainty that comes from a good conscience and being buoyed up already in our present situation with sound hope, we may be able to negotiate with ease this life's sea of prob-

lems and put in at the harbor of God's loving kindness, thus attaining to those good things beyond all telling which the Lord has promised to those who love him, thanks to the grace and mercy of his only-begotten Son, to whom with the holy and adorable Spirit be glory, power and honor, now and forever, for all ages of ages. Amen.[18]

18. A rare variant of the trinitarian doxology with which Chrysostom closes all the homilies.

HOMILY 19

"And Cain said to his brother Abel, 'Come now, let us go out into the open country.'"[1]

NCURABLE [158] WOUNDS RESPOND neither to the harshest of remedies nor to those with benign properties.[2] Just so with the soul: once it falls into bondage and surrenders itself to any sin whatever, it has no interest in recognizing what is for its own good. Even if someone makes a fuss about it over and over again, it is all to no avail; instead, as though with deaf ears it gains no benefit from correction—not because it lacks the ability but because it lacks the will. Not that things are exactly the same in the case of the will as you can observe in the case of bodily wounds; with bodily ailments the natural condition is often stationary, whereas it is not like this at all with the will. Instead, in many cases a villain changes if he wants to and becomes good, and a good person who falls victim to indifference lapses into evil. So the God of all has endowed our nature with free will; he gives evidence of every effort on his part in fidelity to his own loving kindness, and in his knowledge of all the unspoken intentions in the [159] depth of our mind he exhorts and advises us and checks our evil plans ahead of time. To be sure, he does not impose necessity upon us, but in applying the appropriate remedies he allows everything to rest in the intention of the patient.

1. Gen 4.8.
2. An unusually direct opening for Chrysostom: in place of the usual exhortation involving a range of figures for Sacred Scripture and its benefits, there is immediate reference to the body of the previous homily (just as that homily closed with an unusual variation to the otherwise invariable trinitarian doxology). Some particular circumstance may underly the relationship of Homilies 18 and 19.

(2) Accordingly, this is just what happened in the present instance with Cain: see what depths of folly he has fallen into despite such care. You see, he should now have been engrossed in the correction of his sin, once he became aware of it; like a man intoxicated, however, he adds a further wound to his previous suffering and injured condition and refuses the healing applied to him with such care. He hastens the process of bringing his own destruction into effect, beginning with cunning and trickery and by deceiving his brother with beguiling words. Such is the condition of a human being turned animal who goes downhill into wickedness; just as this rational creature enjoys a wonderful status, especially when it makes rapid progress in the practice of virtue, so when it goes downhill into wickedness, it takes on the character of wild beasts. In fact, when it takes on the ferocity of those creatures, this mild and rational creature outstrips their savagery by a large measure.

(3) So let us see here too what happens. "Cain said to his brother Abel, 'Come now, let us go out into the open country.'" The words are those of a brother, but the intention is that of a murderer. O Cain, what are you doing? Don't you know to whom you're talking? Don't you understand that this conversation is taking place with your brother? Don't you realize that he was born of the same mother as you? Have you no notion of the foulness of your scheme? Have you no fear of the judge who is proof against deception? Don't you shudder at the realization of your temerity? Why is it, after all, that you are enticing your brother out into the open country and leading him out of his father's paternal arms? Why are you depriving him of his father's assistance? What is this fresh development, that now you are enticing your brother into the open country and scheming to do something you have not done previously, and on the pretext of friendship feigning brotherly concern, while intending to unleash a warlike assault upon him? What is this madness? What is this fury? Even supposing that you are deranged in mind and make no account of brotherly regard nor recognize the demands of nature itself, still why make an attack in this way

on the person who has done you no wrong? What grudge do
you bear your parents as well that you should want to inflict
such grief on them by becoming protagonist in this dreadful
tragedy and confront them with this violent death? Is this the
gratitude you show them for your upbringing? What wiles of
the devil have drawn you into this deed? Surely, after all, you
can't claim that the favor of the common Lord of all shown
towards Abel caused him to look down on you? Did the Lord
not anticipate your murderous intent and place him under
your authority in subjection to you in those words, "—'His
movement is towards you, and you will be superior to him'"?[3]

(4) This sentence, you see, should be taken to refer to the
brother's subjection. Some people, of course, say that God
addressed such words to Cain in regard to the offering presented by him: "'Its movement'"—that is, the offering's—"'is
towards you, and you will control it'"—that is, you will enjoy
it. So for this reason I have quoted both senses, leaving it to
your judgment to choose for yourselves which seems worth
following.[4] To my mind, anyhow, it seems to refer to the
brother.

(5) "While they were [160] in the open country, Cain set
upon his brother Abel and killed him." A terrible deed, a
dangerous precedent, a loathsome exploit, an unforgivable
sin, a bestial intention of mind. "He set upon his brother
Abel," the text says, "and killed him." O bloody hand! O piteous gesture! Rather, however, it is not the hand that should
be called piteous and bloody but the intention which the limb
responded to. So let us express it this way: O headstrong,
bloody, piteous intention—whatever you call it, you cannot

3. That difficult verse 4.7, as remarked on in Homily 18, n. 16. Notice
also Chrysostom's gift for dramatizing a situation on occasion, using rhetor-
ical devices to explore the emotive and moral possibilities. One has also to
admit that dogmatic significance of events is not always highlighted by Chrysostom to the satisfaction of modern commentators. See Introduction (17)
(FOTC 74).

4. As occasionally elsewhere, Chrysostom can flatter his congregation
with the option for an interpretation of a difficult passage. The "simple faithful" of the Antioch of that time were hardly unlettered, to judge from the
intensely scriptural life he presumes them to enjoy. See Introduction (11)
(FOTC 74).

describe it adequately. How was it that his hand was not paralyzed? how could it manage to grasp the sword and deal the blow? how is it that his soul did not fly from his body? how did it have the strength to put into effect such an unholy outrage? how is it that he did not have second thoughts and reverse his intention? how is it that he did not take stock of his nature? how is it that before beginning the exploit he did not think ahead to its result? how could he bear to see his brother's body gasping on the ground after the attack? how could he bring himself to gaze on the corpse flung to the ground without being immediately devastated by the sight? After all, despite the passing of the years and daily experience of people dying, and though these people suffer in their case the normal end of their life and are on no side related to us, we nevertheless break down; if the person is an enemy, we put an end to our enmity. So much the more, surely, would we be likely to be distraught and lose control on the spot to see a brother, whom we had been conversing with just before, child like us of the same mother and same father, born of the same family, who had attracted the favor of God, lying gasping on the ground, all at once lifeless and inert.

(6) Let us, however, look again, after this unholy deed and this arrogance beyond all excuse, at the great degree of considerateness and love employed by the God of all things. "God said to Cain."[5] How much goodness is this itself a mark of, that the person who had performed deeds like that should be deemed worthy of being addressed! I mean, it frequently occurs that we feel loathing for our relatives when we see them guilty of some such outrage; much more should we marvel at the good God's demonstration of such longsuffering. And rightly so: he is, after all, a physician and a loving father; and like a physician he does everything and employs every skill so as to bring to good health people who have fallen victim to troublesome ailments, and like a loving father he wants in his fatherly benevolence to lead people who have forfeited their natural nobility through indifference back to their former

5. Gen 4.9.

prosperity. So since the extent of his goodness is immense, he
wants to demonstrate his great love even to one whose rashness has taken him to such extremes. That is, he says to him,
"'Where is your brother Abel?'" Beyond all limit is God's
longsuffering: he asks the question, not because he was ignorant, but because he had done the same in his father's case;
after all, there was nothing to prevent him saying the same
thing again. You see, just as he saw Adam hiding through a
sense of shame for his nakedness and asked, "'Where are
you?'" not out of ignorance but to give him grounds for confidence so as to wipe away his sin by confession of his fall (this
being his way, after all, to require of us confession of our sins
at once from the outset and offer us pardon), so now too he
asks Cain in these words, "'Where is your brother Abel?'"
The loving Lord pretends ignorance so that by means of the
question he may cause the man guilty of these sins to be
brought [161] to confession of his guilt and be in a position
to win pardon, perhaps, and love. "'Where is your brother
Abel?'"

(7) So what reply is made by this ungrateful and insensitive
man, headstrong and shameless as he was? He should have
realized that God did not ask the question out of ignorance,
but rather to require of him a confession and to teach us
never to condemn our brethren before proof and to take into
account the Lord's advice; rejecting this attack and knowing
before its irruption the movement of his thinking, he plied
him with precautionary remedies. All this should have brought
him to his senses and to a cessation of his folly, admitting
what had happened, showing his ulcer to the physician and
accepting the remedies he had to give. But for his part he
aggravates the wound and renders the spread of the ulcer
more serious. "He said, 'I don't know,'" the text goes on. See
the effrontery of the reply! Surely you're not addressing a
human being, to feel free to converse with him as an equal?
Don't you know, you poor wretch, who it is you're talking to?
Don't you realize that it is out of his extreme goodness he is
addressing you in his desire to find some excuse for showing
you his characteristic love and with a view to your having no

grounds in future for rendering yourself liable to punishment once he has done all in his power?

(8) "He said," the text tells us, "'I don't know. Surely I'm not my brother's keeper?'" Recognize here, I ask you, the accusation of conscience, and how he was repulsed, as it were, by conscience and did not stop at the words, "'I don't know,'" but added, "'Surely I'm not my brother's keeper?'" as if trying to convince himself. In fact, to judge from the way everything worked out for you as the sequel shows and with regard for the law of nature, you ought in fact be guardian of your brother's welfare. This, after all, is what nature determined and what is required of people in the same family, to be guardian of one another. Even if this was not your intention and you had no wish to be your brother's keeper, why did you turn his assassin and kill the man who had done you no wrong without thinking you had an account to render? Wait a while, however, and you will see him whom you've killed and who lies dead while you are alive and active becoming your accuser and levelling charges at you in a loud voice.

(9) "God said, 'Why have you done this?'"[6] It is a deep meaning that emerges from this question: why have you perpetrated this (the text says)? Why have you committed this unholy deed, this loathsome act, this unpardonable offence, this intolerable folly, this strange and shocking murder, this first assault on the life of a human being at your hands? Why have you committed this awful and terrible crime, which has no sin to match it?

(10) "'The voice of your brother's blood cries out to me from the earth.'" Surely I am not a human being, he is saying, that I hear only that voice that is expressed by mouth? I am God and can respond to someone crying out through his blood, lying on the ground somewhere. Notice how far the voice of this man's blood flies up, reaching from earth to heaven and spanning the expanse of heaven and the heavenly powers, and taking its place at the royal throne itself, lament-

6. Gen 4.10, in a LXX variant that asks for the reason rather than the fact.

ing the murder and condemning the unholy crime. "'The voice of your brother's blood cries out to me from the earth.'" Surely, he is saying, you haven't committed this outrage against a stranger or foreigner? It is against your own brother, who did you no wrong. But perhaps my favor gave rise to this murder in you, and since you could not fight me, you spent your unbridled fury on him. For this reason, assuredly, I will impose such a punishment on you that the outrage will never be lost in oblivion, and the penalty inflicted on you will have as its purpose, that what happened to you will be a lesson for everyone coming later.

(11) [162] "'And now,'" since you have done this, have put into effect what you knew to be wrong and have rushed headlong into murder under the impulse of terrible envy, "'you shall be cursed from the earth.'"[7] Do you see the difference in this curse, dearly beloved? Don't pass it by heedlessly; instead, from the magnitude of the curse come to realize the excess of the outrage. From the difference in the curse you can, if you are of a mind, understand how much greater this sin was than the transgression of the first formed human being. In that case, remember, he said, "'Cursed shall be the soil as you till it,'"[8] and it was on the earth he poured out the curse, to show his care for the human being, whereas in this case, where the crime was deadly, the outrage lawless and the deed unpardonable, he receives the curse in person: "'You shall be cursed from the earth,'" the text says, remember. You see, since Cain perpetrated practically the same evil as the serpent, which like an instrument served the devil's purposes, and as the serpent introduced mortality by means of deceit, in like manner Cain deceived his brother, led him out into open country, raised his hand in armed assault against him and committed murder. Hence, as he said to the serpent, "'Cursed are you beyond all the wild animals of the earth,'"[9] so to Cain, too, when he committed the same evil as the serpent. In other words, just as the devil was moved by hatred

7. Gen 4.11.   8. Gen 3.17.
9. Gen 3.14.

and envy, being unable to bear the ineffable kindnesses done the human being right from the outset, and under the impulse of hatred rushed headlong into the deception that introduced death, so too Cain saw the Lord kindly disposed to his brother, and under the impulse of hatred rushed headlong into murder. Hence the Lord says to him, "'You shall be cursed from the earth.'" You shall be cursed, he says, even on that very earth "'which has opened its mouth to receive your brother's blood from your hand.'" You shall be cursed on the earth, he is saying, which has been forced to receive a shower of this blood so defiled and shed by such an impious hand.

(12) Sacred Scripture then interprets the curse more clearly in the words, "'When you till the soil, it will not proceed to yield its strength to you.'"[10] A remarkable kind of punishment, and a heavy weight of indignation: You will endure the labor, he is saying, you will make every effort on your part and till the soil stained with such blood, but far from experiencing any reward of your many labors you will find all the exertion you expend will be to no avail. Nor will the effects of punishment stop there; instead, "'You will live in lament and trepidation on the earth.'"[11] Once again this is a severe form of punishment, constant lament and trepidation. In other words, because you improperly applied the strength of your body, he is saying, and the vigor of your limbs, for this reason I sentence you to endless shuddering and trembling so that you may have in person not only a constant awareness and reminder of this unholy deed, but also that everyone may see you and learn from this sight, as though by some voice shouting aloud, not to risk similar outrage lest they suffer the same retribution; so the punishment inflicted on you may prove a lesson to everyone never again to defile the earth with such blood. Precisely for this reason I will not impose an abrupt end to your days, lest the event be lost in oblivion; instead, I will cause you to endure a life more distressing than

10. Gen 4.12.
11. Gen 4.12b, where the LXX translates the Hebrew rather differently from our modern versions, relying perhaps more on logic than linguistics.

death so that you may learn from your very labors what it is you have perpetrated.

(13) "Cain said to the Lord: 'My guilt is too great for me to be forgiven.'"[12] There is an important lesson to be learnt here, if we are ready to pay attention, and one very useful for our salvation. "Cain said: 'My guilt is too great for me to be forgiven.'" Behold the complete confession. [163] In other words, such is the sin committed by me, he is saying, that I cannot be pardoned. Someone may say, Behold he has confessed, and confessed with great precision—but all to no avail, dearly beloved: the confession comes too late. You see, he should have done this at the right time when he was in a position to find mercy from the Judge. Remember now, I ask you, what I was saying a short time ago, that on that dread day and before that impartial tribunal each of us will repent of our sins, seeing before our eyes those fearful punishments and the ineluctable chastisements—but all to no purpose, as we have run out of time. In other words, it is before punishment is imposed that penance is appropriate and is so marvellously efficacious. Hence I beseech you, when this remarkable remedy is able to take effect, let us then take advantage of it, and while we are still in this life let us apply the healing power coming from repentance; and let us learn for sure that it will be of no avail to us to repent after the show is over and the time for the contest has passed.

(14) Let us, however, return to our theme. You see, when Cain was asked by the Lord, "'Where is your brother Abel?'" that was the time for him to confess his fault, fall on his knees, pray and ask pardon. At that point, however, he rejected the healing, whereas now, after the sentence, after all was over, after the accusation was levelled at him in a loud voice by the blood that had been shed, he made his confession only to gain nothing from it. That is why the inspired author also said, "He who accuses himself at the beginning of the speech is in the right."[13] Accordingly, had Cain anticipated the Lord's accusation, perhaps he would have been granted

12. Gen 4.13.   13. Prov 18.17.

some mercy on account of the Lord's unlimited goodness. I mean, there is no sin, no matter how grave, that can exceed his mercy provided we demonstrate our repentance at the proper time and beg pardon. "Cain said, 'My guilt is too great for me to be forgiven'"—an adequate confession, but too late.

(15) Cain said, "'If today you drive me from the face of the earth and I must hide from your presence and live in lament and trepidation on the earth, it will happen that anyone finding me will kill me.'"[14] See how these pitiable words lack all conviction for the reason both of their lateness and of their missing the right moment. He said, "'If today you drive me from the face of the earth and I must hide from your presence and live in lament and trepidation on the earth, it will happen that anyone finding me will kill me.'" If you have rendered me accursed on the earth, he is saying, and have personally abandoned me and consigned me to such terrible punishment that I lament and tremble, nothing in future will prevent me being destroyed by anyone who chances upon me, placed as I am in this situation and stripped of your favor. I will be an easy prey, he says, for anyone wanting to do away with me: I am no match for anyone, moving about as I do with limbs uncoordinated and tottering in all directions, and the fact that everyone knows that I have been stripped of your favor will make it easy for anyone who is so disposed to hasten to my destruction.

(16) What, then, is the response of the good and loving Lord? "The Lord God said, 'Not so.'"[15] Do not think, he is saying, things will turn out like this: no one has the right to destroy you if he wants; on the contrary, I will bring you even more intense grief in the course of your life and I will leave you as a lesson for succeeding generations so that the sight of you will prove a [164] warning to them and no one will follow your example. "The Lord God said, 'Not so: anyone who kills Cain will have vengeance exacted on him seven-fold.'" Perhaps I have spoken many words and been the

14. Gen 4.14.
15. Gen 4.15, the LXX misreading the Hebrew "therefore".

cause of great bodily distress to you. But what am I to do? You see, I detect your interest and the keen desire you show, and so I want to move on to what remains and interpret it as well as I can. What is the sense of "'he will have vengeance exacted on him sevenfold'"? Yet once more I am afraid of burying your memory of the text under the plethora of words and of being thought overpowering by you. Still, if you're not too tired, keep up the effort, and we will conclude our treatment of the foregoing text and thus bring our sermon to a close.

(17) "The Lord God said to him, 'Not so: anyone who kills Cain will have vengeance exacted on him sevenfold.' The Lord God put a mark on Cain lest anyone finding him do away with him." Are you afraid, he says, of being done away with? Don't worry, this won't happen: the person who did it would render himself liable to a sevenfold punishment. This, then, is the reason I'm putting a mark on you, lest anyone do away with you unawares and render himself liable to such terrible punishment. We must, however, teach you more clearly how the person doing away with Cain becomes liable to a sevenfold punishment. Give me your attention, I beg you: we have in previous days often addressed your good selves, since it is the time for fasting and we enjoy such serenity; so now too, with our minds free of all upsetting ideas, if we didn't take the opportunity to understand the contents of Sacred Scripture precisely, when would we have another opportunity to grasp them? Hence I beg, implore and beseech you, as though grasping your knees, let us attend with mind alerted to these words so as to gain something fine and elevated, and thus make our way home.

(18) What, then, is the meaning of this phrase, "he will have vengeance exacted on him sevenfold"? First, the number seven has the sense of a multitude in Sacred Scripture, and you would often find it expressed that way, as for example, "The barren woman has borne seven children,"[16] and other such passages. On the other hand, in this case there is refer-

16. 1 Sam 2.5.

ence to the magnitude of the outrage and the fact that what was committed by him is not one sin but seven sins and that for each sin there is need to undergo severe punishment. How then will we number them? By reasoning this way: first, the fact that he envied his brother for the favor he enjoyed from God—something that would have been sufficient, had it been the only factor involved, to have brought ruin upon him; second, that he envied his own brother; third, that he devised a plot against him; fourth, that he committed murder; fifth, that it was his brother he killed; sixth, that he was the first one to commit murder; seventh, that he lied to God.[17]

(19) Did you follow what was said, or would you like us to list them again from the beginning so as to know how each single one of them would have been sufficient to bring on him the severest punishment? After all, who would deem worthy of pardon the man who envied someone who enjoyed favor from God? Behold one sin, the worst and most inexcusable. Next, this one emerges as a worse sin, a brother being the object of envy without doing any wrong. Behold this one too in its turn is not just a casual sin. The third one likewise, his devising a plot to deceive his brother and entice him into the open country without respect for his own kind. The fourth sin is the murder itself that [165] he committed. Fifth, his killing his own brother, born of the same mother. Sixth, his being the first to introduce this kind of killing. Seventh, his presuming to lie to God in the question he asked him. Hence he says, "Anyone attempting to do away with you will render himself liable to a sevenfold punishment." So have no fear of that; see, I'm putting a mark on you lest anyone do away with you unawares. The remission of punishment for your whole life will be instructive for succeeding generations, and what you have committed alone, with no one else present, everyone will know about who sees your lament and trepidation as if you were shouting aloud by your bodily tremors and saying

17. Again Chrysostom the Antiochene is loath to let the literal—perhaps here even literalist—sense of Scripture be set aside in favor of a figurative sense, and hence this elaborate explanation.

and communicating to everyone: Let no one else be rash enough to do the terrible things I have done lest they receive the same terrible punishment.

(20) When we hear this, dearly beloved, let us not pass the words by heedlessly, nor have in mind only the opportunity of assembling here each day and enjoying a spiritual banquet; after all, listening alone is of no advantage without response in terms of action. Instead, let us consider how it was that Cain came to commit himself to this inexcusable and shocking sin, and the fact that he had been rash enough through envy to commit such a crime against the man who had never tried to do him any wrong—or rather to commit murder against his own brother; and instead of simply avoiding evil conduct let us rather take care lest it be done to others. After all, that person is really in dire straits who is bent on bringing his neighbor down. For proof that this is true, notice in this case, I ask you, who is in dire straits—the killer, or the killed? Clearly the killer. Why? Because while the killed even up to the present time is on everyone's lips as a model, is praised and honored as the first witness to truth, as blessed Paul also says, "Though dead Abel still speaks,"[18] the killer on the contrary passed a life more miserable than all other people in those days, and since then has become an object of reproach to everyone and is held out as an example of a man loathsome in God's sight and cursed by Sacred Scripture.

(21) This is true of their lot in this present life which they share together; but of the fate they must meet in the life to come and of the retribution they must receive each individually for his own deeds at the hands of the just Judge, what account could do justice to that, the good or the opposite? No words could describe it, the joyful or the melancholy. In Abel's case, after all, the kingdom of heaven, everlasting tabernacles, the choirs of patriarchs, prophets and apostles and the throng of all the saints will welcome him as one destined to reign for unending ages with Jesus Christ the King, God

18. Heb 11.4—though that epistle gives Abel pride of place for witness to faith rather than truth, and it is through his faith that Abel still speaks.

and the only-begotten Son of God; whereas in Cain's case, the hell of fire and all the other undying torments will receive him as a victim for endless ages along with those who have committed similar crimes to his, and in fact to the degree that greater punishment is decreed by the common Lord of all against those who later were ensnared in these shameful passions. Listen, after all, to Paul's words: "As many as sinned without the Law will also perish without the Law"[19]—that is, they will receive a less severe [166] punishment on account of not having the Law as warning and correction. "As many as sinned under the Law will be judged by the Law": these on the contrary, he is saying, who despite the assistance of the Law committed the same crimes as the others, will fear punishments that are severer and less tolerable. And rightly so, because neither the Law nor the sight of others subjected to such evils brought them to their senses or to a sounder frame of mind.

(22) Hence I beseech you that at least from this present time onwards we learn the lesson for ourselves from the example of others and correct our lives in response to the Lord's instruction and in compliance with his laws; and that the thoughts of our mind not be dominated by hatred, envy, bodily satisfaction, this life's glory and power, pleasures of the palate, or any other unsuitable desire. Instead, let us purge ourselves of every uncleanness or disorder of this life, bid farewell to the most shameful and unseemly passions, and hasten towards that blessed life and those ineffable goods prepared by God for those who love him. May it be our good fortune to be deemed worthy of this, thanks to the grace and love of our Lord Jesus Christ, to whom with the Father and the Holy Spirit be glory, power and honor, now and forever, for all ages of ages. Amen.

19. Rom 2.12—though Paul is not really supporting the distinction Chrysostom is making.

HOMILY 20

"Now, Cain left God's presence and settled in the land of Nod opposite Eden,"[1] and following verses.

OME [166] NOW, let us once more today take up the thread of the reading and apply to you the teaching from this passage, and let us deliver the customary discourse to you from the book of blessed Moses—or, rather, from the sayings of the Spirit which the divine grace has taught us through the mouth of Moses.[2] But, so that the sermon may be clearer to you, it behooves your good selves to recall what has been said already and where we concluded our instruction so that today we may be able to resume it at that point and so touch on the opening words of the reading. You know, of course, that we dealt with the subject of Abel, and showed from the events themselves and from the things which each brother brought as offerings to the Lord how the knowledge of what must be done and what must not be done is implanted in our nature, and the fact that the Creator of all made us independent, that in every case he rewards or condemns us on the basis of intention (on this account, after all, one brother's offering was rejected while the other's gifts were accepted), that thereupon Cain under the impulse of envy rushed headlong to the murder of his brother, that despite this unholy crime and God's wish to summon him to confession of his sins he did not accept this kind of healing remedy but added mendacity to this abominable crime and

---

1. Gen 4.16.
2. One of Chrysostom's frequent statements of his clear conviction of the fact of inspiration of the biblical authors. His thinking on the charism and process of biblical inspiration, however, as with other Fathers, is conspicuously missing. See my article, "terminology."

thus drew upon himself that severe punishment, that he rendered himself stripped and robbed of grace from above and thus remains a salutary lesson for everyone in later times, and that through the sentence he received he addresses himself to the whole human race as if to cry out in loud tones, Let none of you ever attempt anything like this in case you incur these penalties. Do you see the love of the Lord, how by means of the punishment inflicted on Cain he intended not only to bring him to his senses [167] but also to teach everyone in future to avoid in every way this brazen exploit?

(2) Come, let us now press on to what follows and see what it is today as well this blessed author describes to us, inspired as he is by the force of the Spirit. When Cain received the sentence, remember, "He left God's presence," the text says. What does that mean, "He left God's presence"? In other words, on account of that abominable crime he was stripped of the patronage God afforded. "And he settled in the land of Nod opposite Eden." He tells us also the place where he made his dwelling in the future, and teaches us how even Cain did not live far from the garden, for the reason that by being opposite it he might have a constant reminder also of what had happened to his father because of the Fall and also of the magnitude of the crimes committed by him—though he had failed to come to his senses with the punishment inflicted on his father and had himself received terrible punishment. Now, the very place where he dwelt was an unremitting reminder, not only to him alone but to all future generations, of tossing and trembling. The word Nod, you see, is Hebrew, translated as "tossing".[3] So in order that he should find the accusation even in the very place as though recorded on a bronze monument, God settled him there.

(3) Then it says, "Cain had intercourse with his wife; she conceived and gave birth to Enoch."[4] Since they were mortal, it was fitting that they should give all their attention to propagation of children. But perhaps someone may say: How is it

3. Speiser, *Genesis*, 31, suggests "wandering" would have been closer; but Chrysostom's lack of Hebrew did not allow him to question his LXX text.
4. Gen 4.17.

that Cain had a wife when Sacred Scripture nowhere makes mention of another woman? Don't be surprised at this, dearly beloved: it has so far given no list of women anywhere in a precise manner; instead, Sacred Scripture while avoiding superfluous detail mentions the males in turn, though not even all of them, telling us about them in rather summary fashion when it says that so-and-so had sons and daughters and then he died. So it is likely in this case too that Eve gave birth to a daughter after Cain and Abel, and Cain took her for wife. You see, since it was in the beginning and the human race had to increase from then on, it was permissible to marry their own sisters.

(4) This, of course, is the reason why Scripture leaves us to presuppose what was involved when it reports the event in these words only, "Cain had intercourse with his wife; she conceived and gave birth to Enoch, and (Cain) was the founder of a city named after his son Enoch."[5] See how they are now instructed little by little: having become mortal, they want their memory to be kept unfading both through their offspring and from the names of places which they call after their children. Someone may say quite rightly that all such were reminders of their sins and the loss of that glory which both Adam and Eve had the good fortune to enjoy and so had no need of reminders, being superior to them.

(5) "To Enoch was born Gaidad," the text says, "Gaidad begot Maleleel, Maleleel begot Mathusala, Mathusala begot Lamech."[6] See how he skimmed through the genealogies, this blessed author mentioning only the males and making no mention of the females. Instead, just as he said in the case of Cain, that "he had intercourse with his wife" without teaching us anything about where he got his wife, so in just the same way here too he says again, "Lamech took to himself two [168] wives: the name of one was Ada and the name of the other Sella. Ada gave birth to Jobel," the text says; "he was the father of those who dwell in tents and keep cattle. His

5. *Ibid.*, where Chrysostom's variant of the LXX has been made to read less tautologically than the Hebrew and other LXX MSS.
6. Gen 4.18.

brother's name was Joubal; he was the inventor of the harp
and the lyre."[7] Note the precision of Scripture; it taught us
the names of the children born of Lamech's wife and the
occupations they had, as well as the fact that whereas one
devoted himself to keeping cattle, the other invented the harp
and the lyre. "Now, Sella in turn gave birth to Thobel," the
text goes on; "he was a metalsmith, working in copper and
iron."[8] Again it indicated to us the occupation of the child
born of Sella, namely, that he took on the trade of coppersmith. See how stage by stage the things necessary for the
well-being of the human race were provided for. First, Cain
named the city founded by him after the son born to him.
Then, of the sons born of the wives of Lamech, one devoted
himself to keeping cattle while another took on the work of
coppersmith and the third invented the harp and the lyre.
"Thobel's sister was Noeman." What is the meaning of this
strange and surprising statement? Well, now for the first time
it refers to females, making mention of one by name. This
was not done idly or to no purpose; instead, the blessed author has done this to draw our attention to something lying
hidden.

(6) What it is we will keep in store for another occasion,
and for the present press on to what follows. The sequel is,
in fact, no casual addition, but rather calls for a great deal of
effort and very precise interpretation for us to be in a position to discern everything with clarity and gain for ourselves
considerable benefit from the text. "Lamech said," the text in
fact goes on, "to his wives Ada and Sella, 'Listen to my voice,
wives of Lamech, hearken to my words: I killed a man for
wounding me, and a young man for striking me. On Cain fell
sevenfold vengeance, but on Lamech seventy times sevenfold.'"[9] Apply your attention to the utmost, I beseech you,

7. Gen 4.19–21, the LXX describing Jubal somewhat differently from the
Hebrew.
8. Gen 4.22.
9. Gen 4.23–24, where the LXX misinterprets the Hebrew: despite 4.15,
Cain is now seen as the one *on* whom—not *for* whom—vengeance is taken,
ekdikein . . . ek now being employed as elsewhere by the LXX (Num 31.2;

put aside all worldly thoughts, and let us study these words with precision so that nothing may escape us but rather we should proceed to their deepest meaning and be able to light upon the treasure concealed in these brief phrases. "Lamech said to his wives Ada and Sella," the text says, "'Listen to my voice, wives of Lamech, hearken to my words.'" Consider at once, I ask you, from the outset how much benefit this man gained from the punishment inflicted on Cain; not only does he not await accusation from someone else to the effect that he has been guilty of this sin or some worse one, but, without anyone's accusing him or censuring him, he confesses his own guilt, admits his crimes, and outlines to his wives the magnitude of his sin, as if to fulfil the proverb of the inspired writer, "He who accuses himself at the beginning of the speech is in the right."[10]

(7) You see, confession is of the greatest efficacy for correction of faults. Thus, as proceeding to deny guilt after committing sin proves worse than the sins themselves—which was the condition of that man who killed his brother and who when questioned by the loving God did not merely decline to confess his crime but even dared to lie to God and thus caused his life to be lengthened—accordingly Lamech, [169] when he fell into the same sins, arrived at the conclusion that denial would only lead to his receiving a severer punishment, and so he summoned his wives, without anyone's accusing or charging him, made a personal confession of his sins to them in his own words, and by comparing what he had done to the crimes committed by Cain he limited the punishment coming to him.

(8) Do you see the Lord's care for us, how even punishments are the occasion of his love, and that his display of love does not stop short at the person receiving the punishment but results in an efficacious antidote for others, provided they are of a mind to take advantage of its salutary assistance? I

---

1 Sam 24.12). There is some logic in this: the Yahwist, by including "the Song of the Sword" here, has himself thus transformed Cain into an *agent* of vengeance—so perhaps the LXX compromises.

    10. Prov 18.17.

mean, how on earth, tell me, was Lamech otherwise brought
to such confession except by having the constant reminder of
Cain's fate to goad his thinking? "He said," the text reads,
"'Listen to my voice, and hearken to my words.'" See how he
institutes proceedings against himself and issues them with a
summons in this fashion so that they won't idly accept what
he has to say. You see, the sentence, "'Listen to my voice and
hearken to my words,'" was meant by him to imply the following: Apply your attention to the utmost, he is saying, and
heed with precision what I am about to say; I am not going
to talk to you about incidental matters—instead, I will reveal
to you hidden things which no one else knows about except
myself alone and that unsleeping eye, fear of which makes
me eager and anxious to lay plainly before you the crimes
committed by me and the punishments I have made myself
liable to by my unholy deeds. "'I killed a man for wounding
me,'" he says, "'and a young man for striking me. On Cain
fell sevenfold vengeance, but on Lamech seventy times sevenfold.'" A remarkable saying—very remarkable, in fact—
and a highly commendable attitude on the man's part: not
only does he confess the crime and bring the murders he has
committed out into the open, but also by comparing Cain's
crimes with his he imposes the punishment on himself. What
sort of excuse, he is saying in other words, could the man be
deserving of who failed to come to his senses at the sight of
his predecessor's punishment and was even responsible for a
double homicide despite having such a recent reminder? "'I
killed a man for wounding me,'" he says, "'and a young man
for striking me.'" The men I did away with, he is saying, I
wronged not to the same extent as I wronged myself. After
all, on myself I inflicted an ineluctable punishment by committing crimes with no possibility of excuse. I mean, if Cain
became liable to sevenfold punishment for one murder, I
would be justly served to receive seventy times sevenfold punishment.[11] Why and on what account? Cain committed mur-

11. Chrysostom is clearly placing great importance on Lamech's song, as
do modern literary critics, like G. Von Rad in his *Genesis* commentary (1972⁹;

der—fratricide, in fact—yet did so without previous experience of anyone doing so at any time previously or observing anyone else punished for such a crime or feeling the effects of such rage. All of this will be heaped on my head by way of punishment for my two crimes, because I had before my eyes Cain's crime and I could see his punishment to be so implacable and his failure to take so little warning from it. Hence, even if I incur seventy times sevenfold the punishment he did, I will still not discharge my account adequately.

(9) Do you see, dearly beloved, how God created our will independent, and just as we lose our footing if we don't take care, so too we observe what we need to, provided we have a mind to be on the watch? I mean, what was it, tell me, that coerced this man into making his confession? Nothing other than [170] conscience, that judge who is proof against influence. You see, when he fell into indifference and thus put into effect his evil endeavor, immediately conscience raised its voice in accusation of the magnitude of his sins and the extent of the punishment he thus rendered himself liable to. Sin, after all, is like this: before it comes into being and goes to work, it clouds the intellect and deceives the mind; but once it has run its course, it then makes its own stupidity patent to us, the brief and stupid pleasure being replaced in us by unremitting pain, robbing us of peace of mind, and covering the victim in confusion. The loving Lord, you see, appointed us a prosecutor of this kind who would never rest but would constantly be at hand to raise his voice and demand punishment for our sins. This you would see clearly in daily events themselves: the lecher, the adulterer or the person who com-

---

ET London 1972, 111f)—but, partly by preference, partly because of the LXX's misreading of the Hebrew regarding the object of vengeance, Chrysostom's interest in the text is moral, not dogmatic in the way Von Rad sees it: "The Song of Lamech is the third section of the primeval history which the narrator emphasizes. It is a story of the increase in sin and the more and more profound disturbance of the original orders of life with which it goes hand in hand. First, the Fall, then fratricide, and now the execution of vengeance . . ." The mistranslation of the LXX, of course, robs it of this dogmatic significance; but Chrysostom still finds Lamech a figure of considerable moral significance, even if he is no longer the agent but the object of vengeance.

mits any other such excesses, even if he succeeds in escaping everyone's notice, doesn't remain at peace in that condition, but has this savage prosecutor with him and so he is afraid of suspicions, he trembles at shadows, at people who know and people who don't know, and so he suffers perpetual turmoil of spirit and conflicting waves of emotion. Neither is sleep enjoyable for such a person but rather plagued by fear and terror; the table brings no delight, nor can conversation with friends bring such a person out of his depression or dispel his pressing concern. Instead, after that stupid behavior of his he goes about as if he had a public executioner at hand to flay and beat him incessantly, and even if no one is aware of his crime, he suffers those intolerable punishments, having become his own prosecutor and judge.

(10) On the other hand, should a person guilty of such faults have a mind to take advantage of the assistance of conscience, as behooves him, and hasten to make confession of his sins, reveal his ulcer to the physician who cures without reproaching, and in private communion with him without anyone else's knowing tell all in detail, he will achieve a rapid mending of his ways. Confession, you see, means the removal of sins. After all, if in fact the man in question, Lamech, did not shrink from confessing to his own wives the murders committed by him, what excuse would we have if we were not prepared to make a clean breast of our sins to the one who knows them all in detail? Surely it's not because of ignorance that he wants to hear about them! Because he is not ignorant of them, he looks for confession from us while knowing everything before it happens and yet wanting us to have a sense of our faults through confession and to demonstrate gratitude on our part. There won't be the need to outlay expense in this case, will there? there won't be the need to set out on a long journey, will there? this cure won't involve pain and suffering, will it? No, it involves no expense, no suffering, but offers an immediate cure. The Lord, you see, grants remedies for wounds in this way according to the disposition of the patient. Consequently, let the person who is minded to return to health more quickly and be cured of the ulcers of

his spirit approach the physician soberly, and cutting himself off from all worldly concerns let him shed hot tears, give every evidence of insistence, demonstrate a resolute faith and have confidence in the physician's healing arts; he will thus straightway enjoy good health.

(11) Do you see the physician's prodigality which excels the loving concern of all human fathers? It is not something burdensome and demanding that he requires of us, is it? No, simply heartfelt contrition, a lull in our wild ideas, confession of sins, earnest recourse to him; [171] then he not merely rewards us with the curing of our wounds and renders us cleansed of our sins, but also puts to rights the person who beforehand had been weighed down with countless burdens of sin. O the greatness of his love! O the extent of his goodness! When the sinner confesses his sins and begs forgiveness and gives evidence of carefulness in the future, God immediately declares him law-abiding. For clear proof of this, listen to the prophet's words: "Take the initiative in declaring your transgressions so that you may be declared upright."[12] He did not simply say, "Declare your transgressions," but added, "Take the initiative," that is to say, don't wait for someone to accuse you, nor let the prosecutor anticipate you—beat him to the punch by having the first say, so as to deprive the prosecutor of a voice.

(12) Do you see the judge's loving kindness? In the case of human courts, whenever anyone admitted to doing this and anticipated proof of the charges by confessing his crimes, he would perhaps be in a position to escape torture and the torments accompanying it, and even if the case came before a lenient judge he would indubitably receive a sentence of death. In the case of the loving God, on the contrary, the physician of our souls, we meet with ineffable goodness and a liberality exceeding all description. What I mean is this: if we steal a march on our adversary—I mean the devil—who on that dread day will take his stand against us, and already in this present life before our entry into the court we confess

12. Isa 43.26.

our crimes, take the initiative in speaking, and turn accusers against ourselves, we will encourage the Lord not only to reward us with freedom from our sins but also to reckon us among the number of the upright. You see, the man in question, Lamech, made a clean breast of his deeds and condemned himself without the advantage of any law passed to teach him, without having heard any inspired authors, and without any other encouragement except the conviction of his own crimes arising from the judgment rooted in his own nature. So how could we meet with any excuse for not having revealed our wounds to the Lord in all eagerness and received from him healing of them? If we haven't done it now when it is the time for fasting, when we have such serenity of thought, when all indulgence is put aside, at what time will we be able to take stock of our behavior? Hence I beseech you to be ever sober and alert, and spend all this present life with a view to being able by your diligence to avoid that intolerable punishment and keep out of the fire of hell. At this time in particular, however, ought we to do this with all eagerness when on account of the season for fasting we have the advantage of more abundant and insistent teaching.

(13) "Now, Adam had intercourse with his wife Eve; she conceived, bore a son and gave him the name Seth, saying, 'God has raised up for me another child in place of Abel, whom Cain killed.'"[13] Sacred Scripture developed the genealogy as far as Lamech, and then went back to Adam and his wife, and said, "Now, Adam had intercourse with his wife; she conceived, bore a son and gave him the name Seth, saying, 'God has raised up for me another child in place of Abel, whom Cain killed.'" "She bore a son," the text says, "and gave him the name Seth"; [172] the mother was not content with giving the name, but added, "'God has raised up for me another child in place of Abel, whom Cain killed.'" Notice also the mother, how through the name of the child she bore she ensures a constant reminder of that evil deed, and, so that future generations may be in a position to know of the crime

13. Gen 4.25.

committed by Cain, she says, "'in place of Abel, whom Cain killed.'" The comment of a grieving spirit, upset at the memory of what had happened, and while thankful for her new child, yet by the name she gave it erecting a monument, as it were, to her other son. After all, it was no chance sorrow he brought to his parents in raising his hand against his brother and stretching him on the ground before their eyes, a lifeless corpse, whom they had bred and cherished. I mean, if Adam received the sentence, "'Dust you are, and to dust you are to return,'"[14] and "'On the day you eat from it you will truly die,'"[15] still the meaning of the sentence lay in the words alone for the time being and he had no awareness up to that point of what death looked like. Cain, on the contrary, took the initiative against his brother out of hatred, let loose against Abel the rancor that had been gnawing at his vitals, and thus provided his parents with a dreadful spectacle to contemplate. For this reason, assuredly, the mother, who had scarcely lifted her head and was able only at this late stage to find some consolation for that unbearable grief in the birth of a son, offered thanks to the Lord and immortalized the crime of fratricide, thus also inflicting on him the severest of punishments by ensuring the unfailing remembrance of what had been done by him.

(14) Do you see what a terrible evil sin is? how it brings those who commit it into shame and disgrace? do you see how through it he was rendered bereft of grace from above and became an object of mockery for all to see? do you see how even to his parents, committed though they were by nature itself to loving their children, he was transformed into an object of revulsion because of that evil deed? Let us accordingly, I beseech you, shun the sin that brings such evils upon us, and let us choose virtue so that we may win favor from on high and avoid punishment.

(15) "A son was born to Seth," the text goes on; "he gave him the name Enosh. He it was who hoped to invoke the name of the Lord God."[16] See how people are now taught to

14. Gen 3.19.   15. Gen 2.17.
16. Gen 4.26, where the LXX departs from the Hebrew text in some

incorporate an expression of their own gratitude in the
names of their children: Seth, the text says, had a son and
gave him the name Enosh; then, out of a wish to explain to
us the significance of the name, Sacred Scripture adds, "He
it was who hoped to invoke the name of the Lord God."[17]
You see, from this person onwards the blessed author is on
the point of beginning the genealogy, having dismissed the
memory of Cain and also of those who were descended from
him up to Lamech; since he had by the evil of his course of
action besmirched the prerogative granted to him by nature—I mean that of firstborn—he is expunged from the list
along with his descendants. Now Seth, on the contrary, is accorded this distinction—something he did not enjoy by nature—on account of the gratitude in his course of action, and
for the future the position of firstborn is transferred to him,
if not by nature, at least by the attitude revealed in his course
of action, and those descended from him are accorded a place
in the genealogy. Just as the son is called Enosh through invoking the name of the Lord God, so too those who continue
the line from him in future are accorded the same name.
Hence this blessed author concludes the narrative at this
stage and then begins another.

(16) [173] Lest, however, we launch into this narrative and
prolong the instruction to great length, let us, like this blessed
author, bring the sermon to a close at this point and hold over
till next time (God willing) the explanation of what follows.
Just for the time being, however, I want to bring this point to
the attention of your good selves so that you can reap some
benefit from what has been said by us and examine yourselves
daily as to what you have gained from this teaching, and what
from that, and not simply take in our words with your ears

respects—without solving its historical difficulty about the beginning of the
worship of Yahweh, which the E and P narratives in *Exodus* attribute to the
time of Moses.

17. Chrysostom seems anxious to find some etymological connection between the name "Enosh" (Hebrew for "mankind") and the worship of the
Lord (Yahweh, in fact, though word-for-word rendering as *Kyrios* results in a
loss of this point). His argument, however, suggests he is reading some other
sense than the Hebrew into the proper name.

but also rivet them in your mind and make the firm recollection of them your constant concern. In fact, I want you not
simply to be content with them yourselves but also to become
teachers of others so as to be able to exhort them as well,
doing so not only with words but also through your actions
instructing your neighbor in the practice of virtue. I mean,
consider, I ask you, that if you want to gain some little advantage from coming along here each day and achieve the correction of the passions that handicap you, you will ascend
little by little to the very pinnacle of virtue. You see, we will
not cease addressing you each day and making your ears ring
with talk of the noblest way of life so that you may eradicate
those deadly passions—I mean anger, envy and jealousy.
After all, once these have been removed, it will be easier for
the obsession with material goods to find a remedy; and once
the obsession with material goods has in turn ceased, those
improper thoughts and shameful desires will with greater security be suppressed. Avarice, you see, is the root of all
evils;[18] so if we chop out the root and pull it up from the very
bottom, it will be easier for us to get the better of the
branches.

(17) The very peak of evil, after all, and the summit (so to
say) of sin is insatiable desire for possessions; if we were prepared to overcome it, there would be no obstacle to our escaping this obsession and, by so doing, eradicating and
expelling all deadly passions. Don't think it is any great challenge to despise possessions. I mean, when I consider that
many people, through an empty and mindless esteem for
them, expend great amounts of money to no good effect but
only to win the approval of common and often paltry people,
an esteem which fades by evening but before the day is over
brings countless troubles upon them; and that others, on the
other hand, are among the number who are overcome by pagan deception, in their turn yearning after the good opinion
of people and setting much store by it, letting all their possessions go, keeping for themselves only a bit of a cloak and

18. 1 Tim 6.10.

a staff, passing their whole life in this fashion and choosing
to endure all this trouble and distress for the sake of people's
good opinion—when, then, I ponder all this, I know not what
excuse or allowance will be accorded us for not bearing to
give up the least of those things for the sake of the command
given us by God or for the sake of that glory that does not
die and has no end. Instead, we prove worse than those people and fail to understand the difference between such things,
because while they give them up for the sake of the mindless
esteem of their peers, [174] we for our part often choose not
to share the slightest thing with the needy even for the sake
of our Lord, the supplier of our possessions, who promises
us those gifts beyond all telling.

(18) How will our eyes bear to look upon the Judge if we
have so neglected this simple command? I mean, surely I'm
not recommending you to throw all your possessions away.
Make the most of every time of prosperity, satisfy every need,
and what is over and above put to good use by distributing to
those who are hungry or frozen with the cold, and so send it
ahead to your homeland by their hand so as to take advantage
of it there before long. These people, you see, will be in a
particular position to help you in transferring your goods
there so that when you arrive you may find everything arranged to your advantage and you may enjoy greater credit
there, seeing your riches multiplied by your agents—or, rather,
by God's loving kindness. After all, the transaction involves
no problems, does it? It causes no worry or concern, does it?
You have no need of carriers for the transfer, or of guards or
anything else like that; no brigand or robber infests that route
to prey upon the cargo you send. Instead, whatever you put
into the hands of the poor, you put into safe custody, God's
own hand. This hand, of course, is proof against harm and
provides protection for your goods, and when you arrive in
your homeland, in addition to the restoration of your goods
he will commend and reward you, and establish you in complete comfort and enjoyment.

(19) Accordingly, let us, I beseech you, pour out savings to
provide for the poor, and sow seed in good time for the pur-

pose of reaping a harvest at the proper season and not having vain regrets later through putting off the present opportunity. I mean, surely the loving Lord has not blessed you with greater benefits for this reason, that you should squander what has been given you only on your own needs and secrete the rest in safes and chests? It was not for that purpose, but rather that in accordance with the apostolic exhortation your surplus should be used to meet the needs of others. Perhaps your enjoyment extends even beyond what is needful and you spend much money on delicacies, clothing and other sorts of luxurious living, and your generosity extends even to servants and animals, whereas the poor person asks you for none of these things except to assuage his hunger and provide him with his pressing needs and daily bread so as to survive and not perish. You should not desist from doing this, nor think that often you are suddenly robbed and on the point of losing all you have amassed and in some cases sharing it with enemies and rivals; in fact, all the sins, through which you have amassed these things, you take with you as you pass on. What will you then say on that dread day? What excuse will you give for having managed your salvation with such indifference?

(20) So take my advice, and while you still have the opportunity, distribute your superfluous possessions so as to make sure of your salvation there and guarantee a dividend by way of eternal bliss. May it be the good fortune of all of us to enjoy this, thanks to the grace and love of our Lord Jesus Christ, to whom with the Father and the Holy Spirit be glory, power and honor, now and forever, for ages of ages. Amen.

HOMILY 21

"This is the book about the origin of human beings. On the day God made Adam, in God's image he made him; male and female he made them. He gave them the name Adam on the day he made them."[1]

ONDERFUL [175] AND BEYOND TELLING , dearly beloved, is the treasure in the words read just now. I realize that for their part many people take one look at a list of names, pay attention only to the surface of the text, and judge that the words contain nothing more than simply a list of names. For my part, on the contrary, I beg you all not to pass heedlessly by the contents of Holy Scripture. I mean, there is nothing in the writings at this point which does not contain a great wealth of thought; after all, since the blessed authors composed under the inspiration of the divine Spirit, on that account they hold concealed within them great treasure because written by the Spirit. Don't be surprised if in the list of names I guarantee to show you a great wealth of thought hidden there. You see, there is not even a syllable or even one letter contained in Scripture which does not have great treasure concealed in its depths.[2] Hence we must be guided by grace from above and accept the enlightenment of

---

1. Gen 5.1–2, where the priestly editor of the Hebrew text begins his book of generations, or record of Adam's line. The LXX, which before this point has failed to respect the difference between Hebrew *adam* with article and without it to distinguish "human being" from "Adam" (as a proper name) and has preferred the proper name, strangely reverses its pattern in 5.1, still against the Hebrew. Chrysostom's own text here also omits the blessing in 5.2.

2. A classic statement of Chrysostom's principle of the precision, *akribeia*, of Scripture—a principle he adheres to not just by citing it but by examining carefully miniscule items in the text, even down to syllables and letters as he claims (cf. Homily 39 on Abraham's name). See notes 11 and 13 below, and my article, "*Akribeia*."

the Holy Spirit, and only then approach the divine sayings. That is to say, Sacred Scripture does not call into play human wisdom for the understanding of its writings, but the revelation of the Spirit, so that we may learn the true meaning of its contents and draw from it a great benefit.[3] After all, if in daily affairs the writings composed by human beings frequently become corrupt through the passage of time, judging by the date mentioned at the beginning of the text, and still contain great significance in even a single syllable, so much the more in the case of the Holy Scriptures composed by the Holy Spirit can we find this, provided we are alert and do not rush heedlessly on but sharpen our responses and consider everything precisely, proving ourselves no worse than people demonstrating a like enthusiasm for material things.

(2) To draw a comparison with people digging for metal ore: they don't stop short at its first appearance; instead, when they get down to great depth and are in a position to collect nuggets of gold, they expend much effort and vigor in separating them from the soil, and despite that great labor they find only some slight consolation for their pains.[4] Still, even though they know they will gain little return in comparison with their trouble, in many cases despite long hours and much frustration and disappointment of their hopes, they don't give up at this stage: buoyed up by expectation they feel no effect of their efforts. So if they exhibit such zeal in regard to things that are corruptible and passing, to which is attached much uncertainty, much more should we exhibit a like, or even greater, enthusiasm in cases where the wealth is proof against theft and the treasure is not consumed nor is it

3. For Chrysostom not only are the author and text inspired but also the reader, if the inspired text is to be appreciated fully. One effect of such inspiration is that the reader is able to bring a like precision to his study of the precision of the text. See my *Inspiration*, pp. 108–121.

4. One of the several figures (probably not original, as we have seen from De Lubac's survey of similar patristic figures) Chrysostom employs at this point in his homilies to recommend Scripture to his congregation. It is perhaps his favorite figure, as it implies the painstaking study and careful search that exegesis was for the school of Antioch, and highlights as well the great rewards of scriptural reading.

possible for hopes to be disappointed, so that we may be able
to have the good fortune to enjoy the object of our zeal, reap
much benefit in the process, and in the knowledge of God's
ineffable love prove to be grateful to our Lord and also render ourselves immune to the devil's wiles by winning favor
from above.

(3) So come now, let us set forth the words read just now
and examine each one precisely so as to take advantage of the
customary instruction and thus make our way home. "This is
the book about the origin of human beings," the text says.
"On the day God made Adam, in God's image he [176] made
him; male and female he made them. He gave them the name
Adam on the day he made them." Notice, I ask you, the insight of this remarkable author—or rather, the instruction of
the Holy Spirit. I mean, he utters everything to us under the
influence of inspiration; he brought his tongue to the task,
while the grace of the Spirit teaches everything clearly to us
in our human condition by means of him.[5] Consider, then,
how he took the story back to the beginning, and intends to
conduct his narrative all over again, so to say. Why and for
what purpose? Well, he knew that those who were already in
existence had given evidence of much ingratitude and had
not even profited from the fate of the first formed human
being but had descended into the very abyss of wickedness;
his own son had immediately rushed into fratricide from a
motive of envy, and had consequently received that most severe punishment, as we taught your good selves before. Then
those after him in their turn, not even profiting from his punishment, involved themselves in worse evil, as you heard Lamech yesterday describing his own sin to his wives and

5. For Chrysostom the teaching of the human author is the teaching of
the divine author: to find the latter, study the former. In this Chrysostom is
as contemporary in his thinking as Vatican II's *Dei Verbum*—hence its ac-
knowledgment of him. For details of the process of inspiration, however,
Chrysostom is less helpful; his statement here could be taken to support a
mechanical notion of dictation or even possession found among the Fathers,
as emerges also from his commentary on Psalm 45 (PG 55, 183–85)—but
that is a traditional patristic *locus* treated in the customary manner, so we are
none the wiser.

specifying the penalty imposed on him. Finally, he saw bit by bit their wickedness increasing like an evil current about to wash completely over the body, so he stems the tide of wickedness, and doesn't even consider worthy of mention the succeeding generations from Cain to Lamech; instead, as though making a fresh start and wanting to sooth Adam and Eve's grief which the murderer had presumed to inflict upon them with the death of his brother by raising his hand against Abel, he thus begins his account with these words, "This is the book about the origin of human beings. On the day God made Adam, in God's image he made them; male and female he made them. He gave them the name Adam on the day he made them."

(4) Notice how he employs the same words as in the beginning to teach us that he did not even rate worth a mention from now on those generations turned reprobate; instead, he begins the genealogy from the recently born child—I mean Seth—so that from this fact also you may learn how much store God sets by human nature and how he abhors people of murderous intent. You see, he passes over mention of them as if they were people never brought into existence, thus showing us how terrible wickedness is and the fact that those who embrace it do the worst harm to themselves. Behold, in fact, on the one hand, these people are now removed from the list and are judged worthy only of such mention as to have their wickedness immortalized and to become a sober reminder for future generations. On the other hand, he who was unjustly done away with, put to death by a brother's hand, has been a byword on everyone's lips from that time till now, whose memory time has not erased nor has the other brother's accusation been excised; instead, day in day out one is praised to the skies, the other held in everlasting obloquy.

(5) Do you see how much harm is done by wickedness, how much power virtue has, and how one is crushed and dispelled no matter if it goes on the offensive and wages war, while the other, even if attacked and beset with countless insults, shines out the more brightly and resplendently on that account? It would be possible to demonstrate this to your good selves at

this point from many other examples that have occurred to like effect; [177] but lest we lose track for now of the theme we are developing, come now, let us take up again the words in question: "This is the book about the origin of human beings," the text says. "On the day God made Adam, in God's image he made him; male and female he made them. He gave them the name Adam on the day he made them." See how Sacred Scripture begins its account all over again to remind us of the extent of the esteem accorded the newly created human being. "On the day God made Adam," the text says, "in God's image he made him"—that is to say, he appointed him ruler of all visible things. This, after all, is the meaning of "in his image," in respect both of his control and his lordship.[6] You see, just as the God of all has control of all things both visible and invisible, being Creator of everything as he is, so too after creating this rational being he intended him to have control of all visible things. Hence he accorded him also a spiritual being in his wish that he not see death for ever; but since through indifference he fell and transgressed the command given him, out of fidelity to his own loving kindness he did not turn away at this but while stripping him of immortality he placed this creature he had condemned to death in almost the same position of control. Then when the child born to him fell headlong into such awful wickedness and was the first to provide an example of murder, demonstrating that violent kind of death and displaying deep ingratitude by compounding homicide with guile, he decided to bring him to his senses with unremitting punishment so that he should not simply gain something personally from what happened to him but should also teach those coming later both the extent of his crimes and the excess of the impropriety.

(6) Since, however, through great indifference those descended from him gradually involved themselves in worse wickedness, he wanted to console Adam, so to say, for finding

6. See Homily 8, note 13 for mention of modern linguistic and archeological confirmation of Chrysostom's surmise as to the meaning of this key phrase.

himself so desolated not only by his own fall but also by Cain's crime which he saw with his own eyes. Not that they knew what death looked like, even if they had received the sentence: a twofold and threefold grief afflicted him because he saw death introduced into life for the first time, violent death at that, perpetrated by his own son, against his brother, of the same mother and same father as himself, one who had done him no ill. Accordingly, the loving God, wishing to bring him some consolation to compensate him for those griefs, provided him with another son, Seth, and in supplying adequate solace for him by that means he guarantees for the future the beginning of another line from him. Hence the blessed author made that opening remark, "This is the book about the origin of human beings."

(7) Then, notice the way, having promised to outline the origin of human beings, he continues, "Adam was two hundred and thirty years old."[7] Was I not right in saying at the beginning that you can find nothing written idly or to no purpose in Sacred Scripture? I mean, behold here too how much precision this blessed [178] author employs. "Adam had a son of his own in his very image," he says, "and he named him Seth." In the case of the previous child—I mean Cain—on the contrary, he made no such comment except to suggest at the beginning his decline into evil. And rightly so: far from bearing the stamp of his father, he lost no time in taking to wickedness. In the present case, however, the text says, "A son of his own in his very image"—in other words, of the same ilk as his parent, preserving the same stamp of virtue, revealing the image of his father in his actions, capable of reversing by his own virtue the crime of his older brother. You see, it is not in reference to bodily features that Scripture is speaking to us here in the words, "A son of his own in his very image"; it is to do with the disposition of his soul, so that

7. Gen 5.3–5, with that notorious divergence by the LXX from the Masoretic Hebrew text in numbers of years typical also of the Samaritan Pentateuch at this place in the text. Strangely, as if shy of the textual discrepancies, Chrysostom omits reference to this matter of age with such promise for moral comment, and fixes on the names instead.

we may learn that he would not turn out like the other brother.

(8) For this reason, too, his mother in giving her son this name did so with thanks, attributing the birth of a son not to nature or to the process of birth but to the power of God. This it was, you see, that fertilized nature for giving birth, and so the text says, "She gave him the name Seth, saying, 'God has raised up for me another child in place of Abel, whom Cain killed.'"[8] See the precision of the expression; she did not say, God has given me, but, "'God has raised up for me.'" Notice how in outline a premonition of the resurrection is already being suggested to us through this expression. I mean, she spoke as if to say, He has raised up this child for me in place of the fallen one. Even if that one was laid low at his brother's hand (she is saying), still the power of God has raised up this child in place of the fallen one. You see, since the time for the resurrection had not yet come, he raised up, not the fallen one, but another one in his place; hence she said, "'God has raised up for me another child in place of Abel, whom Cain killed.'" Do you see the woman's gratitude? Do you see the Lord's loving kindness? how he envisaged speedy consolation for them? Let us all imitate this, and attribute everything to grace from on high. You see, even if nature takes its course, it does so, not by its own power but in response to the direction of the Creator. Let women not be distressed when they have no children; instead, let them give evidence of a thankful disposition and have recourse to the Creator and direct their request to him, the Lord of nature, not attributing childbirth to the intercourse of the partners nor to any other source than the Creator of everything, who also brings our nature from non-being into being and is able to correct anything deficient. This is exemplified in Eve's making the fact of her grief an occasion for praise when she attributes everything to the Lord in the words, "'God has raised up for me another child in the place of Abel, whom Cain killed.'" Do you see how she was not merely not dis-

8. Gen 4.25.

tressed nor avoided uttering any pained remark (Sacred Scripture, after all, would not have passed it over, if in fact something of the sort had been said by her), but in accepting in noble fashion what had happened she was granted speedy comfort and displayed more intense gratitude by exalting the Lord's kindness?

(9) I mean, take note of the extent of the generosity the Lord gives evidence of on his part: he not only favors her with another son but also predicts at this point that he will be virtuous. "He had a son of his own," the text says, remember, "in his very image." For an immediate insight into the child's virtue, notice him also in turn demonstrating the piety [178] of his attitude in the name of his child. "A son was born to Seth," the text says; "he gave him the name Enosh. He it was who hoped to invoke the name of the Lord God."[9] Do you notice his name, more resplendent than any other diadem, more brilliant than a robe of purple? What in fact could be more blessed than this man adorned by God himself with this title and employing it in place of a name?

(10) Do you see how, as I mentioned at the outset, in these mere names a great wealth of thought lies hidden? That is to say, they reveal in this case not simply the piety of the parents but also the great concern they had for their children, and how from the very beginning they instructed the children born to them through the names they gave them to cling to virtue. They didn't give names casually and by chance, like people today, who say, The child is to be called after his grandfather or greatgrandfather. The ancients, on the contrary, didn't act that way; instead, they took great pains to give such names to their children as not merely led to virtue those receiving them but proved instructive in complete wisdom for everybody else and for later generations too. This we will come to realize gradually as the sermon develops. Accordingly, let us neither give our children any old name, nor

9. Gen 4.26. As mentioned above at footnote 16 in Homily 20, Chrysostom's lack of Hebrew seems to be encouraging him to read more into the name than is justified, as if presuming the following (puzzling) sentence is etymological in basis.

bestow on them the names of grandfathers or greatgrand-
fathers or people of distinguished lineage, but rather of holy
men illustrious for their virtue who enjoyed great confidence
in their relations with God. To be more exact, they should
not trust lightly in those men's names, the parents or the children who have been given these names: a name that is un-
supported by virtuous living is of no benefit—instead, it is
necessary to rest one's hopes for salvation in the practice of
virtue and not to become big-headed over a name or over
one's connection with holy men or over anything other than
the confidence that arises from one's own good deeds. To be
more exact still, we should not become big-headed over this
but rather humble and modest in the situation where we are
able to amass great wealth of virtue. This, you see, is the way
we will personally amass and store up wealth with security,
and win favor from God. For this reason, after all, Christ also
has said to his disciples, "When you do everything, say, 'We
are unprofitable servants,'"[10] deflating their sense of importance in any respect and persuading them to be humble and
not be conceited over their virtuous behavior but realize that
the very greatest virtue of all is to be humble in the practice
of virtue.

(11) Let us, however, return to the theme of the sermon
and see the children born later. It is likely, you see, that as we
proceed bit by bit we will find greater treasure, immense
wealth beyond all telling. The text says: "Enosh (the son of
Seth) was a hundred and ninety years old when he had a son,
Kainan . . .[11] Kainan had a son, Maleleel . . .[12] Maleleel had a
son, Jared . . .[13] Jared had a son, Enoch . . . [14] Enoch was a
hundred and sixty five years old when he had a son Mathusala. Now, Enoch pleased God," the text says; "he lived two
hundred years after having Mathusala, and had other sons
and daughters; Enoch's lifespan was three hundred and sixty
five years. Enoch pleased God, and he was not to be found

10. Luke 17.10.   11. Gen 5.9.
12. Gen 5.12.   13. Gen 5.15.
14. Gen 5.18.

because God had taken him away."[15] Wasn't I right in saying
that as [180] we proceeded we would find immense spiritual
riches beyond all telling in these names? Consider at this
point, I ask you, dearly beloved, the just man's virtue, the
good God's love exceeding all limits, and the precision of Sacred Scripture. "Enoch was a hundred and sixty five years
old," the text says, "when he had a son Mathusala. Now, Enoch pleased God," the text says, "after having Mathusala."

(12) Let both men and women listen and learn about the
just man's virtue, and not consider marriage to be an obstacle
to pleasing God. I mean, it was to this effect that in more
than one place Sacred Scripture made a point of saying that
he had a son Mathusala and then pleased God, and said the
same thing over again in the words, "He pleased God after
having Mathusala," in case anyone thought it was an obstacle
to virtue. You see, as long as we are on our guard, neither
marriage nor bringing up children nor anything else will be
able to stand in the way of our being pleasing to God. I mean,
behold how this man, who as it happens had the same nature
as ourselves, without the guidance of any law or the instructive contents of Scripture or any other inducement to wisdom
gave evidence from his own resources and by choice of such
satisfaction in God's eyes as to live to this day and never experience death even yet. In other words, dearly beloved, had
marriage or the raising of children been likely to prove a
stumbling block on the way to virtue, the Creator of all would
not have introduced marriage into our life lest it prove our
undoing in difficult times and through severe problems.
Since, however, family life not only offers us no obstacle to

15. Gen 5.21–24. In this selection of texts—Chrysostom obviously feeling
the need to push the pace along and omit many details of ages, at the cost
of his habitual principle of the value of Scripture's *akribeia*—his variant of
the LXX generally corresponds to the Hebrew, with two interesting excep-
tions: in v.22 Chrysostom's text supplies the verb "lived" missing from the
Masoretic text and other MSS of LXX (cf. Rahlfs), though he proceeds in
his commentary on the verse to draw a moral point based on a reading where
the verb does not occur at all nor is even presumed; in v.24 the anthropomorphic "walked with God," so full of theological significance for commentators like Von Rad (cf. his commentary, 71–73), appears much more lamely
in the LXX "pleased God."

wisdom in God's eyes as long as we are prepared to be on our guard, but even brings us much encouragement and calms the tumult of our natural tendencies, not allowing the billows to surge but constantly ensuring that the bark dock safely in the harbor, consequently he granted the human race the consolation that comes from this source.

(13) In fact, this good man demonstrates that what has been said by us is true. After having Mathusala, the text says, remember, "Enoch pleased God," and it was for no short period that he followed this virtuous way but, as the text tells us, he lasted two hundred years. Since, after the fall of the first formed, a human being was found to ascend the very heights of virtue and to revoke the sin of our first parents through his own acceptable way of life, see the exceeding love of the good God. When he found someone capable of revoking Adam's sin, he showed through his very actions that it was not out of a desire to inflict death on our race for transgression of the command that he had condemned the person who had been given the command; he took him away during his lifetime to another place. "Enoch pleased God," the text says, "and he was not to be found because God had taken him away." Do you see the Lord's wisdom? He took him away during his lifetime, he did not grant him immortality, in case this should diminish fear of sinning; instead, he let it remain strong in the human race.

(14) Hence once again obscurely, so to say, and imperceptibly he wants the sentence he had passed [181] on Adam to be revoked. But he doesn't make it obvious, so that fear may have the effect of bringing people to their senses. Consequently, he took away Enoch, who pleased him. If, however, someone were anxious to be meddlesome and ask, Where did he take him? Has he continued to live till the present? let that person learn not to follow human reasoning or to pry into God's doings but to believe what is said. In other words, whenever God reveals anything, we shouldn't question what is said but rather treat with the highest regard the words spoken by God, even if they do not correspond to the things that lie before us plain to see. I mean, the fact that God took

him away to another place Sacred Scripture has told us, as well as the fact that God took him during his lifetime without his having experienced death; rather, through the personal satisfaction he found in God's eyes he proved superior to the sentence passed on the race of human beings. But where he took him, or what kind of life he lives now, these further details were not given.

(15) Do you see the Lord's goodness, how on finding the man practicing virtue he did not strip him of the dignity which he had accorded the first formed human being before the transgression of the command? He meant to teach us that, if the latter had not paid greater regard to the devil's deceit than to the command given him, he would have been granted the same reward or even greater. "Mathusala was a hundred and eighty seven years old," the text says, "when he had a son Lamech . . ."[16] Lamech was a hundred and eighty years old when he had a son; he named him Noe, saying, 'This child will surely bring us relief from our labors, from the troubles of our hands, and from the curse the Lord placed on the earth.'"[17] See once again in the name of Lamech's newborn child the greatness of the mysteries, the extraordinary nature of the prophecy, and the good God's unspeakable love. I mean, when by his own prescience he foresees the future, and descries the increase in human beings' wickedness, he foretells by means of the child's name the evils that will come upon all the race of human beings, in the hope that, provided they respond to fear, come to their senses and eschew wickedness, they may choose virtue instead. See also the Lord's longsuffering, how long before the event he makes his prophecy so as to demonstrate his characteristic love and deprive of any excuse those destined to suffer the punishment.

(16) Perhaps, however, someone may say, How did Lamech

16. Gen 5.25.
17. Gen 5.28–29. Chrysostom, again despite his profound interest in the *akribeia* of the sacred text, selects for comment the verses he finds significant; the ages in his text differ slightly from both the Hebrew and LXX, themselves divergent.

come to have such a degree of prophetic power? After all, Scripture doesn't record that he was a person of virtue and remarkable powers does it? Don't be surprised at that, dearly beloved: the Lord, in his wisdom and inventiveness, frequently permits great and wonderful events to be foretold by unworthy people, not only in the Old Testament but also in the New. I mean, listen to the evangelist's words about Caiaphas, the highpriest of the Jews: "He did not give this as a personal opinion, but in his capacity of highpriest that year he prophesied that Jesus was destined to die, not for the person alone but to bring together into one also the nations that had been scattered."[18] You will find something like it occurring again in the story of Balaam also: when urged to curse the people, he not merely did not curse them but even prophesied great and wonderful things, not merely about the people but also about the coming of the Saviour.[19] So don't be surprised if in this case also Lamech in naming his child gives him a name of this kind; instead, attribute it all to God, who arranges everything in his [182] inventive wisdom.

(17) "He named him Noe"; his name, you see, means relief. So he is referring to that destruction that was due to occur so many years later as relief—as Job also says, "Death means relief for man."[20] Since wickedness brings with it great distress of deep intensity, he refers to its removal and disappearance which they were about to experience through that deluge as relief. "He named him Noe," the text says; then it interprets for us the sense of the name by adding, "'Now, this child will bring us relief from our labors'"—meaning he will rid us of evil—"'and from the troubles of our hands,'" meaning again in similar fashion from evil doings, not meaning by this that our hands are troubled but that through their efforts and evil behavior troubles are multiplied. "'And from the curse the Lord placed on the earth'"; this means he will free us from all the evils encumbering us and from the condition of distress and difficulty affecting the earth by the im-

18. John 11.51–52, with some slight variations from the present state of the text.
19. Cf. Num 23–24.   20. Job 3.23 LXX.

position of the curse on account of the fall of the first formed human being. In other words, understand now, I ask you, dearly beloved, how this child proves to be an occasion of instruction for all who see him as he grows up bit by bit: you had only to learn the child's name for the sense of the name to teach you at once the ruin that would fall on people in a future time. You see, had anyone been inspired to make the simple statement that this would happen, the statement would have been consigned to oblivion and not everyone would have known about this intolerable kind of punishment. In this case, on the contrary, this man grew up in the sight of everyone and became a reminder in season and out[21] of God's anger.

(18) To learn with precision how long a time it was that the son continued by means of his name to exhort everyone to shun evil, opt for virtue and thus avoid that awful anger, the text says, "Noe was five hundred years old when he had three sons."[22] See once more another good man with wife and family achieving great satisfaction in God's eyes and opting for the way of virtue in the sight of everyone, hindered in no way either by marriage or by family responsibilities. All this time, however, we must marvel at God's unspeakable longsuffering and the exceeding ingratitude of people of the time: see, this good man continued all those five hundred years shouting aloud and testifying by his name to the impending approach of the deluge on the whole world on account of the extremity of wickedness as he advised. Nevertheless, despite such warning and despite that great number of years the loving God does not inflict the punishment; instead, with an increase in his own longsuffering he adds still further a considerable number of years to his own peculiar forebearance. You see, he had not created the human race for the specific purpose of punishing them—quite the contrary, to regale them with the enjoyment of countless good things. Hence you see him hesitating at every opportunity and loath to act in this matter of punishment.

(19) Lest, however, we overwhelm your memory with a ple-

21. Cf. 2 Tim 4.2.   22. Gen 5.32.

thora of words, let us close at this point and postpone till next time the remainder. All the same, dearly beloved, let us not listen to these things heedlessly; rather, let us learn to take an interest in virtue, make much of finding satisfaction in God's eyes and not give it second place to management of a house, care of a wife, bringing up [183] children or anything else, thinking that these things suffice to excuse lax and careless living, and putting forward those lifeless and ill-considered words, namely, I am a man of the world, I have a wife, I devote myself to the care of my children. This is what a lot of people are inclined to say when we exhort them to take pains over a virtuous life or show enthusiasm for the reading of Scripture. This is not for me, the person says: I haven't left the world, have I? I haven't become a monk, have I? What are you saying, human being that you are? Are you leaving it to them alone to find satisfaction before God? He wants everyone to be saved and come to the knowledge of truth,[23] and he wishes no one to neglect virtue. Listen, after all, to what he has to say by means of the inspired author: "I desire not the sinner's death as much as his conversion and life."[24] No hindrance came to this good man, did it, from intercourse with his wife or family cares?

(20) Accordingly, I beseech you, let us not deceive ourselves, but the more we are embroiled in these cares, so much the more should we take the remedies available in the reading of the Holy Scriptures. I mean, surely the people we've been mentioning were of the same nature as ourselves, and yet had fewer inducements to the practice of virtue. So what excuse could we be granted if while enjoying such great instruction, being favored with so much grace, enjoying assistance from on high, and being in receipt of the promise of those ineffable goods, we did not measure up to the standard of virtue set by those men of old? Were we prepared to remain alert, the matters raised today would suffice to prompt us to love virtue, and never consider anything to be an obstacle to its progress. After all, if people living before the Law arrived at

23. Cf. 1 Tim 2.4.   24. Ezek 18.23.

such heights of virtue on the strength of the instruction innate in their nature, what can we say for ourselves for being found far from virtue despite such assistance, despite the coming of Christ and his countless miracles? Hence, I beseech you, let us not approach the contents of Sacred Scripture idly, but read them with attention so as to gain benefit from them and at least at this late hour be in a position to follow the way of virtue as God would have us do. You see, if we were ready to make this spiritual teaching ring in your ears day in day out, and you were to continue in the same state of indifference, what advantage would come to you from the constant teaching, or what consolation would it be for us to see our effort proving fruitless and no sign of progress stemming from our zeal?

(21) Tell me, after all, are we not composed of two elements—I mean soul and body? So why do we not accord equal attention to both instead of being zealous in treating the body with care, paying money to doctors, ourselves demonstrating much solicitude in its regard, clothing it in rich apparel, supplying it with food beyond what is necessary? We wish it to enjoy constant indulgence and be afflicted with no ailment at all; in the event of some trouble occurring, we apply every means of correcting the problem. This we do in the case of the body—in other words, the lesser element; tell me, after all, what equality is there between soul and body? If, in fact, you want to see the difference, consider how the body comes to be thought of no importance when the soul has left it. Accordingly, you who take such care of the body—for what reason and on what account [184] are you determined to show such disdain for the care of the soul, neither bringing it proper nourishment (I mean the exhortations of the Holy Scriptures), nor applying appropriate remedies to its wounds and the ulcers that sap its strength and undermine its confidence? Instead, you allow it to be overlooked, to waste away with hunger, to be destroyed with ulcers, and to be set upon, so to say, as though by dogs, by those evil and unseemly thoughts, and so to be torn to pieces and lose all its vigor.

(22) Why is it that, as we take care of our body, visible as it

is, we do not take the very same care of our soul, incorporeal and invisible though it is, especially as attention to it is not only easy and trouble-free but also costs us nothing and requires no effort? In the case of attention to the body, on the one hand, there is need of great expense for bodily ailments, paying something to the doctors and the rest for all other assistance (I mean food and clothing), not to mention the majority of people who over and above what is necessary stop at nothing in their spending. In the case of the soul, on the other hand, none of these things is necessary, unless, just as you daily spend money to give nourishment to the body, you are likewise determined not to neglect the soul and let it die of hunger but to provide it with proper nourishment from the reading of Scripture and the support of spiritual advice: "Not on bread alone does man live," Scripture says, remember, "but on every word coming from the mouth of God."[25] If so, you would have an excellent attitude to these matters and would be properly mindful of the element more characteristic of us. So, just as you provide a range of garments for the body and give your attention to food for the various seasons and the diversity of clothing, by the same token don't neglect the soul's nakedness and poverty of good works but likewise clothe it in garments becoming it; thus you ought rapidly to improve its condition and restore it to its natural health.

(23) Now, what are its garments? Almsgiving and generosity in regard to the poor—this is the soul's best covering, this its resplendent mantle. But if you want not merely to provide it with clothing but also adorn it as you do the body, provide it also with the assistance of prayer and confession of sins, and do not cease washing its face with a steady flow of tears. You see, just as you bathe the body's face each day with great care lest any smudge marking its face somewhere should give it an ugly aspect, take the trouble to do the same in the case

___

25. Matt 4.4; cf. Deut 8.3. The LXX, which is being quoted, here and elsewhere renders the Hebrew imperfect by the future where the appropriate English tense would be the present; cf. M. Zerwick, *Biblical Greek* (1960⁴), ET: Rome, 1963.

of the soul also, and bathe it daily by shedding hot tears; by this water it removes the smudge and becomes more resplendent. Because most women through their decadence ignore the instruction of the Apostle when he said, "Don't deck yourselves out in braided hair, or gold, or pearls, or expensive attire,"[26] they go to a lot of expense to do just that—and not women only, but also decadent men drag themselves down to the level of those women's luxury and sport rings on their fingers, as well as decking themselves out with large and heavy jewels, which should make them feel ashamed and want to hide. These men and women, therefore, were they prepared to heed my words, would exchange that gold that brings great harm to both men and women for the adornment [185] of the soul instead and by that means beautify it. I mean, just as gold adornments on the body, even if it be a shapely one, render it more ugly, so even if the soul is unsightly, they transform it to the utmost attractiveness when they are worn.

(24) How, you ask, can gold adornments be worn by the soul? Once more by the hands of the poor. You see, the poor take them and thus become the cause of the soul's attractiveness. Pass your gold to them and deliver them into their belly, and they will give you in return such beauty of soul that you will win the true spouse himself by means of your beauty and will gain for yourself countless blessings through him. After all, when you win the favor of the Lord through your loveliness, you have an abundance of all good things and enjoy untold prosperity. If therefore we wish to win the satisfaction of the Lord, let us abandon the effort to beautify the body and give our attention to the soul's beauty day by day so as to win the favor of the loving God and have the good fortune to enjoy those unspeakable rewards, thanks to the grace and love of our Lord Jesus Christ, to whom with the Father and the Holy Spirit be glory, power and honor, now and forever, for all ages of ages. Amen.

26. 1 Tim 2.9.

HOMILY 22

"Noe was five hundred years old when he had three sons, Shem, Cham and Japheth. Human beings began to be numerous on earth, and daughters were born to them."[1]

THE [185] LEFTOVERS OF YESTERDAY'S MEAL I would like to put before you today—but don't get upset, dearly beloved, at the mention of leftovers: while in the case of material viands after a day or two they frequently lose their freshness and are useless as nourishment; in the case of a spiritual meal there is no cause for anything like that. On the contrary, no matter how much time elapses, it gives all the more evidence of grace and is found to be fresher and more potent. So come now, let us put into effect the promise we made yesterday, discharge our debt of teaching and give evidence of gratitude. You see, the teaching proves to be of advantage not only to those who receive it, as in the case of debts, but also to me as I discharge my debt. Why do I say, to me as I discharge my debt? The nature of this spiritual debt is such that the more it is discharged, the more it grows and brings about an increase in the remainder as well as untold wealth both for the debtor and for the creditors. Do you recognize the new kind of debt and the unusual form of payment? This is the way, you see, with spiritual things: they increase all the more with distribution, and the remainder grows in direct ratio to the number who share in it; the debtor feels no effect of his payment—instead, what he retains increases while the recipients find themselves also in better circumstances.

(2) So, since this is the nature of these spiritual goods, let us in our turn show all zeal and enthusiasm about payment

1. Gen 5.32; 6.1.

68

while you ready your ears for receiving it so that with the recesses of your mind set at rest you may receive the words we say, and in this way go off home. You see, I have in mind once again to bring to the fore the subject of Noe, of God's ineffable love and his longsuffering that surpasses all description. You learnt yesterday how right from his birth [186] this just man was given his name by his father and thus went about providing everyone of that period with a warning of their fate, as if he were shouting aloud and saying in his own words, Refrain from evil, turn to virtue, fear the impending punishment—a deluge will engulf the whole world without exception; the excess of God's anger is extreme, since extreme also is the swell of wickedness. He went on doing this not for a year or two or three, but he kept up this exhortation for five hundred years. Do you see the Lord's longsuffering? Do you see the excess of his goodness? Do you see the intensity of wickedness? Do you see the degree of ingratitude?

(3) It was at this point, as you recall, that our instruction yesterday came to a close; so today we must discover how the loving Lord in fidelity to his own goodness did not stop short at five hundred years but demonstrated a further extension of his care for the people who had sinned in that way. "Noe was five hundred years old," the text says. Sacred Scripture gave us an indication of the significance of the good man's age so that we might learn how long a time he lived exhorting them and how they chose the way of evil and were consumed in it, whereas the good man took a path at variance with them all, displayed the highest degree of virtue and so won favor from God and, while all the others became liable to punishment, he escaped it along with his kin. From this we learn that, provided we remain on the alert and do not lose heart, we will not only come to no harm from dealing with evil people but will even be rendered more careful about virtue. You see, the reason why the loving God arranged things in such a way that everyone good and evil should be in the same situation was in order that the wickedness of the evil might be thwarted, the virtue of the good might shine more brightly, and the slothful might gain benefit from association with the

zealous, if they so wished. Consider, after all, I ask you, the height of this man's virtue, how among such a multitude of people rushing into evil he alone took the opposite direction, placing greater value on virtue than on wickedness and not being made uncertain on the way of virtue by the unanimity of others or their great number; instead, he fulfilled in anticipation the statement due to be made by blessed Moses, that "'you will not join many in evildoing.'"[2]

(4) The strange and remarkable feature is that despite having so many people—everyone, in fact—urging him to evildoing and the practice of wickedness, and despite there being no one to encourage him to virtue, of his own accord he attained to such heights with such a degree of fervor as to proceed in a direction contrary to the vast multitude, without fear or regard for their evil concurrence and without entertaining any notions of the kind that the slothful do. When they see a lot of people displaying the same kind of unanimity, they make this a pretext and excuse for their own sloth in the words, Why should I, tell me, take it into my head to venture something out of step with all these people by differing from such a crowd? After all, surely I don't happen to be better than all these people, do I? What would I gain from opposition of that kind? What benefit would their hatred be to me? Noe had no idle ideas like that and gave them no thought; instead, once more he fulfilled in anticipation that statement of the inspired author, "Better one person doing the Lord's will than a lawless host."[3] After all (he is saying), surely fellowship with this multitude and associating with it in its headlong career into evil will not suffice to deliver me from punishment? He was aware, you see, he was well aware that each of us will be held responsible for our own salvation, and that it is out of the question for someone else to undergo punishment on the sinner's behalf or to have the good for-

2. Exod 23.2.
3. Sir 16.3. Chrysostom's text of the LXX here corresponds to the expanded version written in the margin of Codex Sinaiticus by a corrector, according to Rahlfs—a matter of significance for those endeavoring to isolate Chrysostom's LXX tradition.

tune [187] to receive a reward. Consequently, just as a spark that happens to be burning in the middle of the sea not only is not extinguished but even gives out its light more brilliantly day by day, so the just man proved to be a teacher to everyone by means of his behavior.

(5) Do you see how the Lord created our nature to enjoy free will? I mean, how did it happen, tell me, that while those people showed enthusiasm for wickedness and rendered themselves liable to punishment, this man opted for virtue, shunned association with them and thus felt no effect of punishment? Is it not crystal clear that each person chose wickedness or virtue of his own volition? You see, if that were not the case and independence did not have its roots in our nature, those people would not have been punished nor the others receive reward for their virtue. Since, however, everything has been allowed to remain with our choice owing to grace from on high, punishment duly awaits the sinners, and reward and recompense those who practice virtue. "Noe was five hundred years old when he had three sons, Shem, Cham and Japheth." Notice the precision of Sacred Scripture: when it detailed to us the good man's age, it revealed the excess of the Lord's longsuffering out of a desire to make clear to us again the extremity of the Lord's tolerance and the strong drive of human beings' wickedness.

(6) Let us, however, listen to the very words coming from Moses: speaking under influence of the Spirit, he intends to teach us everything with precision. "Human beings began to be numerous on earth," the text says, "and daughters were born to them." It was not idly that he added the clause, "and daughters were born to them"; rather, its purpose was that we might get an indication of the great multitude. After all, when the mass of roots is as great as that, it follows there must be a great number of branches growing. "Now, when the sons of God saw that the daughters of men were beautiful, they took wives for themselves from them all just as they were inclined."[4] Let us study each expression of this state-

4. Gen 6.2.

ment closely so that nothing of what is hidden below the surface may pass us by. You see, there is need to make a careful study of this passage and confute the fanciful interpretations of those people whose every remark is made rashly—firstly, to repeat what they presume to say, and by demonstrating the absurdity of what is said by them to teach your good selves the true sense of Scripture so that you will not lend your ears idly to people uttering those blasphemies and presuming to speak in a way that brings their own persons into jeopardy. I mean, they claim that this remark is made not about human beings but about angels; these (they say) he called sons of God. Let them demonstrate firstly where angels are called sons of God; they would not, however, be able to show this anywhere. While human beings are called sons of God, angels are nowhere so called. On the contrary, it speaks about angels in these terms: "He makes the winds his angels, fire and flame his ministers,"[5] whereas about human beings, "I said, You are [188] gods,"[6] and again, "Sons have I begotten and raised,"[7] and again, "Israel my firstborn son"[8]—but an angel is nowhere called son, or son of God. What in fact do they claim? To be sure, they really were angels, but because they fell into this lawless way, they lost their status.

(7) Furthermore, another interpretation even more fanciful: Is this not true, then—that they are now fallen, and that this is the cause of their fall? Scripture in fact teaches us differently, that before the creation of the firstformed human being the devil fell from that dignity and with him those whose pretensions outstripped their state, as a sage has also remarked, "Through the devil's envy death entered the world."[9] I mean, tell me: if he had not fallen before the creation of the human being, how could he have envied the human being while retaining his former status? After all, what sense does it make for an angel to envy a human being, the incorporeal being enjoying such great dignity to envy a creature encumbered with a body? Since, however, he had fallen from heav-

5. Ps 104.4.   6. Ps 82.6.
7. Isa 1.2.   8. Exod 4.22.
9. Wis 2.24.

enly glory into utter disrepute, and though incorporeal himself he saw the newly created human being enjoying such
great esteem despite its bodily condition through the love of
the Creator, his burning rage led him into envy, and by
means of the deceit he practiced through the serpent he
caused the human being to be liable to punishment of death.
This, you see, is what wickedness is like; it cannot take kindly
to the prosperity of others. So it is plain for all to see that in
times past the devil and all his company fell from that condition of glory and were numbered among the disreputable.
Is it not a particular hallmark of folly to claim that angels
descended to have intercourse with women, and that incorporeal nature of theirs was reduced to association with cor-
poreal creatures? Or do you not hear the words of Christ
about the being of angels, "At the resurrection they neither
marry nor are given in marriage, but are like angels of
God"?[10] After all, it is not for that kind of incorporeal creature to ever feel the onset of desire. In response to these
people we have to reach the same conclusion, that to admit
this notion into one's mind is the height of absurdity. I mean,
if the saints and people granted the gift of the Holy Spirit
were unable to have a vision of angels (the man of passion,
after all, caught sight of an angel's presence, not his being—
how could he see an incorporeal being?—but rather under-
went a transformation and came close to losing his life in the
process, this man of such calibre and such eminence almost
falling unconscious on the ground),[11] who could be so utterly
deranged as to admit this blasphemous remark and the folly
it betokens, that this incorporeal and intellectual creature
could tolerate intercourse with bodily things?

(8) Lest, however, in raising these matters we ourselves
largely seem to be wasting time to no purpose—come now,
since we have convinced your good selves through these
proofs how this objection has been proved groundless—let us

10. Matt 22.30 in one MS tradition.
11. Chrysostom is here referring to Dan 10 in the Greek version of Theodotion, which differs from the LXX in details such as the mention of Daniel
as "man of passion."

teach you the truth of the material by reading again the words of Sacred Scripture. "Human beings began to be numerous on the earth," the text reads, "and [189] daughters were born to them. Now, when the sons of God saw that the daughters of men were beautiful, they took wives for themselves from them all just as they were inclined." We made the point before in teaching you that it is customary with Scripture to call human beings sons of God. So since these people took their origin from Seth and from his son named Enosh (the text, remember, saying, "He it was who hoped to invoke the name of the Lord God"[12]), those descended from him in future were called sons of God by Sacred Scripture for the reason of their imitation of the virtue of their ancestors up to his time. On the other hand, he gave the name sons of men to those born after Seth, the descendants of Cain and those taking their descent from him. "Human beings began to be numerous on the earth," the text says, "and daughters were born to them. Now, when the sons of God" (the descendants of Seth and Enosh) "saw that the daughters of men" (those born to the other, whom he described by saying that "daughters were born to them") "were beautiful." See how through this expression he indicates to us all their licentiousness; it was not through a desire to raise families that they set about this behavior but out of sheer lechery—"Now, when they saw that the daughters of men were beautiful," the text says. Lust for a shapely figure brought them to this ruin, and a pretty face proved to be for them an occasion of debauchery and licentiousness.

(9) Nor was this enough: the text adds, "They took wives for themselves from them all just as they were inclined." This likewise has the effect of conveying their great licentiousness in the fact that they were ensnared by beauty and had no intention of curbing their unbridled desire; instead, they were captivated and intoxicated by the sight of it, and through their illicit behavior they left themselves bereft of heavenly favor. So that we may learn that they behaved this way neither

12. Gen 4.26.

by the dictates of marriage nor for the sake of raising a family, the text accordingly goes on, "When they saw that the daughters of men were beautiful, they took wives for themselves from them all just as they were inclined." Why was this so? Would anyone lay the blame on the sight of the eyes? Not at all: it wasn't the eye that was the cause of the lapse but the carelessness of choice and the free rein of desire. You see, the purpose for which the eye was created was that through it one should descry God's creatures and praise their Maker. So it is the role of the eye to see, though malicious sight is due to reason, which directs from within. After all, the Lord created the limbs to be of use for us in doing good, and he allowed them to be directed by the spiritual being—I mean the soul. So whenever it inclines to negligence and loosens the reins, like a rider who, unequal to the task of checking the wild impulses of his mounts, gives them the bit and lets himself fall under the hooves of the horses pulling the chariot, our will in just the same manner surrenders itself to wild desires and surrenders itself whenever it is incapable of employing its faculties properly. Hence, when Christ our Lord saw the unreliability of our nature and the indifference of our will, he made a law to protect and curb our inquisitive sight so as to quench the blaze that springs up within us even at a great distance, saying as he did, [190] "The man who has looked at a woman so as to lust after her has already committed sin with her in his heart."[13] Consequently, he is saying, I am forbidding your sight to be unrestricted so that I may preserve you from improper behavior. Do not think, after all, he is saying, that association alone causes sin: it is the intention that brings our condemnation.

(10) So the people in our narrative saw the beauty and were captivated by what they saw. "They saw that they were beautiful," the text says, remember, "and took wives for themselves from them all just as they were inclined." But despite this improper behavior and unrestrained attitude, let us see God's goodness. "The Lord God said, 'My spirit is not to remain

13. Matt 5.28.

forever with these human beings on account of their being carnal. Instead, they will have a life of one hundred and twenty years.'"[14] Such depths of love can be seen in these few words: "The Lord God said," the text reads, "'My spirit is not to remain with these human beings on account of their being carnal.'" He called his exercise of providence his spirit in this verse where he foretells their destruction. So that you may learn that the remark was made to that effect, notice what is added: "'on account of their being carnal'"—that is to say, on account of their devoting themselves to carnal pursuits and not employing properly the properties of the soul, but passing their life just as if they were clad in flesh alone and deprived of soul. You see, it is the unfailing practice of Sacred Scripture to call carnal people flesh, as also to describe people of virtue non-carnal, in the way Paul says, "You, however, are not in the flesh"[15]—not because you are not clad in flesh but because despite being clad in flesh you rise above the thinking of the flesh. So, just as Scripture said to some, for reason of their scorning the concerns of the flesh, "You, however, are not in the flesh," so in the case of others, since they were constantly caught up in carnal concerns, it called them carnal. "On account of their being carnal," I will not continue to allow them to be defiled by sin.

(11) Do you see the depth of his anger? Do you see the extent of the punishment he threatens? Consider how he mingled love with his anger and his threats. You see, this is what our Lord is like: he often threatens, not so as to put his threat into effect but that he may bring us round and never have to put his threat into operation. I mean, if he intended to punish us, why would he announce it beforehand? Since, however, this is not his intention, consequently he is forever delaying and postponing, and he announces it beforehand to give the guilty the opportunity to shun evil, choose virtue, and avoid experiencing punishment. So when he threatened to deliver them to complete disaster (this, after all, is the sense of "My spirit is not to remain with these human beings on account

---

14. Gen 6.3.   15. Rom 8.9.

of their being carnal"—as if to say, "'I won't allow them to live any longer'"), he was not content with putting up with them for five hundred years, the whole lifetime of Noe, when they were instructed by the sound of his name. So he further withholds his anger at this point and sets another deadline for them in the words, I threatened, I spoke up, and I made clear my anger which must be let loose on you for all the sins you have committed; but because I intend to save even those who have committed irreversible wrong and want no one to be lost, accordingly I grant you a further period of a hundred and twenty years so that, provided you are prepared to expunge your sins [191] by conversion to a better way of life and option for virtue, you may avoid experiencing punishment. The text says, remember, "'They will have a life of a hundred and twenty years.'"

(12) The text goes on, "Now, the giants were on the earth in those days. Later, when the sons of God mated with the daughters of men, and children were born to them, these were the giants of old, people of renown."[16] By "giants" in this verse I think Sacred Scripture is referring to men of great physical stature. From these people, the text says, their lines developed. Elsewhere, too, you see, you can find this stated: "Giants come to check my anger,"[17] Scripture says. Some people think that this number of a hundred and twenty years is the limit placed on their life; but this is not the point he is making—rather, his intention is to stress his longsuffering up to this point, which he has displayed in their regard even despite such terrible sins. So let us learn that, in spite of his anger, his threatening and his longsuffering shown them over such a long period of time with a view to their repentance, they not only profited nothing but even persisted in the same ways—hence the words, "When the sons of God mated with the daughters of men, and children were born to them, these were the giants of old, people of renown." Do you see the excess of their ingratitude? Do you see their un-

16. Gen 6.4.
17. Isa 13.3 in a variant of the LXX's preferred reading, "to execute my anger."

responsive spirit? Neither fear of punishment nor the extent
of God's longsuffering won them away from their evil behavior; instead, once they had plunged into the abyss and had
been blinded in their mind's eye, they no longer had the will
to be rescued, immersed as they were in evil desire as if in
some intoxication—just as some sage has said, "When the
godless fall to the depths of evil, they lose all sense of respect."[18] It is a terrible thing, you see, dearly beloved, a terrible thing to fall into the clutches of the devil. I mean, the
soul then, as though caught in a net, and like a boar trapped
in the mire, is likewise caught up in pleasure and, swept along
by its evil habits, it loses all sense of the foul odor of its sins.
Consequently, we must be awake and on our guard so as
never to allow the evil demon any entrance at the outset, lest
he cloud our reasoning, blind the sharp vision of our mind,
and thus as if robbing us of sunlight render us unable to see
the rays of the Sun of Justice and cause us to fall into the
abyss—something that befell those people at that time.

(13) After all, give ear once more to the patience of God's
goodness: "Now, the Lord God saw," the text goes on, "that
the vices of human beings were multiplied on earth."[19] What
is meant by the expression, "Now, he saw"? Had the Lord
been unaware? Not at all; rather, Sacred Scripture explains
everything with our limitations in mind, and so as to teach us
that even despite his extraordinary longsuffering they persisted in the same ways or even involved themselves in worse
evils, it says, "Now, he saw that the vices of human beings
were multiplied." You see, from this evil behavior, as from
some spring, arose as well many other sins in them—hence it
says, "the vices of human beings." I mean, where there is
impurity and licentiousness and such intemperance, it is likely
also that intoxication, drunken violence, extreme dishonesty,
greed and countless other evils will arise. "Now, the Lord God
saw," the text says, "that human beings' vices were multiplied
on the earth, and everyone gave himself up wholly to pon-

18. Prov 18.3 in a variant of the LXX.
19. Gen 6.5.

dering evil all day long." [192] See how each of the expressions reveals the magnitude of the sins. I mean, after making the sweeping statement, "Human beings' vices were multiplied on earth," it added, "Everyone." There is great significance in that word. It is not only the young, the text says, but also the elderly who practice the same vices as the young; not only man but also woman; not only slave but also free; not only rich but also poor.

(14) The word "pondered" also has great force: they were not coerced into this without warning, but gave themselves up to pondering it and made it their intention hour after hour, devoting themselves to evil eagerly, not just tripped up by sin accidentally and by chance once or twice but assiduously involving themselves in it and making a practice of evil—that is to say, it was done by them with great enthusiasm, not casually or carelessly; not for a short time, but day in day out they devoted the whole of their lives to it. Do you see the intensity of the evil? Do you see how they made the affair the object of their care, committing every evil assiduously, and how people of every age gave themselves to the practice of evil? "Everyone," it says—not some callow youth, or naive wretch, but everyone of them immediately and right from the outset took to this wicked contest, all striving to surpass their neighbor in the criminality of their behavior. I mean, consider here, I ask you, the good man's extraordinary wisdom in being able to avoid being harmed amidst such a consonance of evil and to feel no injurious effect from it all. Instead, as though being possessed of a different nature, he adopted that kind of resolute attitude: of his own account he zealously undertook the practice of virtue, shunned their common acquiescence in evil, and remained proof against the ruinous fate descending on them all.

(15) "The Lord God reconsidered," the text goes on, "what he had done in creating the human being on the earth."[20] Notice again the considerateness evident in the concreteness of the expression. "He reconsidered," the text says, instead

20. Gen 6.6.

of, "He regretted." Not that God regrets—perish the thought;
rather, Sacred Scripture recounts it to us in human fashion
so as to teach us that the excess of their sins aroused the
loving God to such anger.[21] "The Lord God reconsidered,"
the text says, "what he had done in creating the human being
on the earth"—in other words, Surely by doing this I have
not been responsible for making him fall into such disaster
and become guilty of his own ruin? By doing this I placed
him in a position of such dignity right from the very outset
and showed such concern for him so that he might choose
virtue and be saved from ruin. But since he did not cooperate
with my loving kindness, it then proved better to put an end
to his evil designs.

(16) "The Lord God thought about it and said, 'I will wipe
off the face of the earth the human being I have made, everything from human being to cattle, everything from reptiles
to birds of heaven, because I have reconsidered what I have
done in creating them.'"[22] All that lay within my power, he is
saying, I have given evidence of: I have brought creatures
from non-being to being, I have implanted in their nature
the knowledge of what is to be done and not to be done, I
have blessed them with free will, I have invoked longsuffering
beyond all telling, and after that long period of time, my anger and the threats I have made, I also set another deadline
in my desire to bring them [193] to a sense of their failings
and to revoke my anger. But since they gained no benefit
from all this, it was necessary to put threats into effect, to
achieve their utter ruin, and to blot out their race like some

21. Anthropomorphisms posed a particular challenge to Chrysostom and
his school in their efforts to maintain that balance between divine transcendence and the human character of the Scriptures, the latter representing
God's gracious *synkatabasis*, "considerateness" (of our limitations, as Chrysostom mentioned above in commenting on Gen 6.5). In this case it is the
pachutēs, the concreteness of the language employed in anthropomorphic
expressions, that demonstrates that considerateness without undermining the
correlative of God's transcendence. See my article, "*sunkatabasis*."

22. Gen 6.7. Again, as in the previous verse, the LXX seems reluctant to
admit openly true regret on God's part, preferring the idea of his having
second thoughts. But cf. James Barr, *The Semantics of Biblical Language* (Ox-
ford, 1961), pp. 252–53.

pernicious leaven lest they become lessons in evil to succeeding generations. "The Lord God said, 'I will wipe off the face of the earth the human being I have made, everything from human being to cattle.'"

(17) Perhaps, however, someone may say, Why is it that in the case of the human being's decline into evil the wild animals too endure the same punishment? For good reason. I mean, surely the wild animals were not created to serve their own needs? Everything was brought into existence for human beings, so once they were removed from the circle, what need would there be of the animals? Hence they also share the punishment so that you may learn the degree of God's anger. Just as in the beginning when the firstformed person sinned the earth received the curse, so too in this case when the human being was on the point of being blotted out the wild animals also share the punishment. Just as, on the other hand, when the human being is pleasing to God, creation also shares the human being's prosperity (as Paul also says, "Creation too will be set free from its servitude to decay with a view to the freedom of the children of God's glory"[23]), so too in this case when the human being is about to be punished on account of the great number of sins and to be consigned to destruction, the cattle also and the reptiles and birds are likewise caught up in the deluge that is due to overcome the whole world. Just as in a household, when the chief steward incurs the wrath of the master, it is likely that all the servants also share in his shame, in just the same way in this case too as with the house, when people fell by the wayside everything in the house and everything lying under the master's control necessarily incurs the same punishment.

(18) "'I have reconsidered,'" the text says, "'what I have done in creating them.'" What great considerateness this remark is filled with! Surely I did not intend, he is saying, to inflict on them such awful punishment? They themselves through the excess of their criminal behavior drove me to this great anger. Then, lest we think that the complete annihila-

23. Rom 8.21 with a slight variation in word order.

tion of humankind is happening and that our race is being eradicated, instead of our learning the great evil that sin is and the great good that virtue is, and that one person doing the Lord's will is better than a thousand lawless people, the text proceeds, "Noe, on the contrary, found favor in the sight of the Lord God."[24] Even if the whole multitude, the text is saying, fell into such terrible wickedness, still at the same time this good man kept alive the spark of virtue, speaking to them all during the whole of this period, exhorting them to give up evil, and keeping himself free of harm from them. Just as they through their behavior drove the loving God to anger, so he too by choosing virtue "found favor in the sight of the Lord God." "God (you remember) is no respecter of persons;"[25] rather, if he finds even one person in such a multitude doing what pleases him, far from scorning him he regales him with his particular providence and shows the greater care for him the more closely he has chosen the way of virtue at a time when there are others who are bent on evil.

(19) Understanding [194] this, then, let our eyes be on one thing alone—pleasing him and bringing ourselves to win grace from on high. Let us not be so beholden to friendship or so enslaved to habit that we neglect virtue; instead, let us take advantage of God's longsuffering as we ought, and while we still have time let us put aside all indifference, yearn after virtue and hate evil. You see, unless we devote ourselves to virtue with longing and enthusiasm and direct extreme hatred towards evil, we will be unable to shun the harm that comes from the latter and gain a hold upon the former. For proof that virtue is of advantage to those that long for it and burn with the desire for it, listen to the inspired author's words: "The judgements of the Lord are true, utterly righteous, and to be desired beyond gold and much precious metal,"[26] not because these things are not so desirable but because with us you can find nothing else more sought after than these sub-

24. Gen 6.8.   25. Acts 10.34.
26. Ps 19.9–10.

stances. Hence he went on to say, "And sweeter than honey and the honeycomb;" in this case also he did not use the comparison for the reason that it is possible to find something sweeter than honey. So, just as in amassing riches people lose their senses out of lust and frenzy, become excited in devoting all their energies to this enterprise, and never have their fill—avarice, after all, being an insatiable addiction, and just as with alcoholics the more wine they take into their system the greater the thirst they burn with—so too the avaricious are unable to check this irrepressible folly, but rather the more they see their wealth increasing, the more they enkindle their appetite, and do not rest from this evil desire until they have fallen to the very depths of wickedness.

(20) Consequently, if these people display to such an intense degree this mischievous enthusiasm, which has proved to be responsible for all those evils, much more should we constantly keep fresh in our mind the judgements of the Lord, more desirable as they happen to be than gold and much precious metal, and consider nothing preferable to virtue; rather, we should excise from our soul these ruinous passions and realize that the fleeting pleasure of this kind is likely to engender everlasting distress and torture without end, and not deceive ourselves nor think that our fortunes begin and end with this present life. You see, even if many people don't admit this in so many words, but claim to believe in the doctrine of the resurrection and future retribution, nevertheless I take notice not of their words but of what they do day by day. That is to say, if you are looking forward to resurrection and retribution, why go chasing the values of this life to such an extent? Why, tell me, do you put yourself to such trouble day in day out amassing more possessions than there is sand on the seashore, not to mention property and dwellings, as well as buying baths, often acquiring these things through robbery and greed, and thus fulfilling that saying from the inspired author, "Woe to those who add house to house, and join field to field so as to steal a march on their neighbor"?[27] Cannot this sort of thing be seen hap-

---

27. Isa 5.8, where the LXX differs from our Hebrew text.

pening day after day? One person says, That house casts a
terrible shadow on mine, and he invents countless pretexts to
get hold of it, while another lays hold of a poor person's property and makes it his own. And what in fact is worse, remarkable and unheard of, and quite beyond excuse, is for a person
comfortably situated in one locality being able to move elsewhere without any good reason for wanting to, either [195]
on account of a change of circumstances or because con-
strained by physical disability; all over the place, in city after
city, he is bent on procuring monuments to his own avarice
and having timeless effigies of his own evil for all to see. He
heaps all sins of this kind on his own head without feeling his
heavy and troublesome burden, whereas enjoyment of them
he leaves for others, not only after his departure from this
life but even here before his demise. You see, no matter what
he wishes, he is stripped of his possessions, they are all squan-
dered, so to say, by his friends and left in tatters without the
smallest part of them falling to him to enjoy. Yet why do I say
enjoy? Even if he wanted, how could he with one stomach
manage to dispose of such an abundance of good things?

(21) The cause of all evils, however, is vainglory and the
desire to give one's own name to property, baths, houses.
What good is it to you, human being that you are, when in
no time a fever comes upon you, your soul suddenly takes
wings and leaves you alone and naked—or, rather, stripped
of virtue but encumbered with injustices, robberies, acts of
greed, groanings, lamentation, orphans' tears, plots, intrigues?
How could you, carrying those heavy burdens of sins weighing upon you, be able to pass through that narrow gate,
which could not admit a load of that size? You would therefore have to remain outside, and lumbered with these burdens to repent all too late, already contemplating before your
eyes the punishments prepared for you, that terrible fire that
is never extinguished and the worm that does not die.[28] If, on
the other hand, we have any sense of our own salvation, let
us, while we still have time, abandon evil ways, concern our-

---

28. Cf. Mark 9.48; Isa 66.24.

selves with virtue and despise vainglory. This, you see, is the reason why it is called vain, because it is quite empty and has no substance or stable foundation: it proves only to be a deceiver of the eyes before it disappears and flies away. Or do we not often see the case of a person who today is escorted by attendants and surrounded by bodyguards, whereas tomorrow he is incarcerated and lodged with brigands? What is more deceptive than this vain and empty glory? Even if in this present life the change in circumstances does not affect the person, death will come upon him to abolish his property completely, the person today swaggering in the public eye, who confines people to prison, the person seated on the throne with great ideas of his own importance, regarding all people as dust under his feet—in a trice he is next found stretched out a lifeless corpse, giving off a stench, the butt of countless insults from those he had wronged and those he had not wronged out of sympathy with their wrong. What could be more pitiable than such a person? While all his possessions are often divided up amongst his enemies and foes, the sins accruing to him from them he carries with him and an account of them is scrupulously required of him.

(22) So, I beseech you, let us shun this vainglory and long for the glory that is true and enduring. Let love of possessions not prove our undoing, nor the flame of passion [196] scorch us, nor hatred and envy consume us, nor rage reduce us to ashes. Instead, let us quench all these evil and ruinous passions in the dew of the Spirit, scorn the things of this life and long for future goods; let us set our thoughts on the future and give close attention to our lifestyle. After all, this was not the purpose of our being brought into this life, that we should only eat and drink. Living is not for eating and drinking, but eating and drinking for living. So let us not reverse the order, nor become slaves of the belly as though created for it nor slaves of the pleasures of the flesh; instead, let us consider the harm coming to us from that source, quell the movements of the flesh and not fall victims of sloth nor allow the flesh to rise up against the spirit. If Paul—a man of such calibre and stature, who traversed the whole world like

a winged creature, who proved superior to bodily necessities and was privileged to hear those secret words that no one else to this day has heard—if he wrote these words, "I punish my body and bring it into subjection lest while preaching to others I myself become reprobate;"[29] if then that man, the object of so great favor, despite such conspicuous prowess felt the need to punish his body, bring it into subjection, submit it to the authority of the soul and place its impulses under the virtue of the soul (people, after all, punish what is rebellious, and bring into subjection what is froward), what then would we say, deprived as we are of these goods, lumbered as we are with the burden of sins, and with nothing to show in addition to this beyond deep indifference?

(23) After all, this war admits of no truce, does it? It has no set time for the assault, does it? At all times there is need for watching and waiting and never being over-confident, since no time has been set for the assault by the one who is waging war and hostilities against us. Let us therefore have our wits about us to stay out of trouble, avoid the snares of the enemy and win God's loving kindness, thanks to the grace and mercy of his only-begotten Son, to whom with the Father and the Spirit be glory, power and honor, now and forever, for ages of ages. Amen.

29. 1 Cor 9.27.

HOMILY 23

"Noe, on the contrary, found favor in the sight of the Lord God. Now, these
are the generations of Noe. Noe was a just man; he was faultless by
comparison with his contemporaries. Noe pleased God."[1]

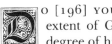O [196] YOU SEE in what has been said already the
extent of God's loving kindness and the surpassing
degree of his longsuffering? Do you see the extremity
of the wickedness of the human beings of that time? Have
you learnt in the midst of this kind of populace how much
virtue the good man had, and that he was quite unaffected
either by their universal decline into wickedness or the fact
that he alone stood out from the crowd of them and traveled
in the opposite direction? In other words, he was like a skillful pilot, controlling the rudder of his mind with great vigilance, not allowing the craft to be submerged under the
violence of the billows of wickedness, but getting the better
of the storm and riding it out at sea as though safely berthed
in port; in this fashion [197] by steering the tiller of virtue he
kept himself clear of the deluge that was about to engulf
everyone in the world. This is the kind of thing virtue is:
immortal, unbowed, proof against the vagaries of this present
life, soaring above the snares of wickedness as though from
some lofty mountain peak and despising all human interests,
it is thus unaffected by any of the material realities that prove
harmful to other people. Like a person stationed on some
high rock mocking the waves as he sees them crashing against
the rock and being immediately dissolved into spray, so too
the person who practices virtue is placed in a safe position
and suffers no unsettling effect from the confusion of worldly

---

1. Gen 6.8–9, with the LXX apparently endeavoring to soften the anthropomorphism in the first Hebrew verb.

affairs, but rather remains firm in serenity of mind, revelling in the tranquility of his own thoughts and aware that the affairs of this life ebb and flow with such rapidity that they differ in no way from the tides in a river. You see, just as you can notice the waves of the sea whipped up at one moment to an incredible height and suddenly brought low again, well in just the same way let us observe people who shun virtue and are mixed up in evil enjoying at one moment lofty notions, adopting a superior pose and being wrapt in the affairs of this life, then suddenly brought low and reduced to utter indigence.

(2) These in fact are the people blessed David, the inspired author, was referring to in the words, "Don't worry when a person becomes wealthy or when the splendor of his house increases, because at his death he will take none of it with him."[2] He is right in saying, "Don't worry." Don't let yourself be upset, he is saying, by the affluence of the rich and the glamor of appearances. After all, before long you will see them laid low, inert, corpses, thrown out to become the food of worms, stripped naked of all their possessions, quite unable to take anything of theirs with them, and instead leaving it all here. So don't get upset to see the events of the moment, nor commend the good luck of the person who shortly is due to be rid of these things. This, you see, is what present affluence is like, and this the true nature of wealth: it doesn't accompany those who pass on from here—instead, they leave it all here behind them, naked and destitute of everything, clad only in their wickedness and the burden of sins they have amassed. In the case of virtue, on the contrary, things are quite different: even here it puts us beyond the reach of those plotting our downfall, makes us invincible, bestows upon us endless enjoyment, does not allow us to be affected by changing circumstances, and when we pass on from here it becomes

2. Ps 49.16–17a; it is significant that Chrysostom impairs the parallelism by omitting 17b, which employs the verb *synkatabainein* in the sense of "going down into the grave," which would not correspond with the usual sense of his favorite notion of *synkatabasis* for the Scriptures, God's loving considerateness (cf. Introduction (20) in FOTC 74).

our traveling companion, especially at that moment when we need its assistance, and on that dread day it renders us great help, softening the gaze of the Judge; as in this life it makes us superior to the direst of fates, so too in the future it snatches from those dreadful punishments those who have virtue to show for themselves. Nor is this all: it even proves to be responsible for our enjoying ineffable blessings.

(3) To prove to you that this is the case and that we are not telling you idle tales and spinning yarns, we shall now endeavor to give a demonstration to your good selves from what has already been proposed. I mean, see how this remarkable person—I mean Noe—at the time the whole human race was provoking the loving Lord to anger against them, was able through his own virtue to avoid feeling the effects of this anger and to win great favor from the Lord. Let us at this point, if you don't mind, discuss the situation of this present [198] life. What I mean is, perhaps some people place no credence in things of the future that cannot be seen with the naked eye. So let us see from the things that happened in this case what befell those that pursued wickedness, on the one hand, and what reward was granted the man who had opted for virtue, on the other. Remember, when owing to the extremity of wickedness the good God condemned the human race to annihilation in the words, "'I will wipe off the face of the earth the human being I have made,'"[3] showing the extraordinary degree of his anger, he delivered the sentence not only against the human race but also against the cattle, the reptiles and the birds. You see, since human beings, for whom these creatures had been created, were due to perish and to disappear from sight, it was appropriate that they, too, should be affected by the punishment with them. Since, therefore, the sentence was unqualified and made no distinctions, you should learn that God is no respecter of persons and that nothing entering our hearts escapes his notice; should he find even a slight excuse put up on our behalf, he shows his ineffable love (Scripture says) that we may not think

3. Gen 6.7.

the destruction of the human race was complete, but may realize that in his characteristic goodness he allows a spark to be saved and a root for the human race, so that once again it should grow up into mighty boughs. "Noe, on the contrary," the text says, "found favor in the sight of God."[4]

(4) Notice the precision of Scripture, how you can't find even a chance syllable contained there to no purpose. After it taught us the excess of human beings' wickedness and the magnitude of the punishment due to be inflicted on its practitioners, it teaches us also about the good man who was able to keep virtue unimpaired amidst such a vast multitude. Virtue, after all, is remarkable even by itself; but when someone proves capable of practicing it in the company of its adversaries, he gives evidence of a much more remarkable degree of virtue. Hence, as though in admiration of the just man, Sacred Scripture says that, in the midst of so many people due to experience God's anger for their wickedness, "Noe, on the contrary, found favor in the sight of the Lord God." "Found favor," to be sure, but "in the sight of God." Not simply "found favor," but "in the sight of the Lord God," so as to teach us that he had this single aim, to be commended by that unsleeping eye and to set no store by men's praise nor their scorn or mockery. You see, it was natural that the person who was bent on practicing virtue in opposition to everybody else would have to incur mockery and scorn, since all those who practice evil are ever accustomed to ridicule those who insist on avoiding it and choosing virtue—something that happens now, too.

(5) Let us have an eye to those many listless people who cannot bear mockery and scorn, but prefer the praise of human beings to true and everlasting glory, ensnared as they are and dragged down by the evil of other people. It is, you see, characteristic of a noble spirit that relies on firm resolve to have the ability to withstand those people anxious to disparage it, and to make no concessions to appeasement of such people; instead, it is accustomed to keep its gaze fixed on that

4. Gen 6.8.

unsleeping eye, to be subject to its approval alone and ignore others', and to consider worthless their praise or censure and rather pass it by like so many shadows and dreams. In the present case the vast majority were generally unable to withstand the scorn of ten, or twenty, or even fewer people, and so were tripped up and came to grief. "There is, you see, a sense of shame that brings on sin."[5] It is, after all, no slight thing to scorn those who mock and ridicule and are bent on making fun of you. Our hero, [199] however, was made of sterner stuff than this: he scorned not only ten, or twenty, or a hundred people but even the whole of the human race, countless numbers of them. Naturally, you see, they all mocked and ridiculed him, treated him like an idiot and abused him in their drunken violence, and perhaps would have even liked to tear him limb from limb, if that were possible. Malice, after all, always goes to wild extremes in its treatment of virtue; not only, however, does it deal it no injury but it even succeeds in making it stronger to resist. Such, you see, is the strength of virtue that in endurance it gets the better of its persecutors and in opposition it proves superior to its opponents.

(6) You can see this, of course, in many situations; still, so that we may offer you some examples—Scripture says, remember, "Give wise people an opportunity, and they will become wiser"[6]—we ought adduce for you examples from both the Old and the New Testaments. I ask you, accordingly, consider Abel: was he not done away with by Cain? Was he not laid low? But don't concentrate on the fact that the killer prevailed and won the day, that he did away with the object of his envy though he had done him no wrong. Instead, think of the sequel, that the victim is on everybody's lips from that day to this, a paradigm for all, his memory undimmed by the passage of all that time, whereas the killer, the victor, even during his lifetime had to endure an existence worse than death, and from that day to this his notoriety has never waned and on the part of everyone he has been the object of condemnation, while his victim day in day out is the recipient

5. Sir 4.21.   6. Prov 9.9.

of words of praise from everyone. And while this is true of
the present life, what words or what thoughts can do justice
to their fate in the world to come? I know, of course, that
with your brains you will find many other such contrasts contained in the Scriptures. This, after all, was the reason they
were composed for our benefit, that we should learn these
things and so shun evil and prefer virtue. Would you like to
discern the same process occurring in the New Testament as
well? Listen to blessed Luke describing exactly the same thing
in regard to the apostles, that after being scourged they went
out from the council rejoicing that they had been judged worthy of being abused for the name of Christ.[7] Of course, the
scourging was no cause of satisfaction, to be sure—rather of
pain and distress; but scourging for the sake of God and the
grounds on which they were scourged gave rise to satisfaction
in them. Their torturers, of course, were utterly at a loss to
know what was happening: listen to their consternation after
the scourging as they ask, " 'What are we to do to these people?' "[8] What are you saying? You have scourged them, inflicted countless tortures on them, and yet you are still at a
loss? Such a powerful and invincible thing is virtue, proving
superior even in the course of suffering such torments.

(7) Lest, however, we make the sermon too lengthy, we must
come back again to this good man and be amazed at the extraordinary degree of his virtue, how he had the fortitude to
ignore this huge multitude's mockery, ridicule, scorn and sar-
casm (I keep mentioning this, as you can see, and will never
give up mentioning it), and to prove superior to it. How did
he manage? I'll tell you: because he had constant regard for
the unsleeping eye, he kept his mind's gaze fixed in that direction, and in future paid heed to all other things as though
they didn't exist. That is the way things are, you see: when
one is smitten with that love, and directs one's whole person
to the search for God, one takes no notice of visible realities;
instead, one has constantly before one's mind the object of

7. Acts 5.41.
8. Acts 4.16. Is Chrysostom deliberately reversing the order of these two
situations in Acts to make a better moral point?

one's love, by night and by day, going to rest and getting up. So don't be surprised if this [200] just man, once he gave that direction to his thinking, took no notice of the people endeavoring to bring him down: giving evidence of his own resources and winning favor from on high, he proved superior to them all. "Noe," the text says, remember, "found favor in the sight of the Lord God." Even though he was not the favorite or darling of any of the human race of the time through his refusal to follow the same route as theirs, nevertheless he found favor in the eyes of the one who haunts the heart, and to him his attitude was acceptable. What harm, after all, tell me, ensued in this case from the mockery and ridicule of his peers, considering the fact that the one who shapes our hearts and understands all our actions proclaimed the man's deeds and rewarded him? On the other hand, what benefit would it be to a human being were he the object of the admiration and praise of the whole world while being condemned on that dread day by the Creator of all and the Judge who is proof against all deceit? Understanding this, therefore, dearly beloved, let us set no store by people's commendation nor seek praise from them in every way; instead, with him alone in mind who examines heart and entrails, let us practice the works of virtue and shun evil.

(8) For this reason, you see, Christ also taught us not to sigh after the praises of human beings and, following many other warnings, he finally brought this charge against us as well: "Woe to you when all people speak well of you."[9] Notice how by the word "woe" he revealed to us the extent of the punishment awaiting such people. This word "woe," after all, is an exclamation of lament, so that it is as if he is lamenting their fate when he says, "Woe to you when all people speak well of you." Notice, too, the precision in the expression: he didn't simply say "people" but "all people." You see, it is not possible for a virtuous person who travels by the straight and narrow path and follows Christ's commands to enjoy the praise and admiration of all people—so strong is the impulse

9. Luke 6.26.

of evil and the resistance to virtue. Consequently, as the Lord
knows that it would be impossible for the person who practices virtue assiduously and accepts praise only from him to
be commended by all people and to enjoy good repute with
them, for this reason he laments the fate of those who neglect
virtue for the sake of such people. You see, commendation
from them would be the clearest indication of not setting
great store by virtue. How, after all, would the virtuous person be commended by everyone if he insisted on rescuing the
wronged from their wrongdoers, the oppressed from their
oppressors? Again, if he were to correct the wayward and
praise the righteous, would it not be likely that while the latter
praised him, the former would revile him? Hence Christ says,
"Woe to you when all people speak well of you." How then is
it not proper to feel admiration and amazement at this good
man for the reason that what Christ taught at his coming this
man prior to him was well versed in by the law innate in his
make-up and put into practice to an extraordinary degree,
and rejecting men's praise he devoted himself to finding favor
with God through the virtue of daily life? The text says, remember, "Noe found favor in the sight of the Lord God."

(9) While, however, this remarkable author told us under
the inspiration of the Holy Spirit that Noe found favor in the
sight of the Lord God on account of the virtue that distinguished him, we need also study the following words and see
the verdict given him by God. "Now, these are the generations of Noe," the text says. "Noe was a righteous man; he
was faultless by comparison with his contemporaries. Noe
pleased God." An unusual style of genealogy; Sacred Scripture [201], in saying, "Now, these are the generations of
Noe," and setting our ears tingling as if on the point of recounting his genealogy—who his father was, whence he took
his lineage, how he came to be in this life and all other details
that people normally give in tracing genealogies—all such it
abandoned, and proving to be superior to custom it says,
"Noe was a just man; he was faultless by comparison with his
contemporaries." Do you see a remarkable genealogy? "Noe,"
it says, "was a man." Notice also the ordinary name given the

good man applicable to us all rather than a title of distinction. You see, since the other people had lost the status of human beings through falling into the pleasures of the flesh, this man (Scripture says) retained the character of a human alone among such a vast multitude. This, after all, is when a man becomes human, when he practices virtue: it is not having the appearance of a human being—eyes, nose, mouth, cheeks and other features—that establishes the human being; these, in fact, are parts of the body. I mean, we would call a human being the man who retains the character of a human being. But what is the character of a human being? Being rational. Why so? Someone will say, Weren't those others rational also? Still, it is not merely this attribute, but also being virtuous and avoiding evil and getting the better of improper passions, following the Lord's commands—this is what makes a human being.

(10) For proof that Scripture's habit is not to bestow the title of human being on those who practice evil and neglect virtue, listen to the words of God, as we were saying yesterday, " 'My spirit is not to remain with these human beings on account of their being carnal;"[10] in other words, he is saying, I regaled these people with a being[11] constituted of flesh and spirit; but as though composed of flesh only, they thus neglect virtue in a spiritual manner and have now proved to belong completely to the flesh. Do you see how on account of their wickedness it calls them flesh and not human beings? Again, as you will probably discover, Sacred Scripture proceeds to name them earth on account of their being completely taken up with earthly thoughts: it says, remember, "Now, the earth was corrupt in God's sight," speaking not about the material earth but naming its inhabitants earth. Elsewhere, however, it names them neither flesh nor earth, nor does it consider them to be in this life for the reason that they are devoid of virtue. I mean, listen to the inspired author as he shouts out aloud in the middle of the metropolis of Jerusalem where there

10. Gen 6.3.
11. The sense seems to require here *ousia* in the text rather than *exousia*, and De Montfaucon suggests the emendation.

were such countless numbers of people, such a vast multitude, "I came and there was no one to be seen. I called and
there was no one to heed me"[12]—not because they weren't
there but because, though being there, they were no better
off than not being there at all. Again in another place it says,
"Hurry about and see if there is someone practicing judgement and righteousness, and I will be gracious."[13]

(11) Do you see how Holy Scripture knows how to call human only the person practicing virtue and doesn't think the
others are human, calling them instead flesh at one time and
earth at another? Hence at this place, too, in promising to list
the genealogy of the good man it says, "Noe was a human
being." You see, he alone was a human being, whereas the
others weren't human beings; instead, while having the appearance of human beings they had forfeited the nobility of
their kind by the evil of their intention, and instead of being
human they reverted to the [202] irrationality of wild animals. Sacred Scripture assigns the names of wild beasts to
human beings, rational creatures that they should be, in the
event of their lapsing into evil and falling prey to irrational
passions; listen for example to its words, "They turned into
rutting horses."[14] See how it gives them the animal's name on
account of their unbridled lust. Elsewhere, on the other hand,
it says, "Poison of serpents on their lips;"[15] here it highlights
their resemblance to the animal's trickery and duplicity.
Again, it calls them dumb dogs.[16] And again, "Like a deaf
adder that blocks its ears,"[17] referring to their stopping their
ears against instruction in virtue. You would find many other
names imposed by Sacred Scripture on people seduced by
their indifference into bestial passions. You can see this not
only in the Old Testament but also in the New;[18] listen to John
the Baptist addressing the Jews, "Brood of vipers, who has

12. Isa 50.2.   13. Jer 5.1 in a variant reading.
14. Jer 5.8.   15. Ps 140.3.
16. Isa 56.10.   17. Ps 58.4.
18. For a similar diatribe against the animal tendencies of those who forsake virtue, based on a similar catena of OT and NT texts, see Homily 12—
another example of the (at times verbatim) resemblance between different
homilies and sermons. See Introduction (2) and (8) in FOTC 74.

shown you how to flee from the wrath to come?"[19] So do you see how here also by naming the animal it implied the duplicity of their intent?

(12) So what could be more wretched than those who practice evil, when they are deprived of the right to be called by the very name of human beings and endure heavier punishment for the reason that despite receiving many promptings from nature they willingly forsook them in their headstrong career into wickedness? Since therefore all the people of that time rendered themselves unworthy of the name and of being called human beings whereas this good man amidst such a dearth of virtue gave evidence of an extraordinary degree of his own virtue, Sacred Scripture begins its account of the man's genealogy with the words, "Now, Noe was a human being." We can find in the case of another good person also this name applied in place of lavish praise, and through this name instead of all other means his meticulous practice of virtue is heralded to the skies. Who is that? Blessed Job, that protagonist of reverence, that world champion, alone capable of tolerating incurable ills, the recipient of countless blows from that evil demon without sustaining injury, like steel able to withstand every blow, not only unbowed by such mighty billows but even emerging superior to the flood, suffering the world's ills in his person yet coming through the experience with even greater lustre. I mean, not only did the rate of the onset of disasters not depress him but it even prompted him to more fervent thanksgiving, and through it all he demonstrated his personal gratitude, dealing the devil a well-deserved blow and showing him that his efforts were in vain and that he was kicking against the goad. Accordingly the loving God praised this holy man for his contests and such difficult struggles, and he sings his praises in addressing the devil, "'Have you taken heed of my servant Job, that there is no one like him on earth, a person beyond reproach, good, true, reverent, proof against any evildoing?'"[20] Do you notice

19. Matt 3.7; Luke 3.7.
20. Job 1.8; in a variant of the LXX.

that he first sings his praises in terms of the name common
to his kind? "'Have you taken heed,'" he says, "'of my servant
Job, that there is no one like him?'"[21] Of course, everyone
was like him, not on the score of virtue but on the basis of
appearance; this, however, is not what makes a human being
—rather, avoidance of evil and practice of virtue.

(13) Do you see which people Sacred Scripture is prepared
to call human beings? Hence, when even from the outset the
Creator of all saw the creature he had made, he said, "'Let
us make a human being in our image [203] and likeness'"—
that is to say, to have control both of all visible things and the
passions arising within him; to have control, not to be controlled. If, however, they forfeit this control and would rather
be controlled than have control, they lose also their human
status and change their name to that of wild animals. Hence,
of course, in this case too Sacred Scripture is anxious to commend this good man's virtue in the words, "These are the
generations of Noe. Noe was a just person." Behold also another remarkable form of commendation, "just": through this
term it suggests this complete kind of virtue. It is customary
with us to apply the word "just" to people practicing every
virtue. Then, for you to learn how he arrived at the very
pinnacle of virtue, which was required of our human nature
at that time also, it says, "a just man; he was faultless by comparison with his contemporaries." He had fulfilled every obligation, the text says, that should be discharged by a person
who had opted for virtue (the sense, after all, of "faultless"),
neglecting nothing, falling short in nothing. It was not that
he did this right and that wrong; rather, he was faultless in
every respect, this after all being required of him. Then, so
as to make the good man appear more conspicuous by comparison, it says, "He was faultless by comparison with his contemporaries"; at that period, amidst his perverted generation,
bent as they were on such terrible evil, prepared to give evidence of not even a trace of virtue.

---

21. This time Chrysostom adopts a different reading of the text, attested
to in our MSS of the LXX.

(14) So amidst that generation, in those times, this just man not only gave evidence of virtue but also proved faultless and perfect in every respect in arriving at the highest pinnacle of virtue. You see, as I said before, it always shows a high calibre of virtue to do the right thing in face of opposition and to give evidence of assiduity amidst discouragement. On this basis, of course, this good person is judged worthy of greater plaudits. Nor does Sacred Scripture cease its commendation at this point: it proceeds to show us the surpassing degree of his virtue and the fact that he received the verdict of heaven when it says, "He was faultless by comparison with his peers," and adds, "Noe pleased God." Such was the calibre of his virtue as to win approval from God. "Noe pleased God," it says, meaning that he proved acceptable to God and was pleasing to that unsleeping eye on account of his good deeds; the conduct of his life attracted divine favor and not only delivered him from the wrath due to fall on everyone but also made him a suppliant for the others. "Noe pleased God," the text says, remember. Who could have a happier lot than Noe's, being in a position to demonstrate such virtue as to have the Lord of all as your eulogist?

(15) Since, therefore, he behaved in this way, his lot was in the view of any thinking person preferable to all riches, any kind of fame, influence or any other human distinction; to the person having sincere love for God this would be more desirable than a kingdom. You see, true kingship is this, being in a position to win the Lord's benevolence and clemency through the excellence of one's lifestyle. After all, the reason we ought to be in fear and dread of hell is not the undying fire, the terrible punishments, the unremitting retribution, but rather offending such a good Lord and finding ourselves outside his benevolence. So likewise we ought to show enthusiasm [204] for that kind of kingship for this reason, out of love for him and to enjoy his favor. You see, as it is worth more than a kingdom to have our loving Lord kindly disposed to us, so it would be a worse fate than hell's fire to fall from his favor.

(16) Do you see how much benefit the good man's mere

name proved to be an occasion of, and how great a treasure
of inspiration this remarkable man's genealogy gave rise to?
Accordingly, let us imitate the norms of Sacred Scripture, and
if we wish to list people's genealogies, let us not cite parents,
grandparents and great-grandparents but expose instead the
virtue of the person with the genealogy. This, you see, is the
best style of genealogy; what good is it to have famous forebears distinguished by virtue if the person himself is bereft
of excellence of life? or, on the other hand, what disadvantage
could it be to spring from lowly and undistinguished parents
and ancestors if the person himself is adorned with great virtue? This good person too, who was of such high calibre and
had won God's favor, did not come from parents of such notoriety: Sacred Scripture doesn't record their virtue. Nevertheless, he prevailed over such stern obstacles, hindered
though he was so severely, and managed to reach the very
pinnacle of virtue, so that you might learn that for the person
prepared to stay alert and on guard and to take good care of
his own salvation, nothing is an obstacle. You see, just as people who slip into indifference are harmed even by chance
events, so if we were prepared to be on the alert, even if there
were innumerable people enticing us to evil, they could in no
way harm us by their efforts, just as this good man too could
not be made lukewarm about virtue despite the number of
those trying.[22]

(17) Accordingly, let no one blame somebody else and im-
pute the guilt to others, but attribute it all to his own negligence. Why do I say to others? Let no one think the devil
himself is sufficient to bar the way leading to virtue: he deceives and undoes the negligent, but he really can't impede
or coerce. Experience itself makes clear that, provided we are
prepared to be on the alert, we can display such resolution
that despite numerous efforts to impel us down the way of

22. As mentioned in Introduction (13) and (17) and frequently in foot-
notes in FOTC 74, the capital sin in Chrysostom's eyes is *rhathumia*, "indifference," "sloth," "neglect," "laxity." From Eve onwards all the Genesis
villains are monuments of indifference, all the heroes exemplars of *prothumia*,
"enthusiasm," as Noe here.

wickedness we will resist their evil design, prove stronger than any steel and block our ears against the inducements of those counseling knavery. Whenever, on the contrary, we become negligent, no matter if there is no one to counsel or undo us, we would be impelled by our own impulse to lay at anchor in wickedness. You see, if responsibility did not rest in our choice and in our control over our attitudes, and if the loving God had not made our nature independent, it would have been inevitable for everyone sharing our nature and affected by the same passions to be all evil or all virtuous. When, however, we see our peers, even those handicapped by the same passions, not afflicted with the same weaknesses as ourselves but ordering nature with steady judgement, surviving wild impulses, reining in desire, suppressing rage, shunning envy, uprooting jealousy, spurning the pangs of greed, thinking little of reputation, mocking all the favor of this world, and setting their heart on true glory and prizing God's approval above all visible goods, [205] is it not patent that in the wake of heavenly grace they are able to achieve these noble feats by their own efforts while we fall victim to our own negligence, betray our salvation and leave ourselves bereft of favor from above?

(18) Hence, I beg you, let us consider these matters, constantly meditate on them, and never blame the devil but rather our own negligent attitude. I say this, not out of a desire to discharge him of any condemnation—perish the thought: he goes about like a lion to seize his prey, roaring and stalking a victim to devour.[23] Rather, my intention is to put us more on the alert lest we think ourselves above reproach, advance readily in this way towards wickedness and utter those frivolous words, Why did God let such a wicked creature loose to ensnare and overthrow us? These words, after all, would be a mark of deepest ingratitude. Instead, take this thought to heart, that the particular reason that he turned him loose was that under the pressure of fear and on the lookout for the enemy's assault we might display great

23. Cf. 1 Pet 5.8.

alertness and constant watchfulness, and in the hope of reward and as guarantee of those ineffable eternal blessings we
might make light of the difficulties of virtue. Why are you
amazed if that was the reason he let the devil loose, caring as
he does for our salvation, anxious to stir us from our indifference, and providing us with some title to reward? His purpose in preparing hell itself was that the fear of punishment
and the unbearable character of its torments might impel us
towards the kingdom. Do you see the Lord's inventive love?
how he does everything and adopts stratagems not only to
save those created by him but also to regale them with ineffable blessings? For this reason, too, he endowed us with free
will, and implanted in our nature and our conscience the
knowledge of evil and of virtue, gave the devil free rein and
threatened us with hell so that we might not have experience
of hell but have the good fortune to reach the kingdom.

(19) Why are you surprised if to this end he has devised all
those stratagems and countless others? He who by nature was
in the bosom of the Father deigned to take the form of a
servant,[24] to submit himself to all other bodily conditions, to
have a woman for mother, to be born of a virgin, to be carried
in the womb for nine months, to be wrapped in swaddling
clothes, to be thought the son of Joseph, Mary's husband, to
grow up gradually, to be circumcised, to offer sacrifice, to
suffer hunger and thirst and weariness, finally to meet his
death, and not simply death but that death thought most
shameful—I mean crucifixion. All of this was accepted for us
and our salvation by the Creator of everything, the one who
never changes, who brings everything from non-being to
being, who looks down upon the earth and makes it tremble,[25] the splendor of whose glory not even the Cherubim,
those incorporeal powers, cannot see but cover their eyes with
their wings as they reveal the marvel to us;[26] he whose praise
angels, archangels and countless hosts forever sing—he it is
who for us and for our salvation deigned to become man,

24. Cf. Phil 2.7.   25. Ps 104.32.
26. Cf. Isa 6.2–3.

plotted for us the way of exemplary living and bequeathed to us adequate instruction by the example he personally gave in assuming the same nature as ours.[27]

(20) Accordingly, what excuse remains for us, [206] now that this example has been set us for our salvation, if we were going to render it all to no avail by forfeiting our salvation through indifference in these matters? Hence I beseech you to be on the alert and not simply follow the pattern set by others, but give careful attention to your own life each day and be clear about what sins you commit and what good deeds you do. Let us in this way proceed to the correction of our sins so that we may win favor from on high, prove acceptable to God like this good man, and have the good fortune to reach the kingdom of heaven, thanks to the grace and love of our Lord Jesus Christ, to whom with the Father and the Holy Spirit be glory, honor and power, now and forever, for ages of ages. Amen.

27. This is one of the passages where Chrysostom's traditional appreciation of the Incarnation emerges most conspicuously (cf. Homilies 27 and 58), providing the basis for his theology of Scripture as the incarnate Word of God. As such it is always balanced, as here, with Chrysostom's other basic conviction, of divine transcendence. On these two verities stood firm Antioch's approach to Scripture. See my article, "Incarnation."

HOMILY 24

"Now, Noe had three sons, Shem, Cham, Japheth. Now, the earth was corrupt in God's eyes, and was filled with lawlessness."[1]

HE [206] BENEFIT THAT CAME to us from the good man Noe's genealogy yesterday was not by chance: we recognized the unusual style of a genealogy, and we saw the good man's praise sung not for the celebrity of his forebears but for the virtue of his own behavior, because of which he also received such a wonderful testimony from Sacred Scripture. "Noe was a just person," it said, remember; "he was faultless by comparison with his contemporaries. Noe pleased God."[2] We concentrated all yesterday's instruction, you recall, on those brief words. It is, after all, the nature of the divine sayings to reveal great riches of thought in a few words, and to bestow untold treasure on those endeavoring to make a precise study of them. Hence, of course, I beseech you, let us never pass heedlessly by the contents of Sacred Scripture, but even if it is a list of names or an outline of history let us descry carefully the treasure hidden there. For this reason, after all, Christ himself said, "Search the Scriptures."[3] The sense of what is written cannot be discovered on the surface at any point but requires of us careful study if nothing of what is concealed in its depths is to escape our

1. Gen 6.10–11.
2. Gen 6.9.
3. John 5.39—something of a manifesto for Chrysostom and his school, who, unlike the Alexandrian tendency to use the scriptural text as a point of departure, instead stay with the text and subject it to close scrutiny, going below the surface to see what is concealed in its depths, as Chrysostom so often claims. For the difference between the two schools, see D. S. Wallace-Hadrill's essay, "The Interpretation of the Biblical Record" in his *Christian Antioch* (Cambridge, 1982), ch. 2.

notice. Now, if the mere naming of our nature—I mean the word "human being" (ἄνθρωπος)—provided the occasion of so much benefit yesterday, how much advantage will we gain if we approach the matters in Scripture with attention and alert mind?

(2) We have, you see, a loving Lord, and when he sees us anxious to learn and demonstrating a keen appetite for understanding the divine sayings, he doesn't allow us to want for anything; instead, he immediately enlightens our thinking, bestows illumination from himself, and in his inventive wisdom he implants in our soul the whole of his trustworthy instruction. Hence, to encourage us to this practice and render us more enthusiastic, he declared worthy of blessing those who give evidence of such keen appetite when he said, "Blessed are those who hunger and thirst after righteousness, because they shall have their fill."[4] See the wisdom in the instruction: he did not merely encourage through the blessing, but also in the phrase, "those who hunger and thirst after righteousness," he taught his listeners the great degree of enthusiasm with which they ought proceed to the study of the spiritual sayings. In other words, he is saying, just as those under the impulse of hunger hurry to food with unheard of enthusiasm, and those burning with great thirst come to drink with alacrity, in just the same way ought we, like people starving and thirsting, come to spiritual instruction. [207] Such people, you see, not only prove worthy of blessing but also secure the object of their desire. "They will have their fill," Scripture says, after all—that is, they will be filled: they will fulfil their spiritual desire. Since, therefore, we have such a Lord, so good, so generous, come now, let us have recourse to him and win favor from him so that he may out of fidelity to his own loving kindness enlighten our thinking with a view to discerning the force of the Holy Scriptures, while you for your part should with great enthusiasm, like people starving and thirsting, receive the spiritual teaching. After all, even though we are lowly and of no account, perhaps the good

4. Matt 5.6.

Lord, anxious as he is to help, will take steps for your sake
and for your salvation to provide us with a sermon in opening
our mouth for his glory and your edification. Accordingly let
us direct all our effort to securing grace from on high, invoke
the one who gives understanding to the blind and helps the
tongue of the mute speak distinctly, and expound the text
read just now so that whatever he supplies out of fidelity to
his own loving kindness we may be able to put before your
good selves.

(3) But give me your full attention, I beseech you, and attend carefully to what is said, putting aside all your worldly
concerns so that we may be able to sow our spiritual seed, as
it were, in a rich and productive pasture, all weeds and thorns
uprooted. "Now, these are the generations of Noe," the text
reads. "Noe was a just man; he was faultless by comparison
with his contemporaries. Noe pleased God."[5] Yesterday the
presentation of our teaching came to a close at this point; so
we need to put what remains before you. "Now, Noe had
three sons, Shem, Cham, Japheth."[6] It was not without purpose that Sacred Scripture indicated to us both the period of
time and the number of the good man's sons: in this case too
it wanted obliquely to bring out the extraordinary degree of
his great virtue. Having said above that "Noe was five hundred
years old,"[7] it then added, "He had three sons," teaching us
the surpassing greatness of his continence, and this despite
the fact that all the people of the time gave themselves up to
such incontinence and gave evidence of much lechery, and all
his contemporaries rushed headlong into evil. I mean, listen
to the words of Sacred Scripture: "Now, the Lord saw that
the vices of human beings were multiplied on the earth, and
everyone gave themselves up wholly to pondering evil from
their youth,"[8] clearly showing us that young people surpassed

5. Gen 6.9.   6. Gen 6.10.
7. Gen 5.32.
8. Gen 6.5, with an individual final phrase replacing "day in day out" as
in Chrysostom's previous quotation of the standard LXX text of this verse
in Homily 22—hardly a surprising "lapse" for a preacher in such a lengthy
quotation, but index again that these homilies were in fact delivered and not
simply composed for delivery.

their superiors in age and the elderly proved by no means inferior to the young in folly, and that the age of innocence demonstrated strong inclination to evil.

(4) So Scripture's purpose is that we may learn how the good man remained alone in fighting the battle of temperance, not to mention his other virtues, while all others displayed great frenzy and fury, until he reached the age of five hundred. You see, after saying, "Noe was five hundred years old," it then adds, "Noe had three sons." Do you see, dearly beloved, the good man's extraordinary temperance? I mean, surely we won't heedlessly pass these matters by; let us instead consider that period of time and the wickedness that surfaced in the whole human race on account of extreme indifference, and notice the degree of virtue and reverence for God that distinguished him in restraining the impulse of desire over such a long period of time, [208] going contrary to everyone else and refraining not only from illicit association but also from what was customary and in fact above reproach. Scripture says, "Noe had three sons, Shem, Cham and Japheth. Now, the earth was corrupt in God's eyes, and was filled with lawlessness." It seems to me the good man was responding to God's plan in both refraining from association at this time and also having these children. I mean, since disaster was about to overwhelm the world on account of the extent of wickedness and the surpassing evil, the loving God by contrast wanted to let the good man survive like some root or leaven so that in the wake of the world's destruction he might be the beginning of people destined to appear later. For this reason he had three children after five hundred years and stopped at that, showing through this conduct that he had acted in accord with the loving kindness which God would show to the human race.

(5) For proof that these words are no idle conjecture, consider the precision of Scripture: when it said that the good man had three sons, it immediately added, "Now, the earth was corrupt in God's eyes, and was filled with lawlessness." Do you see the important distinction being made, beyond all telling, between people of the same nature? I mean, while in

the case of the good man Scripture said, "Noe was a just man, faultless by comparison with his contemporaries," in the case of all the rest it said, "Now, the earth was corrupt in God's eyes, and was filled with lawlessness." It calls the crowd of human beings by the name of the earth. You see, since all their doings were in fact earthly, consequently he implies their lowliness and the excess of their wickedness by the name of the earth. I mean, just as in the case of the firstformed, after his Fall and the loss of the glory that enveloped him previously, God said in submitting him to the punishment of death, "'Earth you are, and to earth you are to return,'"[9] in just the same way here too, since the intensity of their wickedness was extreme, the text says, "Now, the earth was corrupt." It did not simply say, "Now the earth was corrupt," but, "in God's eyes, and it was filled with lawlessness." By saying, "It was corrupt," it suggested all their wickedness. I mean, we can't say that they rendered themselves guilty of one or two sins; rather, they committed every crime with reckless abandon—hence it added, "and the earth was filled with lawlessness." Not idly or by chance did they make evil their practice; instead, they gave evidence of every sin with utter fanaticism. See how for the future it refuses to allow them even the slightest memory but calls them by the name of the earth, highlighting both the excess of their evil and also the magnitude of God's anger. "Now, the earth was corrupt," the text says, "in God's eyes," that is, their whole behavior was at variance with God's directions, going contrary to God's commands and betraying through their own indifference the teaching implanted in their human nature. "And the earth was filled with lawlessness," the text says.

(6) Do you see, dearly beloved, how great an evil sin is, how it even renders human beings unworthy of being called by their own name in future? Listen further to what follows: "The Lord God saw that the earth was utterly corrupt."[10] See again their being called earth. Then, after calling them earth once, twice and a third time, lest anyone make the mistake of

9. Gen 3.19.   10. Gen 6.12.

thinking this was said of the material earth the text goes on, "because all flesh had utterly corrupted their ways upon earth." Even here it did not deign to call them human beings; rather, its intention is by using only the name "flesh" to indicate to us that these remarks are not made about the earth but about people, clad as they are in flesh and expending their energies in earthly pursuits. You see, it is the habit of Scripture, as we often say to your good selves, [209] to give the name "flesh" to those who exhibit a carnal way of thinking and never set their sights on anything lofty, as Paul also says, "Now, those who are in the flesh are incapable of pleasing God."[11] Why is that? Is not the speaker himself clad in flesh? He doesn't mean, however, that those clad in flesh are incapable of pleasing God—rather, those who put no store by virtue but whose thoughts are totally carnal and who are caught up in pleasures of that kind, paying no attention to their soul, incorporeal and intellectual as it is. Sacred Scripture therefore taught us through these words the great number of their sins, the excess of their wickedness, the awful degree of God's anger, and the fact that on account of their studious attention to illicit behavior Scripture called them earth once, twice and a third time and gave them the name flesh, removing from them the name of the nature they shared in common, and demonstrating through the sequel God's ineffable love for us and the extraordinary degree of his considerateness. What in fact does it say? "God said to Noe."[12]

(7) See the surpassing extent of his goodness; like one friend with another he now shares with the good man word of the punishment he is about to inflict on the human race, and says, " 'In my view the whole human race has reached its limit, in so far as the earth is filled with lawlessness on their account. Lo, I am going to destroy them and the earth.' " What does that mean, " 'In my view the whole human race has reached its limit' "? I have shown extreme longsuffering, he is saying, not wanting to inflict the punishment I have in mind to inflict; but since the great excess of their sins brought

11. Rom 8.8.   12. Gen 6.13.

them to the very limit, a stop must now be put to it and their wickedness halted lest it get right out of hand. The text says, remember, "'In my view the whole human race has reached its limit.'" See here too how, as he said before, "everyone ponders,"[13] so too in this case, "'the whole human race.'" In other words, everyone is in agreement, they were hell-bent on lawlessness, he is saying, and it is impossible to find in all that crowd anyone setting any value on virtue. "'In my view,'" the text says, remember, "'the whole human race has reached its limits.'" "'The limit,'" that is, the limit has been passed when the blow had to fall and the spread of the ulcer had to be checked. "'In my view the whole human race has reached its limits,'" just as if there were no one taking notice, and no one likely to require an account of their sins, they gave themselves up to illicit behavior, not considering that it is impossible to escape my notice, the one who has bestowed upon them their existence, favored them with body and soul, and supplied them with an abundance of so many good things. Accordingly, "'in my view the whole human race has reached its limits.'"

(8) Then, as if to offer the good man an explanation and show that the excess of their sins provokes him to such anger, he says, "'in so far as the earth is filled with lawlessness on their account.'" That is to say, surely they've neglected nothing, he means, that could induce them to wickedness? They had given evidence of such extremes that their wickedness then erupted and filled the whole earth with evil. This, to be sure, is the reason I am destroying them and the earth. "'Lo, I am going to destroy them and the earth,'" he says. Since they had anticipated their own destruction through their lawless behavior, accordingly I call down on them utter ruin and bring into effect their disappearance and the earth with them, so that the earth may be able to gain some purification and be cleared of the filth of so many sins.

(9) Consider, I ask you, [210] the kind of spirit this good man was probably in at that point as he heard this from the

13. Gen 6.5.

Lord. I mean, even if he was aware of his own great virtue, nevertheless he did not receive the news without sorrow. After all, good people are a kindly lot, and they would readily put up with anything for the sake of other people's salvation. So how could it be otherwise than that this remarkable man was distressed at these words to ponder already in his mind the universal destruction and the annihilation of the whole of creation, perhaps even without a suspicion of some brighter prospect for himself? You see, at this stage nothing was yet clear to him. Lest therefore his thoughts be completely disturbed and he be unable to pluck some little comfort from amidst all this immensity of depression, God, after teaching him the excess of their wickedness and that the time was now fast approaching for requiring them to undergo a profound setback, said to him, Whereas ruin will overtake them all alike, "'you, on the contrary, make for yourself an ark.'"[14] What is the meaning of "'you, on the contrary'"? Since you have had no part in their evil but have rather pursued your whole life in a virtuous way, accordingly I direct you to build an ark for yourself "'of hewn timber, freshly cut. You will make cabins in the ark, and you will cover it with pitch inside and out. It is to be three hundred cubits long, five hundred wide and three hundred high. You will gather material to make the ark, and round it off a cubit from the top, making a door on the sides and building two or three decks below the waterline.'"[15]

(10) Notice God's considerateness, his ineffable power and his love beyond all telling. His care for the good man emerges in various ways—in directing him to build the ark for himself, in instructing him how to build it, its breadth, its height; he lavishes upon him the greatest encouragement, suggesting to him his hopes of salvation in building the ark and wanting those guilty of such awful sins to be brought by the building

14. Gen 6.14.
15. Gen 6.14–16, with some departures from the Hebrew by the LXX in places, resulting in at least one nonsense phrase, as if the unusual Hebrew word was mistaken for another. The LXX ship is a hundred times the Hebrew one (which Speiser estimates at 43,000 tons), a veritable super-tanker.

of the ark to an awareness of their conduct and to come to a change of heart without experiencing his anger. I mean, it was no brief time that was offered them on this further occasion for a change of heart by means of the building of the ark; it was very lengthy, sufficient (had they not been unresponsive) for them to stoop to a correction of their faults. You see, the chances were that each of them, on seeing the good man constructing the ark, would be ashamed of his responsibility for the work; then, on realizing God's anger, they would come to an awareness of their own sins, provided they were ready to do so. But these people did not even gain anything from the incident, not because it was beyond them but because their wills were set against it.

(11) Accordingly, after God had given the good man instructions about building the ark, he shared with him also the secret of the kind of punishment he was due to inflict on them, and said, You build it as I have directed, while I for my part will arrange things securely in your regard when you complete the building. "'For my part, however—lo, I am about to bring a flood of water upon the earth to destroy all flesh in which there is a breath of life under heaven: whatever is on earth will perish.'"[16] See how through this threat, too, he shows them the magnitude of their sins by saying, I will inflict this punishment on rational and irrational creatures alike. I mean, since they had forfeited their preeminence and had reverted to the behavior of brutes, there would be no difference in the punishment: "'I am about to bring [211] a flood of water to destroy all flesh in which there is a breath of life under heaven.'" Cattle, birds, beasts, fourfooted creatures—everything under heaven will be destroyed. That you may learn that nothing would be spared, he says, "'Whatever is on the earth will perish.'" The world now needs purifying, you see, but don't let this disturb you or unsettle your mind; seeing the incurable condition of the ulcer, I must stem the flow of evil lest they render themselves liable to worse punishments. Hence even in this instance, out of fidelity to my own

16. Gen 6.17.

loving kindness and tempering my anger with goodness, I am applying this punishment in a way that will be painless and not felt by them. You see, it is not that I am ignoring the magnitude of their sins nor what they in fact deserve; rather, I am looking ahead to later developments, and thus I want to impose a fitting punishment on these people and protect from harm those who follow in the future.

(12) So don't be downcast or be afraid when you hear this; even if they are overtaken by a penalty suited to their crime, yet "'I will make my covenant with you.'"[17] Since all your predecessors rendered themselves unworthy and did not prove to have the right attitude to my commands, it is with you I will now make my covenant. The first formed human being, despite so many kindnesses, fell victim to deceit and broke my commands, and the son born to him fell in turn into the same abyss of wickedness, so he too received everlasting punishment in the curse imposed on him. Yet not even his punishment brought those coming after him to their senses; instead, they sinned with such wild abandon as to be declared unworthy of their forebears. Later, of course, I found Enoch preserving the features of virtuous living, and so on account of the great satisfaction he achieved in my sight I took him away elsewhere while still living so as to show others who practice virtue the extent of the rewards they are accorded, and out of a wish that people in future would be imitators of him and follow in his footsteps. So, since everyone is now wholly involved in wickedness and I have found you alone amidst all this throng capable of reversing the transgression of your first parents, it is with you I will make my covenant. After all, the conduct of your life shows you to be trustworthy in regard to respect for the commands I have given.

(13) Then, in case that good man should still have misgivings despite hearing all this, being as he would be the only one to survive, God said further, as though to encourage him, "'You, however, are to board the ark, and with you your sons, your wife and your sons' wives.'" You see, even if these peo-

17. Gen 6.18.

ple were much inferior to the good man in virtue, nevertheless they did not show the excessive wickedness of the others. They enjoyed the benefit of salvation on two grounds in particular. Firstly, for their esteem for the good man: it is the loving God's way to show regard for his own servants and in many cases to grant them the favor of other people's salvation, something he did also in the case of blessed Paul, the world's teacher, who spread everywhere the rays of his own teaching. Remember when he was sailing to Rome, a great storm at sea blew up and all on board were afraid of their lives and despaired of any secure hope because of the violence of the deluge; Paul called on them all in these words: "'Take courage, sirs: there will be no loss of life among you, only the ship. You see, a messenger of the God whom I serve appeared to me this night, [212] saying, Don't be afraid, Paul, God has done you the favor of saving all your company.'"[18] Do you see how the man's virtue had the effect of achieving the salvation of those associates of his? However, it was not merely virtue but also the Lord's loving kindness. In just the same way in the present case also this happened on one account; but it was also on another account, as God wanted some leaven and root to be left of the race that would exist in the future—not because it was impossible for God to fashion humanity all over again and build up the race from a single person, but because he decided in this direction out of fidelity to his own goodness.

(14) Now, notice God's goodness also in the sequel. I mean, as he said in threatening punishment that cattle, reptiles, birds and wild beasts would also perish along with the human race, so too in this instance for the good man's sake he instructed that a pair of each species of these creatures be taken on board the ark so that there would be some seed and foundation for the colonies that would exist later. "'Of all cattle,'" he says, "'of all wild beasts and of all flesh you shall bring two by two into the ark to keep them alive with you; they will include male and female. Of every species of birds

18. Acts 27.22–24.

of all kinds, of every species of cattle, and of every species of reptiles of all kinds on earth, two by two of them all will come aboard to you, male and female, to be kept alive with you.'"[19] Don't pass this by heedlessly, dearly beloved: have a thought for the great apprehension he caused in the good man at the thought of caring for all these creatures. After all, it wasn't sufficient for him to think of his wife, his sons and their wives; rather, he was also given in addition care and nourishment of so many animals. Wait a while, however, and you will see God's goodness and the way he relieves the concern besetting the good man. "'Now, for your part,'" he says, "'take a quantity of all the foods you will eat and load them on board with you; they will serve as food for you and them.'"[20] Don't think, he is saying, you have been left uncared for; see, I have given directions for everything necessary for your nourishment and the beasts' fodder to be put on board the ark to save you feeling the effect of hunger, and want, and the beasts perishing through not having suitable fodder.

(15) For proof of the wonderful commendation he was accorded on this account by the Creator of all, listen to what follows: "The Lord God said to Noe, 'Board the ark, you and your household.'"[21] Then in order that we may learn that he not only saves the good man but also recompenses him for his efforts and rewards him for his virtue, he says, On that account I direct you to board the ark with your household "'because I have found you to be law-abiding in my view by comparison with your contemporaries.'" A wonderful testimony and worthy of trust: what could be better than when the Creator himself, he who brings everything into being, delivers such a verdict [213] on the just man? "'Because,'" he says, "'I have found you to be law-abiding in my view.'" This is true virtue when one gives evidence of it in the view of God, when that eye that is proof against deceit delivers its verdict. Then the loving God teaches us the criterion of virtue that he applied in that case to the just man (not that he in-

19. Gen 6.19–20, with minor discrepancies in listing between Hebrew, LXX and Chrysostom's text.
20. Gen 6.21.   21. Gen 7.1.

tends to apply the same criterion of virtue to everyone but
rather looks for a different standard of virtue according to
different situations), and says, "'because I have found you to
be law-abiding in my view by comparison with your contemporaries'" who have reverted to such terrible evil, those
wicked contemporaries of yours, who have given evidence of
such dreadful ingratitude. "'I have found you to be law-abiding,'" I have discovered you alone to be grateful, I have
found you alone putting much store by virtue; you alone are
seen to be law-abiding in my view, all the others going to
perdition; you I direct to board the ark with all your household; you I bid to take on board the clean beasts seven by
seven. Since he had previously given imprecise directions
about taking on board a pair of every creature, he consequently now says, "'The clean beasts seven by seven, the unclean two by two, male and female;'" then to teach us the
purpose of this he added, "'to continue life throughout the
earth.'"[22]

(16) Now, it is worth investigating in this instance and
seeing how the good man came to know which animals are
clean and which are unclean. I mean, to this point this distinction had never been made which Moses later prescribed
for the Jews. So how did he come to know of it? By himself,
under the impulse of the teaching implanted in his own nature, and later at the dictate of reason as well. You see, nothing of what was made by God is unclean. I mean, how could
we call unclean any of God's creatures, once approval had
been bestowed on them from above and Sacred Scripture had
declared that "God saw all that he had made and, behold, it
was very good."?[23] Now, however, nature under its own impulse gave evidence of this distinction. For proof that this is
true, consider even now, I ask you, how in some places people
abstain from some things as unclean and not customary, while
others in their turn partake of them, custom leading them to
do so. So in this way in the present case also innate awareness
taught the good man what was useful for nourishment, on

22. Gen 7.2–3.   23. Gen 1.31.

the one hand, and what was unclean, on the other—not in
fact but in people's opinion. On what basis, tell me, do we
regard the ass as unclean, even though it feeds on nothing
but hay, whereas we consider the other kinds of animals suitable for eating even though their food includes unclean
items? This is the way the knowledge endowed by God on our
nature becomes a teacher in these matters. Otherwise, however, you would have to say that God in giving him the direction also gave him a clear knowledge of these matters.

(17) But we have said enough about clean and unclean
things. Now another question raises its head for us: why on
earth was he to take the unclean animals two by two, but the
clean seven by seven? Why not six or eight, but seven? Perhaps our sermon is being extended to great length; but if
your strength hasn't failed and you're still willing, we will also
give your good selves a brief instruction on these matters as
far as God's grace allows. You see, many people give many
fanciful interpretations of these matters and take occasion
from them to make observations about numbers. You will
very quickly realize, however, that it is a case not of close
observation but of [214] men's inopportune meddling endeavoring to come up with things which have formed the basis of most heresies. I mean, for the most part (so that we
may be seen from the abundance of evidence to put paid to
those adducing arguments from their own reasoning) we find
in Sacred Scripture a combination of two retained as the preferred number: when, for instance, he sent the disciples, he
sent them two by two, there were twelve of them, the Gospels
are four in number. But there is no need for me to go over
this ground with your good selves, since you've been taught
once before to block your ears to such matters.[24] It is necessary now, however, to say why he ordered the beasts to be
embarked seven by seven. While his direction to embark
more of the clean beasts was given with a view to encouraging
the good man and those with him by reason of their sharing

24. De Montfaucon notes at this point that Chrysostom had good reason
to warn his readers against extravagant theories about numbers by people
like Philo, Clement of Alexandria, and even Eusebius.

in the enjoyment of these creatures, the fact of their going seven by seven would likewise have been a wonderful demonstration of the good man's filial reverence for God, if you were ready to study it. I mean, since the loving God was aware of the man's virtue and the fact that being a just man and the recipient of so much loving kindness from the Lord, including his escape from the effects of this terrible deluge, he intended to show his gratitude after being spared that fate and being set free from the constraints of life on the ark by offering sacrifice in thanksgiving for these events and what had happened to him and thus run the risk in so doing of losing a pair of animals, accordingly in his foreknowledge of the good man's attitude of thanksgiving God bade him put on board seven of every species of bird so that once the catastrophe had reached its end he might implement his purpose without impairing the even number of a species or all the birds together.

(18) You will learn this, of course, when the instruction advances further and we arrive at that part of the text; you will then see the good man has done this. As it is, you have learnt the reason why he was directed to embark the animals seven by seven. In future have no patience with those coming up with fanciful interpretations, contradicting Sacred Scripture and setting up notions out of their own head in opposition to the divine teachings. So, after he had given his directions clearly about the birds, about the clean animals and the unclean animals and their feed, he said to the just man, "'After seven more days, behold, I will send rain on the earth for forty days and forty nights, and I will wipe off the face of the earth all the life I have made, from human beings to cattle.'"[25] Notice, I ask you, in the words spoken at this point the extraordinary degree of his goodness, how in addition to his great longsuffering he now also delivers this forecast seven days ahead out of a wish to bring them to their senses through fear and to lead them to a change of heart. For proof that his purpose in foretelling was that his words

25. Gen 7.4.

might not take effect, consider, I ask you, the Ninevites and consider how great the difference was in the two cases: despite hearing after so many years that disaster was at hand, they did not refrain from wickedness as the Ninevites had. We are, of course, inclined to be indifferent and to postpone reform when punishment lies in the future; but when we are on the verge of something that can cause us pain, then we are likely to humble ourselves and give evidence of change for the better. That in fact is what happened in the case of the Ninevites; when they heard that "after three days Nineveh will be demolished,"[26] not only did they not lose heart but they responded to the warning and practiced such abstinence [215] from evil and gave evidence of such scrupulous confession as to extend the matter of their confession even to wild animals—not that animals go to confession (how could they, after all, lacking speech as they do?) but with the purpose of winning the good Lord's love in their regard by means of these animals. What I mean is that, as the text says,[27] the king's retinue proclaimed a fast and ordered that cattle, beasts and all wild animals should take no food or drink; instead, the whole human race of the time put on sack cloth, including the king seated on his throne, and made long and vehement confession, without being sure that they would escape punishment. They said, you see, "'Who knows if, in fact, God will change his mind about the harm he said he would do us?'"[28]

(19) Do you see pagans' gratitude? do you see how not even the shortage of time led them to be sluggish or made them lose heart? Notice also the people in the present text, who after so great a number of years heard that the deluge would come in seven days and yet were not converted like the Ninevites but rather were unaffected by any condition conducive to confessing that "our own choice was responsible for all

26. Jonah 3.4, where the LXX has three days in place of the Hebrew forty, perhaps (as De Montfaucon suggests) through confusion with the celebrated three day period Jonah spent earlier (2.1).

27. Cf. Jonah 3.7.

28. A paraphrase of Jonah 3.9.

the wickedness." I mean, behold these people—and people they were, too, of the same species as the Ninevites but not of the same disposition. Consequently, they did not meet the same fate: whereas the Ninevites escaped the catastrophe, the good God being content with their conversion in his characteristic love, the others were submerged and overtaken by disaster. The text says, remember, "'After seven more days I will send rain on the earth.'" Then, in his wish to increase their fear, he added, "'for forty days and forty nights.'" Why? Wasn't it possible for him, if he wanted, to send all the rain in one day? But why say in one day? in one moment! He does this of set purpose, however, intending at the one time to instill fear and to provide them with the opportunity of escaping the punishment, even if it be at the very gates. "'I will wipe off the face of the earth,'" the text says, "'all the life I have made,'" from human beings to cattle. See how he makes this forecast once and again, and yet does not make any impact on them. He did all this, however, to teach us that it was just for him to inflict such a heavy punishment on them, and to avoid anyone's making ridiculous imputations by saying that if he had shown more longsuffering, doubtless they would have refrained from wickedness and returned to virtue. Hence he makes clear to us the number of years as well, and orders the building of the ark. After all this he also makes his forecast seven days ahead so as to stop the shameless mouths of those bent on speaking rashly. The text goes on, "Noe did everything the Lord God commanded him."[29] See how here too Sacred Scripture hails the just man's gratitude and obedience, teaching us that he neglected none of the commands but discharged them all, providing a demonstration in this way too of his characteristic virtue.

(20) Accordingly, let us in our turn imitate this good man and be zealous in the discharge of the commands [216] given us by God, and not despise the laws given us by God, but rather retain a lively memory of them and show haste in moving to their practice; let us not be indifferent in managing the

29. Gen 7.5.

affairs of our salvation, especially as the greater measure of virtue is demanded of us the more we have enjoyed his help. Hence Christ also said, "'If your goodness does not exceed that of the Scribes and Pharisees, you will not enter the kingdom of heaven.'"[30] So let us consider this in our own regard, and far from heedlessly passing the saying by, let us think of the degree of punishment that awaits those who not only do not exert themselves to surpass those people but even have less to show than they, who do not refrain from venting their spleen on their neighbor, who do not keep their tongue clean of imprecations, who have no interest in protecting their eyes from harmful prospects, and are unwilling not only to treat kindly the person injuring them but also to show him favor, despite the Lord's direction, "'Let the person anxious to sue you and take your coat have your cloak as well.'"[31] We, on the contrary, often endeavor to wrong our neighbor and even revenge ourselves on the one wronging us, despite the instruction we receive not only to love those who love us (after all, "even the tax collectors do as much," Scripture says[32]) but also to be well-disposed to those who hate us; nor do we show the same degree of love as those who love us.

(21) For this reason I am deeply distressed to see in us such a dearth of virtue, on the one hand, and the intensity of wickedness increasing day by day, on the other, not even the fear of hell arresting our decline into evil nor desire for the kingdom impelling us along the way of virtue. Instead, we are led by the nose, so to say, in the manner of cattle, and have no sense either of that fearful hour or of the laws given us by God, but rather go after people's opinion and seek praise from them, not heeding the words of the gospel, "'How can you believe, when you take credit from human beings and fail to seek that which is found with the only God?'"[33] On the other hand, just as those who seek the former lose the latter completely, so those who depend constantly on the latter don't lose the former either. He had previously promised this, re-

30. Matt 5.20.   31. Matt 5.40.
32. Matt 5.46.
33. John 5.44 with a slight textual variant.

member, when he said, " 'Seek first the kingdom of God, and all these things will be given you as well;' "[34] all these things come to the person who has a longing for that goal. You see, the person who fits his mind with wings to fly away there spurns all present prosperity as though it did not exist. I mean, whenever the eyes of faith descry those ineffable goods, they do not even take notice of visible things—such is the difference in the two kinds of realities. I see no one, however, who esteems unseen realities above visible ones. Hence it is a cause of grief to me and an unremitting ache in my heart that experience has not taught us this lesson, nor have God's promises nor the greatness of his gifts had the effect of converting us to desire for the kingdom; instead, still clinging to the ground we prefer things of earth to those of heaven, the present to the future, those things that disappear before coming into view to those that endure, present pleasure to lasting pleasure, the brief prosperity [217] of this present life to those unending ages.

(22) I know that these words irritate your ears, but pardon me for that. I say this in my zeal for your salvation and my wish that by being a little irritated here you will escape everlasting punishment rather than be somewhat beguiled and suffer unremitting penalty. In other words, if you can put up with my talking and dispel the lethargy that had seized you previously, especially now that this short period of the holy season of Lent remains, you will be able to wipe away your sins and win much loving kindness from God. After all, the Lord has no need of many days or a long time: as long as we are willing, we will even in these two weeks achieve considerable correction of our faults. I mean, if he considered the Ninevites, when they had given evidence of a penance of three days, worthy of such loving kindness, so much the more will he be prepared not to overlook us—provided only that we give evidence of true repentance, give up evil and follow the way leading to virtue. After all, about them—I mean the Ninevites—Sacred Scripture testifies in these words: "God

34. Matt 6.33.

saw that each of them had turned from his evil way."[35] Accordingly, if he sees us also changing course for virtue, turning away from evil and showing zeal for the performance of good works, he will accept our change of direction, rid us of the burden of our sins and lavish upon us gifts of his own. I mean, we are not so anxious for release from our sins or so long after our salvation as he shows enthusiasm for it and hastens to grant us release from them and to bring us to enjoyment of salvation.

(23) Hence, I beseech you, let us stir up our thinking, and let each person be his own examiner as to whether he has anything further to his credit in the time that has passed, whether he gained anything of advantage from this constant instruction, whether he reaped any benefit for strengthening his neighbor, whether he corrected any of his own faults, whether he gained any encouragement to philosophy from our daily exhortation. Let the good person direct attention to improving his good behavior and never relax this commendable performance. If, on the contrary, someone sees himself addicted to the same faults under the influence of a habit that rules his life, let him exert all his powers of reasoning, give an account of his sloth, and not hang back from making progress, but rather arrest the force of the evil habit at this point, stem its tide, put the spur to his powers of thought, apply himself to meditating on that dread day, imagine partaking of that fearful table, the brightness of the flame blazing from it, its searing intensity, the kind of attitude required of the guest, purified of every stain, of every defilement, and avoiding the onset of improper thoughts. Thus we may make ourselves ready in these intervening days and be able to purify ourselves as far as possible, partake of enjoyment there and be judged worthy of those ineffable goods promised to those who love him, thanks to the grace and love of our Lord Jesus Christ, to whom with the Father and the Holy Spirit be [218] glory, power and honor, now and forever, for ages of ages. Amen.

35. Jonah 3.10, paraphrased.

HOMILY 25

"Now, Noe was six hundred years old when the deluge came upon the earth."[1]

WANT [218] ONCE MORE TO TOUCH on the theme I broached to you, brethren, yesterday and set before you again the story of the good man Noe. You see, the good man's wealth of virtue was immense, and it is our duty to study it in detail as far as we possibly can and to draw great benefit from it for you. For your part, strain your attention, I beg you, so that none of the ideas contained there may escape you. It is necessary firstly, however, to remind your good selves to what point yesterday's teaching brought us so that we may resume the sermon from that point and in this way link up what we have said with what now remains to be said.

(2) So how did our instruction conclude? The text says, "The Lord God said to Noe, 'Board the ark, you and your household, because I have found you to be law-abiding before me in this generation. Take on board with you the clean beasts seven by seven, and the unclean two by two. You see, after seven more days I will send rain on the earth for forty days and forty nights, and I will wipe off the face of the earth all the life I have made, from human beings to cattle.' Noe did everything the Lord God commanded him."[2] We brought the sermon to that point and concluded the instruction there. You recall just as well yourselves, of course, that we explained

---

1. Gen 7.6.
2. Gen 7.1–5, with textual differences from the quotation of these verses throughout Homily 24—which goes to document Baur's warning about the Fathers' erratic quotation of Scripture from memory (cf. FOTC 74, Introduction (15).)

124

to your good selves the reason why God directed that the clean beasts be embarked seven by seven but the unclean two by two.

(3) So, come now, today let us move on to the following verses, and see what Sacred Scripture describes to us after Noe's boarding the ark. You see, at this particular time we ought especially display great interest when on account of the season of fasting we have without interruption been enjoying your gracious attendance and have been free of temptation to gluttony, and with our mind alert we have been able to attend with precision to what is said.

(4) There is need, therefore, to say where today's reading takes its beginning. "Now, Noe was six hundred years old," the text says, "when the deluge came upon the earth." Pay attention, I beseech you, and let us not pass this verse by heedlessly; these brief words contain a hidden treasure, and provided we earnestly apply our attention, we shall be able to learn from them both the extraordinary degree of the Lord's loving kindness and the intensity of wickedness of people of that time. "Now, Noe," it says, "was six hundred years old." It was not idly that it taught us the good man's age, or merely for the purpose of our learning that figure itself of the good man's age; instead, because Sacred Scripture had previously taught us to the effect that "Noe was five hundred years old,"[3] and after making known to us his age it had then recounted people's extreme tendency to wickedness and that their mind was set firmly on evil from their youth, accordingly God said, "'My spirit is not to remain with these human beings on account of their being [219] carnal,'"[4] giving them a premonition of the extremity of his anger. Then, so as to give them a sufficient opportunity to change direction and avoid experiencing his anger, he says, "'Instead, they will have a life of a hundred and twenty years,'" as if to say, I will put up with them for another fifty years.[5] You see, in those fifty years the

3. Gen 5.32.   4. Gen 6.3.
5. As De Montfaucon points out here and in Homily 23 where Chrysostom first commented on Gen 6.3, Chrysostom is making a moral point about

just man by means of his own name did not cease reminding
them all and encouraging them, provided they were ready to
heed him, to give up wickedness and change to virtue. Nevertheless, he is saying, even now I promise to put up with them
for a hundred and twenty years so that they may employ the
intervening time properly, shun evil and take up virtue instead. And far from being content with the promise of a
hundred and twenty years, he orders the good man to build
the ark so that the very sight of the ark may also provide
them in turn with an adequate reminder and that no one
would be unaware of the magnitude of the punishment due
to be inflicted. After all, that very fact that that good man
who had reached the very pinnacle of virtue was displaying
such earnestness in building the ark should have been sufficient to put fear and anxiety into everyone with sense and to
persuade them to placate this so kind and loving Lord.

(5) I mean, if those pagans (I'm referring to the Ninevites)[6]—I have to introduce them again, you see, so that by
this means the extraordinary wickedness of these others may
be contrasted with their great responsiveness. You see, our
Lord at that time on that dread day—I mean the Day of
Judgement—delivers his condemnation by bringing forward
these servants and those, when it becomes clear that while all
have enjoyed the same advantages and partaken of the same
goods, not all have shared in the same degree of virtue; instead, he frequently makes a contrast between unequal parties so as to inflict the heavier condemnation on the victims
of indifference. Hence he said in the Gospels, "'Men of Ni-
nevi will rise up at the Judgement with this generation and
condemn them, because they repented at the preaching of
Jonah and, behold, a greater than Jonah is here'"[7]—as if to
say that the pagans did not have the advantage of any such

human sin and divine forbearance to words intended dogmatically; Von Rad
summarizes the Yahwist's intention: "God sets a maximum age beyond which
man, who has increased his vital power in such an ungodly manner, cannot
go" (*Genesis*, 114).

6. De Montfaucon comments here on Chrysostom's weakness for digres-
sions, but admits that this is the longest of them all.

7. Matt 12.41.

solicitude, did not hear the teaching of the prophets, did not
witness signs, did not see miracles, but simply heard words
from one person saved from shipwreck that were capable of
instilling into them a deep sense of despair and of driving
them to such a feeling of helplessness as to make them even
despise the words spoken by him, yet they not only did not
scorn the prophet's words but were wrapt in three days'
remorse[8] and gave every sign of such strict and intense repentance as to revoke the Lord's sentence. These, then, are
the people who will condemn this generation that had the
advantage of the same solicitude, were nourished on the
books of the inspired writers, witnessed each day's signs and
wonders. Then, so as to show also the extraordinary degree
of their unbelief as well as the Ninevites' responsiveness, he
added, "'because they repented at the preaching of Jonah
and, behold, a greater than Jonah is here;'" whereas they had
sight of that unprepossessing person Jonah, welcomed the
preaching he gave, and displayed a most rigorous repentance
(he is saying), these others on the contrary, who had someone
far [220] greater than Jonah and saw the very Creator of all
passing time with them and daily working so many marvelous
wonders—cleansing lepers, raising the dead, setting at rights
disabilities of nature, driving out devils, curing diseases,
granting forgiveness of sins with great authority—not even
the same faith as the pagans did they display.

(6) Let us, however, return to the theme of our sermon so
that you may see both the intensity of one party's ingratitude
and the assiduity of the other's responsiveness, as well as the
fact that whereas the latter agonized over their state for three
days without despairing of their salvation but showing zeal
for repentance, washing away their sins and rendering themselves worthy of the Lord's loving kindness, the others by contrast, while accepting the reprieve of a hundred and twenty
years for repentance, made no further use of that period.
Hence the Lord, on seeing the excess of their wickedness and
observing that they had rushed headlong into grave evil, ap-

8. Cf. note 27, Homily 24.

plied to them rapid correction, removing the depravity of their wicked corruption and taking it out of his sight. For this reason the text says, "Noe was six hundred years old when the deluge came upon the earth." To this point we had learnt that when the Lord's anger occurred and he made this forecast, Noe was five hundred years old. When, however, the deluge was brought upon them, he was six hundred years old, so that a hundred years had passed in the meantime, and yet they gained no benefit from those hundred years, despite the advantage given them of so much instruction from Noe's building the ark.

(7) But perhaps someone might be anxious to find out why God had said, "'They will have a life of a hundred and twenty years,'" and promised to show longsuffering for that length of time, and yet before the completion of that time brought on the disaster. This would be a remarkable demonstration of his loving kindness: when he saw them committing irreparable sins day after day and not only gaining nothing from his ineffable longsuffering but even developing worse ulcers, consequently he cut the time short lest they render themselves liable to worse punishment. And what punishment is worse than this, someone says? That punishment is worse, dearly beloved, more fearful and enduring which lasts into the world to come. In fact, for proof that some people, while not escaping punishment in the next life for making amends in this, will nevertheless endure a lighter one there on account of what happens here and will thus reduce the severity of those sanctions, listen to the words of Christ as he laments the fate of Bethsaida: "'Woe to you, Chorazim,'" he says, "'woe to you, Bethsaida, because if the miracles had taken place in Sodom that took place in you, they would long ago have repented in sackcloth and ashes. Hence I say to you, it will be more tolerable for the land of Sodom and Gomorrah in the day of judgement than for you.'"[9] Do you see, dearly beloved, how in the words, "'more tolerable,'" he showed that those also who paid such a penalty here by enduring that novel and

9. A conflation of Matt 11.21–24.

unusual kind of conflagration would, while still undergoing punishment there, nevertheless have a lighter one on account of their previous experience of such terrible anger here on earth?

(8) So, in the case of the people of Noe's time, lest by aggravating their [221] sins they might render themselves liable to worse punishment, the good and loving Lord, seeing their unrepentant attitude, reduced the period he had promised to allow in his longsuffering. In other words, just as in the case of people giving evidence of gratitude for the goodness characteristic of him he revokes the sentences delivered by him, welcomes their repentance, and lifts the penalty imposed on them, so too in this instance, when he promised to give them either certain goods or a period of repentance, but in fact saw they had proved unworthy, then too in turn he revoked his promises. Hence he said also by the inspired writer: "'At long last I shall speak regarding nations and regarding kingdoms about destroying and overthrowing them; if they should repent, I too will repent of the things I have promised to do to them.'" And again, "'At long last I shall speak regarding nations and regarding kingdoms about rebuilding them; if they should sin, I too will repent of the things I have promised to do to them.'"[10] Do you see how he takes occasion from us for both the love and the anger he shows in our regard? Hence, of course, in this present case, since they had not taken proper advantage of the time, he shortened the period. For this reason, too, blessed Paul spoke against those who were not disposed to respond and were not accepting the offer of salvation given them through repentance: "Do you scorn the wealth of his kindness, his forbearance and his longsuffering, ignoring the fact that God's kindness leads you to repentance? You, on the contrary, in your hard and unrepentant heart are storing up wrath for yourself on that day of wrath, revelation and just judgement."[11] Do you see how this amazing teacher of the world clearly taught us that those who do not take proper advantage

10. A précis of Jer 18.7–10.   11. Rom 2.4–5.

of God's longsuffering offered to us with a view to our repentance render themselves liable to a heavier sentence and punishment? Hence in this case too the loving God, as if explaining and giving the reason why he brought on the deluge before the completion of the time, indicates to use the good man's age, saying, "Now, Noe was six hundred years old." After all, if they hadn't been prepared in those hundred years to repent, what would they have gained from those twenty years beyond going from bad to worse? In other words, to show the extraordinary degree of his ineffable love and goodness, he did not even decline to remind them seven days ahead of time of the onset of the deluge so that they might be stricken with the urgency of the situation and give evidence of some conversion.

(9) See also the Lord's loving kindness, how like a skillful physician he treated the disease in different ways: since their wounds were incurable, he provided them with such a lengthy period of time in his wish that they might come to their senses through the generous amount of time and he might be able to revoke the sentence of his anger. You see, it is always his fashion, concerned as he is for our salvation, to tell us ahead of time the punishments he is due to inflict, with the sole purpose in mind of not having to inflict them. If, of course, he had wanted to inflict them, he would not have told us; but he makes a point of giving us warning so that we may learn of it, be brought to our senses through fear, placate his anger and render his sentence null and void. Nothing, after all, so gladdens him as our conversion and our reverting from evil to virtue. Consider, therefore, how he treated this people's disease, too, first by giving them so much time of reprieve for repentance, then when he saw them unmoved [222] and profiting nothing from the length of time, with disaster at the very gates, so to say, he gives warning, not three days in advance, as in the case of the Ninevites, but seven days. I would, after all, be confident in saying, on account of my knowledge of the excess of our Lord's loving kindness, that even in seven days they could, had they been prepared to give real evidence of repentance, have avoided

experiencing the deluge. Since therefore neither such a lengthy
reprieve nor the urgency of the situation was capable of affecting their evil behavior, he brought on the deluge in Noe's
six hundredth year. "Now, Noe was six hundred years old,"
the text says, "when the deluge came upon the earth." Do you
see, dearly beloved, how much benefit to us knowing the just
man's age proved to be an occasion of, and knowing how old
he was when the deluge came?

(10) Come now, let us move on to the following verses:
when the deluge began, the text says, "Noe, his sons, his wife,
and his sons' wives boarded the ark on account of the flood
from the deluge. The clean birds, the unclean birds, the reptiles—all of them embarked two by two with Noe in the ark,
male and female, as the Lord had commanded Noe."[12] It was
not without purpose that he added the words, "just as the
Lord had commanded Noe;" it was for the sake of adding
further commendation of the just man, both because he had
carried out everything just as the Lord had commanded and
had omitted nothing of what he had been told by him. "It
happened after seven days," just as the Lord had promised,
it says, "that the flood from the deluge came upon the earth
in the six hundredth year of Noe's life, on the twenty seventh
day of the second month."[13] See the precision of Scripture,
how it not only taught us the year of the deluge but also made
clear the month and the day. Then, so as to bring succeeding
generations to a better frame of mind through this narrative
and augment their fear at what had happened, it says, "On
that day all the fountains of the deep burst forth and the
sluice gates of heaven broke open; rain fell on the earth for
forty days and forty nights."[14] See the extent of the consid-

12. Gen 7.7–9, a strange rehearsal of previous verses that succeeds only
in complicating the pictures given already differently by the Yahwist and
Priestly editors. Chrysostom, at a loss like others before him, does his own
simplifying of the text before omitting all but the last safe clause from comment.

13. Gen 7.10–11.

14. Gen 7.11b–12. Von Rad comments on that awesome v. 11b: "Here we
have the same realistic and cosmological ideas as in Gen, ch. 1. According to
the Priestly representation we must understand the Flood, therefore, as a
catastrophe involving the entire cosmos . . ." (*Genesis*, 128).

erateness Sacred Scripture employs here too, describing everything in a human manner: it is not that there are sluice gates
in heaven, but rather that it describes everything in terms
customary with us, as if to say that the Lord simply gave a
direction and immediately the waters obeyed their Creator's
command, fell out of the heavens on all sides and inundated
the whole world.

(11) The fact, too, that he brought on the deluge for forty
days and nights is a further wonderful sign of his loving kindness: his purpose in his great goodness was that at least some
of them might come to their senses and escape that utter
ruin, having before their eyes the annihilation of their peers
and the destruction about to overwhelm them. I mean, the
likelihood is that on the first day some proportion of them
were drowned, an additional number on the second day, and
likewise on the third day and so on. His reason for extending
it for forty days was that he might remove from them any
grounds for excuse. You see, had it been his wish and command, he could have submerged everything in one downpour; instead, out of fidelity to his characteristic love he
arranged for a stay of so many days.

(12) Then it says, "On this day Noe boarded the ark, with
Shem, Cham and Japheth, with Noe's wife, [223] the three
wives of his sons, and all the animals, species by species, as
the Lord God had instructed Noe."[15] When the beginning of
the deluge occurred, it says, according to the Lord's direction,
Noe boarded the ark with his sons, his wife, his sons' wives,
and all the animals species by species. The text goes on, "The
Lord God shut the ark from the outside."[16] Notice in this
place too the considerateness in the expression "God shut the
ark from the outside," to teach us that he had ensured the
good man's complete safety. The reason for adding "from the

15. Gen 7.13–16, with omissions.
16. Gen 7.16, where again the anthropomorphic quality of the narrative
forces Chrysostom to invoke the principle of *synkatabasis*. As Von Rad says,
"That Yahweh himself shut up the ark behind Noah is again one of those
surprising statements of the Yahwist, almost hybrid in its combination of
near-childlike simplicity and theological profundity" (*Genesis*, 120).

outside" to "he shut" was that the good man might not be in the position of seeing the disaster occur and suffering even greater distress. I mean, if he brooded over that terrible flood and set indelibly in his mind the destruction of the human race, the complete annihilation of all brute beasts, and the disappearance, as it were, of people, animals and the earth itself, he would have been disturbed and upset. You see, even if it is the wicked who perish, nevertheless the souls of good people are likely to show compassion when they see people being punished; and you will find each of the good people and the inspired writers making earnest supplication for them, as for example the patriarch did for the Sodomites,[17] and the inspired writers all continued to do. One, for instance, said, "Woe is me, Lord; are you wiping out the remnant of Israel?"[18] while another said, "Will you make people like the fish of the sea, deprived of a leader?"[19] So since without even this the good man was troubled in mind and sick at heart, the Lord, in case the sight of these things should cast Noe into deeper depression, locked him in the ark as though in a prison, lest he have a sight of these events and be terror-struck. In his care for him, therefore, the loving God does not allow him to view the torrent of water nor see the disaster occurring that involved the destruction of the world.

(13) Whenever, on the other hand, I ponder this just man's existence in the ark, I am struck with amazement, and once more attribute it all to God's loving kindness: unless that had strengthened his resolve and had rendered difficult things easy, how would he have been able, tell me, to bear being locked in there like that as though in some dungeon or prison? How could he, tell me, have put up with the awful crashing of the waves? After all, if people who find themselves on board ship driven by sail, watching the pilot seated at the rudder and pitting his own skill against the force of the winds, fear for their very salvation, so to say, and die of fright at the ferocity of the waves, what could you say about this just

17. Gen 18.22–23.   18. Ezek 9.8.
19. Hab 1.14.

man? I mean, finding himself on the ark as though in prison, as I was just saying, he gazed hither and yon, unable to see the sky and having nowhere to direct his eyes, forced to remain inside, with nothing at all to look at that could afford him any comfort.

(14) You see, in the case of people sailing the sea it is possible, even when the billows rise on high, to gain some little comfort by gazing time and again at the sky, descrying a mountain top, and catching sight of a large city; [224] and even if the storm increased in intensity and becomes unbearable for ten days or somewhat longer, yet despite all those storms and those perils, once they are cast up on the shore and get their breath back a little they lose all recollection of those hardships. In the present case, however, it was nothing like that; instead, for a whole year[20] he dwelt in the strange and unusual prison without even being able to breathe the fresh air—how could he, after all, with the ark closed in on all sides? How did he put up with it? How did he last? I mean, even if their bodies had been made of iron and steel, how could they have survived without fresh air, without the breeze, which no less than fresh air exists to invigorate our bodies, without being able to feast their eyes on a glimpse of the sky or the range of colored flowers growing on land? In fact, how did they not lose the sight of their eyes after living in this fashion for so long? And if we were interested in pursuing the matter at the level of human reasoning, we would feel it necessary to consider where they got their supply of drinking water from while living on board the ark. Leaving that aside, how did this good man with his sons and their wives manage to abide living with animals and brute beasts and all the rest? How did he put up with the stench? How did he bear living with them? And why mention that point? How did the brute beasts themselves manage to cope with it without perishing in such a long period of time without being free to enjoy fresh air or move about, but confined in one space? I mean, you know quite well that, as far as our nature

20. A little pardonable exaggeration on Chrysostom's part?

goes as also the nature of the beasts, even if we have the benefit of fresh air and all other things but are confined to one place continuously, there is no way of avoiding our death and demise. How then could this good person last out so long with all these creatures in the ark? In no other way than by the grace from above that makes all things possible. I mean, was it not due to grace from above that the ark was tossed this way and that without being submerged in such a force of water, with no steersman at the helm? You can't say that it was designed like a ship so as to be able to steer a course by some kind of know-how. The ark was shut in on all sides; and by direction of the Creator not only did the force of the water cause it no harm but it rose to the top and guaranteed the safety of its passengers.

(15) So, whenever God does something, dearly beloved, don't insist on inquiring with your human reasoning into whatever he has done: it surpasses our understanding, and the human mind could not succeed in measuring up to it or grasping the secret of what has been created by him. Hence, after hearing that God has so directed, we ought believe and obey what is said by him. After all, being Creator of our nature he transforms and reshapes everything according to his own decision. "The Lord God shut the ark from outside." Great was this just man's virtue and the depth of his faith. Faith, you see, was responsible for the building of the ark, for his putting up with his quarters without resentment, tolerating the hardships of existence with animals and all the wild beasts. On this account blessed Paul called him to mind and to celebrate his virtues shouted aloud, "By faith Noe, forewarned as he was about things not yet seen kept his own counsel as he prepared the ark with a view to saving his own household; by faith he condemned the [225] world, and succeeded to a share of that righteousness that accords with faith."[21] Do you see how faith in God like a safe anchor enabled him to see to the building of the ark and to put up with his quarters? Faith it was, you see, that proved the basis of

21. Heb 11.7.

his salvation; "through it," the text says, "he condemned the world, and succeeded to a share of that goodness that accords with faith." Not that he did the condemning but that the Lord declares the condemnation by comparison; that is to say, those who enjoyed the same advantages as the good man did not share with him the same path of virtue. So it was through the faith that he exemplified that he condemned those who exemplified lack of faith, failing to believe the forewarning.

(16) On the other hand, along with everybody else, I too am amazed at the just man's virtue, and the Lord's goodness and love beyond all telling when I think of how he managed to live among the wild animals, namely, lions, panthers, bears and the other fierce and untamed animals. Call to mind in this connection, I ask you, dearly beloved, the esteem enjoyed by the firstformed human being before the Fall, and consider God's goodness: after his transgression undermined the authority given him, the good Lord by contrast found another man capable of correcting that original image by preserving the imprint of virtue and demonstrating strict obedience to law. So he placed him once more in his pristine position of esteem, as if to teach us through this procedure the extent of the authority Adam had before the Fall. Accordingly the good man's virtue profited from God's loving kindness to restore the former control, and once more the wild animals recognized their subordination. In other words, whenever the animals saw the good man, they lost all thought of their own nature—or, rather, not their nature but their ferocity, and changed to docility the ferocity innate in their nature. Notice this happening in the case of Daniel: encircled by the lions, as though by sheep, he passed his time that way without fear, the good man's trust restraining the wild beasts' nature and not allowing them to demonstrate the characteristics of wild animals.[22] Well, in just the same manner this remarkable man bore his existence with the wild animals with equanimity, and neither the straitened circumstances, nor the protracted length of time, nor being locked in, nor lack of fresh air to breathe

22. A little gloss on Dan 6.22.

caused him to become jaded; instead, through his faith in God everything seemed easy, and thus he lived in that terrible prison as we would in meadows and leafy glades.

(17) In other words, the Lord's command made the difficult things seem simple to him. Such, after all, is the way with good people: when they endure something for his sake, far from attending to the appearance of what occurs, they understand the reason behind it and thus bear everything with equanimity. Likewise by Paul, the teacher of the gentiles, imprisonment, arraignment, daily peril, all those many unbearable hardships were called light, not because they really were so by nature, but because the reason behind their happening produced such an attitude in him that he would not turn back in the face of these oncoming threats. Listen, after all, to what he says: "For the light weight of our passing distress produces in us an eternal weight of glory beyond all comparison;"[23] expectation of the glory we are destined to attain, he is saying, and of that unceasing enjoyment [226] makes us bear without difficulty these hardships one after another and consider them of no consequence. Do you see how love of God reduces the intensity of troubles and prevents our having any sense of them as they befall us? On this account, of course, this blessed man, too, bore everything with equanimity, sustained by faith and hope in God.

(18) "The Lord God shut the ark from outside," the text says. "The deluge fell forty days and forty nights upon the earth, and the ark began to float."[24] Notice once more how he increases our awe through his way of narrating and embroiders the event. "The deluge fell forty days and forty nights," the text says, "the flood deepened and picked up the ark, so that it was lifted above the earth. The force of the water grew stronger and it spread widely on the earth, and the ark was carried above the flood level. The water continued to spread further and further on the land."[25] See how precisely it describes to us the great force of the waters, and

---

23. 2 Cor 4.17.   24. A précis of Gen 7.17.

25. Gen 7.17–19, where the LXX adds "forty nights" to the Hebrew, probably under the influence of v. 12.

the fact that each day the flood increased in extent. "The water continued to spread further and further," the text says, "and covered the highest mountains under heaven. The water rose fifteen cubits, and submerged all the mountains."[26] It was appropriate that the loving Lord arranged for the ark to be shut so that the just man did not see what happened. I mean, if we after so many years and so many generations are aghast simply at hearing Scripture's account of it and are reduced to trembling, how likely it was that that just man would be stricken to see with his own eyes that mighty deep that no one could survive? How, in fact, could he have managed to cope with the vision even for a short time? Would he not, on the contrary, have immediately fainted at his first glimpse as his soul left him, unable to bear any further sight of such an awesome spectacle? I mean, consider, I ask you, dearly beloved, how in our life whenever some little shower falls we go to pieces, worry about all our concerns, even despair of life itself, so to say. So how likely was it that that just man in those circumstances should be distressed to see the flood swelling to such heights? "The flood rose fifteen cubits above the mountains,"[27] the text says, after all.

(19) On this point, I ask you, dearly beloved, recall what was spoken by the Lord when he said, "'My spirit is not to remain with these human beings on account of their being carnal,'"[28] and again, "The earth was corrupt, and was filled with lawlessness,"[29] and "The Lord saw that the earth was utterly corrupt because all flesh had corrupted their ways upon earth."[30] Accordingly, the world needed a complete cleansing; every stain had to be expunged from it, all leaven of the previous wickedness had to be sifted out and no trace of evil left; instead, a certain renovation had to be effected, like some skilled craftsman taking a vase that had aged with time and rusted away, so to say, and putting it into the kiln to ensure the removal of all the rust, thus reshaping and refash-

26. Gen 7.19–20.
27. Chrysostom himself embroidering the text of v. 20 for effect.
28. Gen 6.3.   29. Gen 6.11.
30. Gen 6.12.

ioning it and returning it to its pristine form. In the same way our Lord too cleansed the whole world by the deluge and, so to say, freed human beings from their wickedness, their defilement and all their corruption, leaving the world more resplendent and once more revealing the brightness of its countenance, and not permitting even a trace of the previous ugliness to persist. "The flood rose fifteen cubits above the mountains," says the text.

(20) It is not without purpose that Scripture describes all this to us; instead, its purpose is for us to learn that not only people, cattle, fourfooted beasts and reptiles were drowned but also the birds [227] of heaven and whatever inhabited the mountains, namely, animals and other wild creatures. Hence the text says, "The flood rose fifteen cubits above the mountains," for you to learn that the execution of the Lord's sentence had been effected; he said, remember, "'After seven more days I will bring a deluge upon the earth and I will wipe off the face of the earth all the life I have made, from human beings to cattle, and from reptiles to birds of heaven.'"[31] So, Sacred Scripture narrates this, not simply to teach us the flood level, but that we may be able to understand along with this that there was absolutely nothing left standing—no wild beasts, no animals, no cattle; rather, everything was annihilated along with the human race. Since it was for their sake that all these creatures had been created, with the imminent destruction of the human being it was fitting that these creatures, too, should meet their end. Then, after teaching us the great height reached by the flood waters and the fact that they rose a further fifteen cubits above the mountain peaks, it further adds out of fidelity to its characteristic precision, "There perished all flesh that moved on the earth—birds, animals, every reptile that moved on the earth, every human being—everything that had breath of life, everything on dry land: all perished."[32] That wasn't an idle reference in the words, "everything on dry land;" instead, its pur-

---

31. Gen 7.4 in a version only roughly approximating to the LXX text Chrysostom quoted in the previous homily.

32. Gen 6.21–22.

pose was to teach us that while all others perished, the just man with everyone in the ark alone were saved. You see, in God's design they had previously moved from the dry land and boarded the ark. "All life that was on the face of the earth was wiped out, from human beings to cattle, reptiles, birds of heaven—they were wiped off the earth."[33] See how once, twice and more frequently it teaches us the occurrence of the disaster and the fact that no creatures escaped but rather all were drowned in the flood, both the human race and the animal kingdom.

(21) "Noe alone survived," the text says, "and those with him in the ark. The water was at flood level on the earth for a hundred and fifty days."[34] For all those days, the text says, the water remained at flood level. Consider here again, I ask you, the just man's greatness of soul and the extraordinary degree of his fortitude. What sufferings would he not have endured in having engraved on his mind and having seen with the eyes of his intellect, as it were, the bodies of human beings, of cattle clean and unclean, all alike undergoing death, mingled together without any distinction being made? Further, in addition to this, he pondered within himself the loneliness, the isolation, that distressing existence, with no consolation coming from any quarter, neither from converse, nor from pleasant prospects, nor from knowing with precision how long he was destined to put up with existence in that terrible prison. After all, as long as there was the crashing and booming of the waves, fear was daily sent surging through him. I mean, what likelihood was there that he would suspect any good news when he had before his eyes for a hundred and fifty days the water continuing at such a height, reaching flood level without subsiding in the slightest? Still, he took it all in good part, knowing the Lord's inventiveness and the fact that being Lord of all life he does everything and changes what he wants to, so he bore no resentment against life in those circumstances. You see, God's grace came to lend heart [228] to his enthusiasm and provided him

33. Gen 6.23.   34. Gen 6.23–24.

with sufficient comfort, not allowing him to fall victim to brooding nor dwell on ignoble or unmanly alternatives. In other words, since previously he had made the most of his own resources—his painstaking virtue, his scrupulous sense of goodness, the extraordinary degree of his faith—he was now regaled with the Lord's blessings in abundance: forbearance, fortitude, the ability to bear everything without resentment, putting up with life in the ark, sustaining no harm from the experience, not perishing or being distressed by existence in the company of wild animals.

(22) Let us likewise, therefore, I beseech you, imitate this just man and exert ourselves to bring to bear our resources with a view to making ourselves worthy of the gifts coming from God. This, you see, is the reason he waits for occasions we provide, that he may display great generosity. So, do not let us deprive ourselves of his gifts through indifference; rather, let us make every effort and press forward to take the initiative and follow the way leading to virtue so as to enjoy support from above and be able to attain the goal. You see, it is impossible for us to achieve any good deed without being in receipt of grace from above. Clinging, therefore, to hope in God as though to a firm, secure anchor, let us not have regard for the difficulty of virtue but consider instead the reward following the difficulty and thus meet every challenge easily. Likewise, when a merchant moves out of port and sails on the high seas, it is not only pirates that are on his mind, or shipwreck, or leviathans, or the onset of storms, or continuous tempests, or unforeseen troubles, but also the profits coming his way in the wake of these hazards: nourished by this hope he accepts with equanimity the hardships that beset him so as to gain greater rewards and thus make for his home port. The farmer, too, does not think only of the hardships associated with farming, downpours, bad luck with the soil, a rust plague, a scourge of locusts; instead, he concentrates his thinking on the threshing floor and the sheafs, and so puts up with everything placidly, feeling no effect of the hardships because of his expectation of the yield: even if his hope is uncertain, yet he is nourished by stronger hopes and does not

give up in the face of hardships but brings all his resources
to bear, waiting to gather the reward of his labors. The sol-
dier, too, in turn arms himself and goes into battle thinking
not only of wounds and casualties, enemy raids and other
problems, but imagining victory and trophies coming his way;
thus he equips himself with a panoply of weapons, and despite the great uncertainty and hazard, he banishes all such
thoughts from his mind, sets glowing prospects before him,
banishes all sluggishness, takes up his arms and advances in
formation against the foe.

(23) If therefore, dearly beloved, merchants, farmers and
soldiers on the basis of uncertain hope face numerous hazards and difficulties many and varied, as you heard, and yet
none of them despair in the face of hardship nor shrink back
from brighter prospects, what excuse would we be found worthy of if we desisted from virtue and did not willingly accept
every hardship despite the fact of an assured hope and so
many good things laid up for us and a superabundant reward
for all our achievements? So listen to blessed Paul's remarks
after so many dreadful tribulations, arraignments, imprisonment and [229] daily dying: "The sufferings of this present
life are not worth comparing to the glory due to be revealed
in our regard:"[35] even if each day (he is saying) we suffer
death, something that nature could not endure, even if mind
overcomes matter to gain the prize through the Lord's loving
kindness, we endure nothing comparable to the good things
we are destined to receive (he is saying) or the glory due to
be revealed in our regard. See how great the glory is which
they enjoy who practice virtue, to the extent that it surpasses
anything you could exemplify: were you to ascend to the very
summit, you would still fall short. I mean, what could a human being give evidence of to such an extent as to rival adequately the Lord's generosity? If a man of Paul's quality and
stature said, "The sufferings of this present life are not worth
comparing to the glory due to be revealed in our regard," if
he said, "I die daily,"[36] and again, "I worked harder than all

35. Rom 8.18.
36. 1 Cor 15.31.

of them,"[37] what would we say after being unwilling to put up with incidental hardship for the sake of virtue, and always looking instead for enjoyment and taking care to avoid experiencing distress, even though we know that it is impossible that enjoyment in the next life would come our way otherwise than here in this life showing our desire for it by exerting ourselves? These hardships, you see, are the means of winning God's favor for us, and a little struggle here brings us there great confidence, provided only we are ready to proceed in line with the advice of Paul, the world's teacher.

(24) Consider, dearly beloved, that life's troubles, even if distressing, are still of short duration, whereas the good things that will come to us in the next life are eternal and everlasting. "What we see is passing," Scripture says, "but what is not seen is everlasting."[38] Accordingly, let us endure what is passing without complaint and not desist from virtue's struggle so that we may enjoy the good things that are eternal and last forever. May it be the good fortune of all of us to enjoy them, thanks to the grace and love of our Lord Jesus Christ, to whom with the Father and the Holy Spirit be glory, power and honor, now and forever, for ages of ages. Amen.

37. 1 Cor 15.10.   38. 2 Cor 4.18.

HOMILY 26

"And God was mindful of Noe and of all the beasts, all the cattle, all the birds and all the reptiles that were with him in the ark. And God sent a wind upon the earth, and the water subsided."[1]

REAT [229] AND INDESCRIBABLE beyond all telling is the loving kindness of God revealed in the verses read just now, along with the extraordinary degree of his goodness, which he manifests not only in regard to this rational being—namely, the human being—but also in regard to the species of irrational beings. I mean, being in fact Creator of them all he extends his characteristic goodness to everything created by him, showing us through everything how much care he takes of the human race and the fact that he undertook everything from the beginning and the very outset for our salvation. Accordingly, even if he chastises and punishes, he does both from his very goodness. You see, far from inflicting punishment in rage and anger, it is his wish to put a stop to evil lest it get entirely out of hand. In the present case also, as you have heard, he had no other motive in bringing on the deluge than his concern for the people who had abandoned themselves to such terrible wickedness.

(2) What kind of concern is that, someone will say, that annihilates everyone under the waters? Don't speak rashly, o man [230]; instead, accept with grateful mind what is done by the Lord, and realize in that instance how much concern is evidenced by that happening in particular. I mean, to separate from their wickedness people who have sinned irreparably, who have daily aggravated their wounds and rendered their ulcers incurable—isn't that a mark of the greatest con-

---

1. Gen 8.1, the LXX elaborating the point with the inclusion of birds and reptiles as well.

cern? Isn't the very recourse to punishment replete with loving kindness? After all, for people who in any case are due
to discharge the debt of nature to lay aside their life in this
fashion painlessly by way of punishment and feel no effect of
the events—isn't this a mark of great wisdom and goodness?
Further, if anyone were to learn through reverential consideration what in fact happened, that not only did God treat
the punished with kindness but that those destined to follow
them would reap from it two particular benefits—namely, not
being ensnared in the same troubles, and being rendered
wiser by these events—how much thanks ought they pay to
God for this grace of being brought to their senses afterwards
both through the others' punishment and by the fear of suffering the same chastisement, as well as by the removal of the
leaven of all wickedness and evil and the survival of no one
to instruct them in evil and wickedness? Do you see how his
punishments and chastisements are rather kindnesses, and
demonstrate in particular his concern for the human race?

(3) If anyone were interested in enumerating them from
the very outset, he would find God inflicting punishments in
every instance with this very same purpose. Even in the case
of Adam, when he fell, he did not simply punish him but out
of kindness drove him from the garden. What sort of kindness was that, some one will say, to be expelled from life in
the garden? Don't simply pay attention to the events, dearly
beloved, nor take a casual interest in what is done by God;
instead, gain an insight into the depths of his goodness and
you will find it is this that has motivated him in all his doings.
I mean, tell me, if even after the Fall Adam had continued to
enjoy the same privileges, to what depths would he not have
descended? After all, if he fell a victim to the serpent's deceit
so as to heed all his lavish promises and accept the advice the
devil offered him to make them vain and lead them to hope
for equality with God, drawing them into the sin of disobedience; and if despite that he had continued in the same position of esteem and the same lifestyle, how could he have
failed to consider the wicked demon more trustworthy than
the Creator of all, and have formed extravagant ideas of his

own importance? This, you see, is what human beings are like: when their sin leads them to get the bit between their teeth and feel no fear, they go ahead and fall headlong over the precipice. There are other ways as well, however, by which I can show that it was an example of his loving kindness that God directed him to leave the garden and rendered him liable to the punishment of death, bringing him to his senses and making him more careful in future both by the expulsion and by locating him nearby, and teaching him through these events the deceiver's duplicity. Now the punishment of death he likewise inflicted with this end in view, that in future he might not through disobedience become addicted to sin and commit sins that did not end with death. So does all this not strike you as a mark of the greatest love, both the expulsion from the garden and the imposition of the punishment of death?

(4) I have other means, however, of improving on this explanation. What, precisely? The fact that in venting his anger against him in this way he was not simply investing him with acts of kindness but also intending to bring future generations to a better frame of mind through what was done to him. You see, even if after these events [231] his son (I mean Cain) saw with his own eyes the expulsion of his father from the garden, his fall from that ineffable glory, the magnitude of that curse in the words, "'Dust you are and to dust you are to return,'"[2] and yet did not come to his senses through this but even involved himself in worse evils; if he had not seen what happened to his father, to what depth of folly would he not have plunged? The remarkable thing surely is that in punishing the very person who had committed such terrible sins and besmirched his right hand in execrable slaughter, God tempered the punishment with loving kindness. To learn the magnitude of God's goodness from what happened to Cain: when he insulted God and displayed great disregard for him by intending to make an offering without properly choosing but making his approach casually and as

2. Gen 3.9.

if by chance, God said nothing harsh or severe to him; the sin, at any rate, far from being casual, was extremely heinous. You see, if people wish to show regard for their peers, human beings though they are, by offering them the foremost and most select gifts and are concerned to present them with things that seem to them the most precious of all, how is it that Cain, human being that he was, did not feel it necessary in his offering to God to offer him the most precious and most select gifts? Accordingly, even though he was committing such a grave sin and displaying such extreme disregard, God did not exact vengeance nor did he inflict punishment for what was done; instead, like one friend conversing with another in all gentleness, he thus addressed these words to him, " 'Though you have sinned, be at peace.' "[3] He only showed him his sin and urged him not to go any further. Since, however, that unfortunate man not only gained nothing from such wonderful forbearance but even added worse crimes to the previous ones and rushed headlong to the slaughter of his brother, God was thus showing extreme long-suffering in his regard by first questioning him and giving him the opportunity for explanation; but as he persisted in his shamelessness, then for the sake of bringing him to his senses God inflicted the punishment that had mingled with it great love on his part.

(5) Do you see how, while in the one case he made allowance for Cain when he sinned against him, even though the sin was not casual, in the other case when he raised his hand against his brother he then applied the punishment and the curse. This is what we too should do in our life, in imitation of our Lord: we should discount sins committed against us and make allowance for those who offend us, whereas when someone makes God the object of attack, then we should invoke punishment. Instead—how, I know not—we do everything in the contrary manner: sins affecting God we are not at all concerned to punish, whereas if some chance offense is committed against us, we turn exacting avengers and prose-

3. Gen 4.7.

cutors of that, unaware that by so doing we rather provoke
the loving Lord the more so against ourselves. You see, for
proof that it is customary with God to make allowance frequently for sins committed against himself but to punish with
exceeding severity those sins we commit against our neighbor,
listen to the words of blessed Paul: "If someone has a non-
believing wife, and she is happy to be living with him, let him
not set her aside. And if a woman has a non-believing husband, and he is happy to be living with her, let her not set
him aside."[4] Do you see the extent of the considerateness?
Even if he is a pagan, even if he is a non-believer, yet accepts
the marital situation, she is not to reject him. Further, "Even
if your wife happens to be a pagan, even if she is a non-
believer and yet wants to live with you, [232] don't drive her off.
After all," he says, "how do you know, woman, if you will save
your husband, and how do you know, husband, if you will
save your wife?"[5] See how there is no problem about a person's accepting an unbelieving husband or wife in a marital
partnership. Listen further, however, to Christ's words to his
disciples: "I say to you that everyone who puts aside his wife
except on the score of infidelity causes her to commit adultery."[6] What an extraordinary degree of loving kindness!
Even if the wife is a non-believer, he is saying, or a pagan, yet
accepts the marital situation, accept her; but if she sins
against you and forgets her marriage vows and prefers association with others, you may send her away and reject her.

(6) So with these thoughts in mind let us for our part make
a return to the Lord for his favor to us, and as he is prepared
to make allowances for offenses against him while exacting
vengeance for those against us, and with great severity, in just
the same way let us, too, behave; let us pass over what offenses our neighbor commits against us, but what he directs

4. 1 Cor 7.12–13.
5. 1 Cor 7.16, with an introduction of Chrysostom's own, perhaps in
place of v. 15 stating the 'Pauline privilege,' without which v. 16 fails to have
the force intended by Paul. Yet Chrysostom then goes on to quote Christ in
support of that dispensation, somewhat against the sense of the gospel passage.
6. Matt 5.32.

against God let us take great pains to exact vengeance for.
This, after all, will bring us, too, the greatest benefit, and will
be of no little help to those undergoing correction.

(7) Perhaps our introduction today had been extended to
great length. What is to become of me? It wasn't deliberately
that I went to this extreme; I was carried away with the flow
of the sermon. Since, however, all our talk has been concerned with the deluge, we needed to show your good selves
that even the punishments sent by God are rather acts of
loving kindness than punishments, and so too therefore was
the deluge. I mean, like a kind father he arranges everything
in his care for our kind. But for you to learn both from what
has now been proposed to you and from what was read today
the magnitude of his loving kindness, listen to the very words
of the Holy Scriptures: after blessed Moses taught us yesterday in these words, that "the water was at flood level on the
earth for a hundred and fifty days"[7] (that being the point,
remember, our instruction had reached), he says today, "God
was mindful of Noe, and of all the wild animals, all the cattle,
all the birds and all the reptiles that were with him in the
ark."[8]

(8) Notice once again, I ask you, the considerateness of Sacred Scripture: "God was mindful," it says. Let us take what
is said, dearly beloved, in a sense befitting God, and not interpret the concreteness of the expressions from the viewpoint of the limitations of our human condition. I mean, as
far as that ineffable essence is concerned, the word is improper; but as far as our limitations are concerned, the expression is made appropriately. "God was mindful of Noe," the
text says. You see, since it had narrated to us in what was said
already, as we taught your good selves previously, that the
rain fell for forty days and forty nights, and for a hundred
and fifty days it remained at the same level reaching fifteen
cubits above the mountains, and that while this was happening, the just man happened to be in the ark, unable even to
enjoy a breath of fresh air, with all the brute beasts living with

7. Gen 7.24.   8. Gen 8.1.

him, consequently it says, "God was mindful of Noe." What
is the meaning of "mindful"? It means God took pity on the
just man living in the ark, had mercy on him for the straitened conditions in which he found himself, reduced as he
was to such helplessness and uncertain as to what extreme his
difficulties would extend. I mean, consider, I ask you, what
thoughts he was entertaining after [233] the forty days and
forty nights during which the flood of water poured down,
seeing as he did the waters remaining at the same level for a
hundred and fifty days and not subsiding in the slightest;
what was even more distressing, the fact that he was unable
to see what was happening with his own eyes, since he was
shut in, and because unable to gauge with his eyesight the
extent of the disaster he suffered the greater distress and
imagined worse things each day. I for my part, however, am
amazed how he wasn't overwhelmed by coming to a realization of the destruction of the human race, his own isolation
and that difficult style of existence. Still, the cause of all these
advantages he enjoyed was his faith in God, through which
he kept up his spirits and bore everything without resentment, so that he was nourished by hope and felt no effect of
these troubles.

(9) So, since he had made whatever effort he was capable
of, had given evidence of endurance, and brought his faith to
bear in generous measure in displaying great bravery, notice
the good God's great love for him. "God was mindful of
Noe," the text says. It did not simply say, "He was mindful;"
instead, since Sacred Scripture had previously made clear to
us the testimony to the just man paid by God in the words,
"'Board the ark, because I have found you to be law-abiding
by comparison with your contemporaries,'"[9] consequently it
now says, "God was mindful of Noe." That is to say, he remembered the testimony he had paid him and did not long
neglect the just man; rather, he showed his longsuffering as
long as Noe could bear, and then regaled him with favor from
himself. You see, he knows the limitations of our nature, and

9. Gen 7.1.

when he lets us endure some trial, he allows it to continue for as long as he knows we can endure it so that he may also grant us reward commensurate with our fortitude and give evidence of his characteristic love, as Paul too says, "God, however, is faithful in not allowing you to be tested beyond your capabilities but in providing also with the trial a way out of it so that you can endure it."[10] Since therefore this just man too displayed fortitude and endurance, putting up with confinement in the ark through faith in God, "God was mindful of Noe," the text says. Then, as index of the depths of his loving kindness Sacred Scripture added, "and of all the wild beasts, all the cattle, all the birds and all the reptiles that were with him in the ark."

(10) See how he did everything out of his esteem for the human being: as in the case of the destruction of human beings in the flood he destroyed also along with them the whole range of brute beasts, so in this case too, when he intends to show his characteristic love for the good man out of his regard for him, he extends his goodness to the animal kingdom as well, the wild beasts, the birds and the reptiles. "God was mindful of Noe," the text says, "and of all the wild beasts, all the cattle and all the reptiles that were with him in the ark. God sent a wind upon the earth, and the water subsided." Being mindful of Noe, the text says, and of those with him in the ark, he directed the flood of water to halt so that little by little he might show his characteristic love and now give the good man a breath of fresh air, free him from the turmoil of his thoughts and restore him to a state of tranquility by granting him the enjoyment of daylight and a breath of fresh air. "God sent [234] a wind upon the earth, and the water subsided. The torrents of the depths and the sluice gates of heaven were shut off."[11]

(11) See how it narrates everything to us in human fashion: "The fountains of the deep and the sluice gates of heaven were shut off," the text says, "and the rain from heaven stopped," as if to say that the Lord decided and once again

10. 1 Cor 10.13.   11. Gen 8.2.

the waters kept to their own limits, there was no further
flooding, and instead they gradually subsided. "The water
gave way and flowed off the earth; the water diminished after
a hundred and fifty days."[12] What reasoning could ever manage to grasp that? Let it be (God says); the rain stopped, the
fountains no longer yielded a flood, and the sluice gates of
heaven were shut—how did all this great amount of water
subside? Mighty depths were everywhere—so how could this
huge flood of water suddenly become less? Who could ever
manage to solve this by human reasoning? So what can you
say? It was God's direction that achieved it all. Accordingly,
let us not pry into the secret; let us simply take it on faith
that he gave the command and the depths became shallow,
he issued his direction and once again they checked their onset and respected their own limits which the Lord alone knew.
"On the twenty seventh day of the seventh month the ark
came to rest on the mountains of Ararat. The water continued to diminish until the tenth month; on the first day of the
tenth month the mountain peaks became visible."[13] Notice
how suddenly the change took place and how far the waters
subsided so that the ark could come to rest on the mountains.
Previously, you remember, Scripture had said that the water
level reached fifteen cubits above the mountains, whereas now
it says that the ark came to rest upon Mount Ararat, and then
the water gradually diminished until the tenth month, and
then in the tenth month the mountain peaks became visible.

(12) Consider, I ask you, the just man's equanimity, how he
managed to keep his head for so many months, shut in
though he was as if in complete darkness. "After the forty
days," the text goes on, "Noe opened the window in the ark
he had made and sent out the raven to see if the water had

12. Gen 8.3. Despite his insistence on *akribeia*, Chrysostom does not risk
entering into discussion of the divergent statements of the duration of the
Flood—being unable, of course, to envisage diversity of sources in one narrative.

13. Gen 8.4–5; not unexpectedly in this composite narrative, discrepancies emerge in the texts of Chrysostom, other LXX and Hebrew MSS in the
time references, here and elsewhere.

subsided."[14] See the good man not yet daring to see for him-self; instead, he sent out the raven with the intention of find-ing out through it whether some encouraging transformation could be expected. "It flew off," the text goes on, "but did not come back before the water was dried up from the earth."[15] Sacred Scripture added the word "before," not be-cause it did come back later, but because this is a peculiarity of Sacred Scripture. You would often come across this fea-ture, and we could locate many such examples and bring them to your attention; lest, however, you learn everything from us and become slack in your interest, we will leave it to you to study Scripture and discover where it employs these peculiar usages. But for the present we need to explain the reason why the bird didn't come back. Perhaps, with the waters subsiding, the bird, being unclean, happened upon corpses of men and beasts and, finding nourishment to its liking, stayed there—something that proved to be no little sign of hope and encouragement for the just man. I mean, if that weren't the case and he didn't gain any comfort, it would have come back.

(13) For proof of this, at this point the just man, with ex-pectation enkindled, next sends out the dove, a tame yet friendly bird characterized by great gentleness, with no other diet than seeds, [235] being numbered as it is among the clean birds. "He sent out the dove from him," the text says, "to see if the water had subsided from the face of the earth. The dove found no rest for its feet and came back to him in the ark, because water covered the whole face of the earth."[16] It is worth examining at this point how previously Sacred Scripture said that the mountain peaks had become visible, but now says that the dove found nowhere to rest and came back to him in the ark, because water covered the whole face of the earth. Let us read the verse with precision, and we will know the reason. It did not simply say, remember, "It found no rest," but added, "for its feet," to teach us that even if the

14. Gen 8.6–7.
15. Gen 8.7b. The LXX differs from the Hebrew of v. 7.
16. Gen 8.8–9.

water had partly subsided and the mountain peaks had become visible, still from the abundance of water even the very mountain peaks were muddy or were covered with a muddy slime. Hence the dove was neither able to perch anywhere nor successful in finding food to its liking, so it turned back, teaching the just man by its return that there was still a great flood. "Stretching out his hand," the text goes on, "he grasped it and pulled it in to him in the ark." Do you see the extent of the bird's gentleness, how it returned and by its coming taught the just man to display still some little patience? Hence, the text goes on, "he contained himself for seven days more before sending out the dove from the ark: the dove came back to him towards evening carrying a dry olive twig in its mouth."[17] It is not idly or to no purpose that the phrase "towards evening" occurs here; instead, it is for us to learn that the bird, that had been feeding all day and had found some suitable food, came back in the evening carrying a dry olive twig in its mouth. That is the kind of creature it is, you see, tame and always looking for company—hence, of course, it turned back and by means of the dry olive twig brought the just man great consolation.

(14) But perhaps someone might say: where did it find the olive twig? While the whole incident happened through God's design, both its discovery and the dove's taking it in its mouth and going back again to the just man, yet in this particular case as well that tree is evergreen and it is likely that with the subsidence of the waters the tree still had the foliage on its branches. "He contained himself," the text says, "a further seven days before sending out the dove, which did not proceed to return to him again."[18] See the just man through every event receiving sufficient encouragement; just as he had sound hopes at the bird's return, bringing the olive twig in its mouth, so now too its departure to return no more pro-

17. Gen 8.10–11a.
18. Gen 8.12, in the LXX's literal rendering of the Hebrew idiom (cf. 4.2). It is noteworthy that Chrysostom has thus omitted v. 11b of the LXX and Hebrew, "Noe knew that the water had subsided from the earth," perhaps to avoid a suggestion of superfluity in v. 12.

vided him with a forceful proof of its finding great satisfaction and of the complete subsidence of the waters.

(15) The text goes on, "In the first month of the six hundred and first year of Noe's life the water left the face of the earth. Noe opened the roof of the ark he had made and saw that the water had left the face of the earth."[19] Here once again I am forced to marvel and be amazed at the just man's virtue and God's loving kindness; how could it be, tell me, that in exposing himself to the fresh air and raising his eyes to the sight of heaven he was not blinded and did not lose the sight of his eyes? You are well aware, of course, that this is a particularly common affliction [236] with people who live in dark and gloomy places, if only for a short time in the day, and suddenly decide to look up at the source of light. This just man, on the contrary, lived in the ark as if in complete darkness for an entire year and so many months, and now suddenly looked at the source of light without suffering any such affliction. God's love, you see, came with the endurance granted him, also supplying strength to the body's senses and making them superior to bodily needs. "By the twenty seventh day of the tenth month the land had dried."[20] It is not idly that Sacred Scripture shows such precision: it is for us to learn that by the stage of one day of that year when the just man's endurance was demonstrated the purpose had been fulfilled and the purification of the whole world had been achieved.

(16) Then, when all creation was cleansed as if of some blemish, removing all defilement caused in it by people's wickedness, and its countenance was made resplendent, then finally he directed the just man to disembark from the ark and freed him from that awful prison in the words, "Then the Lord God said to Noe, 'Disembark, you and your sons, your wife and your sons' wives with you, as well as all flesh, from birds to cattle; take off with you every reptile that crawls upon the earth, and increase and multiply on the earth.' "[21]

19. Gen 8.13, with a further instance of disparity in counting.
20. Gen 8.14.
21. Gen 8.15–17.

Notice God's goodness, how in everything he encourages the good man: after ordering him to disembark from the ark along with his sons, his wife, his sons' wives and all the wild animals, then lest great discouragement should gradually overtake him by this further development and he become anxious at the thought that he would be on his own, dwelling alone in such a vast expanse of earth, with no one else existing, God first said, Disembark from the ark, and take off everything with you, and then added, "'Increase and multiply on the earth.'" See how once again this good man receives that former blessing which Adam had received before the Fall: just as he heard when he was created, "'God blessed them in the words, 'Increase and multiply, and gain dominion over the earth,'"[22] so too this man now hears the words, "'Increase and multiply on the earth.'" In other words, just as the former man became the beginning and root of all creatures before the deluge, so too this just man becomes a kind of leaven, beginning and root of everything after the deluge. From this point on, what is comprised in the make-up of human beings takes its beginning, and the whole of creation recovers its proper order, both the soil reawakening to productivity as well as everything else that had been created for the service of human beings.

(17) The text goes on, "Noe disembarked along with his wife, his sons and his sons' wives; and all the animals, all the cattle, every species of bird and reptile crawling upon the earth disembarked from the ark."[23] According to the Lord's direction, the text says, he disembarked from the ark with everything else after receiving the blessing in the words, "'Increase and multiply.'" From then on the just man was living alone in the whole earth along with his wife, his children and their wives. As soon as he disembarks he expresses his own gratitude, and offers thanks to his Lord both for what had happened and for what lay ahead. But if you don't mind, to avoid the risk of lengthening this sermon, let us put off till next time [237] the account of the just man's gratitude and

---

22. Gen 1.28.   23. Gen 8.18–19.

bring the sermon to a close at this point, exhorting your good selves to keep this just man constantly in mind, get to know precisely the beauty of his virtue and become imitators of him. After all, consider, I ask you, how great was the wealth of his virtue from the fact that now for so many days we have been telling his story without even now being able to bring to a close our treatment of him. Why do I say bring to a close? No matter how much we say, we can never reach an end; rather, even if we could say a great deal, even if those coming after could, we would never be in a position to say the last word—such is the nature of the virtue! You see, provided we are willing, this man will be able to instruct all our fellows and lead us all on to the imitation of virtue. I mean, since this just man, even despite living his life amongst such wicked people and being unable to find any soul-mate, was still found to have attained such an extraordinary measure of virtue, what excuse would there be for us who have had no such obstacles and yet are so indifferent about its practice? In other words, don't quote me only his life for those five hundred years and the fact that he lived as the object of scorn and ridicule by the practitioners of evil, but also his existence in the ark. That year, after all, seems to me equivalent to all the previous time; the just man was obliged to endure such terrible hardship there, finding himself in such straitened circumstances, unable to get a breath of fresh air, putting up with life amongst brute beasts and wild animals, and demonstrating through it all the firmness of his resolve, the resoluteness of his decision, and the faith in God he displayed, by means of which he bore everything without resentment or complaint.[24] It was, of course, because of the fact that he brought all his own resources to bear that he enjoyed also the assistance coming from God in abundance. You see, even if he had to put up with the claustrophobia of life in the ark, nevertheless he escaped the terrible flood and that utter devastation.

24. It is for his moral value that Noe is such a significant figure for Chrysostom, monopolizing the Genesis commentary for nine homilies. See FOTC 74, Introduction (13) and (17).

(18) Hence, after that confinement and intolerable imprisonment, he enjoyed both security and freedom from care, and was accorded commendation by God; in turn he discharged his debt of gratitude in deed, and everywhere you will find the first fruits offered by him. As he had made virtue his practice all his life and steered clear of the wickedness of others, and thus did not feel with them the effects of punishment but was alone preserved when all others drowned, so likewise, since he had brought to bear great faith and endured his life in the ark with thankfulness, blessings from God followed in great abundance: once he disembarked from the ark and was restored to his former lifestyle, immediately he was accorded commendation and in turn demonstrated his own gratitude by giving thanks as far as possible, and thus he was granted further blessings from the loving God. You see, this is God's way, when some trifling menial offering has been made by us, yet because we have made it, he showers upon us gifts in abundance. To learn both the extent of human niggardliness and your Lord's prodigality, give your attention, I ask you, to this present case. I mean, if we want to offer anything, what can we do so worthwhile as to give thanks through words? What comes from him he discharges in actions for our benefit. So what comparison is there between [238] actions and words? After all, our Lord, being protected from need, has no need of anything from us except words; he requires this very expression of thanks in words, not because he personally needs it but to teach us to be grateful and recognize the provider of good things.

(19) Hence Paul too said in his letter, "Be thankful;"[25] our Lord looks for nothing from us so much as this practice. Accordingly, let us not be ungrateful, nor allow ourselves to be beneficiaries of his action while showing reluctance to offer thanks to the Lord in word; after all, once more it is to us that the benefit accrues. You see, if we prove thankful in the first instance, we will guarantee a surge of confidence about gaining for ourselves even greater benefits. Only, I beseech

25. 1 Thess 5.18.

you, each day and hour, if it is possible, let us set our minds not only on the common benefits granted by the Creator of all to the whole human race but also those supplied to us privately and individually. Why say those supplied to us privately and individually? Even for those benefits conferred on us in our ignorance let us be thankful. You see, since he is concerned for our salvation, he blesses us in many ways of which we are unaware, often rescues us from perils and confers other blessings upon us. In other words, he is a spring of loving kindness and never ceases providing streams from that source for mankind. So if we keep this in mind and show zeal both in offering thanks to the Lord for his original favors and in preparing ourselves for future favors in such a way that we do not seem to be unworthy of blessings from him, we will be in a position to give evidence of an impeccable lifestyle and avoid the experience of evil. The memory of his blessings will be a sufficient instructor for us in a lifestyle characterized by virtue, and will never allow us to fall victim to indifference and forgetfulness and slip into wickedness. You see, the soul that is alert and on the lookout demonstrates its gratitude not only when things go swimmingly but also when some unfavorable turn of events develops; then it offers equal thanks, not at all enervated by the change in circumstances but rather strengthened by it in the thought of the unspeakable love of God, who having no lack of resources or inventiveness is able even in unfavorable circumstances to demonstrate his concern, even if we are unable to come to a precise understanding of the situation.

(20) Accordingly, let us manage the affairs that affect us in such a way, no matter how things work out, that we make it our one concern to thank him constantly for everything. This is the reason, after all, that we have been made rational creatures and in this we differ from the irrational, that we should offer to the Creator of everything praise, honor and constant glory. His purpose in breathing life into us and giving us the power of speech was that we might have an awareness of the favors done us by him, recognize his lordship, demonstrate our gratitude and offer thanks to the Lord according to our

ability. You see, if people who share the same nature as ourselves render us some mean and paltry favor and frequently
require thanks for the trouble they have gone to, not for the
sake of our gratitude but that they themselves may gain
greater recognition from the affair, so much the more ought
we show gratitude to a greater extent in the case of the loving
God, whose only interest in this being done is our benefit.
[239] I mean, just as in the case of human beings the thanks
offered to benefactors redounds to their credit, so in the case
of the loving God whenever we make such an offering it redounds to our credit, not because he wants the offering to be
made out of a need of praise from us but with a view to the
gain accruing to us once again and our rendering ourselves
eligible for greater assistance. You see, even if we are unable
to do this worthily—how could we, after all, invested as we
are with such natural limitations? Why speak of human nature? Not even the incorporeal and invisible powers themselves, the powers and authorities, the Cherubim and the
Seraphim are able to offer praise and thanksgiving worthily.

(21) Still, it would be proper to offer thanks according to
our ability and constantly glorify our Lord by means of both
praise in word and a virtuous lifestyle. This, you see, is the
kind of praise that would be particularly telling, when we offer our worship on countless tongues. I mean, the virtuous
person leads all of those seeing him to sing the Lord's praises;
and praise from them wins for the person providing the occasion great favor beyond all telling from the Lord. So what
could be a more fortunate lot than our own if we were in a
position of not simply glorifying the good God ourselves with
our own tongue but also of stirring many of our fellows to his
praise in addition to ourselves? Such, you see, is the force of
virtue, that it is able to praise the Creator with countless
tongues. In other words, dearly beloved, nothing could be
compared with a virtuous lifestyle. Hence the Lord too said,
"'Let your light so shine before men that they may see your
good works and glorify your Father who is in heaven.'"[26] Do

26. Matt 5.16.

you see how, just as the light by shining dispels the darkness, so too virtue, when seen, puts evil to flight and by dispelling the darkness of deceit moves the minds of onlookers to praise? Accordingly we ought to exert ourselves to let our good works shine so as to give glory to our Lord. Christ said this, however, not for us to do something by way of display— God forbid—but that we may by a lifestyle characterized by exactness and meeting with his approval provide no occasion of blasphemy to anyone but may through the performance of good deeds encourage onlookers to glorify the God of all. Then, you see, then we will win favor from him to a greater extent and be in a position both to avoid evil and to come into possession of those ineffable blessings, thanks to the grace and love of our Lord Jesus Christ, to whom with the Father and the Holy Spirit be glory, power and honor, now and forever, for ages of ages. Amen.

HOMILY 27

"And Noe built an altar to the Lord, made a choice of all the clean cattle
and all the clean birds, and offered sacrifices on the altar."[1]

ID YOU NOTICE [239] YESTERDAY the loving Lord's
goodness, how he brought the good man out of the
ark, freeing him from life there and releasing him
from that strange and distressing prison, and bestowed on
him the reward for his endurance in the words, "'Increase
and multiply.'"[2] Today let us learn about Noe's gratitude and
his thankful soul, through which once more he invited further and greater favor towards him from God. You see, this
is what God is like: whenever he sees gratitude in response to
initial gifts, [240] he bestows in abundance further gifts from
himself. Accordingly let us in our turn be eager to offer
thanks to the Lord to the best of our ability for the good
things already bestowed on us by him so that we may be accorded greater ones, and let us never forget the blessings
coming to us from God, but rather let us always ponder these
in our mind so that we may be constantly stirred by the memory of them and give thanks, even if their number is so great
that our thinking could never measure up to the challenge of
numbering his kindnesses to us.

(2) After all, how could anyone imagine what has already
come our way, the promises, the events of each day—the fact
that he brought us from non-being to being, that he has
blessed us with body and soul, that he has created us rational,
that he has given us this fresh air to breathe, that he has
formed all creatures for humankind, that he for his part intended from the beginning that human beings should enjoy

1. Gen 8.20.   2. Gen 8.17.

162

life in the garden, have a life free from pain, be relieved of any distress, and while happening to be in bodily condition to enjoy a status not inferior to the angels and those incorporeal powers but even be proof against bodily needs? Then, when he fell victim to the devil's deceit applied by means of the serpent, he did not then abandon the sinner nor cease blessing the transgressor; instead, even through the punishments he inflicted on him, as I said yesterday also, he showed the extraordinary degree of his characteristic loving kindness and laid up for him many samples of his kindness of other sorts and beyond counting. Later, as time passed and the human race multiplied and strayed into wickedness, he saw them incurring wounds that could not be cured, and so he destroyed the doers of evil like some noxious leaven, sparing this good man for the mission of being a root and beginning for the human race.

(3) Notice once again how much generosity he displayed in his regard. From this good man and his sons he made plans for the whole human race to grow into such a vast multitude; he gradually selected the good men—I mean the patriarchs—and appointed them instructors of the rest of the human race, being able as they were by their own virtue to lead everyone onwards and having the power like doctors to cure the afflicted. He led them on, at one time into Palestine, at another into Egypt, both exercising the endurance of his servants and at the same time revealing more conspicuously his own power; in this manner he continued constantly caring for human beings' salvation by raising up prophets and causing signs and wonders to be performed through them. Then (to make my point brief), just as we would never be able to number the waves of the sea, even if we made the effort countless times, so could we neither compass the range of God's benefits which he has given evidence of in regard to our race— finally, however, when he saw the human race despite so much care still needing his great love beyond all telling, and that no great effect had come from the patriarchs, the prophets, those remarkable wonders, the punishments and reminders frequently applied, and those successive captivities, then

as though pitying our race, he sent his only-begotten son
from his fatherly bosom, so to say, and caused him to take
the form of a slave,[3] be born of a virgin, live in our company
and endure our condition [241] in its entirety so that he
might be able to bring from earth to heaven our human race
which lay here below under the weight of its many sins. This
is what astounds the Son of Thunder, realizing as he does the
excess of God's love revealed in regard to the human race,
and so he shouts aloud in the words, "This, you see, is the
extent to which God loved the world."[4] See how much amazement is expressed by the sentence: "This is the extent," he
says, having in mind the magnitude he was about to describe—hence he began in that fashion. So tell us, blessed
John, what was "this extent"? Tell us the measure, tell us the
magnitude, teach us this excessive degree. "This, you see, is
the extent to which God loved the world, that he has given
his only-begotten Son so that everyone believing in him may
not perish but have eternal life."

(4) Do you see the reason for the coming of the Son to be
the following, that those destined to perish would find a
means of salvation through faith in him? How would anyone
through unaided reason have arrived at an understanding of
that great and amazing liberality surpassing all logic which he
lavished on our nature through the gift of baptism, granting
us freedom from all our sins? But what am I to say? Neither
reason suffices to explain it, nor is the mind capable of enumerating the consequences. You see, however much I say,
what remains unsaid is so great that the difference exceeds
the words already spoken. So how would anyone imagine the
way of repentance he has granted to our race in his ineffable
love, and after the gift of baptism those wonderful commands
through which, provided we are willing, we can win favor
from him? Do you see, dearly beloved, the depths of his kindnesses? Do you see that no matter how many we count we

3. Phil 2.7. This is one of those beautiful passages where Chrysostom
develops his thinking on the Incarnation that is the basis also of his theology
of the scriptural Word.
4. John 3.16.

would never be able to tell a fraction of them? After all, how could human tongue manage to cover in words all the things done for us by God? Accordingly, though they are so numerous and so varied, still much greater and beyond all telling are those benefits he has promised in the life to come after change from here to those who tread the path of virtue. To set before us in a few words the extraordinary degree of their magnitude, blessed Paul says, "what eye has not seen, nor ear heard, nor has it entered the human heart, what God has prepared for those who love him."[5] Do you see the extravagance of gifts? Do you see his kindnesses surpassing every human imagining: "It has not entered the human heart," he says. If then we are ready to imagine them and make our thanksgiving according to our ability, we will be able to win his favor to a further degree and be stimulated to virtue even more. Recollection of his benefits, you see, suffices to impel us towards the struggle of virtue, to fit us to scorn all present realities, to long for the one who has conveyed such benefits, and to betray a desire for him increasing day by day.

(5) This was the reason, remember, that this good man, too, enjoyed favor and regard from on high, that he showed great gratitude for previous blessings. To make the point clearer to you, however, we must propose for the consideration of your good selves the beginning of today's reading. When he disembarked from the ark, you recall, in accordance with the Lord's direction, along with his sons, his wife and his sons' wives, and with all the wild beasts and the birds, and he received from God together with his [242] release that wonderful blessing that brought him much comfort in the words, "'Increase and multiply,'" the Sacred Scripture says to teach us the good man's gratitude, "Noe built an altar to the Lord, made a choice of all the clean cattle and all the clean birds, and offered sacrifice on the altar."[6] Notice precisely, dearly beloved, once more in the present words how the Creator of all implanted in nature itself the precise knowledge

5. 1 Cor 2.9, Chrysostom resisting any temptation to improve on the syntax of Paul's OT quotation.
6. Gen 8.20.

we have of virtue. I mean, where, tell me, did the good man acquire this attitude? There was no one else whom he might have had before his eyes. But as in the beginning the child of the first formed human being—I mean Abel—was acting under his own impulse in presenting his offering with great exactness, in just the same way in the present case this good man from his own sound thinking and choice offers thanksgiving to the Lord in sacrifices to the extent of human capability, as he was accustomed to do. See him performing everything with great wisdom; he had need neither of lavish building nor temple, no marvellous house or anything else. You see, he knew, he quite clearly knew that the Lord looks only for one's attitude: building an altar from what lay at hand, and making a choice of the clean cattle and the clean birds, he offered sacrifice and as far as he possibly could he demonstrated his gratitude of his own choosing.

(6) The loving God accepted it and rewarded his attitude, and in turn gave evidence of liberality on his part. Scripture says, "The Lord smelt an odor of fragrance."[7] See how the attitude of the offerer caused the smoke, the odor and any stench arising from it to give off great fragrance. Hence Paul too said in his letter, "Because we are the fragrance of Christ among those being saved and among those being lost; in the one case an odor of death leading to death, in the other case an odor of life leading to life: an odor of fragrance."[8] Don't be upset at the concreteness of the expression; rather, attribute the considerateness of the words to your own limitations, and understand from it that the good man's offering proved acceptable. You see, so that we may be in a position to know even through these very events the Lord's independence of any need and the fact that he permitted these things to happen for no other purpose than encouraging human beings to gratitude, accordingly he allows them to be consumed by the fire so that the offerers too may learn from what happens

7. Gen 8.21.
8. 2 Cor 2.15 plus the final phrase from the Gen text, which De Montfaucon notes other editors have expanded to reproduce that entire clause, against the evidence of the MSS.

that everything happens for their benefit. But for what reason, tell me, does he allow all this to happen? This likewise is an example of his considerateness for human limitations: when human beings gradually slipped into indifference and were on the point of devising gods for themselves and performing sacrifices to them, he took the precaution of ensuring they would offer them to him so that in this way at any rate he could check the likelihood of their being ensnared in the deadly deceit.

(7) For proof that all this was permitted by him out of considerateness, consider in the ensuing period the fact that he allowed circumcision to be legislated, not because it had any power to contribute to the salvation of the soul, but in order that the children of the Jews might wear it as an index of their gratitude, like some sign or seal, and that it would not be possible for them to be involved in dealings with the Gentiles. [243] Hence blessed Paul also calls it a sign in the words, "He gave circumcision as a sign, a seal."[9] You see, for proof that it contributes nothing towards righteousness, behold this good man too, before circumcision had ever been legislated, reaching such a height of virtue. Why mention this? The patriarch Abraham himself before receiving circumcision had been declared righteous on the score of faith alone: before circumcision, the text says, "Abraham believed God, and credit for it brought him to righteousness."[10] Why then, O Jew, do you place great store by circumcision? Learn that before it many people proved themselves good. Abel, for instance, made his offering from faith, as Paul also says: "Through faith Abel made a greater offering to God than Cain";[11] Enoch was taken away, Noe escaped that dreadful flood on the score of great goodness, and Abraham before this was commended for his faith in God. Thus right from the very beginning the human race gained salvation on the basis of faith. The reason, of course, that the loving Lord

9. Rom 4.11, "gave" in Chrysostom's text replacing in ours "received," with Abraham as subject. This passage illustrates two kinds of "considerateness," scriptural and historical.

10. Gen 15.6; Rom 4.3.   11. Heb 11.4.

permitted sacrifices to be offered to him was that, when our
nature was still in an imperfect condition, it might be able to
express its gratitude and at the same time completely avoid
the harmful practice of worshipping idols. You see, if despite
such a display of considerateness many people still failed to
escape disaster, how could anyone have escaped harm from
that unless this had happened?

(8) "The Lord smelt an odor of fragrance." This was not,
however, true of the ungrateful Jews. What was the case with
them? Listen to the words of the inspired writer: "Incense is
an abomination to me"[12]—as if to suggest the malice of the
offerers' intention. You see, just as in the present case the
good man's virtue transformed the smoke and the stench into
an odor of fragrance, so in their case the malice of the offerers caused the fragrant incense to smell like an abomination.
Consequently, let us earnestly take every opportunity, I beseech you, to demonstrate a sound attitude. This, after all,
proves responsible for all our good things. You see, the good
Lord is accustomed to heed not so much what is done from
our own resources as the intention within, on which we depend for our first move in doing these things, and he looks
to that in either approving what is done by us or disapproving
it. So whether we pray, or fast, or practice almsgiving (these,
after all, being our spiritual sacrifices), or perform any other
spiritual work, let us begin with a pure intention in performing it so that we may procure a reward worthy of our efforts.
I mean, it would be utterly pointless for us to undergo the
effort and yet lose the reward through practicing virtue out
of keeping with the laws given by him. It is possible, you see,
it is possible through God's ineffable love to win a crown only
on the score of our intention, without completing the work.
To be convinced of this, consider, I ask you, this example of
almsgiving: when you saw a person in the market place,
evicted and suffering extreme hunger, and you felt compassion for him and raised your mind to heaven in thanking the
Lord both for your good fortune and for the sufferings of

12. Isa 1.13.

the starving person, even if you were not in a position to satisfy his hunger, on the basis of your intention you received your reward in full. Hence the Lord, too, remember, said, "Whoever gives even a cup of cold water on the grounds of discipleship, truly I say to you, he will not lose his reward."[13] Is there anything [244] of less value than a cup of cold water?

(9) In any case, however, it is necessary to raise these matters with your good selves so that you may gain a precise knowledge of them and put into practice the security that arises from gratitude. Listen, after all, to what Christ says: "Whoever gazes at a woman so as to lust after her has already committed adultery with her in his heart."[14] Do you see in this case also condemnation following from the evil intention and punishment inflicted for the thoughtless gaze as if his adultery had been put into effect? Consequently, with this in mind let us in every circumstance look to our intention so that it may ensure that what is done by us proves acceptable. You see, if it turned the smoke and the stench into an odor of fragrance, what effect would it not have on this spiritual worship of ours, and how much favor from above would it not ensure we enjoy? "The Lord smelt an odor of fragrance," the text says. Do you see the good man's actions, how as far as the sight of them was concerned they were in fact paltry, yet were shown to be exceeding great on the basis of his pure intention?

(10) Consider now, I ask you, the surpassing goodness of the loving Lord: "The Lord God took stock and said, 'I will not proceed further to curse the earth for the deeds of human beings, since the human being's mind is bent on evil from youth. So I will not proceed to smite every living being, as I have done, for the future of the earth.'"[15] What a volume of kindness, what magnitude of loving kindness, how ineffable the excess of longsuffering! "The Lord God took stock and said": the expression "took stock" is once again humanly phrased, as if with our nature in mind. "'I will not proceed

13. Matt 10.42.   14. Matt 5.28.
15. Gen 8.21–22a.

further to curse the earth for the deeds of human beings.'"
On the first formed human being, remember, he had placed
a curse in the words, "'Thorns and thistles let it yield,'"[16] and
likewise on Cain in similar terms. So when in this case also he
inflicted such awful destruction, yet for the purpose of encouraging the good man and leading him to take heart and
not be likely to think within himself, what good came of bene-
diction and of the words, "Increase and multiply," if we were
to run the risk again of perishing once we grew to great numbers? (Previously, remember, he had said to Adam, "Increase
and multiply," though still bringing on the deluge)—so to
prevent his having these thoughts and being in constant distress through going over this in his mind, notice instead the
Lord's loving kindness: "'I will not proceed further to curse
the earth for the deeds of men.'" See how he indicated that
he had inflicted the curse on the earth because of their depravity. Then lest we think that he had made this promise
because they had changed for the better, he said, "'Because
the human's mind is bent on evil from youth.'" A strange
form of loving kindness: "'Because the human's mind,'" he
says, "'is bent on evil from youth,'" consequently "'I will no
longer proceed to curse the earth.'" In other words he is saying, While I demonstrated my power once and a second time,
yet since I see evil on the increase, I promise never again to
curse the earth. Then by way of revealing the magnitude of
his love, he added, "'So I will not proceed to smite every
living being, as I have done, for the future of the earth.'"
Notice, I ask you, how in everything he lavishes the greatest
consolation on the good man—or rather, not just on the just
[245] man but out of his characteristic goodness on the whole
nature of humanity ready to come into existence. That clause,
you see, "'So I will not proceed to smite every living being,'"
and "'as I have done,'" and "'for the future of the earth'"
are indicative of the fact that there would no longer be such
a flood nor would such a disaster overwhelm the world. Then
he indicates also the permanence of the blessing: "'For the

16. Gen 3.18.

future,'" he said—that is, for all time I promise never to betray such anger nor cause such chaos either in the confusion of the seasons or the disorder of the elements.

(11) Hence he went on to add: "'Seedtime and harvest, cold and heat, summer and winter shall not be interrupted day or night."[17] Unchangeable, he is saying, will this arrangement be; the earth will never cease supplying its resources to the race of human beings or granting rewards for the hard work of farming, nor will the seasons be interchanged. Instead, cold and heat, summer and winter will be the sequence of each year. You see, since for the period of the deluge a certain confusion occurred in all this arrangement and this good man lived in the ark all this time as if it were one single night, hence God said, Now neither day nor night shall leave its proper course, but rather their service will be uninterrupted to the end of time.

(12) Do you see the comfort quite sufficient and capable of uplifting the good man's spirit? Do you see how much reward he receives for his gratitude? Listen also to what follows as a further example of God's unspeakable generosity. "God blessed Noe and his sons," the text goes on. "He said to them, 'Increase and multiply, fill the earth and gain dominion over it. All the animals of the earth will be in fear and dread of you, all the birds of heaven, everything moving on the earth and all the fish of the sea; I have put them all under your control. Every living creature is there for your food—I have given you them all as I did the green grass—except you are not to eat flesh with its lifeblood in it.'"[18] Here it is proper to marvel at the extraordinary degree of the Lord's goodness; notice, I ask you, once again this good man being accorded the same blessing as Adam, and through his virtue recovering

17. Gen 8.22b, from which Chrysostom detaches those first few words about the earth's future. This time Chrysostom has honored the dogmatic significance of vv. 21–22 in his commentary, so that the modern commentator Von Rad merely paraphrases him: "The contrast between God's punishing anger and his supporting grace, which pervades the whole Bible, is here presented quite untheologically, even almost inappropriately" (*Genesis*, 123).

18. Gen 9.1–4, with a slight assimilation in v. 1 to the similar priestly expression in 1.28, perhaps to reinforce Chrysostom's immediate comment.

the control previously lost—or rather, on account of the Lord's ineffable love. I mean, as he said in the case of the former man, "'Increase and multiply, fill the earth and gain dominion over it; have control of the fish of the sea, the reptiles, the birds of heaven and the animals of earth,'"[19] so now he says, "'All the animals of the earth will be in fear and dread of you, and all the birds of heaven. Every living creature is there for your food—I have given you them all as I did the green grass—except you are not to eat flesh with its lifeblood in it.'" Notice the same rule as that imposed on the first formed man, but differently observed: just as in that case, after entrusting him with control over everything and providing him with enjoyment of things in the garden, he bade him abstain from one tree only, in just the same way in this case, after the blessing and making him an object of fear to the animals and putting the birds under his control, he said, "'Every living creature is there for your food—I have given you them all as I did the green grass.'"

(13) From this the eating of meat takes its beginning, not for the purpose of prompting them to gluttony, [246] but since some of the people were about to offer sacrifices and make thanksgiving to the Lord, he grants them authority over food and obviates any anxiety lest they seem to be abstaining from food on the score of its being consecrated. "'I have given you them all,'" he says, "'as I did the green grass.'" Then, as in the case of Adam he instructed him to abstain from the one tree while enjoying the others, so in this case too, after permitting the consumption of them all without hesitation, he says, "'except you are not to eat flesh with its lifeblood in it.'" So what does this statement mean? It means "strangled," for an animal's blood is its soul. So since they were about to offer sacrifices in the form of animals, he is more or less teaching them in these words that as long as the blood has been set aside for me, the flesh is for you. By doing this, however, he checks ahead of time any impulse of theirs for homicide.

19. Gen 1.28, with variations from Chrysostom's previous text in Homily 10.

(14) To prove this, and also that he does these things out of a wish to make them thereby more cautious, listen to what follows. "'For your own lifeblood, you see, (he is saying) I will require an account of all the animals, and of a man I will require an account for his brother's life.'"[20] What does that mean? Is blood in fact the soul of the human being? It does not say so—perish the thought; instead, it is employing a human form of expression, as if you were to say to someone, I hold your blood in my hands—that is, I have the power of life and death over you. For proof that blood is not the soul of the human being, listen to Christ's words: "'Don't be afraid of those who kill the body but are incapable of killing the soul.'"[21] See the extent of the contrast he made.

(15) "'Whoever sheds someone's blood, his own will be shed in payment for that person's blood, because I have made the human being in God's image.'"[22] Consider, I ask you, how much fear he struck in them with that remark. Even if kinship proves no obstacle, he is saying, nor fellowship of nature restrains you from evil endeavor and, on the contrary, you thrust aside brotherly feeling and become completely committed to this bloody deed, consider the fact that the person has been created in God's image, the degree of honor accorded him by God, and the fact that he has received authority over all creation—and then give up your murderous intent. So what does he mean? If someone has committed countless murders and shed so much blood, how can he give adequate satisfaction simply by the shedding of his own blood? Don't have these thoughts, human being that you are; instead, consider that before long he will receive an immortal body of the kind that will have the capacity to undergo constant and everlasting punishment.

(16) Notice, however, this point as well, how the command was given with precision: whereas in the case of the human being he said, Don't shed blood, in the case of the brute beasts he did not say, Don't shed it, but, "'Except you are not

20. Gen 9.5.   21. Matt 10.28.
22. Gen 9.6.

to eat flesh with the lifeblood in it.'" In one case, Don't shed
it, in this case, Don't eat it. Do you see how little burden is
imposed by his laws? how light and easy his directions? how
he looks for nothing burdensome and demanding from our
nature? Some people, of course, say animals' blood is heavy,
earthy and nauseating; we on the contrary ought show our
observance to arise not from that reason of greater logic but
from the Law of the Lord.

(17) Then, so that we might learn precisely the reason why
he displayed such precision in this direction, and the fact that
in restraining human beings' murderous intent he said, "'You,
however, increase and multiply, [247] fill the earth and gain
dominion over it,'"[23] he did not idly say, "'You, however,'"
but as if to say, Few though you be and few in number, fill
the whole earth and gain dominion over it—that is to say,
have control, authority and enjoyment. Notice God's loving
kindness, how first he bestows great benefits and only then
gives as well law and instruction. Just as in the case of Adam,
after placing him in the garden and granting him so much
enjoyment, he then imposed on him abstinence from the tree,
so also in this case too, after promising never again to inflict
such disaster or display such anger but rather to allow all the
elements to continue unmoved until the end of time, each
keeping to its peculiar course and its particular arrangement,
and after bestowing blessings on human beings, favoring
them with the pristine authority over all the animals, and
guaranteeing them security in their carnivorous diet, he then
said, "'Except you are not to eat flesh with the lifeblood in
it.'" Do you see how he first blesses and displays his ineffable
love and then gives commands? And yet in the case of human
beings this would never happen. People, you see, first want
to give effect to what they have commanded, and they manifest great regard for those who accept their commands and
see to their discharge, and only then reward those showing
complete obedience. With the common Lord of all, however,

23. Gen 9.7, Chrysostom's text again differing from the Hebrew as at v.
1, though Speiser commends the avoidance of obvious dittography in Hebrew "multiply" (*Genesis*, 57).

it is just the opposite: first he bestows blessing and draws our nature to himself with the plenitude of his blessings, and then gives commands that are light and easy, his purpose being to arouse us with his previous blessings and the ease of the commands, and thus cajole us into carrying out the latter.

(18) Accordingly, let us not be indifferent, dearly beloved, nor prove quite reluctant in heeding his commands, when we consider his previous benefits, the ease of his commands and the magnitude of the promised rewards stored up for us after their fulfilment; rather, let us be on the alert and show enthusiasm for the performance of the directions given us by God. Let us not forsake the ways he has given our nature for achieving the salvation of our soul; instead, let us employ as we should the time remaining in our life, and gain for ourselves in advance great confidence, especially at present when there is still part of the holy season of Lent remaining. You see, the number of days remaining is not really small if we are determined to make some improvement in our frame of mind. I said this, however, not because the correction of our faults requires so much time, but because we have such a kind and loving Lord, who has no need of a long time provided we approach him with much warmth and vigilance, warding off from ourselves all worldly cares and relying on grace from above. The Ninevites also, remember, weighed down though they were with such a mass of sins, when they applied themselves to a keen and intense repentance did not need more than three days to arouse God's goodness and to render void the sentence passed against them. Why mention the Ninevites? The thief on the cross did not need even one day. Why mention one day? Not even a brief hour. Such is God's loving kindness in our regard: when he sees the course of our intention, [248] he does not hesitate or delay; instead, he rapidly brings his liberality to the fore and says, "While you are still speaking, I will say, 'See, here I am.'"[24]

(19) Accordingly, he will so treat us if we are prepared to give evidence of a degree of zeal in these few days, capitalize

24. Isa 58.9.

as we ought on the assistance coming from fasting, and make atonement for our indifference by directing fervent prayers to the Lord, shedding warm tears, constantly confessing our sins, submitting our wounds and showing our ulcers as if to a physician and looking for healing from him, as well as bringing to bear other resources of our own—a contrite heart, an exact compunction, generous almsgiving—checking the other passions that disturb our thinking, and ridding our soul of them, not being beset by lust for material gain, bearing neither a grudge against our neighbor, nor hostility against our peers. Nothing, after all, does God so detest and abhor as the person who bears a grudge and constantly maintains hostility in his soul against his neighbor. The harm of this sin is such that it even revokes God's loving kindness! For proof of this, I want to remind you of the parable contained in the gospel, where the man who had received the loan of ten thousand talents from his master fell at his feet and begged and implored him. The text says, remember, "The master took pity on him, discharged him from his obligation and released him from his debt."[25] Do you see the master's compassion? The servant had fallen on his knees and begged a longer time be granted him for repayment. "'Have patience with me,'" the text says, remember, "'and I will pay it all back to you.'"[26] The good master, however, being caring and loving, yielded to the suppliant's prayers and granted not only as much as he asked but more than he had ever imagined. This, you see, is his manner, always to surpass and anticipate our requests. Consequently, when that servant begged for indulgence to be shown and promised to make payment in full, the Lord, who in his goodness overlooks our faults, was then moved with pity, discharged him from his obligation and released him from his debt. Do you see, on the one hand, what the servant requested and, on the other, how much the Lord granted him?

(20) Notice likewise this very man's unreasonableness: whereas he ought to have conducted himself with fellow-feeling to-

25. Matt 18.27.   26. Matt 18.26.

wards his peers in accordance with the marvellous love shown to him, instead he demonstrated the opposite. The text says, "He went out," this very man who had received a remission of a debt of ten thousand talents. Listen carefully, I beseech you: what happened to this man is sufficient to touch our heart and persuade us to rid our thinking of this baleful disease. "This man went out," then, "and found one of his fellow servants who owed him a hundred denarii." Notice how great the difference: in one case the fellow servant owing him a hundred denarii, in the other the master was the creditor, and the sum in question was ten thousand talents, yet on seeing him begging on his knees he yielded. This servant, on the contrary, "took hold of him by the throat and said, 'Pay me whatever you owe.' "[27] What then? The text goes on, "His fellow servant fell to his knees." See how constantly the evangelist repeats this word, "his fellow servant," not idly but for us to learn that there was no difference between them. Yet this man had [249] made the same plea to him that he had made to his master, in the words, " 'Have patience with me, and I will pay it all back to you.' But he ignored his plea and threw him into prison until he paid all that was owing to him."[28] O what an excess of ingratitude! Despite having fresh in his memory the exercise of so much generosity, he still failed to entertain any compassionate thoughts; instead, he first seized his fellow by the throat, then he cast him into prison.

(21) But see what happens. "On seeing this, however," the text says, "his fellow servants were upset; they went and brought to the notice of their master all that had happened."[29] It was not that other servant who grieved (how could he, after all, lying in prison as he was), but his fellow servants, those who, while not being wronged, behaved as though they had been wronged; they were distressed in that way, and went and brought everything out into the open. But now notice the master's anger: "Then summoning him," the

27. Matt 18.28.   28. Matt 18.30.
29. Matt 18.31.

text goes on, "he said, 'Wicked servant.'" You can get a true
picture here of the extent of the damage wrought by the malicious behavior: the master did not call him evil when he was
dishonest about the ten thousand talents, but only at this
point, when he proved harsh to his fellow servant. "'Wicked
servant,'" he said, "'I forgave you all your debt when you
begged me.'"[30] See how he shows the extremity of the man's
wickedness! Surely you could have exerted yourself further?
Did you not speak only paltry words to me, and yet I accepted
your supplication and discharged all that huge debt beyond
all telling? "'Should you also not have had mercy on your
fellow servant as I had mercy on you?'"[31] What excuse could
you claim if, while I the master discharged such a heavy
weight of debts on account of those paltry words, you on the
contrary had no mercy on that fellow servant of equal standing with yourself, nor did you yield to his entreaties, nor did
you recall to mind the favors done you by me and display
some compassion towards him; instead, you proved unmer-
ciful and inhumane, and refused to have pity on your fellow
servant. Hence in this case you are to learn from experience
the extent of the troubles to which you have made yourself
liable. "Falling into a rage the master handed him over to the
torturers." Notice also the master now enraged on account of
his inhumanity to his fellow servant, and his handing him
over to the torturers; what didn't happen previously when the
servant was owing so many debts he now orders to happen.
"He handed him over to the torturers until he paid his debt
in full"[32]—until (the text says) he should repay all those ten
thousand talents which he had previously been forgiven.

(22) Great is God's loving kindness and beyond all telling:
when the servant practiced his wiles in playing the suppliant,
he released him from his obligation; but when he saw him
proving harsh and inhumane, then he revoked his characteristic generosity for the future to show him through the events
themselves that he had wronged him more than he had his

30. Matt 18.32.   31. Matt 18.33.
32. Matt 18.34.

fellow servant. Just as he had thrown his fellow servant into prison until he paid what was owing, so likewise the master handed him over to the torturers until he should repay his debt in full. These words, however, about talents and denarii he did not speak idly; instead, his words are about sin and the immensity of our failings, so that we may learn that, though we are due to pay a debt to the Lord for our countless faults, we receive from him a remission of them on account of his ineffable love. If, however, we prove harsh and inhumane towards our fellow servants and our peers and those who share our nature with us, and do not cancel the faults they commit against us, but rather act badly on the grounds of those peccadillos (after all, whatever the difference between a hundred denarii and ten thousand [250] talents, so much the greater the difference between our sins against the Lord and those done us by our peers), then we will call down on our own heads the Lord's anger, and for the debts of which we have received remission we will force him to require strict accounting under torture.

(23) You see, for us to learn precisely that the Lord constructed this parable for the benefit of our souls, listen to the epilogue: "'This is what your Father in heaven will do to you if each of you does not forgive his brother his failings from his heart.'"[33] Great is the gain from this parable, if only we are prepared to heed it; how could we extend as much forgiveness as is extended to us by the Lord? Whereas we extend forgiveness to our fellow servants—and then only if we are in the mood—it is from the Lord that we in our turn receive remission. Notice also the precision of the expression: he did not simply say, If you do not forgive people their sins, but what? "'If each of you does not forgive his brother his failings from his heart.'" Notice how he wants even our hearts to have the good fortune to enjoy peace and quiet, our thinking to be undisturbed and rid of every passion, and ourselves to demonstrate great loving kindness towards our neighbor. Elsewhere too you can hear him saying this: "'If you forgive

33. Matt 18.35.

people their failings, your heavenly Father will also forgive you.'"[34] So let us not think when we do this that it is to someone else we are doing a good turn or bestowing a great favor on them. It is we ourselves, after all, who reap the benefit of our good dead, and accord great gain to ourselves from the action, just as, if we fail to do it, we likewise do not manage to wrong them but lay up for ourselves the unspeakable torment of hell fire.

(24) Consequently, I beseech you, let us keep this in mind and no longer bear to hold a grudge against those who have done us an injury or otherwise wronged us in some way, nor be badly disposed towards them; instead, let us consider of how much kindness and confidence for us with the Lord they prove to be instruments, and before all else the fact that reconciliation with those who injure us turns out to be a discharge of our sins. Thus let us show all enthusiasm and effort, and out of consideration of the gain accruing from this let us display as much care of those who injure us as if they were really our benefactors. In other words, if we look at things in the cold light of reason, those kindly disposed towards us and those anxious to serve our every need will not succeed in benefiting us as service of those others, which will render us deserving of favor from above and will lighten the load of our sins. Consider, dearly beloved, how important is this virtuous behavior to judge from the rewards promised by the God of all things to those who practice it. He said, remember, "'Love your enemies, bless those who persecute you, pray for those who abuse you,'"[35] since these directions were very demanding and aspiring to the very summit of perfection, he added, "'so that you may be like your Father in heaven, because he makes his sun rise on good and evil, and sends rain on just and unjust.'"[36] Do you see whom that person resembles—as far as is humanly possible—who not only takes no vengeance on those who harm him, but even shows

34. Matt 6.14.
35. Chrysostom here seems to achieve a conflation of Matt 5.44 and Luke 6.27.
36. Cf. Matt 5.45.

zeal in praying for them? Accordingly, let us not deprive ourselves through indifference of such gifts and rewards surpassing [251] all description, but rather evince enthusiasm for
this kind of virtue by every means and, by disciplining our
thinking, respond to God's command.

(25) After all, the reason that I delivered this exhortation
in the present case and brought the parable to the fore, and
the reason for demonstrating the importance of virtuous behavior and the extent of the gain accruing to us from it, was
that while there is still time each of us should exert ourselves,
in the event of there being someone at enmity with him, to
reconcile him by means of assiduous attention. Let no one tell
me that he has made overtures once and a second time but
his enemy has not come round: if we approach this with un-
mixed motives, we will not give up before we prevail through
intense supplication, and thus win him over and turn him
from his hostility to us. I mean, surely it is not he who is the
recipient of gifts from us? It is to us that benefits come: we
win favor from God, we secure remission of sins for ourselves, and gain from this great confidence with the Lord. If
we behave this way, we will be able with a clear conscience to
approach this sacred, awe-inspiring table and pronounce with
confidence those words associated with the prayer. The initiated know what is to be said. Hence I leave it to the conscience of each one to know how by discharging this command we can with confidence utter these words at that fearful
time. If, however, we fall into indifference, what terrible condemnation would we bring on ourselves by doing the opposite
of our words, daring to pronounce the words of the prayer
idly and without thought, fuelling a more intense fire for ourselves, and calling down on us the Lord's anger?

(26) I rejoice and am gratified to see you hearing the words
with pleasure and showing through your applause that you
are anxious to be ready and to put into practice this exhortation of the Lord. This, after all, is physic for your soul, this
is balm for your wounds, this the best way to win the satisfaction of God, this the surest sign of a soul that loves God—to
accept everything on account of the Law of the Lord and not

to be overcome by the limitations of reasoning, but instead to prove superior to passions by recollecting the kindnesses daily done us by God. No matter how much effort we expend, we will be unable to express the least part of the benefits already accorded us, nor those happening to us daily, nor the good things laid up for us on condition of our putting into practice the commands given us from him. Accordingly, let each of us in leaving here perform this good work, show enthusiasm for it as if for the most wonderful treasure and not delay in the slightest. Even if we have to labor, even if we have to search, even if we have to go on a long journey, even if there are certain difficulties, let us dispose of all these problems. Let us make it our concern how we may put into practice the command of the Lord, and thus gain the reward of obedience. After all, surely I am not ignorant that it seems a difficult and burdensome duty to make approaches to the person who nourished grievances and enmity against you, and to stand and converse with him? If, however, you consider the dignity of the promise and the greatness of the reward and the fact that the effect of kindly behavior reaches not only the beneficiary but also you yourself, everything will seem to you light and easy.

(27) Accordingly, let us turn this over in our mind, and so get the better of habit and with pious thinking fulfil Christ's commands so that we may also be judged worthy of rewards from him, thanks to the grace and love of his goodness, to whom with the Father and the Holy Spirit be glory, power and honor, now and forever, for ages of ages. Amen.

HOMILY 28

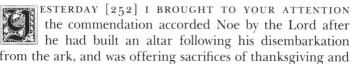

"And God said to Noe and to his sons with him, 'Lo, I am making my covenant with you and with your offspring after you, and with every living being that is with you, including both birds and cattle, and with all the wild beasts of the earth.'"[1]

ESTERDAY [252] I BROUGHT TO YOUR ATTENTION the commendation accorded Noe by the Lord after he had built an altar following his disembarkation from the ark, and was offering sacrifices of thanksgiving and had demonstrated his gratitude. But we were unable to proceed further and deal completely with the reading by showing the loving God's considerateness and care displayed in regard to the good man. I mean, since our sermon had been prolonged to great length, we concluded it rapidly lest your memory be overwhelmed by the plethora of words and the things yet unspoken be impaired by what has been said already. You see, our anxiety was not simply to say a great deal; rather, we wanted to say the kind of things that it would be possible for you to retain in your memory and leave here enriched. After all, if it was likely that we said more than was proper and you gained nothing from what was said, what would be the use of that? Accordingly, in the knowledge that we have undertaken this task for the sake of your benefit, we also consider we have received sufficient reward if we see your progress in grasping our words precisely, and if you store them away in the recesses of your mind, constantly pondering and ruminating on them.

(2) You see, recollection of words already spoken prepares you to receive with greater ease those yet to be spoken, and thus become in the future instructors of others. This, after

1. Gen 9.8–10, the LXX omitting the final phrase of the Hebrew.

all, is the object of all our vigilance and enthusiasm, that you would all become perfect and complete, and that nothing of the contents of the Holy Scriptures would escape you. Acquaintance with them, remember, will also make the greatest contribution to your progress towards an excellent life, provided you are prepared to be sober and alert, and will make you readier for the difficulties virtue involves. You see, whenever it has come to our attention that all of those good people who relied on their considerable trust in God to pass the whole of their life in trials and tribulations and give evidence of great endurance and thanksgiving were as a result found worthy of reward, how could we in our turn fail to show eagerness to travel by the same path as they so as likewise to enjoy the same reward as theirs? Hence I beseech you to make each day some effort both towards your growth in God's grace and to maintaining in security and close observance your previous good behavior, as well as supplying for any omissions, so that in this way you may reach the very pinnacle of virtue to my satisfaction, the building up of the Church and the glory of Christ. Seeing, after all, your insatiable interest in spiritual instruction, I do not cease daily, despite my awareness of my own extreme inadequacy, to offer you nourishment from the Holy Scriptures and to propose for your hearing whatever the love of God provides out of his characteristic benevolence and with a view to your benefit.

(3) So come now, today, too, let us demonstrate to your good selves the extraordinary degree of God's love, which he manifests in regard to the human race, by drawing attention to the very words spoken by God to Noe. "God said to Noe and to his sons." After blessing him and his sons in the words, "'Increase and multiply,'" and entrusting him with [253] control of all the animals and giving him authority to enjoy a share of them in the manner of vegetables for eating, and instructing him not to eat flesh with the blood in it, still caring as he was for the good man and those due to come later and ever anxious to ply our nature with kindness, he added even greater benefits in the words, "God said to Noe and to his sons with him, 'Lo, I am making my covenant with you and

with your offspring after you, and with every living being that is with you, including both birds and cattle, and with all the wild beasts of the earth that are with you, including all that disembarked from the ark. I will keep my covenant with you: no more will all creatures perish in the water of the deluge, and never again will there be a deluge to destroy the whole earth.'"[2] Chances were that the good man was still beside himself and his mind still prey to fear; and it was likely that if some light shower should happen to fall, he would be bound to become distraught and quite upset at the thought of such a deluge overwhelming the world once again. Hence the good Lord took steps to instil confidence into him and all those in future, knowing as he did that even a chance concern would succeed in alarming him, past experience having proved sufficient to frighten him out of his wits. Since therefore the odds were that this blessed man would be utterly terrified at even a passing shower, the good God for this reason, as if taking steps to encourage him and free him from all fear, as well as reduce him to a state of complete security and tranquility, promised never to inflict such dreadful punishment again. This promise he had in fact already made even before the blessing when he said, as you heard, "'I will not proceed to curse the earth.'"[3] Even if people continue their display of wickedness, yet I no longer submit the human race to such terrible punishment. In other words, he shows his ineffable love by making the promise once again so that the good man may be able to take heart and not come to the following conclusion: After first bestowing blessings on the human race and causing us to multiply in number, he brought this ruin upon us.

(4) His purpose, therefore, was to eliminate all apprehension from Noe's thinking and for him to be quite assured that this would not happen again. He said, remember, Just as I brought on the deluge out of love, so as to put a stop to their wickedness and prevent their going to further extremes, so in this case too it is out of my love that I promise never to do

2. Gen 9.8–11.   3. Gen 8.21.

it again, so that you may live free of all dread and in this way see your present life to its close. Hence he said, "'Behold I make my covenant,'" that is, I form an agreement. Just as in human affairs when someone makes a promise he forms an agreement and gives a firm guarantee, so too the good Lord said, "'Behold, I make my covenant.'" He was right in saying, "'I make,'" instead of, Behold I renew the disaster brought on by their sins; "'I make my covenant with you and your offspring after you.'" See the Lord's loving kindness: not only with your generation, he says, do I form my agreement, but also in regard to those coming after you I give this firm guarantee.

(5) Then to show his characteristic generosity he says, "'and with every living being that is with you, including both birds and cattle, and with all the wild beasts of the earth that are with you, including all that disembarked from the ark. I will keep my covenant with you: no more will all the creatures perish in the water of the deluge, [254] and never again will there be a deluge to destroy the whole earth.'" Do you see the extent of the agreement? Do you see the unspeakable generosity of the promises? Notice how once again he extends his loving kindness to the animals and wild beasts—and rightly so: what I have often said before I say again now. That is, since these creatures had been created for the human for that reason they now share the kindness shown humanity. While the covenant with the latter and with the animals seems identical, in fact it is not. This too happens for the human's consolation, you see, so that he may be in a position to know how much esteem he enjoys, since not only is the favor bestowed on himself, but also that all the animals have a share in enjoying the Lord's generosity on his account. "'No more will all creatures perish,'" the text says, "'in the water of the deluge, and never again will there be a deluge to destroy the whole earth.'"

(6) Do you see how once, a second time, and more frequently he promises never again to inflict such an awful disaster, so as to eliminate fear from the good man's thoughts and cause him to be optimistic about the future? Then, con-

sidering not his own nature but our limitations, he is not content with the verbal promise, but demonstrates his considerateness in our regard by supplying also a sign valid for all time and capable of freeing the human race of this terrible fear, with the result that even if a heavy shower should fall, even if a wild storm should break, or if the tide should reach to a flood, not even then would we be able to feel fear but rather feel confidence by contemplating the sign given us. "Then the Lord God said to Noe: 'This is the sign of the covenant which I am making between me and you.'"[4] See the great regard he displays for the good man; like one person speaking with another, he makes his agreement with him in just the same fashion in the words, "'This is the sign of the covenant which I am making between me and you, and with every living creature that is with you for all generations.'" Do you see that the sign due to be given to every creature is made valid for eternal generations? Not only does he give the sign to all creatures alike, but he also makes it never-ending and coterminous with the duration of the world. So what is the sign? "'I am putting my bow in the clouds, and it will act as a sign of a covenant between me and the earth.'"[5] See, along with the verbal promise he also gives the sign, namely, the rainbow, which some people say is caused by the sun shedding its rays on the clouds. In case my word is not sufficient, he is saying, behold I also give a sign that I will never again inflict such an awful punishment; so when you see the sign, you will be freed of fear. "'When I bring clouds on the earth, my bow will be visible in the clouds, and I will remember my covenant between me and you and every living being of every kind.'"[6] What are you saying, O blessed author? I will recall (he is saying) my covenant—that is, the guarantee, the promise—not because he needs to recall it, but for us to fix our eyes on that sign given us and thus suspect no trouble; instead, by remembering at once God's promise we are able to be confident that we will suffer nothing like that again.

4. Gen 9.12.   5. Gen 9.13.
6. Gen 9.14–15.

(7) Do you see God's considerateness, how much care he shows our race, the great extent of the loving kindness he has displayed, not because he saw the change in human beings but for the purpose of teaching us through every event the extraordinary degree of his [255] goodness? "'Never again will there be a deluge to wipe out every creature;'"[7] never again will there be a downpour like that. Since he knew the human race were afraid of that, see how he constantly makes the promise as if to say, Even if you see a great rush of water falling, don't suspect any trouble in that event: "'There will be no deluge to wipe out every creature,'" never again will the human race experience anger like that. "'My bow will be in the clouds, and sight of it will remind me of an eternal covenant between God and all living beings of every kind.'"[8] Notice the utter ordinariness of the language he employs out of a wish to induce confidence and security in the human race. I will see, he says, that I remember my covenant. Does that therefore mean that sight jogs his memory? This is not the conclusion we are to come to—God forbid—but that when we see the sign, we may take heart at God's promise, especially as it is impossible for God's promises to fail.

(8) "God said to Noe," the text goes on, "'This is the sign of the covenant I made between me and all creatures that are upon the earth.'"[9] You recognized, he is saying, the sign I gave of agreement between me and every creature living on the earth. Worry your head no longer, nor upset your thinking; instead, fix your gaze on this and allow yourself the luxury of firm hope, let all those coming after you enjoy comfort from this sign, and let sight of it provide the basis for confidence that never again will such an awful deluge destroy the world. I mean, even if people's sins are intensified, nevertheless I will keep these promises I have made: I will vent no longer such terrible anger on everyone. Do you see the excess of his goodness? Do you see the extent of his considerateness? Do you see the degree of his care? Do you see his promise of

---

7. This time Chrysostom quotes v. 11 in a different form—a common enough departure for a preacher.

8. Gen 9.16.   9. Gen 9.17.

generosity? After all, he did not simply extend his kindness
to two or three or even ten generations; instead, he promised
it would last as long as the duration of the universe so that
we might be the wiser for each instance, both the fact that
they suffered such terrible punishment for the enormity of
their sins and also the fact that we were accorded such marvellous promise owing to his ineffable love. People of sense,
you see, are drawn to obedience of commands rather by kindnesses than by punishments.

(9) Accordingly, let us not prove ungrateful; even if before
we gave evidence of any good, or rather while we were actually practicing things deserving of punishment, he granted
us such lavish kindness, what great generosity would he still
not accord us from his richness provided we prove grateful,
demonstrate our thanks for his previous favors and work a
great change for the better? If he bestows favors on us despite
our being unworthy and is kindly disposed towards sinners,
what good things would we not meet with, provided we desist
from evil and follow virtue? You see, the reason why he takes
the initiative in laying up for us many blessings and grants a
further opportunity of pardon to sinners instead of immediately inflicting penalties is this: that through every means he
may win us over, in every way ply us with blessings, in every
manner show us longsuffering. Frequently, however, while he
punishes some by every means, his intention is to encourage
others so that they may be brought to their senses through
fright at the unfortunate and avoid experiencing punishment. Do you see his inventive love, how everything done by
him happens with this sole object in view [256]—our salvation?

(10) So with this in mind let us not be remiss, or neglect
virtue, or bypass the laws laid down by him. You see, if he
sees us repentant and at peace and quite resolved on making
a start, he both comes to our aid with resources of his own
by rendering everything easy and light for us and also does
not allow us even to feel the effects of the effort virtue involves. I mean, whenever the soul directs its faculties towards
God, it can no longer be deceived by the appearance of visible

realities; instead, it passes them all by and takes less careful
note of these things that fall under our gaze than of those
realities that are not seen by our bodily eyes and are not subject to change but remain constant, as it is their nature to be
fixed and unmoved. Such, you see, are the eyes of the mind:
they concentrate uninterruptedly on those latter realities and,
contemplating everything of this present life in the light of
the radiance from them, pass them by as if some dream or
shadow, no longer subject to deception nor able to be beguiled. Instead, even if they see wealth, they immediately
mock it in their knowledge that it shifts from one person to
another with less reliability than any runaway slave and, far
from being constant, it brings countless troubles on its pos-
sessors, drives them to the very brink of disaster (so to say)
and throws them over. Should they happen to espy some bodily beauty, they still do not lose their balance but consider its
susceptibility to death and corruption and the fact that disease suddenly attacks and blights that beauty completely and,
before the onset of disease, age takes effect and renders re-
pulsive and ugly the face that was previously beautiful, whereas
death, on the other hand, makes its assault and utterly wastes
the body in its prime. Should they see someone clad in glory
or sovereignty or scaling the very pinnacle of honors, and
enjoying complete health and happiness, they ignore him as
someone with no sure or firm foundation but only an inflated
esteem for things that will leave him high and dry more
surely than the currents of a river. After all, what is of less
value than all the glory of this present life when it is compared to the grass in flower? "All human glory," Scripture
says, remember, "is like grass in flower."[10] Do you see, dearly
beloved, how clearly the eyes of faith see when the mind is
directed to God? Do you see how they can be beguiled by no
visible reality? Instead, they have an accurate assessment of
things and are subject to no deception.

(11) If you don't mind, however, let us once more resume
the thread of our sermon, put a few matters before you and

10. Isa 40.6 LXX.

bring our instruction to a close so as to fix in your minds the remembrance of what has been said. When, as you recall, Sacred Scripture completed its account of the divine sign, its intention once again was to teach us the matters related to the good man and his sons in saying, "Now, the sons of Noe who disembarked from the ark were Shem, Cham and Japheth. Now, Cham was father of Canaan. These three were Noe's sons; beginning with them people spread out over the whole earth."[11] It is worth enquiring at this point why in mentioning the three sons of Noe, Sacred Scripture added, "Now, Cham was the father of Canaan." Don't think, I beg you, this detail was tossed in to no purpose: there is nothing of the contents of Sacred Scripture which is spoken without some purpose that involves great benefit concealed beneath the surface. So why did it draw this to our attention by adding, "Now, Cham was the father of Canaan"? It intends in this way to hint to us the extraordinary degree of his intemperance by the fact that not even the magnitude [257] of the disaster nor the terribly straitened conditions in the ark caused him to control himself; instead, even though his elder brother had not yet at this stage had children, he indulged himself in incontinence at a time when the world was in the grip of such awful distress and disaster, and gave himself up to intercourse; far from putting a check on the impulse of desire, already from the very outset the depravity of his attitude had become clear. So, when a little later his son Canaan is due to receive the curse for the disrespect towards the father of the family, Sacred Scripture had already anticipated its announcement on that account and revealed to us the name of the child at the same time as the intemperance of its father; the purpose was that when you later see him giving evidence of ingratitude towards his father, you would be in a position to know that right from the very beginning he was the kind of person not to be restrained even by the disaster. I mean, deep apprehension is sufficient to quench pleasure of all kinds, and there is nothing so capable of checking this flame and fury as depth of appre-

11. Gen 9.18.

hension and excess of ill fortune. So when this person in the midst of such troubles displays such a frenzy and lust for siring offspring, what excuse could be made for him?[12]

(12) At this point, however, another question arises for us, that well known one that is bandied about everywhere: why does the son receive the curse when it is the father who is guilty of sin? But in case we are now making the sermon too long, we will leave this point to next time, so that when we reach that place in the text we may then also offer whatever solution God provides. You see, there is nothing of the contents of Sacred Scripture, as I said before, that you can find written there without some reason. So for the time being we know that it was not idly or by chance that Moses mentioned the son's name in saying, "Now, Cham was the father of Canaan. These three were Noe's sons; beginning with them people spread out over the whole earth." Let us in our turn, dearly beloved, not pass this present verse idly by, but rather grasp from this very remark as well the greatness of God's power. "These three were Noe's sons," the text says; "beginning with them people spread out over the whole earth." How could they have sufficed for that? How could the whole world come into existence from these few? How did their bodies manage to survive? There was no doctor to apply healing, no other kind of therapy. You see, there were not even any cities yet founded; instead, after the awful distress of their life in the ark they disembarked shrivelled up, as it were, after being shut in, so how could they have failed to expire after having the misfortune of being in such terrible isolation and unspeakable solitude? How did they not perish? Tell me, after all, would not fear and anxiety unhinge their mind and derange their thinking?

(13) Don't be surprised, dearly beloved: God it was who was managing everything, and the Creator of our nature was removing all these difficulties, and that direction of his in the words, "'Increase and multiply, and fill the earth,'"[13] also

12. Chrysostom asks the same question of the text's reference to Canaan here as do modern commentators, but with much greater moral elaboration.
13. Gen 1.28.

granted them this increase. The Israelites, too, when they were confined in Egypt working with clay and making bricks, all the more in these circumstances did they grow into a vast multitude, and neither the pitiless and cruel command of Pharaoh requiring male children to be cast into the river, nor the rest of the ill treatment they endured from their task-masters [258] was successful in reducing their numbers; rather, they grew in numbers even further. Grace from above, you see, was bringing everything to a successful conclusion through adversity. Accordingly, when God gives his command, don't seek to subject things to examination according to human procedures: he is, after all, superior to our nature and so has no need of human procedures, but even through the very obstacles he causes things to flourish. In just the same way in the present case, too, he peopled the whole world from these three men. The text says, "Beginning with these three, people spread out over the whole earth." Do you see God's power? Do you see how, even though the obstacles were many, there was nothing to thwart his will?

(14) You can see the same thing happening in the case of the faith: despite such adversaries, despite such conspirators and the opposition of kings, tyrants and mobs directing their every effort at quenching the spark of faith, through these very conspirators, through their anxiety to impede progress the flame of religion was fanned to such an extent as to engulf the whole world, inhabited and uninhabited. I mean, if you travel as far as India, as far as Scythia, to the very end of the world, even to the great Ocean, everywhere you will find the teaching of Christ illuminating the souls of all people. You see, the strange and remarkable thing is that the preaching of religion reformed even the barbarian races themselves; they developed a thirst for knowledge, they gave up their old ways and adopted religion instead. Just as the Creator of all caused the number of human beings to multiply through these three men, in just the same way in the case of the faith, he won over the whole world through eleven men—fishermen, illiterate, untutored, not even bold enough to open their mouths. These illiterate, untutored fishermen stopped the

mouths of philosophers, and like winged creatures traversed the whole world sowing the teaching of religion, pruning away the thorns, rooting out inveterate habits, and in every place planting Christ's laws. Neither the fact of their being few in number, nor their lack of tutoring, nor the severity of what they commanded, nor the fact that the human race was in bondage to inveterate habits was sufficient to prove an obstacle to them; instead, grace paved the way for removing all these difficulties, and so they achieved everything with ease by gaining a firmer resolve through the very obstacles. When on one occasion they were scourged, you recall, they went off rejoicing, not simply on account of the scourging, but "for the fact that they had been thought worthy to suffer dishonor for the name of Christ,"[14] whereas on another occasion when they were thrown into prison and were set at liberty by the angel, they still continued the same practices: going as far as the temple they sowed the word of their teaching, landing the people in their net in the cause of religion. Arrested again, they not only did not lose their resolve on that occasion but displayed even greater outspokenness, rising amidst a mob that raged and ground its teeth to declare, "'God must be obeyed rather than men.'"[15]

(15) Do you see the extent of their outspokenness? Do you see these untutored fishermen scorning such demented crowds that were ready to wreak death and destruction? When, however, dearly beloved, you hear this, attribute its occurrence, not to these men, but to grace from above which gave them strength and stimulated their readiness. Even blessed Peter himself, when he restored the use of his limbs to the man who was lame from his mother's womb, [259] to the amazement and wonder of everyone at their gifts, made no secret of his own gratitude in saying, "'Gentlemen, why are you staring at us as if we are responsible for his walking through our own power or religious spirit?'"[16] Why is it, he is saying, that you are amazed and astounded at what has happened? I

14. Acts 5.41.   15. Acts 5.29.
16. Acts 3.12.

mean, surely we aren't the ones who have worked this miracle, or restored him to health by our own power and made him walk, are we? Why are you staring at us? We have contributed nothing beyond making our tongues available, whereas the one who has achieved it all is the Lord and Creator of our nature. He is "the God of Abraham, Isaac and Jacob," whom you entitle patriarchs; he is the one "whom you betrayed and disowned before Pilate when his verdict had been to acquit him"—he it is who has achieved this, the one "whom you disowned, holy and good though he is, and asked for a murderer to be spared you, whereas you condemned the author of life, but God raised him from the dead and we are his witnesses. Through faith in his name this man, whom you see and know, his name has restored to vigor; faith which comes through him gave the man full strength in the presence of you all."[17]

(16) What exceeding great forthrightness of speech! How unspeakably efficacious the power of the grace vouchsafed them from on high! This blessed man's outspokenness would have been the clearest testimony of the Resurrection. What greater sign could anyone seek to have than this when the one, who before the Crucifixion could not withstand the threat of a mere girl now rises in opposition, to the Jewish people in this fashion and on his own berates them despite their uncontrolled fury and utters such things as were capable of rousing their fury to greater heights? Do you see, dearly beloved, how this also in the present instance demonstrates what I was saying in the beginning? When anyone is on fire with love for God, no longer can he bear to see the things that fall under the gaze of these bodily eyes of ours; instead, he employs other eyes—I mean the eyes of faith—and in everything he has his sights on those other realities and he keeps his mind directed towards them. He walks on earth as though all his business was in heaven, and in this way discharges all his duties, being unhindered in the pursuit of virtue by any human preoccupation. Such a person, you see,

17. Acts 3.13–16.

no longer has an eye for life's attractive features, no longer its harsh and difficult features, but passes them all by in pressing on towards his true homeland. Just as the contestant in this bodily race who runs with great concentration sees none of his opponents, no matter how many times he comes across them, but keeps his mind intent on the race, and thus easily overcomes everything in pressing on towards the goal he has set himself, in just the same way the person keen to run the race of virtue and desirous of leaving earth to reach heaven surrenders all visible things here below, becomes engrossed in the race and does not stop nor allow himself to be hindered by any visible thing before he succeeds in arriving at the very summit. In other words, to the person so disposed, whatever in this present life has a frightening aspect becomes contemptible; such a person has fear neither of sword, nor precipice, wild animals' teeth, torture, arrest by executioner, nor any other of life's hardships; instead, even if he sees the way strewn with burning coals he treads it as though he saw only meadows and gardens; even if he spies some other form of punishment besetting him, he does not become [260] numb at the sight nor turn back. Desire for future realities, you see, has transformed his attitude: as though clad in a body accidentally and for no purpose, he proves superior to passions, and guarded by grace from above he does not even feel the effect of bodily distress.

(17) So I beseech you: with a view to being able to bear without difficulty the effort which virtue involves, let us give evidence of great love of God, and by devoting our attention in that direction let us not be deflected by any of this life's concerns in our course towards that goal. Instead, let us keep in mind the constant enjoyment of future blessings and thus bear without distress the hardships of the present life: let insult not disturb us, nor poverty oppress us, nor bodily ailment sap the energy of our soul's purpose, nor scorn and derision on the part of the majority render us listless in practicing virtue. Let us rather shake off all these irritations like dust, adopt a noble and elevated attitude, and thus take a stance of great fortitude to all problems. As we recommended

to your good selves yesterday, let us with all zeal be reconciled with our enemies and dispel the remaining passions from our soul: should untimely desire beset us, let us ward it off; should choler arouse our anger, let us suppress its upsurge with the singing of spiritual exhortations and thus show in its true light the ruin that passion brings. "A man of quick temper," Scripture says, remember, "is not honorable;"[18] and again, "The person who is angry with his brother without cause shall be liable to the hell of fire."[19] Should desire for money unbalance our thinking, let us be quick to shun this noxious ailment and expel it for what it is—the root of all evils. Let us be zealous in correcting each of the passions that beset us, so that by avoiding harmful ways and practicing those that are good we may on that dread day be judged worthy of God's loving kindness, thanks to the grace and mercy of his only-begotten Son, to whom with the Father and the Holy Spirit be glory, power and honor, now and forever, for ages of ages. Amen.

18. Prov 11.25 LXX.   19. Matt 5.22.

HOMILY 29

"Noe, the first tiller of the soil, planted a vineyard. He drank some wine and got drunk."[1]

Y NOW [260] WE HAVE REACHED the final stage of our presentation dealing with the just man. Hence, I beseech you, summon up your attention and heed my words precisely. From today's reading, you see, it is possible to reap benefits that are not small or accidental: what happened to people of former ages proves to be a subject of the greatest instruction for us, provided we are ready to be alert. This, I mean, is the reason that a record has been kept of their sins, that we may shun the latter and emulate the former—and not only to this end, but as well Sacred Scripture shows you good people often failing, and sinners giving evidence of radical conversion, so that from both sources we may achieve sufficient assurance, the man who stands firm not being over-confident once he sees the just losing their step, nor the man in sin not despairing thanks to the prospect of many people making amends and managing to ascend to the very summit. So let none of you, I beg you, grow over-confident, even should they be conscious of their many achievements, but rather be anxious, [261] heeding the recommendation of blessed Paul's words, "So let the one who seems to stand firm take care not to fall."[2] Let the one who has slumped to the very depths of evil not despair of his own salvation, but rather consider God's unspeakable love and

1. Gen 9.20–21, where Speiser suggests the Hebrew would be better translated, "Noe, a man of the soil, was the first to plant a vineyard." Chrysostom's commentary shows he, too, grasped that sense, despite the LXX text.
2. 1 Cor 10.12.

also heed God speaking through the inspired author, "Does whoever falls rise again; does the one who turns away return?"[3] and again, "I don't wish the sinner's death as much as his turning from evil to live."[4] Do you see, dearly beloved, how every item written in Sacred Scripture has been recorded for no other purpose than our benefit and the salvation of the human race?

(2) With this in mind, then, let each of us apply the remedies from Scripture appropriate to ourselves. This, you see, is the reason these matters are freely proposed to everyone: people of good will are able to apply the fitting remedy to the ailment that is threatening them and secure a rapid return to health—provided someone doesn't resist the healing processes of the treatment, but rather gives evidence of personal gratitude. There is, after all, no ailment of soul or body besetting the human race which cannot come to healing from this source. Why is that, tell me? A person comes to this source burdened with care and the pressure of affairs, and on that account is overwhelmed with despair on entering— only to hear at once the words of the inspired author, "Why are you grief-stricken, my soul, and why do you disquiet me? Hope in God, for I shall praise him, my God, the help of my countenance";[5] receiving sufficient encouragement from this, he goes away throwing off all that faintheartedness. Likewise another person is oppressed by poverty and at his last gasp, depressed at seeing others flush with money, full of their own importance and putting on airs; this person in turn hears the words of the same inspired author, "Cast your care upon the Lord, and he will sustain you";[6] and again, "Don't worry when someone becomes rich and the luxury of his house increases, because at his death he will not take any of it with him."[7] Another person, too, is in dire straits through being subjected to scheming and calumnies, and finds life insupportable, unable to find human help from any quarter; but this person too is instructed by this blessed author in the

3. Jer 8.4.
4. Ezek 18.23 in a LXX variant.
5. Ps 42.5–6.
6. Ps 55.22.
7. Ps 49.16–17.

midst of such terrible difficulties not to take refuge in human resource—listen, after all, to his words, "While I remembered them in prayer, they spoke calumnies against me."[8] Do you see from what source he looks for assistance? Other people, he is saying, concoct schemes and calumnies and plots, whereas I take refuge in the unassailable rampart, in the firm anchor, in the haven waves cannot threaten—that is, in prayer, by means of which all difficulties are made light and easy for me.

(3) Still another is despised and scorned by those who formerly cultivated him, and is deserted by his friends, and this worries him and disturbs his peace of mind. This person, too, however, will hear the words of this blessed author, provided he is willing and approaches this source, "My friends and neighbors came and took a position against me, those close to me kept their distance; those bent on taking my life did violence to me, those intending evil against me talked sweet nothings but had their mind on trickery all the day."[9] Do you see them concocting schemes to the very death and declaring war to the finish? In other words, the phrase, "all the day," means all during life. So what was he doing while they were scheming and plotting these things? "I, however," he says, "am like a deaf person, I do not hear, and am like [262] a mute not opening his mouth; I became like one who does not hear and has no reproof on his lips."[10] Do you see the extraordinary degree of his wisdom, how he survived difficult ways? While his opponents were concocting schemes, he even blocked his ears so as not to hear; while they at no time ceased sharpening their tongue and uttering gossip and lies, he checked their folly with his silence. Why did he cast himself in this role, giving the impression of being a deaf mute with neither ears nor tongue, especially as they were plotting these stratagems? Listen to his explanation for such wisdom: "Because I had placed my hope in you, Lord."[11] Because I depended on my hope in you, he is saying, it was of no inter-

---

8. Ps 109.4.
10. Ps 38.13–14.

9. Ps 38.11–12 LXX.
11. Ps 38.16.

est to me what was done by them: your grace is sufficient to
undermine all that, to render their plots and schemes futile,
and to allow none of the plans hatched by them to take effect.

(4) Do you see how it is possible to find in Scripture a remedy appropriate to every trouble afflicting the human race
and go off healed, to dispel every depression that life causes
and not be brought low by any circumstance befalling us? For
this reason I beseech you to make your way here frequently,
and attend carefully to the reading of the Holy Scriptures,
not only while you are present here but also at home by taking the sacred books in your hand and receiving the benefit
of their contents with assiduity. Great, you see, is the advantage accruing from this: first, this very fact of the tongue's
being brought to reform through reading; then the soul too
is given wings and becomes elevated, glowing with the light
of the Sun of Justice, freed at that time from the harm of evil
thoughts and enjoying great peace and tranquility. What
bodily nourishment is for the maintenance of our strength,
reading is for the soul. You see, its nourishment is spiritual,
and it both invigorates the mind and makes the soul strong,
better attuned and wiser, no longer allowing it to fall victim
to irrational impulses but even rendering its wings light and
transferring it to heaven itself, so to say.

(5) Accordingly, let us not neglect such a great advantage,
I beseech you; instead, let us show all zeal in attending to the
reading of the holy Scriptures in our home as well, and when
we come along here let us not waste our time in gossip and
idle talk, but rather respect the purpose for which we have
come, by rousing ourselves and heeding what is being read
so that we may gain greater advantage and so take our leave
from here. If the chances were that in coming here you would
further waste your time in idle and unprofitable conversation
and wend your way home after receiving no further benefit
from the spoken word, what would be the good of that? I
mean, how could it be other than illogical if, on the one hand,
we went off to a secular festival and were enthusiastic about
gaining everything possible from the festival before heading
home, and had spent our money on this while, on the other

hand, when we come here we show no enthusiasm about gaining any advantage or paying attention to our soul before departing, especially as there is no call to be involved in expense but only to bring an eagerness and attentive attitude? Lest, therefore, we prove worse than people attending secular festivals, let us be zealous to give evidence of careful attention and alertness [263] so as to take away with us as we go from here food for the journey; thus we shall not only manage for ourselves but also be of assistance to others and be in a position to direct our wife, our household, our neighbors, our friends and even our enemies. Spiritual teachings, you see, are like that: matters applicable to everyone are proposed, nor is any distinction made in them except in so far as one person brings an attentive mind to the task and outdoes his neighbor in fervent enthusiasm.

(6) Since, therefore, the benefit accruing from the present teachings also is so considerable, come now, let us put before you the text we have read, reap the benefit arising from it, and thus make our way home. "Noe, first tiller of the soil," the text goes on, "planted a vineyard. He drank some wine and got drunk." Notice how the very beginning of this reading proves to be an occasion of much benefit to us. You see, whenever we hear that this just man, perfect though he was and recipient of testimony from on high, drank wine and got drunk, how much zeal should we now show, immersed as we are in such terrible sins of all kinds, in shunning the harm that comes from drunkenness? And yet this just man's becoming victim of this vice is not the same thing as our falling into the same habit: there are many factors that suggest this good man deserves forgiveness. I say this not to defend drunkenness but to show that the just man came to grief not through intemperance but rather from ignorance. For proof that it was not out of rashness that he got to know how to drink wine, listen to the very words of Scripture, which also offer an excuse in the expressions used. "Noe, first tiller of the soil," the text says, "planted a vineyard. He drank some wine and got drunk." That very word "first" shows that he made the first discovery of wine drinking, and through ig-

norance and inexperience of the proper amount to drink fell
into a drunken stupor. This is not the only relevant factor;
being also in the grip of deep depression he wanted to derive
from this indulgence consolation for himself, as a sage also
has said, "Let people in distress have wine and those in pain
strong drink,"[12] which shows that nothing can prove such a
good remedy for depression as recourse to this, aside from
the fact that in some cases intemperance undermines the benefit coming from it. Who can deny that this just man was
deeply distressed to see himself so isolated, people's bodies
strewn about before his eyes and the one tomb serving them
as well as cattle and wild animals?

(7) It is, after all, the practice of the prophets and the just
to grieve not only for themselves but for the rest of mankind.
If you're inclined to check that, you will find them all giving
evidence of this compassion—for example, you can listen to
Isaiah's words, "Don't put yourself out to comfort me for the
destruction of the daughter of my people";[13] or Jeremiah, on
the other hand, "Who will pour water on my head, and provide a fountain of tears for my eyes?"[14] or Ezekiel, "Alas,
Lord, will you destroy what remains of Israel?"[15] or Daniel
lamenting in these words, "You have made us few in number
by comparison with the gentiles";[16] or Amos, "Think better
of this, Lord";[17] or Habakkuk, "Why do you show me pain
and trouble?"[18] and again, "You will make people like the fish
of the sea."[19] You can even listen to the words of this blessed
author Moses himself: "If you forgive them their sin, do so;
but if not, wipe me out also";[20] and again when God promised
to entrust him with responsibility [264] for a greater nation
in the words, "Let me be: I will destroy this people and make
you into a great nation,"[21] Moses did not choose this alter-

12. Prov 31.6.   13. Isa 22.4.
14. Jer 8.23 LXX.   15. Ezek 9.8.
16. Does Chrysostom have in mind Dan 3.37 in the LXX?
17. Amos 7.3 LXX.   18. Hab 1.3.
19. Hab 1.14, where the future sense is otiose and not reproduced in
modern versions.
20. Exod 32.32.
21. A paraphrase of Exod 32.10.

native, considering instead command over them preferable. The world's teacher, blessed Paul, too said, "I would wish myself to be lost to Christ for the sake of my brethren, my kinsmen by race."[22]

(8) Do you see how each of the just demonstrated great compassion for his fellows? Now consider in the situation of this just man, too, how much it was likely he was experiencing and how he was overcome with depression to see both the intensity of the awful solitude, and the earth itself, which previously had been bedecked with numerous plants and beautified with flowers, and now suddenly like plucked foliage turned out to be bare and empty. So, since the intensity of his depression was so profound through finding little encouragement for himself in his situation, he gave himself up to cultivation of the soil—hence the text says, "Noe, first tiller of the soil, planted a vineyard."

(9) It is worth enquiring, however, whether he personally invented the growing of crops at this stage, or if this was the result of creation right from the very outset. While it is likely that this was created right from the very outset on the sixth day, when "God saw all that he had made, and lo, it was very good"[23] ("God," the text says, remember, "rested on the seventh day from all the works he had done"[24]), yet the usefulness of crop-growing was hardly known. You see, if crop-growing had been known right from the very outset, or its produce obvious, doubtless Abel would have made a libation of wine as well in making his offerings. But as ignorance still prevailed regarding the use of produce, they did not take advantage of crop-growing. Noe, however, being inventive in regard to farming, and given to great industry, probably tasted even the fruit, pressed some bunches of grapes, made wine and had a draught of it. Since he had neither tasted it before, nor knew anyone else who had partaken of it, he didn't know how much he should take nor the manner in

22. Rom 9.3. Chrysostom is finding it difficult to stay with the day's reading, and has indulged in a lengthy introduction and digression, assembling a vast mosaic of biblical texts.
23. Gen 1.31.   24. Gen 2.2.

which to take a share and so, through ignorance he was surprised into drunkenness. A further reason, however, was that since a carnivorous diet had been introduced into life, now wine drinking was, too. But notice, dearly beloved, how little by little the organization of the universe is provided for, each person proving to be an inventor of some skill from the beginning under the influence of intelligence from God implanted in nature; in this way he introduced practice of skills into life. The first man, remember, invented cultivation of the soil; after him one invented the tending of flocks, another the raising of cattle, one music, another metalwork; this just man, on the other hand, devised vinedressing from the instruction implanted in his nature. "Noe, first tiller of the soil, planted a vineyard. He drank some wine and got drunk." Notice how the remedy for depression, the restorative for his health, when through ignorance he went to excess, not only did not help him, but even harmed his constitution.

(10) [265] Perhaps, on the other hand, someone might say, Why was vinedressing, source of such terrible wickedness, introduced into life? Don't idly blurt out what comes into your head, o man: vinedressing is not wicked nor is wine evil—rather, it is use of them beyond the norm. You see, dreadful sins arise not from wine but from one's depraved attitude and through undermining the benefit that should naturally come from it because of intemperance. The reason that now after the deluge he shows you the use of wine is that you may learn that before using wine the human race had both come to grief in unbridled licentiousness and given evidence of extremity of sinfulness before wine had even appeared. This was also that, when you see the way wine is used, you would not attribute it all to wine but to the depraved intention bent on evil. Consider especially where wine has proved useful, and tremble, o man: in this consideration the basis of the good things involved in our salvation is worked out. Those who have an insight into spiritual realities understand this saying.

(11) "Noe, first tiller of the soil, planted a vineyard. He drank some wine and got drunk, and lay naked in his dwell-

ing." A terrible thing, you see, dearly beloved, a terrible thing
is drunkenness, capable of dulling the senses and drowning
the mind: man, rational and entrusted with responsibility for
all creatures though he is, is thus shackled with unbreakable
bonds and brought low like a motionless corpse. Worse in fact
than a corpse: a corpse happens to be incapable of either
good or evil, while the inebriate is incapable of good but more
capable of evil; he lies there, an object of ridicule to all
alike—wife, children, even the neighbors. I mean, whereas
one's friends consider their own shame and hide their head
in embarrassment, one's enemies on the contrary gloat over
it and pour out ridicule and curses, as if uttering these words:
has that fellow the right to draw breath? Beast! Pig!—and
even harsher words than that. Inebriates, you see, are worse
off than men returning from war with bloodstained hands
and themselves on stretchers: such men are perhaps praised
by many people on account of their spoils, their victories,
their wounds and their bloody exploits, whereas inebriates are
declared wretched, branded as despicable, and made the object of countless insults. After all, what could be more despicable than the person addicted to drink, reeking of it to high
heaven day in day out, having lost the judgment of reason?
Hence the warning of some sage, "Human life begins with
bread and water, clothing and a dwelling to cover one's ugliness,"[25] so that even if one falls a victim to drunkenness, one
does not make a public spectacle of oneself but is kept out of
sight by one's friends and not left to be an object of mockery
and ridicule for everyone.

(12) "Noe, first tiller of the soil, planted a vineyard," the
text says. "He drank some wine, and got drunk." The word
for drunkenness, dearly beloved, is not always used in Sacred
Scripture for that failing only, but also for satiety. So you
could say about this just man that, far from falling victim to
drunkenness through intemperance, he was brought into that
condition through satiety. Listen, after all, to David's words:
"They will become intoxicated from the richness of your

25. Sir 29.21.

house"[26]—that is, they will be filled. On the other hand, those who give themselves up to drunkenness never have their fill; the more wine they imbibe, the more they burn with thirst, and indulgence proves to be a constant fuelling of their thirst; by the time all that remains of the pleasure [266] has disappeared, the thirst proves to be unquenchable and leads the victims of drunkenness to the very precipice.

(13) "He planted a vineyard," the text says; "he drank some wine, got drunk and lay naked in his dwelling." See this happening to him, not somewhere out in the open, but in his dwelling. The reason Sacred Scripture indicated to us that it was "in his dwelling" was that you might see from the sequel the gravity of the wickedness of the one who drew attention to his nakedness. "Cham, the father of Canaan," the text goes on, "saw their father's nakedness; he went out and told his two brothers outside about it."[27] Perhaps if there had been others present, he would have mentioned his father's predicament to them too—such was the son's depravity. You see, for the reason that you might learn that right from the very beginning he was corrupt in attitude, it was not by chance that Scripture said that Cham saw his father's nakedness. Instead, why? "Cham, the father of Canaan, saw." Why, tell me, does he mention his son's name at this point too? For you to learn that he was intemperate and incontinent, and with the same inclination with which he gave himself to procreation in such a terrible situation, he now vented his insolence on his father.

(14) "He went out," the text says, "and told his two brothers outside." Notice, I ask you, in this case, dearly beloved, how his evil behavior is rooted not in human nature but in his attitude and inclination; they had the same nature, notice, they were brothers and had the same father, were born of the same pangs, fell under the same parental care, and yet did not betray the same inclinations: whereas one plunged headlong into evil, the others abided by their duty of respect for their father. Perhaps, however, in mocking and ridiculing his father's predicament he drew attention to it without heeding

---

26. Ps 36.8.   27. Gen 9.22.

the words of some sage, "Don't seek notoriety from your father's dishonor."[28] Yet his brothers didn't behave that way;
instead, what? On hearing this, "Shem and Japheth took a
cloak, put it on both their backs, went in backwards and covered their father's nakedness; with their faces turned away
they did not see their father's nakedness."[29] Do you see these
sons' right attitude? While one drew attention to it, the others
refrained even from looking at it; instead, they moved with
gaze averted so that they might do the right thing by covering
their father's nakedness. Notice also their restraint as well as
their right attitude: they neither railed at him nor upbraided
him but, when they heard his words, they made it their one
concern to right the situation speedily and give evidence of
behavior directed at respecting their father. "With their faces
turned away," the text says, "they did not see their father's
nakedness." Great was the sons' respect, and this is shown to
us not only through their act of covering their father but also
through their not bearing to see him.

(15) Accordingly, let us learn from this case also and gain
from both instances by imitating the latter two sons and shunning the example of the former. After all, if the man who
drew attention to obvious nakedness rendered himself liable
to a curse and by forfeiting the respect he shared with his
brothers was condemned to serve them (if not himself in person, at least all his offspring), what fate awaits those who draw
attention to the sins of their brethren, not merely not con-
cealing them but even making them more conspicuous and
by this means blowing the sins up out of all proportion? You
see, whenever you publicize a brother's fault, you not only
make him more shameless and perhaps more lethargic in his
progress towards virtue, but you also render the listeners
more indifferent and encourage [267] them in their sloth—
and not merely this, but also the fact that you are responsible
for God being blasphemed. Still, no one is unaware how
heavy the punishment this brings those who are responsible.
So let us, I beg you, avoid Cham's example, and instead imi-

28. Sir 3.10.   29. Gen 9.23.

tate the sense of shame shown by these respectful sons in regard to their father's nakedness; let us in that fashion keep under cover our brethren's sins, not for the purpose of encouraging them to indifference but that we may thereby in particular provide them with an even better occasion of ridding themselves promptly of that terrible affliction and of returning to the path of virtue. You see, just as such return is rendered easier for a sober person by the fact of having not many witnesses of his private failings, so when a person has passed the point of blushing and sees that the whole world knows him to be guilty of evil, it is not easy for him to reform; instead, like someone falling into the depths, submerged under countless waves, he will have greater difficulty in managing to emerge, but rather then sinks into despair and gives up the effort to return.

(16) Hence, I beseech you, let us not draw attention to our neighbors' faults; should we learn about them from others, far from being anxious to see their nakedness, let us rather, like the rightminded sons, conceal them, cover them up, strive to raise the fallen person by exhortation and advice, instructing him in the magnitude of God's love, the extraordinary degree of his goodness, his boundless compassion, so that like them we may enjoy greater commendation from the God of all, who wants "all to be saved and to come to the knowledge of truth,"[30] who wants not so much "the death of the sinner as his conversion to life."[31] "They did not see their father's nakedness," the text says. See how right from the very beginning they fulfilled these obligations from the law innate in their nature and thus anticipated their imposition in the law drafted for the instruction of the human race, as is legislated for in the words, "Honor your father and your mother, that it may be well with you,"[32] and, "Whoever reviles father or mother is to be put to death";[33] this had already been fulfilled in their behavior. Do you see how nature had in anticipation arrived at adequate instruction?

30. 1 Tim 2.4.
32. Exod 20.12.

31. Cf. Ezek 18.23.
33. Exod 21.17.

(17) "Noe, however, came out of his drunken sleep," the text goes on, "and got to know what his youngest son had done to him."[34] "Noe, however, came out of it," it says. Let those who spend their life in their cups heed the gravity of the error, and let them avoid the harm that comes from drunkenness. "Noe, however, came out of it," the text says. What is meant by "he came out of it"? What we usually say of the possessed when they are in a fit, that so and so came out of the demon and was freed from his tyranny, this too is what Scripture implied in the present instance. I mean, voluntary intoxication is really a demon, clouding the intellect more severely than any demon, and robbing its victim of any sense of values. You see, whereas we frequently have pity on the possessed person when we see him, we react quite differently to the drunk: we show anger and annoyance, and heap curses on him. Why on earth do we do that? Because, whereas the wicked demon's victim [268] involuntarily does what he does, whether it be kicking, or tearing garments, or screaming certain insults, and deserves excuse, the drunk, on the other hand, does not deserve excuse, no matter what he does; instead, he finds in family, friends and neighbors harsh accusers on the score that willingly and of his own accord he adopted evil ways and surrendered himself to the tyranny of drunkenness. I say this, not for the sake of condemning the just man: there were many grounds for conceding him excuse, most of all his never falling into the same faults again, which would be the clearest sign that in his former sin he was a victim not of indifference but of ignorance. After all, had he been a victim of indifference, it would surely have been inevitable for him to be ensnared by that passion again.

(18) I mean, had he fallen victim to the same fault, far from keeping silent, Scripture would have let us know about it. You see, Sacred Scripture has one purpose and goal, to pass over no detail of events but rather to instruct us in them truthfully: it is neither moved by envy to pass over the virtues of good people, nor by charity to cloud over their sins like-

34. Gen 9.24.

wise; instead, it brings everything to our notice so that we may have some record and instruction, and so that, should we in turn fall victim to some fault, we may be careful never to fall into the same fault again. I mean, the fact of sinning is not so harmful as persisting in sin. So don't take notice of the fact that the good man got drunk but that this didn't happen to him again. Pay attention, I ask you, on the contrary to those who waste their days in taverns and die a daily death, I could almost say; when they come to, they don't then avoid the harm coming from that practice but dedicate themselves to it as though to some task or exploit. Furthermore, however, you would keep in mind also the fact, this just man, even if drinking and becoming intoxicated through inexperience and ignorance of the due amount to imbibe, nevertheless was a good person with much virtuous behavior to his credit, and so could have kept under cover the sin that occurred by accident; in our case, on the other hand, beset as we are with countless other passions, what comfort could we gain for ourselves, tell me, when we sink ourselves in drunken stupor along with those other sins? Who would allow us excuse when we have not even come to our senses through experience?

(19) "Noe, however, came out of his drunken sleep," the text says, "and got to know of what his youngest son had done to him." What is meant by "what he had done"? It refers to something grave and intolerable. After all, keep in mind that having espied within the house his father's predicament, he ought to have kept it quiet, but instead he went out and bruited it abroad, making a laughing stock of his father as far as he could in his shameful intent. Whereas he should have called them inside the house if he was bent on reporting his father's nakedness and have blurted it out that way, instead he went outside and blurted it out, with the result that, had there been a crowd of other people there, he would have made them as well witnesses of his father's predicament. That is why the text says, "what he had done"—namely, he demonstrated that disrespect towards his father, was unmindful of the respect due from children for their parents, drew at-

tention to sins, wanted to suborn his brothers and make them
join him in his disrespect. "What his youngest son had done
to him," the text says. Actually, he wasn't the youngest: he
was the second, ahead of Japheth; still, even if he was ahead
of him [269] in age, yet he was more juvenile in his attitude,
rashness demoting him in order. That is to say, since he wasn't
prepared to respect the limits of his position, he lost the precedence conferred on him by nature: just as through the depravity of his inclination he surrendered what he possessed
by nature, Japheth through his sound attitude acquired what
he did not possess by nature.

(20) Do you see how you can find nothing in Sacred Scripture that is contained accidentally or by chance? "What his
youngest son had done to him," the text says. "He said,
'Cursed be Canaan: he shall be a menial slave to his brothers.'"[35] Lo, we have come to the question mooted on all sides:
you can hear lots of people asking, Why is it that, though the
father was at fault in publicizing his parent's nakedness, it is
the son who bears the curse? I beseech you, then, listen carefully and heed the solution of the problem: we will tell you
whatever divine grace provides with your salvation in mind.
"He said, 'Cursed be Canaan: he shall be a menial slave to
his brothers.'" It was not idly or to no purpose that he made
mention of the son but for some hidden reason: it was his
intention both to curse him for the sin of disrespect he had
committed against him and at the same time not to undermine the blessing already bestowed by God, the text reading,
remember, "God blessed Noe when he disembarked from the
ark and his sons as well."[36] So, in case it should seem he had
cursed the man who had once fallen under God's blessing,
for the time being he omitted mention of the disrespectful
one while applying the curse to his son.[37]

(21) To be sure, someone will say, while this shows that the

---

35. Gen 9.25.   36. Cf. Gen 9.1.
37. Chrysostom seems to be shifting the basis of his explanation of this
difficulty compared with Homily 28; n. 12 there contrasts his other, moral
explanation with the dogmatic and literary explanations of modern commentators.

reason he did not curse Cham was that he had enjoyed blessing from God, nevertheless why is it that, though he was the
sinner, the other man had to pay the penalty? This doesn't
happen idly, either: Cham did not endure less punishment
than his son, he too felt its effects. You know well, of course,
how in many cases fathers have begged to endure punishment in place of their children, and how seeing their children
bearing punishment proves a more grievous form of chastisement than being subject to it themselves. Accordingly, this
incident occurred so that Cham should endure greater anguish on account of his natural affection, so that God's blessing should continue without impairment, and so that his son
in being the object of the curse should atone for his own sins.
You see, even if in the present instance he bears the curse on
account of his father's sin, nevertheless it was likely that he
was atoning for his own failings. In other words, it was not
only for his father's sin that he bore the curse but perhaps
also for the purpose of his suffering a heavier penalty on his
own account. After all, for proof that parents are not punished for their children, nor children for their parents, each
being liable for the sins he has committed, you can find frequent statement among the inspired authors—as, for instance, when they say, "The teeth of the one eating sour
grapes shall be set on edge,"[38] and, "The soul that shall die
is the soul that sins,"[39] and again, "Parents shall not die for
their children, nor children for their parents."[40]

(22) Accordingly, let none of you, I beseech you, be ignorant of Sacred Scripture's point and be rash enough to find
fault with what is written; instead, accept its words with a
grateful mind, marvel at the precision of Sacred Scripture,
and consider the grave evil sin is. I mean, behold the man
sharing the same birth pangs as his brothers, born of the
same womb, [270] yet made their slave by the onset of sin,
robbed of his freedom and brought into subjection—hence

38. Jer 31.30, which is found at 38.30 in the LXX.
39. Ezek 18.20.
40. Deut 24.16. Again a series of scriptural testimonies support Chrysostom's moral point.

the origin of his subsequent condition of servitude. Before this, you see, there was no such indulgence, people being pampered in this way and needing others to minister to their needs; rather, each one looked to his own needs, there being great equality of esteem and complete absence of discrimination. When sin entered the scene, on the contrary, it impaired freedom, destroyed the worth inherent in nature and introduced servitude so as to provide constant instruction and reminder to the human race to shun the servitude of sin while returning to the freedom of virtue. You see, for the fact that servant and master both stand to gain benefit arising from this incident, provided they are willing, let them give due thought—the servant, on the one hand, to the fact that he entered servitude for the reason that Cham rushed headlong into such impertinence, while the master in turn should consider that servitude and command arose from no other source than Cham's display of a depraved intention and his fall from the equal esteem he enjoyed with his brothers.

(23) If, however, we are on the alert, these evils that came into life as a result of the sins of our forebears will in no way be able to harm us, going no further than the level of terminology, as they do. While it was the first formed human being who through the Fall brought on the punishment of death and was responsible for spending his life in pain and distress, and it was he who was the cause of servitude, Christ the Lord on the contrary came and permitted all these evils to occur only at the level of terminology, provided we are of the right mind. You see, death is now not death but only carries the name of death—or, rather, even the very name has been abolished. I mean, we no longer call it death, but sleeping and dreaming. Hence Christ himself said, "'Our friend Lazarus is asleep,'"[41] and Paul, writing to the Thessalonians said, "About those who are asleep, brethren, I don't want you to be ignorant."[42] Servitude in turn is likewise only a name: the one who commits sin is a slave. For proof that Christ came to remove it and left it existing only at the level of terminology,

41. John 11.11.   42. 1 Thes 4.13.

or rather even cancelled its very name, listen to Paul's words: "But those who have believers for master should not show them less respect because they are brethren."[43] Do you see how the advent of virtue caused those previously subject to the brand of slavery to be brought into the kinship of brotherhood?

(24) The text reads, "'Canaan shall be a menial slave to his brothers.'" You did not exercise your position properly, he is saying, nor have you gained any advantage from your parity of esteem; hence I intend you to come to your senses through subjection. This had happened also in the beginning in the case of the woman: though of equal status with her husband, she did not exercise well the position given her, and consequently she had her authority removed and heard the words, "'Your yearning will be for your husband, and he will be your master.'"[44] Since you do not know how to exercise control well, learn to be controlled well rather than controlling badly. This, of course, was the reason the character in the present incident also receives the punishment with a view to his coming to his senses and he personally suffers the penalty through his son, so that you may learn that, even if he was then elderly, nevertheless the penalty would be passed on to his son—something that made his life bitter and painful as he pondered the fact that after his own death his son was due to pay the penalty for his doings. [271] I mean, for proof that the son's life was inherently depraved and all his successors proved to be abominable in their decline into evil, listen to Scripture's words in the form of a curse: "Your father was an Amorite and your mother a Hittite;"[45] likewise someone else's taunt, "You offspring of Canaan and not of Juda."[46]

(25) You see, it is now worth hearing, on the other hand, following the punishment inflicted on the one who drew attention to his father's nakedness, what rewards were bestowed on those who accorded their father such respect and defer-

43. 1 Tim 6.2.   44. Gen 3.16.
45. Ezek 16.3, Chrysostom strangely omitting the pointed opening of the jibe, "Your origins are from the land of Canaan."
46. Dan 13.56.

ence. "Noe said," the text goes on, "'Blessed be the Lord the God of Shem, whose slave Canaan shall be.'"[47] This, someone may perhaps say, is not a blessing of Shem. His being blessed is in fact deliberate: whenever God is thanked and blessed through human beings, then it is usual that more ample blessing falls on those through whom God is blessed. Accordingly, in blessing God he made Shem beneficiary of greater blessing and became the cause of richer reward for him than if he had bestowed the blessing on himself.[48] In other words, just as he grants us generous favors from himself when he is blessed through us, so likewise when through us other people blaspheme against him our condemnation proves to be greater on that account for providing the occasion. Accordingly, let us be anxious, I beseech you, to live in such a manner and give evidence of such intensity of virtue that all who see us will raise hymns of blessing to the Lord God. You see, good and loving as he is, he wants to be praised through our in-strumentality, not because he personally expends any effort with a view to his own glory, being protected against need as he is; instead, his purpose is that we may provide him with occasions for granting us greater favor from himself. "'Blessed be the Lord the God of Shem, whose slave Canaan shall be.'" Do you see how the paternal chastisement is shown to be more a reprimand than chastisement? Noe was a father, after all, and a loving father at that, and he had no wish to inflict the due penalty but rather to stop the evil from going further. For this reason, he says, I sentence you to servitude so that you may have a constant and ineluctable reminder.

(26) Then he says, "'May God enlarge Japheth's territory, may he dwell in the tents of Shem, and let Canaan be their slave.'"[49] Once again a wonderful eulogy this, containing per-haps some treasure below the surface. I mean, if it was not idly or to no purpose that his father imposed his name on

47. Gen 9.26.
48. If Chrysostom's argumentation seems convoluted, he is doing no worse than modern commentators like Von Rad and Speiser, who at least, like Chrysostom, resist the temptation to alter the difficult text.
49. Gen 9.27.

Noe but rather to foretell by means of the name the deluge due to occur, far less was it idly or by chance that this good man bestowed his blessings. In other words, through these blessings, Shem's and Japheth's, I am inclined to think he is suggesting the calling of the two peoples—through Shem the Jews, on the one hand, the patriarch Abraham coming from him, after all, whence the Jewish race developed, whereas through Japheth, on the other hand, came the calling of the gentiles. Notice, after all, that this blessing foretells as much. "'May God enlarge Japheth's territory,'" the text says, remember, "'May he dwell in the tents of Shem.'" We see this fulfilled in the case of the gentiles; while, on the one hand, he refers to all the gentiles in the phrase, "'May he enlarge the territory,'" on the other hand, through the words, "'May he dwell in the tents of Shem,'" he means that the gentiles were in possession of things prepared for the Jews and provided for them. "'Let Canaan be their slave.'"

(27) Do you see how great were the rewards the former received for their rightmindedness, [272] and the extent of the disrespect the latter flaunted about by means of his indiscretion? Let us constantly have this graven on our minds so that we may, on the one hand, succeed in becoming careful imitators of the former while, on the other hand, we may avoid the latter's depravity of attitude and extraordinary indiscretion.

(28) The text continues, "Noe lived three hundred and fifty years after the deluge. Noe died after a lifespan of nine hundred and fifty years."[50] Don't think, however, that Sacred Scripture indicated this to no purpose; rather, notice in this instance as well the good man's continence in the fact that, through enjoying security and prosperity, and attaining such a long life after disembarking from the ark, he still refrained from procreation. Scripture, you observe, did not make mention of his having further children than these three. Take note likewise in this text of Cham's extreme intemperance in the fact that he did not even come to his senses by seeing his

50. Gen 9.28–29.

father's remarkable display of continence, but even did the exact opposite in everything to his father. Consequently and quite properly the whole race springing from him was sentenced to servitude so as to receive some check to this depraved attitude.

(29) Then Sacred Scripture goes on from this point to tell of the children born to the sons, in these words: "Now, Cham became the father of Chous"; and further, "Now, Chous became the father of Nebrod, who was the first on earth to be a mighty hero; he was a mighty hunter in the Lord's sight."[51] While some people say the phrase, "in the Lord's sight," means being in opposition to God, I on the contrary do not think Sacred Scripture is implying this—rather that the person was strong and brave. But the phrase, "in the presence of the Lord God," means created by him, receiving from him God's blessing, or the fact that God was on the point of arousing our wonder through him by creating such a remarkable creature and displaying him before us on the earth. He too, however, in his turn in imitation of his forebear did not take due advantage of his natural preeminence but hit upon another form of servitude in endeavoring to become ruler and king. You see, there wouldn't ever be a king unless there were people being ruled; but in that case freedom is seen for what it really is, whereas slavery is most galling in conditions of freedom, the more power is exercised over free people. See what ambition is guilty of: observe bodily strength not keeping to its limits but constantly lusting after more and clutching for glory. You see, the orders he gave were not those of a leader; rather, he even builds cities with a view to ruling over the enemy.

51. Gen 10.6, 8–9. Despite his protestation elsewhere about the relevance of genealogies from the viewpoint of his beloved *akribeia* (Hom. 2 *in Oziam*; PG 56, 110), Chrysostom now, as if suddenly aware of the amount of attention he has lavished on Noe and his family (nine homilies), rushes ahead and even truncates his habitual moral conclusion, all unaware of the importance given to this Table of Nations by modern commentators like Von Rad, who sees it as "a document of amazing theoretical power. . . . For Biblical theology the inclusion of the table of nations means a radical break with myth" (*Genesis*, pp. 143, 145).

(30) "From that land came Assur," the text goes on, remember, "and he built Nineveh."[52] Notice further in this text, I ask you, how the wickedness of forebears does not leave its mark on our nature: these Ninevites, who won God's mercy through their repentance and cancelled the Lord's sentence, had as ancestor that parricide Cham, then that tyrannical and arrogant person Nebrod as kin, from whom came Assur. On the other hand, it is said there were perhaps others among them who were soft and pampered, leading a decadent and corrupt life, abandoning themselves to intoxication, ribaldry, revelry and jesting—yet since they were determined to give evidence of an exact repentance, the wickedness of their forebears [273] left no mark on them. Instead, they won such great favor from on high that up to this day the practice of their repentance is celebrated.

(31) Accordingly, let us too imitate them and learn that our forebears' wickedness does not leave its mark on us, provided we are ready to be on the alert, nor can our forebears' virtue be of any use to us if we are guilty of indifference. So let us show great zeal in embracing virtue and give evidence of a grateful attitude, so that we may enjoy the same blessing as Shem and Japheth and remain free from the curse and the servitude that Canaan incurred and not become slaves of sin. Instead, may we take advantage of the true freedom and come by those ineffable blessings, thanks to the grace and love of our Lord Jesus Christ, to whom with the Father and the Holy Spirit be glory, power and honor, now and forever, for ages of ages. Amen.

52. Gen 10.11.

HOMILY 30

"The whole world had the same language, and everyone used the same words."[1]

O, [273] AT LONG LAST we have reached the end of the holy season of Lent, we have completed the voyage of fasting and now, thanks to God's grace, we have put into port. Don't become careless on that account, however; instead, let that be an occasion for our giving evidence of so much the greater enthusiasm and vigilance. Navigators, too, when they are on the point of entering port after crossing countless seas, with full sails and cargo brought out of the hold, then most of all exercise great concern and anxiety lest the ship crash on to some reef or rock and render their previous trouble useless. Runners behave in this way, too; when they approach the end of the course, then most of all they exert their keenest effort so as to reach the finish-line and be awarded the prize. Prize-fighters as well, despite countless fights and victories, exert the greatest effort when they are wrestling for the prize so that they may win the purse and go home. So, just as navigators, runners and prize-fighters in each case stretch their enthusiasm and vigilance to the limit at the point when they are close to success, well, in just the same way ought we too, now that we have arrived at this great week, give thanks to God's grace, intensify the devotion of our prayers and give evidence of precise and thorough confession of sins, practice of good works, generous almsgiving, fair dealing, even-tempered behavior and every other virtue, so that we may arrive at the Lord's Day with these good deeds and thus enjoy the Master's generosity.

---

1. Gen 11.1. Chrysostom, with his moral purpose, is not likely to rush over this chapter as he did the Table of Nations.

(2) We call the week great, not because it has a greater number of hours—other weeks having many more hours, after all—nor because it has more days, there being the same number of days in this and the other weeks, of course. So why do we call this week great? Because in it many ineffable good things come our way: in it protracted war is concluded, death is eliminated, curses are lifted, [274] the devil's tyranny is relaxed, his pomps are despoiled, the reconciliation of God and man is achieved, heaven is made accessible, human beings are brought to resemble angels, those things which were at odds are united, the wall is laid low, the bar removed, the God of peace having brought peace to things on high and things on earth. This, then, is the reason we call the week great, because in it the Lord lavished on us such a plethora of gifts. This is the reason many people intensify their fasting as well as their sacred watching and vigils, and practice alms-giving, thus showing by their behavior the regard they have for the week. After all, since the Lord in this week has regaled us with such great goods, how are we too not obliged to demonstrate our reverence and regard as far as we can?

(3) Emperors, too, in fact, by their own action declare the extent of the reverence they have for these august days by ordering everyone involved in civic administration to suspend business, the doors of the courts to be closed and all kinds of strife and dispute to be eliminated so that we may have the chance to proceed to our spiritual duties in complete peace and quiet. And not only this: they also give evidence of further generosity by releasing from their chains those confined in prison, and thus imitating their Lord to the extent of human capacity. Just as he (as Scripture tells us) releases us from the harsh prison of our sins and offers us enjoyment of countless goods, in just the same way ought we to become imitators of the Lord's mercy as far as we can. Do you see how each of us demonstrates the reverence and regard we have for the days that have been made occasion of such great benefit for us? Hence I beseech you, now above all times let us dispel all worldly thoughts, keep the eye of our mind clear and alert, and in this fashion attend here; let no one come to

church cluttered up with worldly concerns if the purpose is to gain the due reward of our effort and thus go off home.

(4) So come now, let us spread before you the customary feast and regale your good selves with what we read before from blessed Moses by drawing to your attention the text itself just read and demonstrating the precision of Sacred Scripture. When it brought the story of Noe to a close, remember, it then began the genealogy starting with Shem in the words, "Sons were born to Shem, ancestor of all the sons of Eber and younger brother of Japheth."[2] Then, after giving the list of names, it says, "Two sons were born to Eber: the name of one was Phalek because in his time the earth was divided."[3] Notice how by the naming of the child it gave a hint of the sign due to occur before long, so that when you see the event take place you will not be amazed now that you have previously seen the child's name foreshadowing it. You see, after it listed the children later born to these people, it adds, "The whole world had the same language, and everyone used the same words"[4]—referring not to the earth but to the human race, with the intention of teaching us that all mankind had the same language. "The whole world had the same language," it says, "and everyone used the same words." "Lips," literally meaning language, and "words" likewise has the same meaning, so that it is saying that everyone had the same language and idiom. For proof that the reference is to language [275] in the verse, "The whole world had the same language," listen to the words of Scripture elsewhere: "Venom of asps is on their lips."[5] Scripture is accustomed to refer in this way to language by the word "lips."

(5) "When they travelled from the east, they found open country in the land of Sennar and settled there."[6] Notice how the human race, instead of managing to keep to their own boundaries, always longs for more and reaches out for greater things. This is what the human race has lost in particular, not being prepared to recognize the limitations of their own con-

---

2. Gen 10.21 in Chrysostom's variant of the LXX.
3. Gen 10.25.   4. Gen 11.1.
5. Ps 140.3.   6. Gen 11.2.

dition but always lusting after more and entertaining ambitions beyond their capacity. In this regard, too, when people who chase after the things of the world acquire for themselves much wealth and status, they lose sight of their own nature, as it were, and aspire to such heights that they topple into the very depths. You could see this happening every day without others being any the wiser from the sight of it; instead, they pause for a while, but immediately lose all recollection of it and take the same road as the others and fall over the same precipice. This is exactly what you can see happening to these people in the present instance: "When they travelled from the east, they found open country in the land of Sennar and settled there." See how in gradual stages it teaches us the instability of their attitude: when they saw the open country (the text says), they packed up and left their previous dwelling and settled down there.

(6) Then it says, "Each one said to his neighbor, 'Come, let us make bricks and bake them in the oven.' Brick acted as stone for them, and their mortar was bitumen. They said, 'Come, let us build ourselves a city and a tower with its peak reaching to heaven; let us make a name for ourselves lest we be scattered over the whole earth.'"[7] See how they failed to take proper advantage of their common language, their vain plan for this life proving the source of their troubles. "'Come,'" the text says, "'let us make bricks and bake them in the oven.' Brick acted as stone for them and their mortar was bitumen." Notice how much security they wanted to be able to count on in their building, unaware that "unless the Lord build the house, in vain do its builders labor."[8] "'Let us build a city for ourselves,'" the text says—not for God but "'for ourselves.'" See the intensity of their wickedness: despite having a fresh memory of that recent disaster, they fell into such terrible folly. "'Let us build ourselves a city,'" the text says, "'and a tower with its peak reaching to heaven.'" By the mention of heaven Sacred Scripture meant to bring to our attention the excess of their temerity. "'Let us make a

7. Gen 11.3–4.   8. Ps 127.1.

name for ourselves,'" the text says: do you see the root of
their wickedness? So that we may enjoy an undying reputation, the meaning is, so that we may be in a position to be
remembered in perpetuity; such will be our performance and
achievement that we will never pass into oblivion. Let us do
this "'lest we be scattered over the face of the whole earth.'"[9]
While we are still in this situation, the meaning is, let us put
into effect what we have resolved, to leave an indelible memory for ourselves with succeeding generations.

(7) There are many people even today who in imitation of
them want to be remembered for such achievements, by
building splendid homes, baths, porches and avenues. I mean,
if you were to ask each of them why they toil and labor and
lay out such great expense [276] to no good purpose, you
would hear nothing but these very words—so as to ensure
their memory survives in perpetuity and to have it said that
"this is the house belonging to so-and-so," "this the property
of so-and-so." This, on the contrary, is worthy not of com-
memoration but of condemnation: hard upon those words
come other remarks equivalent to countless accusations—"belonging to so-and-so the grasping miser, despoiler of widows
and orphans." So such behavior is calculated not to earn remembrance but to encounter unremitting accusations, achieve
notoriety after death, and incite the tongues of onlookers to
calumny and condemnation of the person who acquired these
goods. But if you're quite anxious for undying reputation, I
will show you the way to succeed in being remembered for
every achievement and also, along with an excellent name, to
provide yourself with great confidence in the age to come.
How, then, will you manage both to be remembered day after
day and also become the recipient of tributes even after passing from one life to the next? If you give away these goods
of yours into the hands of the poor, letting go of precious
stones, magnificent homes, properties and baths. This is undying reputation, this remembrance proves for you provider

9. Chrysostom's text of vv. 3–4 at these places shows the variations that
one would expect of a preacher's less than perfect recall.

of countless treasures, this remembrance relieves you of the burden of sins, and procures for you great confidence with the Lord. After all, consider, I ask you, even the very words everybody would be likely to say about the dispenser of such largesse—so generous and kind, so gentle and good. Scripture says, remember, "He distributed his goods as gifts to the poor; his righteousness lasts forever."[10] That, after all, is what material wealth is like: the more it is given away, the more it remains, whereas if it is clung to and locked up in safe keeping, it destroys even the people who cling to it. "He distributed his goods as gifts to the poor," it says, remember. But listen to what follows as well: "His righteousness lasts forever." It took one day for him to distribute his wealth, and his goodness continues for all time and earns an undying remembrance.

(8) Do you see reputation extending to the end of time? Do you see reputation accompanied by great and ineffable blessings? Let it therefore be our concern to be remembered for edifices of this kind. I mean, those made of stone, far from bringing us any advantage, even mock us more loudly than an imperishable memorial. Whereas we take our leave with the sins accruing from them upon us, the buildings themselves we leave here, nor do we win from them even the slightest reputation of any value; rather, we incur slander, while the title immediately passes to someone else. This, you see, is the way things are: property passes from one person to another, from him to someone else, and so on. Today the house is said to belong to so-and-so, tomorrow to somebody else, and later to someone else again. We deceive ourselves quite deliberately to think that we have complete ownership, unmindful that we enjoy only use of things and willy-nilly must pass them on to other people; the fact that these are people we would prefer not to have them, I will pass over for the time being. In short, though, if you long for remembrance, this is what you must concentrate on: listen to how the widows remembered Tabitha, and how they surround Pe-

10. Ps 112.9.

ter, weeping and showing him tunics and cloaks which Dorcas had made while she was with them. Do you see the buildings pulsing with life, emitting cries and possessed of such virtue as even to bring back from death to life? In fact, when they surrounded Peter and gave a vent to a flood of hot tears by way of begging for the means of subsistence, Peter (the text says) sent everyone outside and fell on his knees in prayer; then he raised her up, called the faithful [277] including the widows and set her in their midst as large as life.[11] If you want to be remembered and are anxious for true repute, imitate her, and build edifices like that, not going to expense on lifeless matter but displaying great generosity in regard to your fellow human beings. This is the remembrance that is worth admiring and brings great benefit.

(9) Let us, however, return once more to our theme and see the temerity of the men of that period; their vices, in fact, will prove a lesson for us, provided we are prepared to be on the alert. "'Let us build a city for ourselves,'" the text says, "'and a tower with its peak reaching to heaven; let us make a name for ourselves lest we be scattered over the earth.'" Do you see how in all cases they give evidence of the depravity of their attitude: "'Let us build a city for ourselves.'" Notice, however, even after such a terrible disaster how they put their hand to evils that are no less grave. So what will happen? How will they be shaken loose of this folly? Out of fidelity to his characteristic love God promised never again to inflict a deluge; these people, on the contrary, were not brought to their senses even by his punishments nor were they improved by his kindnesses.

(10) Hence, listen to what follows so as to learn the magnitude of God's ineffable love. "The Lord God descended," the text goes on, "to see the city and the tower that the sons of men were building."[12] See how human a fashion Scripture uses in narration! "The Lord God descended," the text says— not for us to think in human fashion, but so that in this way

11. Cf. Acts 9.36–41.
12. Gen 11.5. The anthropomorphism prompts Chrysostom, as usual, to a warning of the true purpose of such "considerateness" in language.

we may be instructed never to condemn our brother idly nor convict them on hearsay unless we gain some clinching evidence beforehand. You see, this is the reason why everything happens, on God's part, and why he employs such wonderful considerateness with a view to the instruction of the human race. "The Lord God descended," the text says, "to see the city and the tower." Notice him not checking their folly at the outset but employing much longsuffering and waiting for them to put into effect all their wickedness, and only then thwarting their attempt. You see, lest anyone should be able to say that, while they had made plans, they had not put their designs into effect, he waits until they implemented their plans and only then shows them how vain their exploits are. "The Lord God descended," the text says, "to see the city and the tower that these creatures were building." See the excess of loving kindness: he let them toil and labor so that experience of these matters might prove a lesson for them.

(11) When he saw the wickedness developing and the disease intensifying, he did not allow it to reach its goal; instead, he revealed his characteristic goodness and, like an excellent doctor who sees the complaint becoming aggravated and the ulcer turning incurable, he performs an immediate excision so as to remove completely the source of the complaint. "The Lord God said," the text goes on, "'Lo, they are all of one race and tongue (that is, one language and one idiom). They have begun this exploit, and now they will leave undone none of the things they have planned to do.'"[13] See the Lord's loving kindness: since he is on the point of putting a stop to their exploit, he first offers an explanation and, as it were, demonstrates the magnitude of their sin and the excess of their ingratitude, as well as the fact that they had abused their common language. "'Lo, they are all of one race and one tongue,'" the text says, remember. "'They have begun this exploit, and [278] now they will leave undone none of the things they have planned to do.'" This, you see, is his custom, when he is on the point of inflicting punishment, to show first

13. Gen 11.6.

of all the magnitude of the sins as if offering an explanation, and only then to apply the corrective. In the case of the deluge, too, remember, when he was about to put into effect that awful threat of punishment, Scripture says, "Now, the Lord God saw that men's vices were multiplied, and everyone gave himself up wholly to pondering evil from his youth."[14] Do you see how he first showed the excess of their wickedness, and only then says, "'I will destroy the human being'"?[15] In like manner in this case too, "'Lo, they are all of one race and tongue, and have begun this exploit.'" If despite their advantage of such similarity of thought and language they rushed headlong into such awful folly, how would they avoid worse crimes with the passage of time? "'They will leave undone,'" the text says, remember, "'none of the things they have planned to do:'" nothing will succeed in checking their impulse—rather, they will be anxious to put into operation everything planned by them in case they should shortly be punished for things already perpetrated.

(12) You will find the same thing happening in the case of the first formed human: in that case, too, when God was on the point of expelling him from life in the garden, he said, "'Who told you that you are naked?'" and again, "Lo, Adam has become like one of us in knowing good and evil. Now there is risk that at some time he may put out his hand and pick fruit from the tree of life, eat it and live forever.' The Lord God sent him out of the garden."[16] In this case he says, "'Lo, they are all of one race and tongue. They have begun this exploit, and now they will leave undone none of the things they have planned to do. Come, let us go down there and confuse their speech, so that they will be unable to understand one another's language.'"[17] Notice once again the considerateness of the expressions; "'Come,'" it says, "'let us go down.'" What is the force of these words? Does the Lord

14. Gen 6.5, Chrysostom quoting from memory and adding a phrase not found in his text in Homily 22, though his commentary there seems to suppose such an addition.

15. Gen 6.7.   16. Gen 3.11, 22–23.

17. Gen 11.6–7.

need assistance for making correction? or help in their destruction? No, not at all; on the contrary, just as Scripture had already said, "The Lord descended," to teach us through this means that he saw in precise detail the excess of their wickedness, in this text too in the same way it says, "'Come, let us go down.'" This remark, however, is made as if to those of equal status: "'Come, let us go down and confuse their speech, so that they will be unable to understand one another's language.'" Like an everlasting memorial, he says, I am setting in place for them such terrible punishment that would last forever and no length of time would suffice to bring them forgetfulness of it. In other words, since they abused their similarity of language, I intend them to come to their senses through their difference in language.

(13) This, in fact, is the way the Lord is accustomed to behave. This is what he did in the beginning in the case of the woman as well: she had abused the status conferred on her, and for that reason he subjected her to her husband. Again, too, in the case of Adam, since he drew no advantage from the great ease he enjoyed and from life in the garden, but rather rendered himself liable to punishment through the Fall, God drove him out of the garden and inflicted on him everlasting punishment in the words, "'Thorns and thistles let the earth yield you.'"[18] So when the people in the present case, who had been dignified with similarity of language, used the privilege given them for evil purposes, he put a stop to the impulse of their wickedness through difference in language. "'Let us confuse their speech,'" he says, "'so that they will be unable to understand one another's language,'" his purpose being that, just as [279] similarity of language achieved their living together, so difference in language might cause dispersal among them. How could people lacking the same language and converse live in conformity with one another? "The Lord God dispersed them from there across the face of the whole earth, and they stopped building the city and the tower."[19] See God's loving kindness in the extent of the help-

18. Gen 3.18.   19. Gen 11.8.

lessness to which he reduced them; from then on they resembled lunatics: when one gave a direction, another responded in different fashion. Hence "they stopped building the city and the tower. That is why it was given the name Confusion, because there it was that the Lord God confused the languages of the whole earth, and from there the Lord God dispersed them in all the earth."[20] Notice the extent of the action taken to ensure remembrance of it would last for all time: first the conflict of tongues, or rather prior to this the giving of the name—the name Phalek, remember, which Eber gave his son, means division. Next, the place name: the place was called Confusion, which is what Babylon means. Then, Eber kept the same language as he had had before, so that this too should prove an unmistakable sign of the conflict.[21] Do you see how many means he wanted to use to keep the memory fresh and prevent the present event from being consigned to oblivion? You see, from that time on a father was obliged to tell his child the reason for the difference in languages, and a child would want to know the reason for the place name; the reason, of course, why the place was called Babylon, which means "confusion," was the fact that it was there that the Lord God confused the languages of the whole earth and from there he dispersed them. I think the place name implies both things, that he confused the languages and from there they felt the effects of dispersal.

(14) Dearly beloved, you have heard what gave rise to their dispersal and the conflict of tongues. Let us, I beseech you, avoid imitating them, and make proper use of advantages provided for us by God; let us have human nature in mind and keep our ambitions on the level that is proper for human beings, being mortal as we are. With our thoughts on the evanescence of this present life and how short is our time in

20. Gen 11.9. The LXX does not attempt to parallel the word play in the Hebrew on "Babylon," though Chrysostom shows his awareness of it.
21. This gratuitous comment of Chrysostom's gives rise to some perplexity in his editors. But perhaps Chrysostom is just stating, as do modern commentators, "Eber is the eponymous ancestor of the Hebrews" (Speiser, *Genesis*, 70).

this life, let us store up for ourselves abundant grounds for confidence through the performance of good deeds by giving evidence not only of the severity of our fasting in keeping with these days of Lent but also of the generosity of our alms-giving and our ardent prayers. Prayer, you see, ought always be joined to fasting. For the truth of this, listen to Christ's words, "This kind leaves only in response to prayer and fasting"[22]; and again in the case of the apostles Scripture says, "With prayer and fasting they commended them to the Lord, in whom they were believers;"[23] the Apostle further says, "Don't deny each other, except in prayer and fasting."[24] Do you see how fasting needs help from this quarter? Then it is, you see, that prayers are raised with devotion, when the mind becomes more elevated, is burdened with nothing, and is encumbered by no evil weight of lechery. Prayer, in fact, is a wonderful shield, great security, a rich treasure, a mighty harbor, safe refuge, provided we approach the Lord with attention, [280] withdraw our mind from distraction on all sides and press our suit without allowing our soul's enemy any inroads. I mean, since he knows that at that time we have the power to discuss matters relevant to our good, confess our sins, show our wounds to the physician and come by efficacious healing, then it is especially that he goes on the offensive and tries every strategem to trip us up and force us into indifference.

(15) Hence, I beg you, let us be on the alert, realize his wiles and at that time especially show so much zeal for driving him off as if we saw him before us with our own eyes, for expelling every thought that disturbs our peace of mind, and for devoting ourselves completely to raising attentive prayers so that not only the tongue may speak but also the mind may be in step with the words. I mean, if the tongue pronounces the words but the mind is miles away, busy with some domestic concerns and concentrating on other public affairs, we gain no advantage at all—instead we possibly incur greater

22. Matt 17.21.   23. Acts 14.23.
24. 1 Cor 7.5 elliptically.

condemnation. After all, if in our approach to a mere human being we display such concentration as frequently to have eyes for no others nearby, but concentrate our attention and fix our eyes on him alone, much more should we do this in the case of God and persevere in prayer unremittingly and without interruption. This, in fact, is the reason Paul wrote in these words, "With a prayer for every occasion let us pray in spirit."[25]—not only in word and with untiring persistence, he says, but also in our very soul, "in spirit." In other words, let your requests be spiritual, he says, let your mind be alert, let your attention be concentrated on the words. Ask for the kind of things it is usual to ask of God so that you may gain what you ask; to the same end maintain your constant vigil, alert, keeping your attention undimmed, no yawning or switching your mind in one direction and another, but working out your salvation in fear and trembling. "Blessed is the person," Scripture says, remember, "whose piety puts him in awe of everything."[26]

(16) Prayer is a great good: someone conversing with a virtuous person gains no little advantage from the experience, so how much good will the one communing with God be granted? Prayer, after all, is conversing with God. For proof of this, listen to the words of the inspired author: "Let my conversation be pleasing to God,"[27] that is, may my converse seem acceptable to God. I mean, he is able to offer help before we ask for it, isn't he? Still, he waits so as to take occasion from us for daily bestowing on us providential care from himself. Accordingly, whether we have our requests granted or not, let us persist in asking, and render thanks not only when we gain what we ask but also when we fail to. Failure to gain, you see, when that is what God wants, is not worse than succeeding; we do not know what is to our advantage in this regard in the way he does understand. The result is, then, that succeeding or failing we ought to give thanks. Why are you surprised that we don't know what is to our advantage?

25. Eph 6.18.   26. Prov 28.14.
27. Ps 104.34.

Paul, a man of such quality and stature, judged worthy of
ineffable blessings, did not know what was advantageous in
his requests: when he saw himself beset with trouble and di-
verse tribulations, he prayed to be rid of them, not once or
twice but many times. "Thrice I besought the Lord,"[28] he
says, remember. "Thrice" means he besought them frequently
[281] without success. So let us see how he was affected by it:
surely he didn't take it badly? He didn't turn fainthearted,
did he? He didn't become dispirited, did he? Not at all. On
the contrary, what? God said, " 'My grace is sufficient for you;
my power has its full effect in infirmity.' "[29] Not only did he
not free him of the troubles besetting him, but he even allowed him to persevere in them. True enough; but how does
it emerge that he did not take it badly? Listen to Paul's own
words when he learnt what the Lord had decided: "I will
gladly boast of my infirmities."[30] Not only, he says, do I no
longer seek to be rid of them, but I even boast of them with
greater satisfaction. Do you see his grateful spirit? Do you see
his love for God? Listen to what he says: "You see, as for
praying for what we ought, we are at a loss."[31] It is not possible, he says, for us—human beings that we are—to have a
precise knowledge of everything. So we ought yield to the
Creator of our nature, and with joy and great relish accept
those things that he has decided on, and have an eye not to
the appearance of events but to the decisions of the Lord.
After all, he who knows better than we what is for our benefit
also knows what steps must be taken for our salvation.

(17) Accordingly, let it be our concern to persevere constantly in prayer and, far from being depressed by a slow
response, let us give every sign of longsuffering. He postpones response to our requests not to deny us but with the
intention of instructing us in the way of entreaty and out of
a wish to draw us to him uninterruptedly. Likewise when a
loving father is entreated many times by his child, he does not
accede immediately—not from any unwillingness to give but

28. 2 Cor 12.8.   29. 2 Cor 12.9.
30. Ibid.   31. Rom 8.26.

to encourage the child's entreaty by this means. With this in mind, then, let us never give up our effort by desisting from our approach to him or from the entreaties we make. After all, if the woman's supplication got the better of that harsh, insensitive judge who had no respect even for God, and provoked him into assisting her,[32] how much more can we provoke our Lord into assisting us if we are minded to imitate that woman, since he is so gentle and loving, so compassionate and caring for our salvation? Accordingly, let us condition ourselves to be not easily distracted from the task of assailing him constantly with our prayers day and night, and especially at night, when there is no one to hinder us, when there is great peace of mind, when there is complete repose, all hubbub left outside the house, no one likely to put us off or distract us from entreaty, when our mind happens to be set at rest and is able to propose everything precisely to the physician of souls. I mean, if blessed David, king as he was as well as inspired author and beset with so many worries, clad in mantle and crown, could say, "At midnight I rise to praise you for the rulings of your justice,"[33] what should we say who, despite leading a private and carefree life, don't even do the same as he? In other words, since by day he had much on his mind, a great mass of business, terrible confusion, and could not find a suitable time for the proper kind of prayer, the time of respite which others devote to sleep, lying on soft beds, tossing and turning; on the contrary the king, though caught up in such responsibility, devoted the time to prayer, conversing privately with God, directing sincere entreaties [282] to him of the most intense kind, and thus he achieved whatever he set his mind to: through these prayers he was successful in wars, inflicting defeat and adding victory to victory. He enjoyed, you see, an invincible weaponry, an ally from on high sufficient not merely for battles conducted by human beings, but also for the cohorts of the demons.

(18) So, let us in our turn imitate this man, the peasants the prince, we with our carefree and peaceful life the man in

32. Cf. Luke 18.2–5.   33. Ps 119.62.

mantle and crown, but still rivalling the lifestyle of monks. I mean, listen further to his words in another place, "My tears became my bread day and night."[34] Do you see his soul finding itself afflicted with unremitting remorse? My nourishment, he is saying, my bread, my food was nothing other than my tears by night and day. Again, "I am distressed with my groaning, I drench my bed with tears night after night."[35] What will we say for ourselves in our own defense, we who are reluctant to give evidence of the same degree of remorse as this king beset by so many affairs of state? What, after all, tell me, could be more comely than those eyes rendered so beautiful with the coursing of tears as if with some pearls? You have seen the king giving himself to tears and prayers both by night and by day; see, too, the world's teacher locked in prison and put into the stocks along with Silas, yet praying all night, in no way prevented from so doing either by the pain or by his bonds, but so much the more giving evidence of a more ardent love for God: "Paul and Silas," the text says, remember, "were praising God in the middle of the night."[36] David in his royal estate and kingly mantle spent all his life in tears and prayers; the Apostle, snatched to the third heaven, vouchsafed ineffable mysteries, finding himself in prison offered the Lord prayers and hymns in the middle of the night; the king rose at midnight to sing praise, the apostles offered prayers and hymns in the middle of the night.

(19) Let us too imitate these men, building a wall around our life with the habit of prayer and letting nothing ever prove an obstacle to us. There is, in fact, nothing that can be an obstacle to us provided we are on the alert. Listen, after all, once more to the words of the world's teacher: "In every place raising pure hands in prayer, without anger or conflict."[37] If you keep your mind purified of improper passions, you can, whether you are in the market place, at home, on a journey, appearing in court, at sea, at the hotel or in the workplace—wherever you are, you can call on God and ob-

34. Ps 42.3.   35. Ps 6.6.
36. Acts 16.25.   37. 1 Tim 2.8.

tain your request. Mindful of this, I beseech you, let us give evidence of assiduity in fasting and prayer, and gain for ourselves the assistance this brings, so as to be regaled with favor from God, live out the present life in a manner pleasing to him, and in the life to come be granted some measure of his loving kindness, thanks to the grace and mercy of our Lord Jesus Christ, to whom with the Father and the Holy Spirit be glory, power and honor, now and forever, for ages of ages. Amen.

HOMILY 31

"Tharra took his sons Abram and Nachor, his son Haran's son Lot, and his
daughter-in-law Sarah, his son Abram's wife, and led them from the land
of Chaldea to journey into the land of the Canaanites. He went as far as
Charran and settled there."[1]

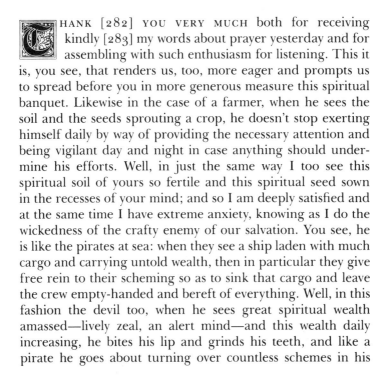HANK [282] YOU VERY MUCH both for receiving
kindly [283] my words about prayer yesterday and for
assembling with such enthusiasm for listening. This it
is, you see, that renders us, too, more eager and prompts us
to spread before you in more generous measure this spiritual
banquet. Likewise in the case of a farmer, when he sees the
soil and the seeds sprouting a crop, he doesn't stop exerting
himself daily by way of providing the necessary attention and
being vigilant day and night in case anything should undermine his efforts. Well, in just the same way I too see this
spiritual soil of yours so fertile and this spiritual seed sown
in the recesses of your mind; and so I am deeply satisfied and
at the same time I have extreme anxiety, knowing as I do the
wickedness of the crafty enemy of our salvation. You see, he
is like the pirates at sea: when they see a ship laden with much
cargo and carrying untold wealth, then in particular they give
free rein to their scheming so as to sink that cargo and leave
the crew empty-handed and bereft of everything. Well, in this
fashion the devil too, when he sees great spiritual wealth
amassed—lively zeal, an alert mind—and this wealth daily
increasing, he bites his lip and grinds his teeth, and like a
pirate he goes about turning over countless schemes in his

1. Gen 11.31 in an expansion of the LXX text, presumably to provide his
audience with some of the details Chrysostom has lost by omitting the genealogy in this ch. 11. Speiser notes (*Genesis*, 79) that this LXX spelling of
the city we know as Haran retains a form older than the Hebrew; the NT
also adopts it (Acts 7.2, 4).

mind so as to discover some slight chink in our armor, render us empty and bereft, and strip us of all our spiritual wealth.

(2) For this reason, pray, let us stay alert, I beseech you, and the more our spiritual resources increase, the more let our spirit of vigilance be intensified; let us strengthen our defences on all sides against his assaults, and through an irreproachable lifestyle let us win favor from God and thus render ourselves superior to the devil's shafts. He is, remember, an evil beast, and has manifold wiles: when he does not succeed in enticing us to wickedness from the outset and ensnaring us through deception (after all, he doesn't apply force or constraint—far from it—but only deception: when he sees us indifferent, he trips us up), when, then, he does not succeed in undermining our salvation in an open way through wickedness itself, frequently through the very works of virtue that we perform he casts his net and unbeknown to us plunders all our wealth. What, then, is it that I am saying? You see, it is necessary to explain it very clearly so that you may be instructed in his schemes and avoid the harm coming from them. When he sees us showing no interest in barefaced wickedness but rather shunning licentiousness and embracing sobriety, and furthermore rejecting greed, showing distaste for injustice, scorning indulgence, and instead devoting ourselves to prayer and fasting and showing zeal for almsgiving, then he devises another scheme by which he can undermine all our resources and render such good deeds fruitless. I mean, those who with great effort survive his wiles he causes to form an inflated opinion of their good deeds and have regard for human glory, his purpose being to make them lose true glory. You see, the person who has some experience of spiritual things and loses sight of them to consider human glory takes his reward from that source already and no longer has God as his debtor; he enjoyed commendation from the people from whom he sought to be praised, and so deprived himself of the rewards promised from the Lord, preferring the passing [284] esteem of his peers to that of the Creator of all.

(3) The Lord himself anticipated this in his teaching on

prayer, almsgiving, and fasting in these words: "When you fast, anoint your head and wash your face in case your fasting becomes obvious to people instead of your Father in secret, and your Father who sees in secret will reward you";[2] and again, "When you give alms, don't blow your own trumpet," he says, "as the hypocrites do in the synagogues and the open streets so as to be praised by people. Truly, I say to you, they already have their reward."[3] Do you see how the person looking for the former reward loses the latter, whereas the one who practices virtue and aims at avoiding people's attention will gain recompense from the Lord publicly on that dread day. "Your Father," the text says, "who sees in secret will reward you publicly." Don't worry, he says, about the fact that not a single human being commended you, and you practiced virtue unnoticed; instead, set your mind on this fact that the Lord's generosity will be so great before long, not in a private fashion nor in secret—rather, he will sing your praises and reward you in the presence of the whole human race from Adam till the end of time, and will bestow on you recompense for your works of virtue. So what degree of excuse would those people deserve who submit to the effort virtue involves, and then for the sake of that passing, vain and futile glory that comes from their peers deprive themselves of esteem from on high?

(4) Let us therefore make ourselves secure, I beseech you, and whatever spiritual deed we have the privilege to perform let us be careful in every way to conceal it completely in the recesses of our mind so that we may win the regard of that unsleeping eye and not render ourselves unworthy of the Lord's esteem for the sake of the esteem of human beings and the flattery often given with favors in view. Both failings, you see, are ruinous and a risk to our salvation—performing spiritual deeds while having an eye to human glory, and nourishing self-importance from whatever good one is able to achieve. Hence it is necessary to be quite alert and to apply to ourselves unremittingly the remedies from Sacred Scrip-

2. Matt 6.17–18.   3. Matt 6.2.

ture so as not to fall foul of these ruinous weaknesses. You
see, even if a person was above reproach in countless ways
and accomplished every virtue, and yet became filled with
self-importance, that person would be the most pitiable and
wretched of all. This was made clear to us in what that well-
known Pharisee went through, flattering himself by comparison with the Publican and frittering away all the wealth of
his virtue through his own words, rendering himself empty-
handed and bereft, and suffering a startling and novel shipwreck: having reached the very port he lost all his precious
cargo.[4] In other words, suffering this misfortune from prayers offered wrongly is like meeting with shipwreck in the
middle of the harbor. For this reason, of course, Christ too
instructed his disciples in these words: "When you have done
everything, say, We are unprofitable servants,"[5] to forewarn
them in his wish that they keep themselves at great distance
from that ruinous passion. See, dearly beloved, how the person with his mouth open for human glory and performing
the works of virtue on that account has no benefit from it
either, and the fact that despite practicing every example of
virtue, if he seems to give himself credit for it, he finishes up
empty-handed and bereft of everything?

(5) So, let us shun all these ruinous weaknesses, I beseech
you; let us concentrate on that unsleeping eye, and neither
have the same values as our peers nor seek after the commendation that comes from them, [285] but rather be content
with the commendation that comes from the Lord. "His
praise is not from human beings but from God,"[6] says Scripture. The more we advance on the way of virtue, the more
we cause ourselves to be temperate and restrained. You see,
even if we advance to the very pinnacle of virtue, we will
(provided we compare this in all gratitude to the kindnesses
coming from the Lord) see clearly that we have contributed
not even the slightest part of the benefits coming to us. Each
of the saints, after all, was conspicuous for this. For proof of

---

4. Cf. Luke 18.9–14.   5. Luke 17.10.
6. Rom 2.29.

it, listen to the world's teacher, that towering spirit, how despite such great achievements, despite such wonderful testimony from above ("This man is a vessel of election as far as I am concerned," Scripture says, remember[7]), he does not lose sight of his own failings but ponders them insistently, and the sins for which he was quite sure he had received forgiveness in baptism he does not even allow himself to forget but cries aloud, "I am the least of all the apostles, I am not worthy to be called an apostle."[8] Then for the purpose of our learning the extraordinary degree of his humility, he added, "for the reason that I persecuted the Church of God."

(6) O Paul, what are you doing? In his characteristic generosity the Lord relented and cancelled all your sins—and are you reviving them? Yes, I know, he says, I am aware of the Lord's forgiveness of me—yet whenever I recall my doings and see the ocean of the Lord's loving kindness, then I realize perfectly that it is due to his grace and loving kindness that I am what I am. After saying, remember, "I am not worthy to be called an apostle for the reason that I persecuted the Church of God," he added, "by the grace of God, however, I am what I am";[9] while I did betray such terrible folly, he says, yet his ineffable goodness and grace granted me forgiveness. Do you see his contrite spirit, constantly recalling the memory of his sins before baptism? Well, let us in our turn imitate this, and our sins after baptism let us remember each day, constantly recall them in our memory and never allow them to recede into oblivion for us. They will prove sufficient restraint, you see, to lead us to reform and self-control. Why do I mention Paul, a man of such quality and calibre? Are you prepared to see also those people in the Old Testament particularly blessed in this regard, showing restraint despite countless deeds of virtue and outspokenness beyond telling? Listen to the words of the patriarch, despite his converse with God, after the promise made to him: "'As for me, however, I am dust and ashes.'"[10]

7. Acts 9.15.   8. I Cor 15.9.
9. I Cor 15.10.   10. Gen 18.27.

(7) Since, however, I have made mention of the patriarch, let us put before your good selves today's reading, if you don't mind, so as to explain it and thus see the extraordinary degree of the good man's virtue. "Tharra," the text says, "took his sons Abram and Nachor, his son's son Lot, and his daughter-in-law Sarah, his son Abram's wife, and led them from the land of Chaldea to journey into the land of the Canaanites. He went as far as Charran and settled there. Tharra lived two hundred and five years in Charran, and died in Charran."[11] Let us attend precisely to the reading, I beseech you, so as to manage to grasp the sense of the writings. Note, in fact, right in the beginning there seems to be a question in the words used; whereas this blessed author—Moses, I mean —says, [286] "Tharra took Abram and Nachor and led them from the land of Chaldea to journey into the land of the Canaanites. He went as far as Charran and settled there," blessed Stephen used the following words in praising the Jews: " 'The God of glory appeared to our father Abraham when he was in Mesopotamia before he settled in Charran . . . and after his father died he led him there to settle.' "[12] So what does that mean? Is Sacred Scripture contradicting itself? Not at all; rather, you need to understand from this that since the son was godfearing, God appeared to him and bade him move there. His father Tharra, though he happened to be a heathen, nevertheless for the affection he had for his son agreed to accompany him in his migration; he went to Charran, settled there and thus ended his life. Then it was that the patriarch moved to Canaan at God's bidding. Of course, God did not transfer him from there until Tharra passed on.

(8) It was then, remember, after the latter's demise, Scripture says, "The Lord said to Abram: 'Go forth from your country, your kindred and your father's house, onwards to a land that I will show you. I will make you into a mighty nation; I will bless you and magnify your name, and you will be blessed. I will bless those who bless you and curse those who

11. Gen 11.31–32, the LXX extending Tharra's lifespan by inserting the former "in Charran" in v. 32.
12. Acts 7.2, 4.

curse you; all the tribes of the earth will be blessed in you.'"[13]
Let us study each of these words precisely so as to see the
godfearing character of the patriarch's attitude. Far from
passing the expression idly by, let us consider how much force
there is in the direction. "'Go forth,'" he says, "'from your
country, your kindred and your father's house, onwards to a
land that I will show you.'" Leave behind you, he is saying,
what is obvious and accepted, and choose rather what is not
clear or apparent. Notice how from the very beginning the
good man was trained to prefer the less obvious to the more
obvious, and future realities to those which are to hand.

(9) It was, in fact, no slight thing that he was ordered to
do—to leave his country where he had lived for so long, all
his kindred and the whole of his father's household, and go
to a place he didn't know and didn't understand. I mean, he
didn't explain what the place he wanted him to migrate to
was like; instead, he put to the test the patriarch's godfearing
spirit with the vagueness of his command: "'Onwards to a
land that I will show you,'" he says. Consider, I ask you,
dearly beloved, how the command required a detached attitude that was not handicapped by any attachment or habit.
If in these days, despite the growth in religion, there are
many people so hidebound by custom that even under pressure of necessity they would times without number opt to
endure everything rather than move from the place where
they first had their home (something you can see not only in
the case of people generally but also in the case of those who
have fled public hubbub and chosen the life of monks), well,
much more at that time was it likely that the good man had
difficulty with the command and found it unpalatable? Go

13. Gen 12.1–3, verses of whose significance Von Rad says: "The transi-
tion from primeval history to sacred history occurs abruptly and surprisingly
in vv. 1–3. All at once and precipitously the universal field of vision narrows;
world and humanity, the entire ecumenical fulness, are submerged, and all
interest is concentrated upon a single man . . . What is promised to Abraham
reaches far beyond Israel; indeed, it has universal meaning for all generations on earth" (*Genesis*, 150). For us it is significant that Chrysostom, with
his more moral and less dogmatic concerns, has taken 31 homilies to exhaust
the primeval history and reach the patriarchal narratives.

forth, he says, leave your kindred and your ancestral home,
"'onwards to a land that I will show you.'" Whom, in fact,
would these words not have disturbed? He reveals to him neither the place nor the country; he just tests the just man's
attitude with his vague command. You see, if anyone else had
been so bidden, anyone of a hundred, he would have said:
All right, you bid me leave the country I'm now living in, my
kindred, my ancestral home. Why don't you make clear to me
[287] the country you order me to travel to, so that I may be
in a position to know how great the distance? How, after all,
tell me, is it going to become clear that that place will be
shown to be better and more prosperous than the one I'm
leaving?

(10) The just man, on the contrary, neither said any of
those things nor contemplated them; instead, with a full realization of the magnitude of the command he preferred
what was unclear to what he was in possession of. If, of
course, he did not have a lofty intention and wise attitude and
had not been schooled in every way to obey God, he would
have found no little further obstacle in the fact of his father's
death. You know, after all, that many people often choose on
account of their families' tombs to die in those same places
where their forebears finished their days. Accordingly, it was
likely that this good man, had he in fact not been extremely
godfearing, would also have reasoned this way: My father left
his home for love of me, ignored longstanding customs,
proved superior to all other claims and came as far as this
place (as if to say, For my sake he finished his days in exile),
so shouldn't I in turn be anxious to pay him the same com-
pliment after his death instead of leaving my father's tomb
with his kindred and going off? Still, none of these considerations proved sufficient to blunt his purpose; rather, his
love of God made everything appear light and easy to him.

(11) Perhaps he could have given thought to this consideration (if, that is, he had wanted to submit his personal interests to human reasoning), namely, how can I make tracks at
my age, hastening as I now am towards the end of my days?
Unaccompanied by my brother, and not having my kindred

with me, but separated from all those who by family ties are
my support, how can I in this desolate and lonely condition
take possession of a foreign place without even knowing
where my wandering will stop? If it should be my misfortune
to lose my life halfway through the journey, what will be the
good of this terrible upheaval? Who will lay out for burial this
old man, this refugee, friendless and homeless? Perhaps my
wife will summon the neighbors to show some compassion
and meet necessary expenses from some voluntary contribu-
tions. Would it not be far preferable for me, with so little time
left to me to live, to end my days remaining here rather than,
in my old age, be dragged hither and yon, the object of everyone's jibes, as though incapable at my advanced age of living
in tranquility instead of shifting from place to place and
never stopping anywhere?

(12) This just man, on the contrary, far from entertaining
any of these thoughts, hastened to obey the command. Perhaps, however, someone would say that these words were sufficient encouragement for him, "'Onwards to the country that
I will show you. I will make you into a mighty nation and I
will bless you.'" Had he not been godfearing, well, this very
remark would have been particularly effective in rendering
him slow to respond; he could have said, had he been like
most people, Why do you guide me to a foreign land and bid
me take possession of someone else's country? If you really
intend to make me great, why on earth not do it to me here?
Why would you not grant me blessing while living in my ancestral home? If it should be my misfortune, before the destination you intend, that I perish from being overcome by the
effort of the journey and end my days, what good comes to
me from your promises?

(13) He was loath, however, to give thought to any of these
notions; instead, he was like a loyal servant in having ears
only for the command. He obeyed it without any meddlesome
curiosity and was in fact perfectly assured [288] that God's
promises were unfailing: "'I will make you a great nation; I
will bless you and magnify your name, and you will be
blessed.'" The scope of the promise is extraordinary: "'I will

make you a great nation; I will bless you and magnify your name.'" Not only will I place you at the head of a great nation and cause your name to be great, but as well, "'I will bless you and you will be blessed.'" I will favor you with so much blessing, he says, that it will last for all time. "'You will be blessed'" to such an extent that everyone will be anxious to thrust themselves into your company in preference to the highest honor. See how God right from the very beginning foretold to him the notoriety he would later confer upon him. "'I will make you a great nation;'" he said, "'I will magnify your name, I will bless you and you will be blessed.'" Hence the Jews too found in the patriarch grounds for self-importance and endeavored to establish their kinship with him in the words, "'We are children of Abraham.'"[14] For you to learn, however, that on the basis of their evil ways they are in fact unworthy of such kinship, Christ said to them, "'If you were children of Abraham, you would do the works of Abraham.'"[15] John, too, son of Zechariah, when those anxious to be baptized flocked to the Jordan, said to them, "'Brood of vipers, who warned you to flee from the wrath to come? Bear fruit that benefits repentance, and don't presume to say, We have Abraham for our father. I tell you, after all, that God can raise up children to Abraham even from these stones.'"[16] Do you see how great his name was in everyone's estimation? For the time being, however, before the sequel the just man's godfearing qualities are demonstrated in the way he believed the words coming from God and accepted without demur everything, difficult though it seemed.

(14) "'I will bless those who bless you,'" he said, "'and curse those who curse you; all the tribes of the earth will be blessed in you.'" See God's considerateness in giving him an index of such great love: I will consider as friends those friendly to you, and as enemies those showing enmity to you—something even children hardly manage to achieve in regard to their parents, treating as friends and enemies the

14. Cf. John 8.33.   15. John 8.39.
16. Matt 3.7–9.

same people as they do. Marvelous, therefore, dearly beloved, is God's favor for the patriarch; I will bless those who bless you, he says, and curse those who curse you. "'All the tribes of the earth will be blessed in you.'" Notice the addition of still further liberality: all the tribes of the earth, he says, will be anxious to be blessed in your name, and on the basis of your title will rank their own status more elevated.

(15) Do you hear, dearly beloved, the command the Lord gave to this Chaldean, this old man, ignorant as he was of Law, unacquainted with Prophets and beneficiary of no other teaching?[17] Do you see the scope of the commands? How he stood in need of a sublime and youthful spirit to perform them? Now consider the patriarch's rightmindedness in the way Scripture [289] makes it clear to us: "Abram set out as the Lord God had told him, and Lot traveled with him."[18] It did not simply say, "Abram set out," but "as the Lord God had told him." He did everything, it says, in accordance with the command. God told him to leave everything, kindred and house together, and he left them; he told him to go to a land he did not know, and he agreed; he promised to make him into a mighty nation and to bless him, and he believed that this too would happen. As the Lord God had told him, so he set out—that is to say, he believed the words coming from God, with no hesitation or uncertainty, but rather with mind and purpose firmly decided he set out; hence he enjoyed great favor from the Lord.

(16) "Lot traveled with him," the text adds. Although God had said, "'Go forth from your country, your kindred and your father's house,'" why did he bring Lot with him? It was not that he was disobedient to the Lord; but perhaps because Lot was young and Abram held the place of a father in his regard, and because he was reluctant on the grounds of love and equity to be separated from the good man, Abram could not bear to leave him behind out of this sense of responsibility. From now on Lot took the place of a son to him, since at

17. Whether or not Chrysostom is referring to the threefold division of the Hebrew Bible, there seems some little prolepsis on his part here.
18. Gen 12.4.

his advanced age he was without children owing to Sarah's infertility. In particular the youngster's values were quite in keeping with the just man's: does this not emerge from the fact that, in associating himself with the just man when he had the choice of the two brothers, he showed great insight in making the wise decision as to which of his uncles it would be to whom he should entrust his fortunes? Likewise his choice of exile was itself further proof of the nobility of his values; even if eventually he seemed to fail in some matters when he appropriated the prime lands,[19] nevertheless he lost no time in following the good man's footsteps. Hence the good man took him as companion in his travels, and Lot enthusiastically preferred exile to life at home.

(17) Then, for us to know that it was to no youngster that the Lord's commands to the patriarch were addressed but to someone already pressing old age, a stage when most people are inclined to be reluctant about traveling, Scripture adds, "Now, Abram was seventy-five years old when he left Charran." Do you see how, far from age or anything else capable of winning him over to remaining at home proving a deterrent for him, his love for God proved superior to everything. You see, whenever a soul is alert and vigilant, it cuts through all obstacles and becomes completely the possession of the loved one; it is not upset by any apparent difficulties in its path, but passes them all by, not stopping until it gains the object of its feverish search. For this reason, too, of course, this just man, though vulnerable to impediment from old age and many other factors, broke through all restraints like a young man in his prime, impatient of any obstacle, and thus pressed on in haste to implement the Lord's command. No other way is open to you to implement your plan, after all, if you really want to give evidence of some deed of manly valor, than to make a direct assault initially on everything likely to offer you resistance in such a project. Such, in fact, this good man realized clearly, and he gave every impediment the slip, entertaining no thought of custom, kindred, ancestral home,

19. Cf. Gen 13.11.

burial grounds or even old age, concentrating on one thing alone—how to succeed in fulfilling what was commanded by the Lord. There was scope for recognizing in the exploit plenty of grounds for alarm, a man of advanced age going into exile with his wife, [290] herself by now well on in years, and a pack of servants, not knowing where his journeyings would finish up. Still, if anyone cautiously entertained thoughts like that, what extreme difficulties there were in the journey in those times: it wasn't possible, as it is today, to mingle with people without apprehension and so to engage in travel lightly, since every place had a government different from the next and there were difficulties for people traveling from one lot of rulers to the next, as you passed from kingdom to kingdom almost as each day passed.

(18) So this would have been sufficient obstacle for the good man, too, if he had in fact not had great love and obedience of the command. But as it was, he broke through all these impediments like a spider's web: his faith stiffening his resolve, and with reliance on the trustworthiness of the guarantor, he took to the road. "Abram," the text goes on, "took his wife Sarah, his brother's son Lot, and all the possessions they had acquired in Charran, and set out to travel to the land of Canaan."[20] See the precision of Scripture in the way it recounts everything to us so that we may learn through every detail the good man's godfearing qualities: "He took his wife Sarah," the text says, "his brother's son Lot, and everything they had acquired in Charran." It was not without purpose that it said, "everything they had acquired in Charran"; rather, it was for us to learn that the patriarch carried nothing with him from the Chaldeans, but bequeathed all those legacies to his brother and left in the condition of carrying only the things he had been able to acquire in Charran. Now, the remarkable man did this, not to show the esteem he had for those latter possessions, nor because he happened to resemble a miser, but for the purpose of being able to show

20. Gen 12.5. Chrysostom omits the mention given by the Hebrew and LXX among the list of Abram's possessions of the people (*psyche*) they had also acquired.

everyone through his prosperity God's provident care for
him: the one who uprooted him from the land of the Chaldeans and in turn bade him move his dwelling from there
was the same who day by day increased his prosperity and
removed every problem, with the result that this itself proved
to be an index of his godfearing attitude—that he traveled
along that route carrying such things with him. Each single
onlooker, you see, very likely wanted to find out the reason
for the just man's departure. Then, being told that he was
going into foreign parts at God's bidding and had left behind
his own property, they learnt the truth of it from the events
themselves and came to know the godfearing qualities of the
just man's obedience as well as the extraordinary degree of
God's provident care for him.

(19) "He set out," the text says, "to travel to the land of
Canaan." How did he come to know that the destination of
his traveling would be the land of the Canaanites whereas
the effect of the command was, "'Onwards to the land I will
show you'"?[21] Perhaps God revealed this as well to him by
bringing into his mind an image of the land he wanted him
to move to. In other words, his reason for speaking vaguely
in giving him the order, "'Onwards to the land I will show
you,'" was to reveal to us the just man's virtue. Then, after
he had expended his own resources with great generosity,
God in his turn communicated to him knowledge of the land
where he wanted him to settle. You see, since he foresaw the
extent of the just man's virtue, consequently he uprooted him
from his home, bidding him take not even his own brother,
because he wanted Abram to become instructor at that time
to everyone in Palestine and shortly after to those in Egypt.
Do you see how the roots of virtue and the roots of evil are
not to be found in nature but in the disposition of the will?
See, after all, these two, the patriarch and Nachor, [291] were
in fact brothers in the order of nature, whereas they were not

21. Chrysostom with his characteristic 'precision' detects the inconsistency
and does not 'pass it idly by'; his solution, of course, cannot invoke the find-
ings of modern criticism as to the presence of various editorial hands at this
point.

so by disposition: although the latter rivaled his brother in virtue, yet he had been ensnared in error ahead of time, whereas Abram demonstrated daily to everyone through his own behavior his progress in virtue under God's help.

(20) "Abram reached the land of Canaan, and traveled through the length and breadth of the land as far as the place of Suchem by the lofty oak."[22] Scripture informs us of the part of the country where the good man now settles. Then, for us to learn what conditions were like there, it adds, "Now, the Canaanites inhabited the land at that time." It was not without purpose that blessed Moses communicated this further fact; instead, it was for us to learn in this case, too, the patriarch's wise attitude in that, as these places had already been overcome by the Canaanites, he was forced to reside wherever luck would have it, in the manner of a nomad and refugee, like some despicable outcast. Yet he made no difficulty of this condition nor said, Why should this be? I passed my days in Charran in such esteem and attention—and now I'm obliged to go about on sufferance like an exile, a refugee, a stranger, and look for repose in a wretched hovel; and far from being able to find it there, I am obliged to pass my time in tents and shacks, and put up with all other kinds of hardships. Is this all God meant when he said, "'Onwards, and I will make you into a great nation'"? It's a promising beginning for me, to be sure; what improvement is there to look forward to? This, however, wasn't the way the just man presumed to express himself or consider changing his mind; on the contrary, with mind quite made up and unshakable faith he trusted in God's promises and constantly maintained an unflinching resolve—hence he was in turn promptly rewarded with encouragement from on high.

(21) But in case we protract the instruction to great length, let us stop at this point and conclude the sermon, leaving the recommendation with your good selves—to imitate this just man's attitude. Observe the comparison: this just man, despite its being a most unlikely invitation, was asked to leave

22. Gen 12.5b–6.

one country for another and displayed such obedience, without age proving an obstacle or any of the other factors we
have enumerated, and without his being made slow to obey
by the inconvenience of the time or any other thing capable
of discouraging him, and on the contrary the old man broke
through all hindrances and sped off in haste like a sprightly
youth, in the company of his wife, his brother and his retinue,
to give effect to the command issued by God. We, on the
other hand, are not called to leave one country for another,
but to leave earth for heaven; we don't display the same enthusiasm about obeying, but rather propose in many cases
trifling and pointless excuses, nothing being sufficient to win
us over—neither the magnitude of the promises, nor the vile-
ness of visible realities in being earthly and passing, nor the
dignity of him who invites us. Instead, we give evidence of
such indifference as to prefer these passing realities to those
that last forever, earth to heaven, and things that fade even
before being espied to those that can never come to an end.
To what extreme, after all, tell me, would our folly reach in
amassing these possessions? What madness is this, to be beset
each day by pressing desire without at any time having one's
fill but rather being in worse condition than drunken sots? I
mean, just as they burn the more [292] with thirst the more
deeply they drink their wine, and kindle a harsher flame, so
too do these people fail to check their desire by surrendering
themselves to the tyranny of the desire for possessions, but
rather the flame is fanned more ardently and the furnace
kindled more savagely, the more possessions they acquire.

(22) Don't we see that our predecessors, despite their gaining possession of the whole world, so to speak, were snatched
from it naked and bereft after gaining this solitary legacy;
that an account was demanded of them for their guilt and
responsibility for everything? While essential differences were
frequently distinguishable, each person nevertheless took his
leave burdened with the sins of all, carrying punishment for
them along with deep wrath, and unable to find any consolation from any quarter. Why, then, tell me, are we so careless
in regard to our own salvation and have as little interest in

our own soul as if it were someone else's? Don't you listen to Christ's words, "What will a person give in exchange for his soul?" and again, "What good will it be for a person if he gains the whole world but suffers the loss of his soul?"[23] After all, surely you have nothing equal in value to it. Even if you mention the whole world, you'll be saying nothing. What good is it, as Christ said, to gain the whole world and yet suffer the loss of our souls, which is more part of us than anything else? This soul of ours, therefore, which is so important, which requires us to be so caring in its regard—why do we neglect it to such an extent that it is daily torn asunder, sometimes beset with our desire for material possessions, sometimes cut to pieces with licentiousness, at other times put to shame with anger, and tortured in divers fashion with every single passion, and why do we never or only at the last moment show it any consideration? Who would any longer judge us worthy of excuse or acquit us of imminent punishment?

(23) For this reason, I beseech you, while we still have time, let us cleanse the soul's filth with generous almsgiving, and by this means quench the fire of our sins. Scripture says, remember, "Water will extinguish a blazing fire, and sins are purged away by alms."[24] Nothing, in fact, nothing else will be so successful in snatching us from the fire of hell as generosity in this. If we give evidence of it in accord with the laws given us by him, without doing anything for effect but rather out of love for God, we will be able both to wash away the filth of our sins and also win loving kindness from God, thanks to the grace and mercy of his only-begotten Son, to whom with the Father and the Holy Spirit be glory, power and honor, now and forever, for ages of ages. Amen.

23. Matt 16.26.   24. Sir 3.30.

HOMILY 32

"And the Lord appeared to Abram and said to him, 'I will give this land to your descendants.' He built an altar on the spot to commemorate the Lord's appearance to him."[1]

REAT [292] AND BEYOND ALL TELLING, dearly beloved, is the treasure in the words read just now, and deserving of heightened attention and a mind active and alert so that we may pass over nothing of the riches hidden in these brief phrases. You see, the reason that the loving God did not allow all the contents of the Scriptures to yield themselves spontaneously clear and obvious at first glance with scant reading was that he might disturb our sloth and we might show signs of alertness [293] and thus reap the benefit of them. It normally happens, after all, that matters discovered with effort and research are riveted more firmly in our minds, whereas what is discovered with ease soon flies away from our heart. So, far from showing indifference, I beseech you, let us stir up our thinking and make a thorough and in-depth study of the writings so as to be in a position to gain some greater benefit from them and thus go off home.

(2) The Church of God, in fact, is a spiritual market and a surgery for souls, and, like people going to market, we ought acquire an abundance of good things from here and go home the better for it, and like patients at a surgery we ought receive various remedies for the passions afflicting us and go off. I mean, our purpose in assembling each day is not simply to gossip inconsequentially with one another and then all part; rather, it is for each of us to learn something worthwhile, get healing for our troublesome ailments and take our leave in that condition. After all, how would it not be utterly

1. Gen 12.7.

254

absurd for us to send our children to school, expecting of them day after day some advantage from their lessons, and never to regret their going there idly and to no purpose if we do not see them making some improvement—whereas, on the other hand, we at our mature age attend this spiritual school without giving evidence of an eagerness equal to theirs, even though the lessons here redound to our good as far as the salvation of our souls is concerned? So let each of us, I beseech you, examine his conscience daily as to the advantage derived from this day's sermon, and the next day's, and so on, lest we too seem to be attending here idly and to no purpose.

(3) Now, for the fact that this discharges me of all responsibility (after all, I bring all my resources to the task and leave nothing undone as far as in me lies) whereas it proves to be the basis of greater condemnation for those who come in ill-humor or attend without care or have no wish to make an improvement, listen to the words of Christ to the man who buried the talent: "Wicked servant, you ought to have lodged my money with the bankers and at my coming I could have expected it with interest,"[2] whereas about the Jews, "If I had not come and spoken to them, they would have no sin—but as it is they don't have any excuse."[3] In the present case, however, our concern is not whether we are free of blame; instead, we are anxious for your advancement, and we consider our contentment spoilt, even if we are guiltless on countless scores, if you in your turn do not give evidence of an enthusiasm commensurate with our efforts. This, after all, is the basis of our contentment, seeing your growth in spirituality. I know, of course, that by God's grace you are filled with understanding and can admonish others; in keeping with Paul's advice,[4] however, I serve you with fresh reminders, stir up your zeal and enthusiasm and ceaselessly supply you with this encouragement in the wish that you become mature and fully developed. After all, I consider it no little demonstration

2. Matt 25.26–27.   3. John 15.22.
4. Chrysostom probably has in mind passages in Paul such as Rom 15.15; Col 4.12; 1 Cor 14.20.

of your advance in God's eyes to attend here daily with such great eagerness and have an insatiable appetite for spiritual teaching. You see, just as appetite for bodily nourishment would be an index of perfect health, so desire for spiritual teaching is a quite unmistakable proof of health in terms of the soul. Hence, of course, knowing as I also do of your love and the fact that, even should I prolong the instruction a thousand times, I would be unable to match your [294] enthusiasm and bring you a surfeit of this spiritual nourishment, I will as far as in me lies not cease providing you daily for your good with whatever God's grace supplies and fixing in your mind the teachings of the holy Scriptures.

(4) So, come now, today too let us entreat the loving Lord to direct our tongue in discovery of what we seek, and let us lay before you the customary instruction by proposing to your good selves those very words previously read out. "The Lord God appeared to Abram," the text says, "and said to him." Wasn't I right in saying at the outset that a great treasure is contained in these brief words? I mean, notice at once the strange and unusual opening of the expression: "The Lord God appeared to Abram," it says. This is the first time we find this stated in Scripture, "he appeared." Neither in the case of Adam, nor Abel, nor Noe, nor anyone else did Sacred Scripture employ this expression. So why is the expression, "he appeared," used? And how is it that elsewhere Scripture says, "No one will see God and live"?[5] How, then, would we interpret the words of Scripture, "He appeared"? How did he appear to the just man? Surely he didn't see his true being? No—God forbid. What, then? He was seen in the way he alone knows and in the manner possible for Abram to see. In his inventiveness, you see, our wise and loving Lord, showing considerateness for our human nature, reveals himself to those who worthily prepare themselves in advance. He explains this through the sacred author in the words, "I gave many visions and took shape in the works of the inspired

___

5. Cf. Exod 33.20. Chrysostom illustrates in this passage the Antiochene process of wrestling with each item of the text.

authors."[6] Isaiah in his turn saw him seated, something that is inapplicable to God, since he doesn't sit down—how could he, after all, with his unique nature being incorporeal and indefectible? Daniel too saw him, as the Ancient of Days;[7] Zechariah had a different vision of him,[8] and Ezekiel in turn a different one.[9] This is the reason, therefore, that he said, "I gave many visions," that is, I appeared in a way suited to each one.

(5) So in the present case, after he uprooted the just man from his home and bade him go into a foreign country where he arrived and roamed around in the manner of a nomad and a stranger, since the Canaanites still occupied the land, and was looking around to see where he should take up his abode, the good Lord wished to console him and strengthen his resolve lest he lose enthusiasm and doubt the promise already made to him, "'Go forward, and I will make you into a great nation.'" The good man, after all, had before his eyes happenings that were contrary to promise, and himself amongst the most contemptible and abject of men, a forlorn survivor, without means of finding a haven. So to stimulate his resolve, "The Lord appeared to Abram," it says, "and said to him, 'I will give this land to your descendants.'" You see, although the just man, who was in fact in his old age, had no children on account of Sarah's sterility, he promises to endow the child born to him with the land. Consider, I ask you, God's loving kindness, how in his foreknowledge of the just man's virtue he wants to bring him to the notice of everyone and, like some hidden pearl, make him conspicuous in this way. In heaping promises on promises and making these wonderful offers he postpones their fulfilment somewhat so that the patriarch's godfearing qualities may be demonstrated [295] by the fact of his seeing things turning out contrary to promise for the time being without the blessed man's being alarmed or dis-

6. Hos 12.10, a key text for Chrysostom's theology of the incarnation of the Word in Scripture.

7. Dan 7.22.   8. Zec 1.

9. Ezek 1ff. See Introduction (18) in FOTC 74 for comment on Chrysostom's expectations of his congregation's familiarity with the Bible.

258 ST. JOHN CHRYSOSTOM

turbed, but rather keeping his resolve undeterred in his belief that without doubt what was once promised him by God
was in fact firm and secure. Let us, however, scrutinize everything in detail so that in this way we may learn both the good
God's inventive wisdom and the care he showed in regard to
the just man, as well as the patriarch's love for the Lord. "The
Lord God appeared to Abram," the text says. How did he
appear? In the way God alone knows, and in the way it was
possible for Abram to see him. You see, I don't cease saying
this, ignorant as I am of the way it happened; I am content
to listen to the words of Scripture, "The Lord God appeared
to Abram, and said to him, 'I will give this land to your descendants.'"

(6) Keep precisely in mind the promises made by God, so
that when you see the just man beset by various circumstances, you may discover the extraordinary degree of his
good sense, the fibre of his courage, and the firm and stable
quality of his love for God, and that you may learn the lesson
from what happened to this just man never to regard it as a
case of abandonment by God when you see someone beset by
trials from the ungodly or other tribulations of this life. Instead, have a mind to the diversity of God's designs and leave
all to his unsearchable providence. After all, he allows this
good man, as godfearing as he was and so exemplary for his
great obedience, to suffer so many trials which you are pres-
ently quite well aware of, not out of disregard for his servant
but in his desire to reveal his virtue to everyone else. It is, in
fact, customary with him to do this to each of the just ones:
as many of you as are familiar with the reading of the holy
Scriptures will be in a position to discover the truth right
from the beginning and find God disposing of the life of his
servants in this way. So how would it not be a mark of extreme ingratitude to consider this concession by God a case
of abandonment and not to regard it as an extraordinary sign
of great care and ineffable love? Accordingly, to show the excess of his power he realizes these two objects from this incident: he renders obvious to everyone his servant's endurance
and courage as well as the inventiveness of his providence

even amidst inauspicious circumstances, and after success had almost been despaired of he directs affairs as he wishes without being impeded by difficulties occurring in the process. "The Lord God appeared to Abram," the text says, "and said to him, 'I will give this land to your descendants.'" A wonderful promise, particularly welcome to the just man: you appreciate how people who reach old age, especially if they have passed their whole life childless, long for children. So the Lord God gave him this reward for his obedience in heeding the words, "'Leave your country,'" without delaying or postponing but responding to the command and putting into effect what had been ordered—hence he says, "'I will give this land to your descendants.'"

(7) Consider how through this statement he stirred Abram's thinking and supplied him with a recompense that matched his difficulties. This was the reason, of course, that the good man demonstrated his personal gratitude by immediately taking steps to offer thanksgiving. "He built an altar on the spot to commemorate the Lord's appearance to him," the text says. See the indication of his godfearing attitude: the very spot where he had been accorded converse with God he consecrated [296] and gave evidence of thanksgiving as far as he could. This, in fact, is the meaning of the phrase, "He built an altar"—that is, he gave thanks for the promises made to him. Just as people under the influence of affection often build homes whenever they happen to meet people kindly disposed to them, and many have even founded cities and named them after their association with kindred spirits, well, in just the same way this just man, on the spot where he had been accorded a vision of God, "built an altar to commemorate the Lord's appearance to him, and moved on from there," the text says. What is the meaning of "moved on from there"? That after consecrating the place at that stage and dedicating it to God, he departed from there and transferred to another place, the text says, "to the mountain east of Bethel and pitched his tent there"[10]—in other words, it says, he

10. Gen 12.8.

erected a temporary dwelling. See how frugal he was, how unencumbered, to move in this way without difficulty, accompanied by both wife and household. Let men heed this, let women heed it; often when we have occasion to go into the open country, we think of countless pieces of equipment and get involved in many and varied tasks for the sake of bringing along many things that, far from being of any use, are pointless and idle, and we bring with us and encumber ourselves with things that are the object of our attention merely for show.

(8) Not so this just man, however. Instead, what? After being accorded converse with God, he consecrated the place and built an altar; then he moved elsewhere with complete ease. "He pitched his tent there, with Bethel to the west and Aggai to the east; there he built an altar to the Lord and called on the name of the Lord." See how in every way he displays his own godfearing attitude: he built the altar there on account of the promise made him by God, consecrated the place and moved on; but there in turn, after pitching his tent, "he built an altar to the Lord and called on the name of the Lord." Do you see his reasonable attitude? do you recognize the advice given in his letters by the world's remarkable teacher, blessed Paul, in the words, "In every place raising your hands in prayer,"[11] being put into practice by the patriarch ahead of time in building an altar in every place and offering thanksgiving to the Lord? He knew, you see, he knew well that the God of all looks for nothing more from the human race, despite his countless kindnesses beyond all telling, than a grateful attitude and knowing how to render thanks for his favors.

(9) Let us see once more, however, how in this case the just man moves on. "Abram moved on and traveled until he pitched camp in the desert."[12] Notice once again his godfearing attitude and his great wisdom. Once again, the text says, he left there and "pitched camp in the desert." Why did he move on from there? Perhaps because he could see some of

11. 1 Tim 2.8.   12. Gen 12.9.

the inhabitants were not pleased with his being there. Hence, of course, he showed the extraordinary degree of his tolerance and the way he set great store by peace and treated no one shabbily by choosing the desert as his territory. "He traveled," the text says, "until he pitched camp in the desert." That is a strange expression for Sacred Scripture to use: as it is normal to use the expression in the case of war, so too in the present case it is said of [297] the just man that he pitched camp so as to show the patriarch's unencumbered condition; since, just as soldiers with ease pitch camp now in one place, now in another, so too this just man, though accompanied by his wife, his nephew and such a large household, made these transfers with greater ease. Do you see his unencumbered life in his old age accompanied by wife and household? Yet what particularly strikes me with admiration is the fortitude of his wife: when I consider the frailty of womankind, and ponder how she made those transfers with ease in the company of the just man, not grumbling about it herself nor proving an obstacle to the just man, I reckon that she was endowed no less than the just man with a courageous and highly motivated intention. We will grasp this in particular as we move on to what follows in the reading.

(10) Did you notice how after hearing, "'I will give this land to your descendants,'" the just man, far from settling down, moved from one place to another, and, in turn, from there to still another place? See him driven also from the desert, however, not by men but by the pressure of famine: "There was a famine in the land."[13] Let this be heeded by those people who speak idly and unguardedly, playing the soothsayer and maintaining that when so-and-so arrived, famine struck, and when so-and-so left, it stopped. See, there was a famine on the arrival of the just man, a severe famine, though the just man did not panic nor suffer any human reaction nor attribute responsibility for the famine to his own arrival. But when he saw nature under constraint and famine in control, "Abram went down into Egypt," the text says, "to sojourn

13. Gen 12.10.

there, because famine raged in the land." Consider how progress was proving more gradual for the just man; the Lord
was providing that he should be teacher not only for the inhabitants of Palestine but also for those in Egypt, and that he
should make the light of his own virtue conspicuous to everyone. You see, since he was like a hidden lantern concealed in
the land of the Chaldeans, God shifted him from there so
that he might conduct those seated in the darkness of error
towards the way of truth. Perhaps, however, someone may say,
Why didn't he arrange for those in the land of the Chaldeans
to be brought through him to religion? While it is likely that
his providence was exercised through other channels for their
salvation as well, yet listen to the words of Christ, "No
prophet is without honor except in his own country."[14] So to
give effect to his own promise made in the words, " 'I will
magnify your name,' " he allows famine to occur for that purpose, and in this way necessity to bring him to Egypt, so that
people there also may learn how great is the man's virtue. In
other words, famine, like a jailer brandishing bonds, uprooted them from the desert and drove them into Egypt.

(11) But let us now see the sequel and the extent of the
problem the just man was embroiled in, so that we may discover his courage and his wife's good sense. You see, when
they had covered a large part of their journey and then found
themselves close to Egypt, the good man became anxious and
spoke to his wife in fear and trembling for his very life, as
you might say. "When Abram was on the point of entering
Egypt," the text goes on, "he said to his wife Sarah: 'I'm
aware that you are a very beautiful woman. So it will happen
that, when the Egyptians see you, [298] they will say, She is
his wife, and they will kill me, but spare your life. Consequently say, I am his sister, so that things may go well for me
on your account, and my life will be spared thanks to you.' "[15]
Do you see from these words the extent of the alarm and
dread into which the good man fell, without at all losing his
clarity of thought, or having panic spread to his frame of

14. Matt 13.57.   15. Gen 12.11–13.

mind, or giving voice to such thoughts as, What's happening? We're not abandoned, are we? Surely we're not deceived? The Lord hasn't deprived us of his providential care, has he? Would the one who said, " 'I will magnify you, and will give this land to your descendants,' " leave us at this stage like this, to fear the worst and fall into flagrant risk to life?

(12) No such thoughts did the just man entertain; instead, his one concern was how to manage to devise some stratagem to find a solution to the famine and escape the hands of the Egyptians. " 'I'm aware,' " the text reads, " 'that you are a very beautiful woman.' " See how great was the woman's beauty, even though they had then reached old age, how she was still blooming despite her great age, and bore the flush of beauty on her face despite such awful trouble and misfortune endured on the way in moving from place to place, shifting from the lands of the Chaldeans to Charran, from there to Canaan, and from there in turn to Chananea, and so from there and finally to Egypt. So what man, even the most sprightly, would not have been devastated by these unending movements? Yet this remarkable woman, with the splendor of her beauty still upon her despite such wear-and-tear, instilled into her husband an extremely severe alarm—hence his words, " 'I'm aware that you are a very beautiful woman. So it will happen that, when the Egyptians see you, they will say, She is his wife, and they will kill me, but spare your life.' " Consider how he trusted in his wife's behavior, and wasn't afraid she would ever become conceited because of their compliments; rather, he offered her further persuasion in these terms: " 'Lest they kill me while sparing your life, consequently say, I am his sister, so that things may go well for me, and my life will be spared thanks to you.' " Since it was no ordinary thing he was requiring of her, he meant to win her over with the explanation he supplied by inclining her to compassion and persuading her to play her part convincingly. " 'So it will happen,' " he said, " 'that, when the Egyptians see you, they will say, She is his wife, and they will kill me, but spare your life.' " He didn't say, They will abuse you; at that stage he didn't want to frighten her with his remarks, espe-

cially as he had qualms about God's promise. Hence he said, "'They will spare your life. Consequently say, I am his sister.'"

(13) Consider, I ask you, the extent of the panic the just man's mind had probably fallen into when he urged this course on his wife. I mean, you know perfectly well how there is nothing more depressing for husbands than having their wives fall under suspicion of this kind. Yet the good man shows all anxiety and takes every step to ensure the adultery is put into effect.[16] Don't, however, dearly beloved, rashly condemn the good man; rather, gain from this a particular insight into his great sagacity and courage—yes, his courage in nobly withstanding and overcoming turmoil of mind to the extent of planning such stratagems. For proof, after all, that nothing is more difficult to bear than this, listen to the words of Solomon: "A man's jealousy is intermingled with rage: he will have no mercy on the day of vengeance, nor will his enmity be sated in return for many gifts";[17] and again, "Jealousy is harsh as Hell."[18] Let us, however, notice many people falling into such madness that they did not even spare their own wives, but as well oftentimes caused the death of both the adulterer and themselves. [299] So extreme is the fury of this behavior and so unrestrained is jealousy as to cause the person once snared in this passion to be oblivious even of his own salvation. On the one hand, it is possible to recognize in this incident the just man's courage and, on the other hand, his keen sagacity in being able, despite finding himself in such an awful predicament as though snared in nets, to find this way by which the evil might be made less severe. You see, if he had said that she was his wife and had not enacted that artifice by employing the name 'sister', she would have been wrested from the just man once the beauty of her appearance seduced the Egyptians' lecherous mind, and the good man

16. Chrysostom has none of the unease about accepting the obvious interpretation of Abram's action shown by some modern commentators like Speiser (but not Von Rad)—though, as usual, he is not above a little rationalizing as well.

17. Prov 6.34–35 in Chrysostom's abbreviated text.

18. Song 8.6.

would have been killed so as not to remain as witness of the
crime. So since these two unfortunate events were ineluctably
due to occur owing to men's incontinence and the king's tyranny, Abram said, for the purpose of their being able to find
some small consolation amidst utter helplessness, "'Say, I am
his sister;'" this may rescue me from danger. After all, as far
as I am concerned, whether you say you are my sister or my
wife, there will be no preventing the ineluctable conclusion
that they will proceed to your abduction on account of your
beauty of form, whereas there is a chance for me to escape
their designs if you employ the name 'sister'. Do you see the
just man's sagacity, how despite being in their clutches he
could still find some way to plan how he might manage to
prove superior to the Egyptians' plot?

(14) Furthermore, conclude from this, I ask you, both the
just man's endurance and his wife's goodness. His endurance,
on the one hand, in not losing his temper and saying, Why
do I bring her with me, proving as she is the cause of such
disaster for me? What advantage, after all, is there for me in
the relationship, now that I am on the point of risking everything for her sake? What good is it to me when she not only
brings me no comfort but is even the cause of death itself to
me through her very beauty? He neither said nor thought
any such thing; instead, he rejected any such thought and
doubted in no way God's promise, concerning himself with
one thing only—how to succeed in escaping the foreseen danger. Consider in this case, I ask you, dearly beloved, God's
ineffable longsuffering, how in no way did he assist or console
the just man, but rather allowed his trouble to come to a head
and increase, and permitted him to come to the end of his
tether, at which point he displayed his characteristic providence. "'Consequently say,'" Abram said, "'I am his sister,
that things may go well for me on your account, and my life
will be spared thanks to you.'" This is what the good man
had said—not the mark of a person about to breathe his last
(Scripture says, after all, "Don't fear those who destroy the
body but are unable to destroy the soul"[19]); rather, his re-

19. Matt 10.28.

marks on this occasion to his wife were according to habit. "'So that things may go well for me on your account,'" he said, "'and my life will be spared thanks to you'"—as if to say to her, Say, I am his sister, in case you cause my flight from famine in Canaan to lead me into the clutches of the Egyptians. So prove to be the cause of my salvation, "'so that things may go well for me on your account.'" Piteous words: great was his fear on account of Egyptian passion and also because of the fact that the tyranny of death had been let loose. Hence the good man chose even to be an accomplice in his wife's adultery, as if playing the role of adulterer in his wife's shame, so as to avoid death. Its face, you see, was fearsome: its brazen gates had not yet been broken, its edge had not yet been blunted.

(15) Do you see the bond of love between husband and wife? Do you see [300] what trust the husband had in imposing to such an extent on his wife, and the degree of cooperation he received from his wife? She neither demurred nor complained; instead, she did everything to carry off the deception. Let husbands and wives take note and imitate their harmony, the bond of their love, the depth of their devotion, and let them emulate Sarah's self-control. Because, despite her old age, she not only remained so conspicuous for beauty but also rivaled the just man's virtues, she was consequently rewarded with so much providential care from God and with reward from on high. Accordingly, let no one point the finger at a beautiful appearance nor make those brainless remarks, Beauty ruined such-and-such a woman, beauty proved the cause of so-and-so's disaster. Beauty wasn't the cause—far from it—it is a work of God; rather, depraved will is the cause of every evil. Do you see this remarkable woman dazzling in every respect, with beauty of soul and beauty of feature both, following in the good man's footsteps? Let women imitate her: lo, despite everything—elegant appearance, sterility, advanced age, a condition of prosperity, so much shifting and traveling, constant problems coming in rapid succession—nothing unhinged her thinking; instead, she remained on an even keel. For this reason, of course, she won reward worthy

of her endurance, to succeed in her extreme old age in bearing a child in her infertile womb and elderly frame.

(16) "'So that things may go well with me on your account,'" Abram said, "'and my life will be spared thanks to you.'" There is no recourse left me for survival, he is saying, other than your being prepared to say, "'I am his sister.'" In other words, perhaps I will escape the threatening danger, and thanks to you I will now stay alive and attribute to you my life henceforth. His words were sufficient to win his wife over and engage her compassion. This really is wedlock, being associated not only in fair times but also in risky situations; this is a sign of true love, this is a hallmark of really genuine affection. A gleaming diadem atop the head does not so well betoken the king as this blessed woman's splendid example was revealed in her very responsiveness which she showed in regard to her husband's proposal. So who would not be amazed at the thought of her utter acceptance? Who could adequately extol her for her readiness, despite her remarkable continence and at this advanced age, to expose herself to adultery and accept intercourse with a barbarian for the sake of saving the life of the just man to the extent her own compliance made possible?

(17) Wait just a moment, however, and you will see God's inventive providence. You see, he gave evidence of such longsuffering thus far for the purpose of rendering the good man's virtue even more conspicuous and so that through what happened there, not only people in Egypt but also people in Palestine might be instructed as to the extent of the favor the patriarch enjoyed from the Lord of all. The text goes on, remember, "When Abram entered Egypt, the Egyptians noticed that his wife was very beautiful. Pharaoh's courtiers saw her, sang her praises to Pharaoh and brought her into Pharaoh's household. On her account they treated Abram well: there came into his possession sheep, cattle and asses, slave boys and girls, mules and camels."[20] See how those things which the just man placed no store in previously came

20. Gen 12.14–16.

into his possession. You see, as he entered [301] Egypt, "the Egyptians noticed that his wife was very beautiful"—not simply beautiful but such as to win the hearts of all who saw her through her extraordinary beauty. "Pharaoh's courtiers saw her and sang her praises to Pharaoh." Don't pass this sentence idly by, dearly beloved; instead, marvel how none of the Egyptians laid a hand on the woman, stranger though she was and a traveler from foreign parts, nor did they abuse her husband; on the contrary, they went in and gave a report to the king. Now, this happened so that the matter should be more public and that when retribution was taken on the ruler, not just any private person, this event would be bruited abroad.

(18) "They brought her into Pharaoh." Immediately the just man was separated from his wife, and she was personally conducted to Pharaoh. Notice the extent of God's longsuffering, how not at the beginning or from the outset does he give evidence of his characteristic providence, but rather permits everything to happen, letting the woman fall almost into the jaws of the beast, and only then makes his power felt by everyone. "They brought her into Pharaoh's household." In what state of turmoil was the woman's mind at that time? How disturbed was her thinking? What kind of storm broke upon her? How did she not suffer shipwreck instead of remaining unmoved like a rock, awaiting grace from on high? Yet why single out this woman for mention? What state of mind was the just man probably in at her introduction into Pharaoh's household? "On her account they treated Abram well"—as her brother, that is: "there came into his possession sheep, cattle and asses, slave boys and girls, camels and mules." All these things that he was given for his keep and by way of a bribe, however—what a conflagration did they not enkindle in him? How did they not burn into his mind and inflame his thinking as he considered the motive behind the gifts?

(19) Do you see the perils reaching almost the very limit? Do you see how by the norms of human logic no hope of reversal of fortunes was now left? Do you see how by human reasoning the situation was to be despaired of? Do you see

how the woman had fallen into the very jaws of the beast? Now observe God's ineffable love in this incident, and marvel at the extraordinary degree of his power. The text goes on, "God afflicted Pharaoh and his household with terribly severe afflictions over Sarah, Abram's wife." What is the meaning of "afflicted"? It means imposed punishment for his rash and evil exploit. "Severe afflictions"—not merely "afflicted" the king, but "with severe afflictions." Since the rash deed was no slight matter but extremely serious, the punishment was accordingly severe. "And his household": why did all the members of his household share in the punishment when the king alone had sinned? This too did not happen without purpose: the intention was to reach the king's folly in this way, too. You see, there was need of a particularly severe chastisement so that the chastised might desist from his depravity. How was that a fair thing, you will say, for them to be punished on his account? It wasn't only on his account that they received punishment; rather, it was likely that they too had been involved in arranging and effecting the crime that was about to be committed. After all, did you hear what Scripture said before, that "Pharaoh's courtiers sang her praises, and brought her into Pharaoh's household." You saw them having played the role of panders in regard to the [302] just man's wife by way of favor to the king. For this reason, of course, not only he personally but also all his retinue shared in the punishment, so that they might learn that their unseemly behavior was not directed simply at a stranger or some person of no account but at a man who was the object of God's special concern and accorded such marvellous care by him. Hence, therefore, God depressed his thinking with the extreme severity of the punishment, checked him in his loathsome exploit, dissuaded him from his irrational impulse, halted his lecherous intent, contained his undisciplined desire, reined in the fury of his lust.

(20) Consequently, see him now: with how much reasonableness the king now speaks, the tyrant to the stranger as though to some nomad whose wife he had ventured to abduct. Scripture was right in saying, "He afflicted Pharaoh and his household over Sarah, Abram's wife." Along with the pun-

ishment came the realization that she was the just man's wife; though she had been taken into Pharaoh's household, she still remained in fact the just man's wife. "Now, Pharaoh summoned Abram and said to him, 'Why did you do this to me?'"[21] Notice the kind of words the king utters: "'Why did you do this to me?'" he says. Did I do something to you, stranger that I was, no one's friend, come under pressure of famine, to the king, the tyrant, the ruler of Egypt? What did I do to you? You abducted my wife, you scorned me as a stranger, spurned me, treated me as of no account; a helpless victim of your unrestrained lust, you were bent on putting into effect your plans in my regard. So what did I do to you? You did terrible things to me, he said, and committed crimes against me. See how great was the reversal of fortunes: the prince says to the peasant, "'Why did you do it to me?'" You have turned God against me, he says, you have brought his anger upon me, you have made me liable to punishment, you have caused me to pay the penalty with all my household for my efforts against you. "'Why did you do this to me in not letting me know that she is your wife? Why on earth did you say, She is my sister? I took her for my wife.'"[22] I had in mind to take her, he says, as a sister of yours. How did you come to learn that she was the good man's wife? The avenger of such awful disorder, he it was who brought this to my knowledge. "'So why did you do this to me in not letting me know that she is your wife? I took her for my wife'" and was on the point of sinning. Thinking she was your sister I had her in my company and ventured to put this into effect.

(21) Notice how the severity of the punishment depressed his thinking to the extent of leading him to offer an excuse to the just man and show signs of every care for him. And yet had God's grace not been active in appeasing his mind and instilling fear into him, the consequence would have been that he would have flown into an even worse temper to the extent of evening the score with his deceiver, the just man, wreaking his vengeance on him, and bringing him to the ul-

21. Gen 12.18.   22. Gen 12.18b–19a.

timate peril. He did none of this, however; fear quenched the
fire of his anger, and his one concern was to show signs of
care for the just man. He now knew, you see, that it was impossible that this could be an unimportant man if he enjoyed
such marvelous favor from on high. "'Now, behold, your wife
is before you; take her and be off with you.'" In other words,
now that I know she is your wife, not your sister, lo, she's
yours; I meant no harm to your union, and did not rob you
of your wife. On the contrary, "'behold, your wife is before
you—take her, and be off with you.'"

(22) What imagination could adequately conceive amazement at these events? What tongue could manage to express
this amazement? A woman dazzling in her beauty is closeted
with an Egyptian [303] partner, who is king and tyrant, of
such frenzy and incontinent disposition, and yet she leaves
his presence untouched, with her peerless chastity intact.
Such, you see, God's providence always is, marvelous and surprising. Whenever things are given up as hopeless by human
beings, then he personally gives evidence of his invincible
power in every circumstance. A comparison can in fact be
made with that marvelous and unusual situation of seeing
the man of passion[23] surrounded by those dreadful wild
beasts without coming to any harm, but emerging from the
pit unscathed as though encircled by sheep, along with the
three young men in the furnace, harmed in no way by the
fire as if passing their time in a meadow or garden, and
emerging from it just as if they were graven pillars. Well, in
just the same way the present event deserves our wonder in
that the just man's wife suffered no abuse from the Egyptian
king, tyrant and lecher that he was, but emerged safe and
sound. God, you see, it was who effected it all, who gives
support when none is forthcoming and can always bring
things from desperate circumstances to sound hope.

(23) "'Now, behold, your wife is before you; take her and
be off.'" Don't think, he is saying, that you have been injured

---

23. Cf. Dan 3. As mentioned above at Homily 22, n. 11, Chrysostom
employs here the version of Theodotion, which differs from the LXX in
details such as the reference to Daniel as "man of passion."

by us. In fact, whereas our actions were done out of ignorance, behold, we now know the calibre of your protector; the
anger descending on us has taught us the extent of the favor
you enjoy from the God of all. So take your wife and be off
with you. Now the just man was an object of dread to them,
on account of which they hastened to ply him with great attention so as to propitiate his Lord by favors done to him. Do
you see, dearly beloved, the extent of his patient endurance?
In this connection, I ask you, remember those words which
the patriarch used when he was about to approach the confines of Egypt: "'I'm aware that you are a very beautiful
woman. So it will happen that, when the Egyptians see you,
they will kill me but spare your life.'" So, with those words in
mind, consider what actually happens in this case, and marvel
both at the just man's endurance and at the power of the
loving God in causing the good man to depart with such distinction after entering the country with such terrible fear and
dread. "Pharaoh gave his men instructions about Abram, to
escort him and his wife, all his possessions, and Lot with
him."[24] Now the good man leaves with pomp and circumstance and with plentiful supplies, and turns out to be a
teacher not only of the people in Egypt through what had
occurred, but also of those along the way and the inhabitants
of Palestine. I mean, people who saw him traveling down under pressure of the famine, moving with fear and trembling,
and now in turn with such notoriety, prosperity and wealth
came to know of the power of God's providence in his favor.
Who ever saw anything like it? Who ever heard of it? He left
to find relief from famine—and came back like this, bedecked with wealth and untold distinction.

(24) Don't be surprised, dearly beloved, nor marvel at what
happened; rather, marvel, be stunned and glorify the power
of the common Lord of us all. See also Abram's descendants
going down, on the one hand, into Egypt in the same fashion
under pressure of famine, and in turn leaving there in pros-

24. Gen 12.20, the LXX including Lot, perhaps under the influence of
the next verse.

perity after terrible servitude and hardship. This, after all, is the extent of the Lord's inventiveness: when he allows terrible things to reach a climax, then it is that in turn he scatters the storm and brings peace and quiet and a complete change of fortunes so as to teach [304] us the greatness of his power. "Now, Abram left Egypt, he and his wife and all his possessions, and Lot in his company, and he went into the desert."[25] You would be right in applying to this just man those words that blessed David used of those who returned from the captivity in Babylon: "Though they sow in tears they will reap in joy. They went their way and wept as they cast their seed, but in returning they will come in joy, carrying their sheaves aloft."[26] Did you see his downward journey to be beset with worry and fear, with the fear of death heavy upon him? Now see his return marked by great prosperity and distinction! The just man now, you see, was an object of respect to everyone in Egypt and in Palestine. After all, who would have failed to show respect for the one who so enjoyed God's protection and was accorded such wonderful care? Quite likely what befell the king and his household escaped no one's attention. His purpose, you see, in permitting everything and in allowing the just man's trials to reach such a point was that his endurance might appear more conspicuous, his achievement might win the attention of the whole world, and no one would be unaware of the good man's virtue.

(25) Do you see, dearly beloved, the magnitude of the benefit coming from his trials? Do you see the greatness of the reward for his endurance? Do you see both man and wife, advanced in age though they were, giving evidence of so much good sense, so much courage, so much affection for one another, such a bond of love? Let us all imitate this, and never become dispirited nor consider the onset of tribulations to be a mark of abandonment on God's part or an index of scorn; rather, let us treat it as the clearest demonstration of God's providential care for us. I mean, even if we have the burden of sin weighing upon us, we will be able by showing

---

25. Gen 13.1.   26. Ps 126.5–6.

great endurance and thankfulness to make them less burdensome; if we don't have many sins, in our turn too we will likewise enjoy greater favor from on high if we render thanks. Our Lord, you see, is loving and is interested in our salvation, and for this reason he gives us the opportunity of the onset of tribulations in the manner of some sort of exercise and training so that we in our turn may show what we are capable of and thus enjoy more generous favor from him. Knowing this, let us not grow slack under trials nor offer resistance to distress, but rather even rejoice, according to blessed Paul, who says, "Now I rejoice in my distress."[27] Do you see his grateful spirit? If he rejoiced in distress, could he ever then have been a victim to depression? If what caused depression in others provided him with grounds for contentment, consider, I ask you, the condition of his soul.

(26) For you to learn that there is no other way available to gain the good things promised us and be found worthy of the kingdom of heaven than by passing the present life in distress, listen to the apostles speaking to recent converts to the faith. "After making many disciples," the text says, "they returned to Lystra and to Iconium and to Antioch, strengthening the disciples' spirits and exhorting them to remain steadfast in the faith by telling them that we must enter the kingdom of heaven through great distress."[28] So what excuse can we make if we are unwilling to bear in a spirit of nobility, courage and thankfulness whatever befalls us, now that we see that there is no other way open to us to gain our salvation than by traversing this path? For proof, after all, that in passing the present life in distress none [305] of the just ones endured anything novel or unusual, listen to Christ's words, "In the world you will have distress, but take heart."[29] That is, in case on hearing this they should become depressed, he communicated to them immediately some encouragement in promising them grace from himself: "But take heart," he said, "I have overcome the world." You have with you, he

---

27. Col 1.24, where Chrysostom reads "distress" for "sufferings."
28. Acts 14.21–22.   29. John 16.33.

means, the one who lightens the weight of grief, who does not allow you to be overwhelmed by the onset of tribulations, who with the trial brings also escape from it, and does not permit difficulties to beset you beyond your strength.[30] Why are you upset? Why are you worried? Why are you greatly vexed? Why so faint of heart? After all, provided we apply all the resources at our disposal—our endurance, patience and thankful attitude—surely he will never allow us to be the object of scorn? Even if things reach a sorry pass, they are no match for our Lord's wisdom, are they? Let us give evidence of our own good will and have a faith that is unalloyed, knowing as we do the inventiveness of the protector of our souls. And he, who knows what is for our good far better than we, will arrange things appropriately to such an extent that they will turn out as they should in his designs and for our good, so that we may gain the reward of our endurance and be thought worthy of loving kindness on his part, thanks to the grace and mercy of our Lord Jesus Christ, to whom with the Father and the Holy Spirit be glory, power and honor, now and forever, for ages of ages. Amen.

30. Cf. 1 Cor 10.13.

HOMILY 33

"Now, Abram was very rich in cattle, silver and gold. He journeyed to
where he had come from, into the desert as far as Bethel, to the place where
his tent had formerly been, between Bethel and Haggai, to the place of the
altar which he had made there in the beginning."[1]

EEING [305] YOUR GATHERING here today with such
enthusiasm and your interest in listening to me, I
want to discharge the debt I owe your good selves. I
am aware that you for your part have possibly forgotten
everything on account of the lapse of many days in the meantime and the fact that we have directed our sermon to other
themes. The arrival of the sacred festival interrupted our series: it was not appropriate for us while celebrating the Lord's
Cross to have instruction on other matters; instead, each time
we felt the need to lay before you a table suited to the occasion. This, of course, was the reason why, when the day of
the Betrayal arrived, we interrupted the sequence of our instruction in response to need and directed our words to the
betrayer, and then in turn proposed for your consideration
thoughts about the Cross. Then, when Resurrection day
dawned, it behooved us to instruct your good selves on the
Lord's Resurrection, and next to provide you in the days following the Resurrection with a demonstration of it through
the wonders that happened afterwards, when we took up the
Acts of the Apostles and from there laid before you the customary feast, offering particular exhortation day after day to
those who had just been granted the favor of baptism.

(2) So now we must remind you of the debt and at long last

---

1. Gen 13.2–4. This homily, as our Introduction explains and Chrysostom points out below, was delivered after a long gap for Easter and other
occasional sermons. Cf. Introduction (1) & (8) in FOTC 74.

proceed to discharge it. You see, even if you are not aware of the kind of debt on account of your being plagued with many cares, like having care of your wife, being concerned for your children, [306] being anxious for daily nourishment, and beset with many other worldly preoccupations, we on the contrary, being hampered by no such worries, can recall the debt to your mind and take steps to discharge it. Don't be surprised if we give evidence of such readiness to repay: this debt is of a kind different from material wealth. I mean, in the latter case the debtor would never be quick to display his readiness to repay, realizing that repaying his debt reduces his own means while increasing the wealth of his creditor. In the case of this spiritual debt, however, it is nothing like that; by repaying his debt the debtor is, on the contrary, all the better off, and the creditors' profit is greater. Hence, in the former case defaulting on debts is frequent, whereas in the latter case great gain accrues to both parties, both debtor and creditors. This is what Paul, too, says in his exhortation on love, "Don't owe anyone anything except to love one another,"[2] to show that this debt is always reckoned to be due for repayment, not for withholding. You, too, must not be negligent about keeping yourself in readiness to receive repayment: this makes us better off in making repayment, and will prove to be an occasion of greater benefit to you, too. Since, then, this is what this kind of debt is like, the more we pay back the more we increase our wealth according to our greater repayment—come now, let us teach you also the basis of the debt so that you in your turn may more enthusiastically receive what we say, accept our readiness to make repayment, and reward us by attending to our words with enthusiasm.

(3) What, then, is the basis of our debt? You remember clearly that we brought to your attention the story of the patriarch—the journey he took down into Egypt on account of the famine, the abduction of Sarah perpetrated by Pharaoh, God's anger against him arising from his care for the just man, against him and all his household, care shown by lead-

2. Rom 13.8.

ing the patriarch to make the return journey from Egypt with great wealth. "Pharaoh gave his men instructions about Abram," the text says, remember, "to escort him and his wife, all his possessions, and Lot with him. Now, Abram left Egypt with his wife and all his possessions and Lot in his company, and he went into the desert."[3] At that point we cut short the sermon, and altered the topic by devoting all the intervening days to instruction on subjects relevant to the occasion. Hence our task today is to link up with the sequel and to join the verses yet to be read to what has already been commented on, like fitting together one whole body; this is the way, you see, that our treatment of the subject will be easily taken in by you.

(4) For our words to be clearer to you, however, it would be worth our while also proposing to your good selves the very beginning of today's reading. The text reads: "Now, Abram was very rich in cattle, silver and gold. He journeyed to where he had come from, into the desert as far as Bethel, to the place where his tent had formerly been, between Bethel and Haggai, to the place of the altar which he had made there in the beginning. [307] Then Abram called on the name of the Lord God." Let us not rush idly by this reading, but rather recognize clearly the precision of Sacred Scripture in recounting nothing to us as of no importance. "Now, Abram was very rich," the text says. Consider first of all this very fact that its habit had been to convey nothing idly or to no purpose, nor in this case is it without reason that it calls him rich: nowhere else had it made mention of his being rich—this was the first time. Why, and to what purpose? For you to learn the inventiveness of God's wisdom and providence displayed in favor of the good man, as well as his boundless and extraordinary power. The man who had gone into exile in Egypt under the pressure of famine, unable to sustain the privations of Canaan, suddenly became rich—and not just rich but very rich, not only in cattle but also in silver and gold.

3. Gen 12.20–13.1.

(5) Do you see the extent of God's providence? Abram left to find relief from famine, and came back not simply enjoying relief from famine but invested with great wealth and untold reputation, his identity well-known to everyone: now the inhabitants of Canaan gained a more precise idea of the good man's virtue by seeing this sudden transformation that had taken place—the stranger who had gone down into Egypt as a refugee and vagabond now flush with so much wealth. Notice how he had not become less resolute or devoted under the influence of great prosperity or the abundance of wealth, but rather he pressed on once more to that place where he had formerly been before going down into Egypt. "He went into the desert," the text says, "to the place where his tent had formerly been, to the place of the altar which he had made there in the beginning. He called on the name of the Lord God." Consider, I ask you, how he was a lover of peace and quiet, and was constantly attentive to divine worship. The text says, remember, that he went down to that place where he had previously built the altar; by calling on the name of God he already right from the very beginning fulfilled in anticipation that saying of David, "I would rather be of no account in the house of my God than take up residence in sinners' dwellings."[4] In other words, solitude turned out to be preferred by him for invoking the name of God, instead of the cities. After all, he well knew that cities' greatness is not constituted by beauty of buildings nor by multitude of inhabitants, but by the virtue of the residents—hence too the desert proved to be more desirable than the cities, adorned as it was by the just man's virtue and thus a more resplendent vision than the whole world.

(6) "Lot, who accompanied Abram," the text goes on, "had flocks, herds and cattle. The countryside could not manage to support their living together, since their company was numerous, and they could not dwell together."[5] Not only had there been an increase in wealth in the patriarch's favor, but "Lot too had flocks, herds and cattle." Perhaps on the one

4. Ps 84.10.   5. Gen 13.5–6.

hand Abram, being generous, was in the habit of favoring his
nephew with these things, while on the other hand other people would supply him with them out of regard for the patriarch. "The countryside could not support them," the text
says, "because their company was numerous." Notice the
abundance of their possessions proving at once responsible
for their separation, creating a division, sundering their harmony, and undoing the bond of kinship. "Trouble developed
between Abram's herdsmen and Lot's herdsmen. Now, the
Canaanites and the Pherezites inhabited the land at the
time."[6] Notice how the relatives [308] are responsible for the
first signs of separation: invariably this is the source from
which spring all problems—discord among brethren. The
text says, remember, "Trouble developed between the herdsmen." They are the ones who provide the occasion for separation, who sunder the harmony, who give evidence of bad
feeling. "Now, the Canaanites and the Pherezites inhabited
the land at that time." Why did it mention that to us? Because
it had said that, "the countryside could not manage to support their living together," Sacred Scripture wanted to teach
us the reason why it could not support them, namely, because
it was still occupied by these peoples.

(7) But let us see the patriarch's godfearing attitude in
quenching by his characteristic restraint the fire that threatened to break out. "Abram, however, said to Lot, 'Let there
be no trouble between you and me, nor between my herdsmen and yours, for we are brothers.'"[7] See the extraordinary
degree of his humility, see the height of his wisdom: the elder,
the senior, addresses his junior and calls his nephew
"brother," admits him to the same rank as himself and retains
no special distinction for himself; instead, he says, "'Let there
be no trouble between you and me, nor between my herdsmen and yours.'" Nor would it be proper, after all, for this to
happen, he says, since we are brothers. Do you see him fulfilling the apostolic law, which says, "Already, then, the verdict
has completely gone against you for having lawsuits with one

6. Gen 13.7.   7. Gen 13.8.

another. Why not rather suffer wrong? Why not rather be defrauded? Instead, you do wrong and defraud, and this to your own brethren."[8] All these admonitions the patriarch observes in fact by saying, "'Let there be no trouble between my herdsmen and your herdsmen, because we are brothers.'"[9] What could be more peace-loving than such a spirit as this? It wasn't idly, of course, or to no purpose that I mentioned at the outset that his reason for preferring solitude to the whole civilized world was a love for peace and quiet. See him in this case, too, when he noticed the herdsmen completely at odds, how right from the very beginning he tried to quench the fire that threatened to break out, and put a stop to the rivalry. You see, it was important for him in his role of teacher of wisdom sent to the inhabitants of Palestine, far from providing any bad example or offering any encouragement, rather to give them all the clearer instruction through the clarion call of his restraint in manners and to convert them into imitators of his own virtue.

(8) "'Let there be no trouble,'" he says, "'between you and me, between my herdsmen and yours, for we are brothers.'" Remarkable restraint in those words, "'between you and me.'" Notice how he addresses Lot on terms of equality—and yet I have the impression that the outbreak of trouble had no other origin than in the refusal of the patriarch's herdsmen to allow Lot's to enjoy the same privilege as they. The just man, however, handles everything with restraint, demonstrating the remarkable degree of his own good sense, and teaching not only those present at the time but also everyone in future never to settle our differences with our relatives by feuding. Their squabbling brings great disgrace on us, and instead of the trouble being attributed to them, the blame reverts to us. So what fittingness could there be for brothers, sharing in fact the same nature, the same links of kinship and [309] due at that point to dwell near to each other, to engage in hostilities when it was expected of them to play the role of

8. 1 Cor 6.7–8.
9. This time Chrysostom quotes the verse in a slightly different LXX text.

teaching all these people restraint, gentleness and complete good sense? Let people who judge they are above such reproach give heed to this example when on the grounds of relationship they connive at their relatives' larceny, rapacity, scheming beyond measure, both in the city and in the country, confiscation of one person's farm and another's home, and on that basis they show such scoundrels even greater favor. I mean, even if the felony was the work of someone else, still you shared personally in the guilt of the crime, not only by taking satisfaction in the deed and considering your own stocks to be increased by it and your wealth to grow greater, but also in not preventing the crime that was about to take effect. After all, the person who is in a position to forestall the criminal and does not do it is no less liable to punishment than the criminal.

(9) Far from deceiving ourselves, therefore, I beseech you, let us personally shun larceny, rapacity and the temptation to add to our wealth from these sources, and let us teach our relatives not to commit this kind of thing. In fact, instead of leaving us free of guilt, this would bring us heavier condemnation: to win our favor these people betray their own salvation by committing a crime, thus involving us in their own ruin. If, however, we are prepared to be on the alert and we disentangle ourselves from the ensuing disaster, we will also extricate them from the evil venture. Don't, pray, address to me those frivolous words, "That's got nothing to do with me; I've cheated no one, have I? I had no idea! Someone else committed the crime, I took no part in it." That's pretext and excuses. If you want to prove you had no part in the crime, that you weren't an accomplice, and didn't take the role of an agent of rapacity, repair the damage, solace the victim, restore what has been stolen. This, you see, is the way to clear yourself of charges and reform the culprit, by showing that the crimes committed by him were contrary to your intention, and by comforting the victim you will not allow him to be overwhelmed by the depression that he would likely succumb to owing to the robbery.

(10) "'Let there be no trouble,'" the text reads, "'between

me and you, and between my herdsmen and yours, for we are brothers.'" Do you see the mild manner? do you see the restraint? Listen as well to the sequel so as to come to know the extraordinary degree of his good sense. How, then, was the threat of trouble put to rest and the outbreak of hostility quenched? " 'Lo, all the land lies before you. Part from me; if you go to the left, I'll go to the right; if you go to the right, I'll go to the left.' "[10] Notice our hero's good sense and the extent of his deference. Prior to this, however, dearly beloved, consider, I ask you, how great is the harm ensuing from wealth and the disagreement from great prosperity: their flocks grew bigger, great wealth accrued to them, and immediately harmony between them was disrupted—where there had been peace and the bonds of affection, now there was trouble and hostility. You see, whenever it is a question of mine and yours, there are grounds for the utmost trouble and a basis for hostility; by contrast, where this isn't the case, habits of peace and harmony exist together without any confusion.

(11) To grasp this, listen to what blessed Luke says about those embracing the faith from the beginning: "They all had one heart and one soul,"[11] he says, not that they all had one soul (how could they, after all, being in different bodies?), but because they give us an example of the most highly developed harmony. Had the good man not been most longsuffering and skilled in practicing good sense, he would have lost his temper and [310] said to Lot, What is the meaning of such frenzy? Your kindred haven't dared raise their voice against my retainers, have they? Have they not considered the distance between us? I mean, what is the cause of your prosperous circumstances? Is it not my provident care? But who thrust you into public notice? Was it not I who took pride of place in your regard, and acted as a father to you in every respect? Is this the reward you bestow on me for the great attention I have showered on you? Was this what I could expect for bringing you everywhere with me? All right, granted

10. Gen 13.9.   11. Acts 14.32.

you have in mind none of the things that have come your way at my hands: should you not at least have shown regard for my age and respected my grey hairs? Instead, you took no notice of your herdsmen debauching my herdsmen, all heedless of the fact that as resentment against them reverted to me, so their froward behavior would be turned home to you.

(12) None of this, however, did the just man deign to allow to enter his mind; rather, rejecting any such thought, his single concern was how to quench the hostility threatening to flare up, and how he might arrange their dwelling without any trouble by devising a separation free from recrimination. "'Lo,'" he said, "'does not all the land lie before you? Part from me; if you go to the right, I'll go to the left; if you go to the left, I'll go to the right.'"[12] See the just man's restraint: he shows Lot by his behavior that far from doing this by choice or out of a wish for them to be parted, it was rather under pressure of hostility and for the purpose of avoiding a continual feud in the household. Consider how, by means of his words, he allays the ill feeling, giving Lot complete right of choice and offering him all the territory in the words, "'Lo, does not all the land lie before you?'" Choose whatever you wish, and I will be ready with great contentment to accept the part you have left for me. Tremendous wisdom on the just man's part: in every way he tries to be no burden to his nephew. His meaning is, after all, Since what I didn't want has taken place—the need for a parting of the ways so as to allay the outbreak of hostility—accordingly I give you prior right of choice and confer on you complete authority so that you may choose whatever land you decide is more desirable and leave the rest to me. Did anyone ever deign to do as much for a very brother of his own, such as the patriarch was shown to do in favor of his nephew? Even if he, for his part, had taken the initiative in exercising his choice, and after choosing the principal portion had permitted the other man what was left over, would it not have been a great thing done even in this manner? Yet, on the contrary, he wanted to show the

12. Again Chrysostom recalls his text inexactly.

extent of his virtue and satisfy the young man's desire so that
he should have no grounds for resentment from the separation; so he completely ceded the right in the words, " 'Lo, all
the land lies before you; part from me' " and choose whatever
you wish.

(13) Accordingly, it behooved the nephew, who had experienced such restraint, to show respect for the patriarch in
return, and cede to him the exercise of choice. You see, it is
usual with practically all of us, whenever we see our opponents at the point of concocting some stratagem against us or
struggling to usurp pride of place, not to allow ourselves to
be bettered or give way to them. On the other hand, whenever we see them giving ground and conceding every right to
us in conciliatory terms, out of regard for their great restraint
we desist from hostility and reverse our position by ceding
them every right, even if the person at odds with us seems
inferior. Accordingly, Lot, too, should have behaved this way
[311] in regard to the patriarch, yet on account of his youth
and being a prey to waxing greed he usurped what he
thought to be the best parts and made his choice on that
basis. The text goes on, "Lot looked about and saw that all
the region of the Jordan was well-watered, up as far as Zo-
gora (this was before God's destruction of Sodom and Gomorrah), like the garden of God and like the land of Egypt.
Lot chose for himself all the region of the Jordan; he moved
off from the east, and the brothers parted from each other."[13]
Do you see the extraordinary degree of the just man's virtue
in not allowing the root of the trouble to grow; instead, at
once he dug out the weed about to flourish and destroyed it.
By employing great restraint and demonstrating unspeakable
contempt of other things for the sake of virtue, did he not
show everyone how peace and freedom from hostility are in
fact more estimable than all his wealth?

(14) I mean, in case anyone should condemn the just man
for proving ill-disposed towards Lot or believe he uprooted
him from his home, led him into foreign parts and now

13. Gen 13.10–11.

drives him from his new home, or think he does this out of enmity, instead of our all learning that it is under the impulse of peace that he does it, he even yielded the choice to Lot and made no objection when he chose the prime land, so that everyone would be in a position to know the goodness of our hero's attitude and the object of his peaceable disposition. Another wonderful design in particular had been provided for so that many good effects might follow from his example, namely, that Lot might be taught through the events that it had not been proper for him to make the choice, that the people of Sodom might come to know Lot's virtue, and that despite the separation the promise made to the patriarch might take effect as the words said, "'To you and your descendants I will give this land.'" We shall see this as we gradually proceed, Sacred Scripture making everything clear.

(15) "Abram stayed in the land of Canaan," the text goes on, "whereas Lot settled in the cities of the region, pitching his tent in Sodom. Now, the people of Sodom were very wicked sinners in God's sight."[14] Do you observe Lot having regard only for the nature of the land and not considering the wickedness of the inhabitants? What good, after all, is fertility of land and abundance of produce when the inhabitants are evil in their ways? On the other hand, what harm could come from solitude and a simple lifestyle when the inhabitants are more restrained? The summit of blessings, you see, is the uprightness of those who dwell in a place. Lot, however, had eyes for one thing only, the richness of the countryside. Hence Scripture's desire to indicate to us the wickedness of those who dwelt there in the words, "Now, the people of Sodom were very wicked sinners in God's sight"; not merely "wicked" but also "sinners," and not simply "sinners" but also "in God's sight," that is, the extent of their sins was extreme and their wickedness superabounded—hence it added as well, "very wicked in God's sight." Do you see the extremity of the evil? Do you see how great an evil it is to usurp pride of place and not to consider what is for the com-

14. Gen 13.12–13.

mon good? Do you see what a great thing is deference, ceding pride of place, taking second place? Take note, in fact: as the instruction develops we shall see that the one who took the pick of the best places gained no advantage from it, whereas he who chose the lesser became more resplendent day by day [312] and, with his wealth increasing, he became the attraction of all eyes.

(16) Lest we prolong the sermon to great length, however, let us terminate it at this point and postpone the sequel to next time while giving you this exhortation, to imitate the patriarch by never aspiring after the first places but rather heeding blessed Paul's words, "outdoing one another in respect,"[15] especially our superiors, and being anxious to take second place in everything. This, in fact, means filling first place, as Christ himself said, "'Whoever humbles himself will be exalted.'"[16] So what could parallel this, when by ceding pride of place to others we ourselves enjoy greater esteem, and by showing them special honor we bring ourselves into the highest honor? Accordingly, I beseech you, let this be our particular concern, to imitate the patriarch's humility, and by following in the steps of this man who displayed such wonderful good sense before the time of the Law, let us, who enjoy grace itself, advance in virtue. It really is, in fact, a genuine instance of humility that this remarkable man gave in regard to the person far inferior to himself, not only on the score of virtue but also of age and all other respects. Consider, after all, that the elder man gave way to the younger, the uncle to the nephew, and the recipient of such wonderful favor from God to the one who so far had nothing worthwhile to show for himself; what the latter should have said as befitting a younger man addressing his senior and his own uncle, this the patriarch said to his junior.

(17) So let us in our turn show signs of respect not only for our superiors or those who happen to be our equals. This, you see, would not be humility; whenever you do what is imposed by necessity, it is not humility but duty. True humility

15. Rom 12.10.   16. Luke 14.11; 18.14.

it is, on the contrary, when we defer to those who seem to be our inferiors and give pride of place to those judged to be of much lower estate. If we view these things aright, however, far from judging anyone to be our inferior we shall consider all people our superiors. I say this not in the light of our condition of being overwhelmed by countless failings; rather, even if someone is convinced of his good deeds beyond number, unless the conviction he has about himself is that he is the last of all, he would gain no benefit from all his good deeds. This, you see, is humility, when someone has grounds for complacency but lowers and humbles himself and keeps pride in check. Then, in fact, he will reach true heights, according to the promise of the Lord in the words, "'Whoever humbles himself will be exalted.'" Accordingly, I beseech you, let us all take every effort to reach the heights that are scaled by humility so that we may enjoy from the Lord the same favor as that just man Abram and be accorded those ineffable blessings, thanks to the grace and loving kindness of our Lord Jesus Christ, to whom with the Father and the Holy Spirit be glory, power and honor, now and forever, for ages of ages. Amen.

HOMILY 34

"The Lord said to Abram after Lot's parting from him, 'Lift up your eyes,
and from where you now are look north and south, east and west: all the
land you see I will give you.'"[1]

ESTERDAY, [312] DEARLY BELOVED, you learnt of the
patriarch's extraordinary humility, you saw the remarkable degree [313] of his restraint. It was no
slight thing for the old man, who had performed so many
good deeds and enjoyed so much favor from the Lord of all,
to display towards the younger man, his nephew, such equality of esteem as to cede to him pride of place and take second
best, and put up with everything for the sake of heading off
conflict and eliminating the grounds of rivalry. Let us all be
anxious to emulate this conduct, never threatening our relatives nor entertaining grandiose notions; let us give evidence
of deep humility by deferring to them, let us rather make it
our concern to take second place in behavior and speech, not
even reacting against those who do us wrong, even if they
happen to be beneficiaries of ours (this, after all, is the most
excellent philosophy), nor even being provoked by their arrogance, even if those feuding with us are our inferiors—
rather, let us allay their ill feeling by restraint and meekness.

(2) Nothing, you see, is more efficacious than this, nothing
is more potent. This brings our soul into lasting tranquility,
as if causing it to find haven in port, and proving to be for
us the basis of complete repose. Hence Christ too delivered
that divine instruction in the words, "Learn from me, for I
am meek and humble of heart, and you will find rest for your
souls."[2] Nothing, you see, brings the soul into repose and
great peace to such an extent as meekness and humility. This

1. Gen 13.14–15.   2. Matt 11.29.

would prove to be for its possessor more valuable than any diadem, this would be more to one's credit than any notoriety or glory. I mean, what could be more desirable than being freed from the threat of conflict arising within one's own person? I mean, even if we enjoy peace and respect many times over outwardly while alarm and disturbance arise within us from the tumult of our thinking, no benefit comes to us from peace on the outside—just as nothing would be more pitiable than a city suffering the treason of the citizens within its walls, no matter if you fortified it with countless ramparts and fortifications.

(3) Accordingly, I beseech you, let us make this our special concern, to keep our soul undisturbed, to bring it to a state of peace, to free it from all alarm so that we ourselves may enjoy complete repose and may be gentle with our acquaintances. This, in fact, is a particular mark of the person endowed with reason: mildness, restraint, gentleness, humility, tranquillity, not being pulled and tugged like a slave either by anger or by the other passions, but through the use of reason prevailing over interior impulses, preserving our natural nobility and not falling victim to the frenzy of brute beasts through indifference. To learn the power of gentleness and restraint, and how virtue alone suffices to render the person who practices it devotedly worthy of those ineffable encomiums, listen to the eulogy bestowed to blessed Moses on that account, and the crown awarded him for that reason: "Moses was the mildest of all people on the earth,"[3] Scripture says. Do you see the greatness of the encomium, which conferred on him equality of esteem with the whole human race—or, rather, gave him precedence over all mankind? Again, Scripture says about David, "Be mindful, Lord, of David and all his meekness."[4] On that score, too, the patriarch won much greater favor from on high, and by exerting himself from his own resources he was accorded greater blessings from the loving Lord. You will come to realize this when we propose to you the sequel [314] to yesterday's words and unfold for

3. Num 12.3.   4. Ps 132.1.

your good selves the passage read at the outset. You see, when Abram gave evidence of great restraint in giving pride of place to Lot and yielded to him the right of choice, he willingly chose second place for the sake of avoiding all rivalry; hence notice the extent of the reward he immediately enjoys from God and the way he regales the patriarch with recompense in excess of his considerable wealth. This, you see, is what our Lord is like: when he sees us exerting ourselves even slightly of our own accord, he plies us with generous rewards on his account, and demonstrates such great generosity as to surpass by a great margin what has been done by us.

(4) You will find this done by him in each of the works accomplished by us. I mean, what, tell me, could be more worthless than two pennies? Yet despite that, he caused that widow who made an offering of the two pennies to be celebrated from that time to this all over the world.[5] Why do I say two pennies? If you give only a cup of cold water, even for that he will award great recompense, always rewarding for their intention those who practice virtue.[6] You could see this done by him also in the case of the offering of prayers: if someone prays with fervor, immediately he will say to him, "While you were yet sleeping, lo, I was at your side."[7] If, however, one gives evidence of greater insistence and earnestly offers petitions with great desire and ardent zeal, he likewise exalts and rewards him for his petition. This he did also in the case of the Canaanite woman;[8] when he saw her great persistence and constancy, he first of all exalted and, so to say, crowned her with commendation, making her famous throughout the whole world; then with great generosity he surpassed the extravagance of her petition, saying to her, " 'O woman, great is your faith.' Then he added, 'May your wish be granted.' "[9] If we wanted to single out every example of the holy Scriptures, in every case we would see the Lord's

---

5. Cf. Luke 21.1–3.   6. Cf. Matt 10.42.
7. Isa 65.24.   8. Cf. Matt 15.22–28.
9. Matt 15.28. This is proving to be a typically wide-ranging scriptural introduction to the day's theme.

great generosity. The patriarch had a precise understanding of that: well aware that the person giving way in unimportant matters would be better off in matters of greater consequence, as you heard yesterday, he yielded to Lot and chose for himself the worse region so as to remove the grounds of rivalry, demonstrate his own virtue and leave the whole family in peace.

(5) But let us see from what has just been read what reward he receives from the Lord for such restraint. "God said to Abram," the text says, "after Lot's parting from him, 'Lift up your eyes, and from where you now are look north and south, east and west; all the land you see I will give to you and your descendants forever.'" See the promptness of God's providential recompense demonstrated in favor of the good man: Sacred Scripture wants to teach us the extent of the reimbursement the patriarch was accorded for such humility from the loving God, and so after saying that Lot took his leave and went off to the land he had selected on the score of its beauty, it immediately added, "The Lord God said to Abram." Then, for our precise realization that he said this by way of rewarding him for what had been done for Lot, it added, "God said to Abram after Lot's parting from him," [315] as if to say the following words to him without demur, You ceded the beautiful region to your nephew on account of your great restraint and thus gave evidence of your eminent humility and showed such concern for peace as to put up with anything for the sake of preventing any rivalry coming between you—hence accept from me a generous reward. "'Lift up your eyes,'" he said, "'and from where you are now look north and south, east and west; all the land you see I will give to you and your descendants forever.'" Do you see the recompense exceeding in great measure what had been done by Abram? The loving Lord uses the same words as Abram himself in his act of deference: as he had said, "'Lo, does not all the land lie before you? Part from me; if you go to the right, I'll go to the left; if you go to the left, I'll go right,'" so the Lord said, "'Lift up your eyes, and from where you now are, lo, all the land you see I will give to you and your descendants forever.'"

(6) Observe in this instance the extraordinary degree of his generosity: whereas you gave him the right of choice (he is saying), ceding the region he wished to take for himself while being content for your part to accept what was left over, I am displaying such generosity as to hand over to you all the land that falls under your gaze on all sides, north and south, east and west—all the land you see; and not only this but also "'to your descendants forever.'" Do you see the generosity worthy of God's goodness? do you see how Abram was granted as much as he had conceded? Let us learn from this incident to show great generosity in almsgiving so that we may be granted great rewards in return for giving meager alms. I mean, what parity is there, tell me, between giving a little money and winning remission of sins? Between feeding the hungry and enjoying confidence on that dread day and hearing those words that earn right of entry to the kingdom, "I was hungry, and you gave me something to eat"?[10] The one who showed you such generosity was not beyond alleviating that person's need, was he? His reason, however, for allowing him to be afflicted by need was that he might win great reward for his endurance and you might store up for yourself confidence on the basis of almsgiving.

(7) Do you see the Lord's loving kindness, how he arranges everything with our salvation in mind? So when you consider that it is for you and your welfare that that person is beset with want and perishing from starvation, don't pass him by heartlessly, but prove a faithful steward of what has been entrusted to you by the Lord so that by alleviating the poor person's need you may win such favor from on high. And praise the Lord for allowing that person to live in need for the sake of you and your salvation in order that you may be able to find the way to be in a position both to wash away your sins and by managing properly what has been entrusted to you by the Lord to be accorded that commendation which exceeds all thought and description. You will hear, in fact, "Well done, good and faithful servant, you have been faithful

10. Matt 15.35.

in a few things, I will set you over many; enter into the joy of your Lord."[11] Understanding this, let us look on the poor as our benefactors, able to afford us the basis of our salvation, and let us give with generosity and a joyful spirit, never being tardy in our offering, but conversing with them with great restraint and showing great meekness. "Incline [316] your ear to a beggar," remember, "and respond peaceably to him in meekness"[12] so that even before your gift, you may lift his spirit from the dejection of great need with the gentleness of your words. Scripture says, remember, "a kind word is better than an offering";[13] so speech is able both to lift the spirit and bring it much comfort.

(8) Accordingly, let us not simply have the recipient in view in showing generosity in almsgiving, but consider who it is who takes as his the kindnesses shown to the poor person and who promises recompense for favors done; and thus let us direct our attention to him while showing all zeal in making offerings with complete enthusiasm, and let us sow generously in season so that we may also reap generously. Scripture says, remember, "he who sows sparingly shall also reap sparingly."[14] Let us consequently sow these good seeds with no sparing hand so that in due season we may reap generously. Now, after all, is the time for sowing, which I beseech you not to pass by, so that on the day of harvesting the returns of what was sown here we may gather the fruits and be regaled with loving kindness from the Lord. Nothing, you see, nothing else of our virtuous deeds will so succeed in quenching the fire of our sins as generosity in almsgiving: it causes the remission of our sins, proves the guarantee of confidence for us and ensures the enjoyment of those ineffable goods.

(9) This is enough talking, however, to encourage you and to show you that by giving alms, meager though they be, we receive great rewards from the Lord. By this stage, you see, the sermon has gone to an exhortation in almsgiving because,

---

11. Matt 15.23.   12. Sir 4.8.
13. Sir 18.16.
14. 2 Cor 9.6. Chrysostom is still skirting around the day's theme with his allusions to other parts of Scripture.

as you recall, we told you that the patriarch ceded part of the country to Lot, letting him have the most beautiful area in the region while taking the worst land for himself, and so he was accorded such generosity from God that the promise made him by God surpassed all thought and imagination. The text says, remember, " 'Lift up your eyes, and from where you are, lo, all the land you see to north and south, I will give to you and your descendants forever.' " You ceded part of the country to your nephew, he says; lo, I promise you the entire country—and not only this, but also I guarantee to give it to your descendants, and forever, or in other words in perpetuity. Do you see how he outdoes himself in his benefactions? Since he knew that the patriarch longed for this in particular, and that nothing else would so arouse his enthusiasm, he said, This favor, too, I will bestow upon you—that those descended from you will succeed to possession of the land and will have control over it in perpetuity.

(10) Then in case Abram should have regard only to his own condition, his advanced years and Sarah's sterility, and thus lose confidence in the promise instead of trusting in the power of the one making the promise, he said, " 'I will make your descendants as numerous as all the grains of sand in the world; if anyone can number the grains of sand in the world, your descendants too will be numbered.' "[15] No doubt the promise went beyond human nature; not only did he promise to make him a father despite so many impediments but also to extend the gift to such a multitude as to be compared with all the grains of sand in the world, and the multitude to be beyond number, wishing as he did to demonstrate the extent of the remarkable increase by the comparison. [317] Notice how the loving Lord gradually exercises the just man's virtue. After saying previously, " 'I will give this land to your descendants,' " he now says in turn, " 'I will give it to your descendants forever, and I will make them as numerous as all the grains of sand in the world.' " For the time being the reality of the promise extended only to words, and much time would

15. Gen 13.16.

elapse in the meantime, the purpose being that we might
learn the godfearing quality of the patriarch's attitude and
the extraordinary power of God. You see, the delay and post-
ponement was intentional, so that those in receipt of the
promise might reach extreme old age and, so to say, lose all
hope for the time being according to human logic, and only
then have the experience of their own limitations and come
to recognize the remarkable degree of God's ineffable power.

(11) Now, consider, I ask you, in this disposition of time the
resoluteness of the patriarch's attitude in bypassing all human
considerations, directing his thinking to the power of the person who made the promise and not being alarmed or concerned. I mean, you know how, when someone makes a
promise on one or two occasions without ever putting into
effect what was promised we become less enthusiastic about
placing any further trust in the person making the promise.
While, however, this would be possible in the case of human
beings, yet with God, who manages our affairs with great
wisdom, once he promises—no matter if countless obstacles
interpose—we should have regard for the greatness of God's
power and keep our spirits up, our resolve strengthened, and
know that the words spoken by him will without fail take effect. There is nothing, you see, which will ever succeed in
frustrating his promises—he is God, after all, with whom all
things are possible, and hence he directs affairs in the direction he wishes, being able to find ways where there are none
and, despite our despairing, leading us to sound hopes so that
in this way we may learn the extraordinary degree of his inventive wisdom. "'Arise,'" he said, you see, "'and travel
through the length and breadth of the country, because I am
going to give it to you.'"[16] See how in every development he
aims at instilling in the just man a deep sense of security:
Arise, he says, travel about and get to know the size of the
country you are about to occupy, and so that you may enjoy
great satisfaction, buoyed up by the prospect of occupation.
You see, I am going to give you as much land as you traverse,

16. Gen 13.17.

so that you may realize that you did not give up as much as you are now about to receive. So don't think the worse part was left to you when Lot usurped what seemed the prime areas. On the contrary, before long you will know by the way things turn out that his choice of the prime areas was not to his advantage; and he will come to realize for himself what a mistake it was to set his heart on those prime areas. For the present, however, take possession of the reward of the humility and restraint you showed to your nephew, accept the promise, and now get to know all the land of which you are ruler, and which before long you and your descendants will possess in perpetuity. " 'And to your descendants forever,' " he said, remember.

(12) Wonderful the extent of the promise; remarkable the depths of generosity of the Lord of us all; extraordinary the degree of the reward conferred by him in his mercy and love on this blessed man and on the descendants destined to be born to him! Hearing this and amazed at God's unspeakable goodness, the patriarch "struck camp and moved on until settling [318] at the oak of Mambre which is at Chebron."[17] After accepting the promise, the text is saying, and following Lot's parting, he changed his camp site to the vicinity of the oak of Mambre. Notice his sensible attitude, his high sense of responsibility in effecting the transfer with ease and making no difficulty of changing from place to place. I mean, you will not find him shackled and hidebound by any custom, something which frequently affects a great number of people, even those considered wise and those generally free of concerns: should the occasion require them to change and move in a different direction, even in many cases for a spiritual matter, you would find them troubled, beside themselves, regretting the change on account of their being prisoners of habit. The just man, on the other hand, wasn't like that: he showed good sense from the very outset, and like a stranger or pilgrim he moved from here to there and from there to the next place, and in all cases his concern was to give evidence of his godfearing attitude in his actions.

17. Gen 13.18.

(13) You see, when he changed his camp to the vicinity of the terebinth grove of Mambre, immediately "he built an altar there to the Lord."[18] Do you see his sense of gratitude? I mean, once he set up camp, without delay he made an offering in thanksgiving for the promise made to him. On each spot where he made camp you will find him preoccupied with this concern above all, building an altar, offering prayers, and fulfilling the apostolic law bidding us pray in every place with pious hands raised on high.[19] Do you see his soul carried aloft to the love of God and proving grateful for all his favors? Far from waiting for the promises to take effect, he even gives thanks and does all in his power to give evidence of gratitude for the favor ahead of time and thus to encourage his Lord to fulfill his promises.

(14) Let us also imitate and trust in God's promises, not allowing time to undermine our resolve, nor any obstacles to intervene in the meantime to weaken our determination. Trusting instead in God's power as if we already had before our eyes the revelation of the promises, let us give evidence of unalloyed faith. Extraordinarily great, you see, are the promises the Lord has made to us, too, surpassing our imagination—I mean enjoyment of the kingdom, a share in those ineffable goods, life with angels, escape from hell. On the other hand, let us never lose confidence because these things are not visible to bodily eyes; rather, let us consider the fidelity of the one promising and the greatness of his power, and thus view them with the eyes of faith and on the basis of what has already been given let us maintain sound hope in what is to come. The reason, after all, that we have been blessed with many favors here is that we may be encouraged by the former to have confidence in the latter. He who gave his own son out of love for us, how will he not grant us everything else? As Paul also says, "He who did not spare his own son but handed him over for us all, how will he not grant us everything else as well along with him?"[20] If he gave his son for us sinners, if

18. Ibid.   19. Cf. 1 Tim 2.8.
20. Rom 8.3.

he favored us with the gift of baptism, if he granted us forgiveness of previous sins, if he laid down for us a way of
penance, if he devised countless other means to our salvation,
[319] clearly he will provide the good things stored up for us
in the time to come. After all, he who prepared these things
before our coming into existence out of his characteristic
goodness, how will he not grant us also enjoyment of them?
I mean, for proof that he did prepare these good things for
us in advance, listen to his words to those standing on his
right: " 'Come, you who enjoy my Father's blessing, take possession of the kingdom prepared for you before the beginning of the world.' "[21] Do you see the excess of goodness, the
great degree of loving kindness he displays towards the human race in preparing for us enjoyment of the kingdom even
before the beginning of the world?

(15) Let us therefore not prove ungrateful nor render ourselves unworthy of such wonderful gifts, but rather love our
Lord as we ought and do nothing to impair his favorable regard for us. After all, it wasn't we ourselves who initiated the
process, was it? He took the initiative in displaying towards
us his great love beyond all telling. So would it not be absurd
for us not to love as far as lies in our power the one who loves
us so much? You see, for love of us he endured everything
without demur, being torn as it were from the paternal bosom
and willing to take on the form of a slave,[22] passing through
every human experience, submitting to abuse and indignity
at the hands of Jews, and finally accepting the cross, the most
shameful death, so that he might set us free through faith in
him as we go crawling on the earth and weighed down with
countless burden of sins. All this, in fact, blessed Paul had in
mind, that fervent lover of Christ, who like a winged bird
traversed the whole world, who in his zeal gave evidence of
the faculties of incorporeal creatures, though in bodily form
himself, and thus minded he shouted aloud, "The love of

21. Matt 25.34.
22. Cf. Phil 2.6–7, introducing a catena of Pauline texts that illustrate his
regard and fellow-feeling for the Apostle.

Christ, you see, constrains us."[23] See his uprightness, see the extraordinary degree of his virtue, see his fervent love. "The love of Christ," he says, "constrains us," that is, urges, impels, coerces us. Then, wishing to explain what had been said by him, he says, "convinced of this, that if one person died for all, then all have died, he did die for all so that the living might live no longer for themselves but for the one who died and rose for them."[24] Do you see how appropriate it was for him to say, "The love of Christ constrains us"? He is saying, you see, If he died for the sake of us all, he died for the purpose that we the living might live no longer for ourselves but for him who died and rose for us.

(16) Accordingly, let us heed the apostolic exhortation, not living for ourselves but for him who died and rose for us. How, you might say, will we be able to avoid living for ourselves? Listen to this blessed man's words again: "Now, it is no longer I who live, but Christ who lives in me."[25] See how, while still striding the earth and clad in mortal flesh, he was in the condition of a dweller in heaven who lives in the company of incorporeal creatures. Hence he said further in another place, "Now, those who are Christ's have crucified the flesh with its passions and lusts."[26] So this is what is meant by not living for ourselves but for the one who died and rose for us, when we are in this life like corpses and are not distracted by any visible realities. You see, the reason the Lord was crucified was that we might exchange this life for the next—or rather, that we might through this life earn the next for ourselves. The present life, after all, provided we are prepared to be sober and alert, leads us to the enjoyment of eternal [320] life; and we will be able, if we are willing to maintain some little vigilance and open wide our mind's eye, to keep alive in ourselves through every eventuality some understanding of the rest to be enjoyed there, and thus bypass and fly above visible realities while straining our attention to those of the next life that last forever. So this blessed man said by way

23. 2 Cor 5.14.   24. 2 Cor 5.14–15.
25. Gal 2.20.   26. Gal 5.24.

of instructing us, "The life I now live in the flesh I live by
faith in the Son of God, who loved me and gave himself up
for me."[27]

(17) See his ardent spirit, see his mind borne aloft on
wings, see his imagination inflamed with love for God! "The
life I now live," he says, "I live by faith." In other words, he
says, Don't think I'm at work on some concern for the things
of this present life; even if my condition is in the flesh and I
am bound by the needs of nature, yet I live by faith, faith in
Christ, spurning all present realities, bypassing everything
through hope in him, and keeping my mind fixed on him.
Then, for you to learn the excess of his love, he says, "I live
by faith in the Son of God, who loved me and gave himself
up for me." Notice the extraordinary degree of his gratitude.
What are you saying, O blessed Paul? A little earlier you said,
"Who, far from sparing his own son, actually gave him up
for us all,"[28] and now you say, "Who loved me"—are you
claiming as your own the benefit meant for all? Yes, he says:
even if the sacrifice was offered by him for the whole human
race, yet on account of my love for him I claim the deed for
my benefit. This was also the way the Old Testament authors
spoke in saying, "O God, my God";[29] admittedly he is God of
the whole world, but it is peculiar to love to claim as one's
own what belongs to all. "By faith in the Son of God," he says,
"who loved me." What are you saying? Did he love you alone?
The whole human race, of course, he says, yet I owe him
thanks just as if I alone was loved. "And who gave himself up
for me." What now: was he crucified for you alone? Does he
not say himself, "When I have been lifted up, I shall draw
everyone to myself"? Didn't you yourself say, "He gave himself up for us all"? Yes, he replies; I am not contradicting
myself in this, but confirming my love.

(18) Notice further something else he teaches us in these
words: earlier he had said of the Father, "He gave him up for
us all"; now he says, "He gave himself up." The former

27. Gal 2.20.   28. Rom 8.32.
29. Cf. Pss 22; 118.

expression was intended to show the unity of thought and
esteem between Father and Son, since he says in another
place also, "Proved obedient to the point of death,"[30] in each
case expressing his faith in the Passion.[31] In the latter case,
on the contrary, he employed the phrase "gave himself up"
to show that he willingly embraced suffering, not acting out
of necessity but from the wish and determination to take on
the salvation of the whole human race, and so he endured
the Cross. So what degree of love will we manage to demonstrate in a worthy manner towards him who has shown such
rich love in our regard? I mean, even if we deign to expend
our very soul in obeying his laws and observing the commands given by him, we would not even then succeed in
reaching the measure of the love he showed for our nature.
In his case, after all, it was a matter of God accepting this
fate for the sake of human beings, and the master for his
servants, and not simply for his servants but for those giving
evidence of ingratitude and grossly implacable hostility. Whereas
he took the initiative in [321] displaying such kindness towards those unworthy creatures so frequently remiss, we, on
the contrary, will go to no great pains, whatever demonstration we are able to give, to make some return to the one who
has taken the initiative in our regard by such wonderful acts
of kindness. I mean, whatever comes from us, should it in
fact follow eventually, is by way of response and indebtedness,
whereas his actions are grace and favors, a wonderful degree
of giftgiving.

(19) Consequently, with all this in mind let us love Christ
as Paul loved him; far from allowing ourselves to take much
account of present realities, let us constantly keep the love for
him fixed firmly in our soul. This is the way, you see, to show
scorn for everything of the present life, this is the way to live
on earth as if in heaven, neither puffed up by successes here

30. Phil 2.8.
31. De Montfaucon suggests this translation of "Passion" for Chrysostom's *oikonomia*, normally used by him in the sense of "the divine plan":
"*oikonomia* is taken to refer to the Incarnation when the sermon deals with
Christ, but here it refers to the Passion, as emerges from what follows."

nor dejected by failures. Instead, we will pass by everything here and be carried up to the Lord as the object of our love, not troubled by the waiting itself but making our own the words of that blessed man, "The life we now live in the flesh we live by faith in the Son of God, who loved us and gave himself up for us," so that we may pass the present life without harm and be found worthy to enjoy the good things to come, thanks to the grace and loving kindness of our Lord Jesus Christ, to whom with the Father and the Holy Spirit be glory, power and honor, now and forever, for ages of ages. Amen.

HOMILY 35

*"Now, it happened that in the region of Amarphath king of Sennaar,
Arioch king of Alasar, Chodologomor king of Elam, and Tharthak king of
the nations made war with the king of the Sodomites."*[1]

THE READING [321] OF THE HOLY SCRIPTURES, dearly
beloved, is a great blessing. This it is that arouses the
soul to an appreciation of wisdom, this directs the
mind to heaven, this brings the man to a thankful attitude,
this prevents our getting excited over any earthly reality, this
brings our thinking to rest in the world beyond and ourselves
to do everything with a view to reward from the Lord and to
deal with the trials of virtue with great readiness. From this
source, you see, you can gain a precise understanding of the
providence of God's prompt retribution, the fortitude of
good people, the Lord's goodness and the greatness of his
rewards. From this source you can be stirred to ardent imitation of noble men's good sense in not fainting under the
struggles of virtue but rather maintaining hope in God's
promises before their realization.

(2) Hence, I beseech you, let us practice the reading of the
holy Scriptures with great zeal. This, after all, is the way to
fortify our knowledge, too, if we are assiduous in applying
ourselves to their contents. I mean, it is not possible for the
person who is in touch with the divine message in a spirit of
zeal and fervent desire ever to suffer neglect; rather, even
should a human teacher not come our way, the Lord himself

1. Gen 14.1–2. Commentators generally highlight the unique character of
ch. 14 for its digression into world history and its amount of puzzling an-
nalistic detail. Chrysostom has little antiquarian interest, and moves rapidly
to Abraham and Melchizedek, so that—unusually—he deals with the whole
chapter in one homily. Like his modern counterparts, however, he does feel
the need to account for the atypical material.

would come from on high to enlighten our minds, shed light on our thinking, bring to our attention what had slipped our notice, and act as our instructor in what we have no knowledge of—provided we are prepared to contribute what lies in our power. Scripture says, remember, "Do not call anyone on earth your teacher."[2] When therefore we take an inspired book in our hands, let us concentrate, collect our thoughts and dispel every worldly thought, and let us in this manner do our reading with great devotion, with great [322] attention so that we may be able to be led by the Holy Spirit towards the understanding of the writings and may gain great benefit from them.

(3) Even that pagan eunuch of the queen of Ethiopia,[3] remember, despite being in all his glory and riding along in his chariot, did not neglect that opportunity for reading; instead, with the inspired author in his hand he put much effort into reading, even without understanding the contents. Nevertheless, because he brought to bear all that lay within him—his enthusiasm, his earnestness, his attention—he chanced upon a guide. Consider, I ask you, what a great effort it was not to neglect reading even while on a journey, and especially while seated in a chariot. Let this be heeded by those people who don't even deign to do it at home but rather think reading the Scriptures is a waste of time: claiming as an excuse their living with a wife, conscription in military service, caring for children, attending to domestics, and looking after other concerns, they don't think it necessary for them to show any interest in reading the holy Scriptures. I mean, look at the case of the eunuch, a pagan to boot, both facts sufficient to induce indifference in him, and as well as that his public image and abundance of wealth, plus the fact that he was on a journey and traveling in a chariot (after all, it's not easy to pay attention to reading when you're traveling like that—quite the contrary, it's extremely difficult). Yet his desire and great enthusiasm made light of all these problems, and so he gave himself

2. Chrysostom's textual variant of Matt 23.8.
3. Cf. Acts 8.26–40.

to reading without muttering the words many people mutter these days: I don't understand the contents, I can't grasp the full sense of the words, why should I go to this trouble all to no purpose by reading without having someone capable of guiding me?

(4) None of these considerations counted for anything with that man, barbarian in language though he was, yet sage in his thinking; instead, he judged that, provided he gave evidence of all that lay within his power, he would not be overlooked but would rapidly enjoy grace from on high, and so he gave himself to reading. Hence the loving Lord, seeing his desire, did not ignore him, did not leave him unprovided for, but immediately sent him a mentor. In your case, on the other hand, I ask you, consider God's wisdom in waiting for the man first of all to bring to bear his own resources and only then he demonstrated his characteristic assistance. Since, therefore, the eunuch had discharged himself of all his capabilities, then the angel of the Lord appeared to Philip and said, "'Up now, and travel to the road that leads down from Jerusalem to Gaza (a desert road).' Lo, an Ethiopian, eunuch and minister of Candace, queen of the Ethiopians, who had gone to worship at Jerusalem, was on the return journey seated in his chariot, and he was reading the prophet Isaiah."[4] See how precisely the writer of the book described things to us, saying "Ethiopian" so that we should know he was a barbarian; then he said "minister" to show he in fact enjoyed the highest rank and pomp. "Who had gone to worship at Jerusalem," he said: notice also the reason for his journey, sufficient to reveal his godfearing attitude of mind—I mean, how long a journey he undertakes so as to pay adoration to the Lord. You see, they were still of the mind that worship was conducted in one place only, and consequently traveled long distances to offer prayers there; for this reason, of course, he arrived at the place of the temple and [323] Jewish cult so as to pay adoration to the Lord.

(5) After putting into effect what he had longed to do, the

4. A précis of Acts 8.26–28.

text says, "he was on the return journey, seated in his chariot and reading." Then Philip approached him and said, "'Do you really understand what you're reading?'"[5] Do you see his spirit of devotion, persisting with his reading while not understanding the contents, and anxious to chance upon a mentor to guide him? You see, the apostle straightway stimulates his longing by the question he asks; the fact that he deserved to meet someone to guide him towards understanding of the contents emerges from his very reply. I mean, when the apostle said, "'Do you really understand?'" and came close in his lowly condition, he was not put off, he made no objection, he did not consider himself disgraced in the way many foolish people react, often preferring to remain in unbroken ignorance through a sense of shame in admitting their ignorance and having to learn from those able to instruct them. This man, on the contrary, had none of those reactions; instead, he made his response with great restraint and discretion, showing his state of soul in the words, "'Well, how could I, unless someone shows me?'"[6] Not only did he reply with restraint and continue on as well, but he showed us the virtue in his own behavior by issuing an invitation in those words— the minister, the barbarian, seated in his chariot, inviting the man of lowly mien, despicable in attire, to mount and ride with him. Do you see his enthusiasm of spirit? Do you see the extraordinary degree of his piety? Do you see the barbarian's godfearing attitude in fulfilling that saying of a certain wise man, "If you see a man of understanding, pay him an early visit, and let your foot wear out his doorstep"?[7] Do you see how fitting it was he was not scorned? Do you see how fitting it was he enjoyed favor from on high? Do you see how he omitted nothing that was due to be performed on his part? For that reason he chanced upon his mentor at that point and gained a precise knowledge of the efficacy of Scripture's contents, shedding light on his mind.

(6) Have you noticed how great a good it is to practice the

5. Acts 8.30.   6. Acts 8.31.
7. Sir 6.36.

reading of the holy Scriptures with earnestness and zeal? The reason, in fact, that I have brought to your notice the story of this barbarian as well, is in case we are all ashamed to turn imitators of the Ethiopian, of the eunuch, of this person who did not neglect spiritual reading even on a journey. This barbarian is capable of proving a teacher of us all, those living a private life, those enlisted in military service, those who happen to be surrounded with pomp and circumstance, people in general, not only men also women as well, as much those who live the monastic life as those who spend all their time at home. From him we could learn that no time proves an obstacle to the reading of the divine sayings; rather, it is possible not only at home but also moving about in public, making a journey, being in the company of a crowd and involved in business affairs, to give oneself earnestly to these sayings so that by bringing our own resources to bear, we too may promptly chance upon a mentor. Our Lord, you see, discerning our enthusiasm for spiritual matters, far from ignoring us, supplies illumination from above and enlightens our mind. Accordingly, let us not neglect reading, I beseech you; rather, whether we recognize the efficacy of the contents [324] or are unaware of it, let us apply ourselves to it assiduously. Constant attention to it, after all, creates an indelible memory; and it often happens that what we could not discover today in our reading we all of a sudden come across the next day in returning to the task as the loving God in unseen fashion sheds light on our mind.

(7) Enough, however, of these present remarks of ours aimed at promoting your constant practice of the reading of the holy Scriptures. Listen to what is now said for you to learn, on the other hand, that in all other matters as well it is customary for the Lord, when we have contributed what we have to offer, to supply generously in his turn what comes from him, and that what he did in the case of Bible reading by dispatching with great promptness a mentor for the barbarian he likewise does in the case of people bent on practicing virtue. To make the point clearer for you, however, it would be appropriate to bring to your notice again the inci-

dent concerning the patriarch and to make the connection at
this point with what was said yesterday. You know, of course,
from what has already been said how for the great instance
of humility that he showed in Lot's favor by yielding pride of
place to him he enjoyed a great reward from above, receiving
a promise surpassing in great measure what had been done
on his part. Let us now see as well, however, from the words
read today another instance of the just man's virtue, so that
proceeding in this way we may discover God's unspeakable
providence shown in his regard. You see, with the intention
of instructing us all through the patriarch's good sense, he
allows him first of all to give evidence of the godfearing character of his own attitude on each occasion, and then confers
the recompense on his part, so that we too may show zeal in
imitating the patriarch by committing ourselves to efforts of
virtue and thus putting ourselves in the way of its rewards.

(8) Now, however, it is time to propose for your consideration the contents of today's reading. In fact, it hardly requires commentary—the very reading of the text suffices to
reveal the extraordinary degree of the good man's virtue.
"Now, it happened," the text reads, "that in the reign of
Amarphath king of Sennaar, Arioch king of Alasar, Chodologomor king of Elam, and Tharthak king of nations made
war with Balak king of Sodom, Barsak king of Gomorrah,
Sennaar king Adamah, Sumobor king of Seboim, and the
king of Balak (that is, Segor). All the latter joined forces in
the salt valley (that is, the Salt Sea)."[8] Note the precision of
Scripture in recording the names of the kings and their peoples—not without purpose but for you to learn from their
names their barbaric character. These men, it says, remember, made war on the king of Sodom and the others. Then it
also teaches us the cause of the war, what gave rise to it. "For
twelve years," the text says, remember, "they had been in
thrall to Chodologomor king of Elam, but in the thirteenth
year they rebelled. In the fourteenth year, however, came
Chodologomor and those kings supporting him and they slew

8. Gen 14.1–3.

the giants in Astaroth and Karnaim, the powerful nations along with them, the Ommaioi in the city of Shaveh, the Horites in the mountains of Seir as far as the terebinth of Pharan, which is in the wilderness. They reversed direction and came to the spring of judgment, which is [325] now Kadesh, and slew all the rulers of Amalek and the Amorites dwelling in Hazazontamar."[9]

(9) Let us not idly pass these words by, dearly beloved, nor consider the account to be of no value. It was of set purpose that Sacred Scripture recounted everything to us with precision so that we should learn the might of these barbarians and the degree of valor they displayed and with how much ferocity they involved themselves in war so as to clash even with the giants—that is, men powerful in bodily stature—and put to flight all the peoples dwelling there. You see, just as a swollen torrent sweeps away everything in its path and destroys it, in just the same way the barbarians fell on these peoples and destroyed them completely with the result that they put to flight the rulers of the Amalekites and all the others. But perhaps someone may say, What good is it for me to know about the might of the barbarians? It was not idly or to no purpose that Scripture mixed these matters in with its account, nor is it without point that we are now bringing it to your attention and directing you in turn to recall their valor; rather, our purpose is that from the ensuing instruction you may learn both the extraordinary degree of God's power and also the patriarch's virtue.

(10) So, against these forces that had gained such power and had routed so many peoples, "There went out to do battle the kings of Sodom, Gomorrah, Adamah, Seboim and Balak (that is, Segor); they took up battle positions in the Salt Valley against Chodologomor, Tharthak, Amarphath and Arioch—four kings against five. Now, the valley is salty, pits of bitumen."[10] Then, for us to learn how they were terror-

9. Gen 14.4–7. Chrysostom's habitual reminder of the precision of Scripture in these verses is made with tongue in cheek, his obvious lack of interest in historical geography and legendary characters appearing in the unusual rapidity of commentary.

10. Gen 14.8–10.

stricken at their boldness and the might of their power and
were sent fleeing, Scripture says, "The kings of Sodom and
Gomorrah took to flight and chanced upon the place of the
bitumen pits, while the remainder took to the hill country."
Do you see how great was the might of these men? How they
managed to terrify their enemies just by their very sight and
caused them to be sent fleeing? Now see how with complete
ease they put to flight all their foes, took all their possessions
and departed. "Now, they seized the hill country, all the
horses of the men of Sodom and Gomorrah and all their provisions, and departed. Now, they also seized Lot, Abram's
nephew, and his accoutrements, and made off. He had, you
see, been living in Sodom."[11]

(11) Notice that what I said yesterday has come to be true,
that Lot, far from being better off for his choice of the better
parts, rather had learned from experience not to set his heart
on the better parts. You see, not only did no benefit come to
him from it but, lo, he was even led away into captivity and
learnt the lesson through experience that it was much better
for him to enjoy the just man's company than to be parted
from him and undergo these great trials even if living inde-
pendently. I mean, he parted from the patriarch and thought
he enjoyed greater independence, had the good fortune to
enjoy the better parts and experience great prosperity—and
all of a sudden he becomes a captive, dispossessed, without
hearth or home. The purpose was for you to learn what a
great evil division is, and what a great good harmony is, and
that we ought not hanker after pride of place but love to take
second place instead. "Now, they seized Lot and his accoutrements," the text says, remember. How much better was it to
be in the company of the patriarch and accept everything
[326] for the sake of not sundering the mutual harmony than
be separated and while choosing the better parts be immediately beset with such awful perils and fall into the clutches
of barbarians?

11. Gen 14.11–12, with an apparently inadvertent insertion of the hill
country into the list of booty, under the influence of the previous verse—to
judge from comparison with the Hebrew and LXX.

(12) "One of those who escaped came and told Abraham the traveler. Now, he was camped near the oak of Mambre the Omorite, brother of Eschol and Aunan, who were confederates of Abram."[12] How was it that the patriarch had no knowledge that such forces of war were on the rampage? Perhaps he chanced to be at a great distance from the conflict, and for that reason knew nothing of it. "Now, someone came and told Abraham the traveler," the text says, to remind us that he got the news on his return from Chaldea. You see, because he had his camp across the Euphrates, consequently he was described also as traveler. Right from the outset his parents gave him this name, suggesting to him ahead of time his movement from there; in other words, he was also called Abram because he would one day cross the Euphrates and enter Palestine.[13] Notice how his parents, all unaware, and unbelievers to boot, gave the child the name under the influence of God's inventive wisdom, as was also the case with Lamech giving Noe his name. This, after all, is a characteristic of God's loving kindness, oftentimes to foretell even through unbelievers events due to happen a long time later. So, the text says, someone came and told the traveler what had happened, the capture of his nephew, the great power of those kings, the sack of Sodom and the shameful flight. "Now, he was camped near the oak of Mambre the Omorite, brother of Eschol and Aunan, who were confederates of Abram." Perhaps at this point, however, someone might wonder, Why was it that the just man Lot, alone of the fugitives from Sodom, was taken into captivity? Far from occurring idly or to no purpose, this was for Lot to learn through the events themselves the patriarch's virtue, and that others might also be saved, and that he might learn not to hanker after pride of place but yield to his betters.

12. Gen 14.13.

13. Chrysostom is thus taking issue, like his editor De Montfaucon and modern commentators after him, with a significant textual obscurity—the meaning of the word we have rendered "traveler" for *perates* in his LXX text, translating a Hebrew form based on the consonants *hbr*, which some would read as "Hebrew" and thus detect another sign that the strange ch. 14 came from a non-Israelite source. Cf. Speiser, *Genesis* 102–109.

(13) Now, let us at this point hear the sequel so as to learn both the just man's virtue and God's assistance beyond all telling. Give careful heed, however, to what is said, and strain your attention to the utmost. Great, you see, are the benefits to be derived from this, especially to learn the lesson in this case from what happened to Lot that we need never be at a loss if, on the one hand, good people encounter trials while, on the other, scoundrels and rascals escape them, nor should we in any way hanker after pride of place nor regard anything preferable to association with good people; instead, even if it means servitude, we should consider association with men of virtue to be more desirable than being at liberty. Along with these lessons, however, we can also learn from this incident the patriarch's great tolerance, the extraordinary degree of his affection, the greatness of his bravery, his scorn for wealth, the unspeakable power of God's assistance to him. The text reads, "When Abram heard that his nephew Lot had been captured, he called up the retainers of his own household to the number of three hundred and eighteen and gave chase as far as Dan, falling upon them by night, himself and his retainers, and he continued to strike them as far as Chobal, which is west of Damascus. He recovered all the cavalry of the Sodomites, and rescued his nephew Lot, all his accoutrements, his people and his women."[14]

(14) Consider in this case, I ask you, dearly beloved, [327] the greatness of heart exemplified in the just man's virtue: trusting in the power of God he was not cowed by the force of the enemy when he learnt of the rout they had caused, firstly by falling upon all the tribes and prevailing against the Amalekites and all the others, and then by engaging the Sodomites, putting them to flight and seizing all their property. The reason, you see, why Sacred Scripture described all this to us ahead of time, as well as all they achieved through their bravery, was that you might learn that the patriarch prevailed against them, not by physical strength, but through faith in God, and achieved all this under the protection of help from

14. Gen 14.14–16, differing in details from the Hebrew.

on high, not by wielding weapons and arrows and spears or by drawing bows or raising shields, but with retainers of his own household.

(15) Why was it, someone may ask, that he called up retainers of his own household to the number of three hundred and eighteen? For you to learn that he did not simply take everyone but only retainers of his own household, men raised by Lot, so that they might wreak their vengeance with much relish, like men entering this conflict for their own lord. "He fell upon them by night," the text says, "himself and his retainers, and continued to strike and pursue them." It was, you see, a hand from on high that joined in the attack and assisted in directing the battle—hence they had no need of weapons or fighting machines; instead, he had only to heave into sight with his retainers to smite some and cause others to take to flight, doing both in complete security without harassment from anyone, and he recovered the cavalry of the king of Sodom, his nephew Lot, all his accoutrements and the women. Do you see why it was permitted that while the others fled Lot alone should be taken captive? For two reasons: so that the patriarch's virtue should become manifest, and that on his account many others also might find salvation. Then he returns bearing a great prize of distinction, Lot, and parading as well as him the cavalry, women and accoutrements, announcing in a clear voice and proclaiming more loudly than any trumpet that it was not by human power nor by force of numbers that he had won the prize and achieved victory but had done everything with aid from on high. Do you see in every event the just man being conspicuous and demonstrating to everyone on every occasion God's providence in his regard? Now you see him also zealous to prove a teacher of reverence for God to the Sodomites: "The king of Sodom," Scripture says, remember, "came out to meet him on his return from the slaughter of Chodologomor and the kings with him."[15] Notice the extent of his virtue and his enjoyment of assistance from God; the king comes out to meet

15. Gen 14.17, omitting the place reference in 17b.

this stranger, advanced in years, and shows high regard for him. He had learnt, you see, that the advantage of kingship is as nothing to the person bereft of assistance from on high, and that nothing could be more efficacious than God's hand raised to assist.

(16) The text goes on, "Melchisedek, king of Salem, brought out bread and wine. Now, he was a priest of God the most high."[16] What is conveyed to us by this comment, "king of Salem" and "priest of God the most high"? He was, for one thing, king of Salem, the text says; blessed Paul, after all, said the same in drawing attention to him when writing to the believers amongst the Hebrews, calling to mind both his name and his city of origin, and at the same time he plumbed the significance of his name [328] and employed some degree of etymology in saying, "Melchisedek, king of righteousness."[17] You see, in the Hebrew language the word *Melchi* means kingdom and *Sedek* righteousness; then, moving on to the name of the city he says, king of peace, Salem after all meaning peace.[18] On the other hand, he was a priest, possibly self-appointed, this being the way with the priests of the time, you see; so in fact he had either been accorded the honor by his peers on account of his preeminence in age, or he had made it his business to act as a priest, like Noe, like Abel, like Abraham when they used to offer sacrifices. In a particular manner he was to prove a type of Christ.[19] Hence Paul too understands him in this role in the words, "With no father, with no mother, with no family history, lacking beginning of days and end of life, he yet resembles the Son of God and remains a priest forever."[20] How, you ask, is it possible for a

---

16. Gen 14.18.   17. Heb 7.2.

18. The imperfect accuracy of these derivations suggests what we already know of Chrysostom's acquaintance with Hebrew, namely, that he had not been introduced to it by his teacher Diodore, and so was at the mercy of rough equivalents. See Introduction (3) and (15), in FOTC 74.

19. A rare venture into typology by Chrysostom, the Antiochene, and only with the encouragement of Scripture itself. His school would discourage him from exploring other Scriptural senses than the literal in the manner of the great Cappadocians, and his commentary on the Psalms finds him embarrassed at times by these restraints. See my *Inspiration*, pp. 128–149.

20. Heb 7.3.

person to have no father or mother, and to lack beginning of days and end of life? You heard that he was a type; well, neither marvel at this, nor expect everything to be found in the type. You see, he would not be a type if he were likely to contain every feature that occurs in reality. So what does the saying mean? It means that, just as the former is said to have no father or mother on account of there being no mention of his parents, and to have no family history on account of there being no history for him, so too Christ, on account of his having no mother in heaven nor father on earth, is said to have no family history and in fact has none.

(17) See how, in the respect he showed the patriarch, a mystery is suggested to us: he brought out bread and wine. Now that you see the type, consider the truth, I ask you, and marvel at the force of Sacred Scripture in foretelling from the very outset things yet to happen. "He blessed Abraham," the text goes on, "in the words, 'Blessed be Abraham by God the most high, who created heaven and earth. Blessed be God the most high, who delivered your enemies into your hands.'"[21] He not only blessed him but also praised God; in the words, "'Blessed be Abraham by God the most high, who created heaven and earth,'" he also highlighted to us God's power from his creatures. If he in fact is God, creator of heaven and earth, those worshipped by human beings would not be gods; Scripture says, remember, "Let those gods perish who did not make heaven and earth."[22] The text reads, "'Blessed be God, who delivered your enemies into your hands.'" Notice, I ask you, how he not only celebrates the just man but also acknowledges God's assistance. After all, without grace from above he could not have prevailed over such might of those besetting him. "'Who delivered your enemies,'" the text says: he it is who caused everything, he it is who rendered the strong powerless, he it is who brought down the armed hordes

21. Gen 14.19–20. Chrysostom's text, though not the LXX generally, seems to slip into the fuller name Abraham at this point, at least for a while—though, predictably, Chrysostom will make great play of the formal name change when it occurs at Gen 17.5 in Homily 39.
22. Jer 10.11.

through those unarmed—from that source is the grace forth-coming that provides you with such power. "'Who delivered your enemies into your hands,'" the text says.

(18) Do you see how it shows his peaceableness and his love for Lot in indicating that even Abraham regarded his peers as enemies for what they had done to his nephew. "He gave him a tenth of everything,"[23] the text adds. Paul says this, too: "Now, consider how great this man is, to whom the patriarch Abraham even gave a tenth of the spoils";[24] that is to say, from the spoils which he had acquired he rewarded Melchisedek, apportioning him a tenth of everything he had taken, thus already at that stage proving for everyone a teacher of the need to demonstrate great generosity and offer up the first fruits [329] of what has been provided us by God. Then the king of Sodom, struck by the patriarch's magnanimity, said to him: "'Return me my men, but keep the equipment for yourself.'"[25] A fine gesture of gratitude on the king's part—but notice the just man's sound thinking: "Abram, however, said to the king of Sodom, 'I will raise my hand to swear before God the most high, who made heaven and earth, not to take even string or shoelace of all your goods, in case you were to say, I gave Abram his wealth.'"[26] The patriarch's contempt for material wealth was intense. Why is it with an oath that he rejects the offer in the words, "'I will raise my hand to swear before God the most high, who created heaven and earth'"?[27] He wants to give the king of Sodom two lessons, that he is above the gifts offered by him and gives evidence of great wisdom; he is anxious to prove an instructor for him in reverence, as if to teach him in these

23. Gen 14.20b.   24. Heb 7.4.
25. Gen 14.21.
26. Gen 14.22–23. The future tense of the oath makes little sense, and again (cf. Homily 15, n. 8 above) arises from LXX misreading of Hebrew verb forms.
27. Again Chrysostom quotes the verse in a slightly different form from before, raising the question: is this the mark of a preacher whose recall is not always word-perfect (cf. Introduction (15), in FOTC 74), and is it irreconcilable with the view that the homilies represent a text prepared for delivery but not actually preached in their present form?

words, I am calling him to witness that I will take nothing of yours—namely, the Creator of all—so that you may come to know the God over all and not regard as gods the things shaped by human hands. This, in fact, is the maker of heaven and earth, he also determined the course of this war and was the cause of victory. So don't expect me to be ready to take anything you've offered me. It was not, you see, for a reward that I wreaked vengeance; instead, in the first instance it was out of love for my nephew, and then from the very nature of a good man that I should wrest from the clutches of barbarians people wrongfully abducted.

(19) "'I will not take even string or shoelace of all your goods'"—that is to say, not even a chance item, nothing worthless or anything thought beneath contempt. I mean, people are accustomed to call a shoelace the tip of the shoe because it comes to a point; in fact, barbarians normally use this kind. Then he states the reason for his refusal, "'In case you were to say, I gave Abram his wealth.'" I have on my side the supplier of countless goods, I enjoy much favor from on high, I have no need of wealth from you, I don't want human resources, I am content with the regard God pays me, I know the generosity of his gifts towards me. Having yielded to Lot worthless scraps, I have been granted great promises beyond telling, and now by not accepting wealth from you I earn for myself greater wealth and win further grace from him. This in my opinion, at any rate, was the reason why he took the oath in the words, "'I will raise my hand to swear before God the most high,'" namely, that the king should not think that he was simply putting up a pretence about what was likely to happen, but should rather be quite clear about his not taking the least bauble from him. He was honoring that command given by Christ to the disciples, "Freely you have received, freely give."[28] In other words, he is saying, Surely I have contributed nothing to the course of the war other than consent and encouragement, whereas the victory and the spoils and everything else has been his work in his invisible might.

28. Matt 10.8.

(20) Then, in case the king should think that it was out of scorn or contempt that he did not accept what was offered by him, and to show even in this the mildness and good sense of his thinking, he said, I will take nothing "'except what my young men consumed and the portion for the men who accompanied me, Eschol, Aunan and Mambre—they will take a portion.'"[29] These I will allow to take a portion, he says, since they have given evidence of deep friendship. [330] "These," you see, the text says,[30] "were Abram's confederates," that is, joined in friendship; this shows their option to share the perils with him. Hence, with the intention of rewarding them, he is even prepared to take some portion, and in this once again he fulfills the apostolic law in the words, "The worker deserves his fare."[31] I mean, he lets them take no more than their due: "'except what my young men consumed and the portion for the men who accompanied me, Eschol, Aunan and Mambre—they will take a portion.'" Do you see the precision of the patriarch's virtue both in giving evidence as well of good sense in the matter of his disregard and scorn for wealth, and at the same time in doing everything so as not to appear to have acted from pretence or contempt and thus to have entertained grandiose notions about winning the victory?

(21) Well, let us in turn imitate this, I beseech you, and take pains to keep ourselves free of the temptation either to bask in a desperate glory on the pretext of virtue or to neglect virtue on the pretext of humility. Instead, let us in all cases keep to the middle course and base the good works done by us on humility as a kind of foundation and basis so that our practice of virtue may be established securely. This, after all, is real virtue when it has humility associated with it. I mean, the person who has laid down this foundation securely will be able to construct his edifice to whatever height he wishes. This is the greatest security, this an impregnable fortification,

29. Gen 14.24.
30. Chrysostom's perhaps—unless De Montfaucon is misreading the MSS —but not the Hebrew or the LXX otherwise.
31. Matt 10.10.

this an unassailable tower, this supports every structure, not
allowing it to be toppled by force of winds nor by onset of
hurricanes nor by assault from gales; instead, it renders it
safe against every attack and equips it as if with steel. In this
way humility preserves virtue from defeat and wins for us
great reward from the generosity of the loving God. This was
the way the patriarch received such an extent of God's wonderful promises. I mean, you will be aware from what follows
in the text due to be read later how, with God's permission,
even in this case he scorned the gifts made to him by the king
of Sodom and thus was accorded wonderfully ineffable gifts
of God. For this virtue he was not alone in being conspicuous,
but along with him all other good people. To the extent that
you are industrious in reading the holy Scriptures you will be
able to discover this happening in every case. You see, whenever our loving Lord sees us scorning the things of this present life, he provides us generously with these as well, and
also stores up for us the enjoyment of future goods. This you
can observe happening also in the case of wealth, the glory
of this present life and all perishable things.

(22) Accordingly, let us despise this world's wealth so as to
be able to find the true wealth, let us scorn the empty glory
of this life so as to enjoy that other genuine, dependable kind;
let us mock this world's prosperity so as to attain to those
other ineffable blessings; let us consider present realities of
no value so as to be able to direct all our energies towards the
desire for what lies ahead. You see, it is not possible for the
person attached to present realities ever to entertain the desire for those other ineffable blessings; as though some film
lies over his body's eyes, [331] so the longing for this world
dulls his intellect and does not allow him to see at a glance
anything that is to his advantage. Nor, on the other hand,
could the person who has the desire for those other sure and
dependable blessings set his heart on those perishable, decay-
ing things that are whisked away even before they have taken
form. I mean, the person consumed with longing for God
and possessed of desire for what lies ahead sees the situation
of this world with different eyes, and knows that this present

life is all sham and deception and is no different from dreams. Hence blessed Paul too said as much in his letter, "The form of this world is passing away,"[32] to show us that every human thing only exists in appearance and passes away like a shadow or dream, having about it nothing true, nothing firm. So how could it be other than an infantile attitude to go after shadows and give importance to dreams, and cling to these things that shortly afterwards pass away? "The form of this world is passing away," he says, remember. When you hear it is "passing away," why do you still go after it any longer? When you hear that all human things only exist in appearance and are in fact destitute of true meaning, why do you willingly submit to a deception, and not rather consider their transient and insubstantial condition and bypass them, while transferring your desire to those other realities that are everlasting, fixed and dependable, susceptible of no change? You see, if you are to understand the point of view of the world's teacher, observe him further in another place intending to demonstrate the worthlessness of all the glitter of this world by the kind of language he employs when he says, "Visible things," even if you cite abundance of wealth, glory, reputation, power and influence, even kingship itself and wearing a crown and a lofty throne—all these "visible things are transient,"[33] giving evidence of a short time's duration, not affording us enjoyment for long. So what do you want us to seek after if all these visible things are in fact transient? Those others that are not visible, he says, not these visible ones but those that are not seen by these bodily eyes of ours. And who would offer us this advice, you ask, to bypass visible things and seek after those that are not seen? Let the very nature of things, he says, instruct you that while the former, even if in fact visible, nevertheless rapidly pass away, the latter, even if in fact we cannot now see them, nevertheless are in reality everlasting, have an eternal duration, know no conclusion, suffer no ending, experience no change, remain solid and immovable. Perhaps I may even seem to be a nuisance

32. 1 Cor 7.31.   33. 2 Cor 4.18.

offering this advice day in day out to no purpose—but what am I to do? Great is the harm wrought by wickedness, great the tyranny of possessions, great the dearth of virtue. Hence I am anxious to get the better of the disease if only by dint of frequency of exhortation and lead those attending here to complete recovery. You see, the reason that we take pains to engage in the explanation of the Scriptures, bring to your notice the virtues of the just, and never leave off echoing the same message is that we may be able through all these means to urge you on to imitation of these good people.

(23) At this late stage, at any rate, let us show some care for our own salvation and take proper advantage of the opportunity given us in light of the appointed day in our life; while there is yet time, let us make every effort in the direction of repentance and correction of our faults, let us use the abundance of our wealth for the betterment of our souls and spend the surplus on those in need. After all, why is it, tell me, that you allow your silver and gold to be consumed [332] by rust, whereas it ought to be emptied into the bellies of the poor so that by lodging it in that safe deposit at the appropriate time you may enjoy assistance from it when you particularly need comfort from it, and that those who are nourished on it at your hands may on that dread day open the doors of confidence to you and welcome you into their eternal dwellings?[34] Let us, on the contrary, not allow our garments to be consumed by moths and rot away to no purpose in the cupboard while so many people are needy and go about naked; let us instead put the naked Christ ahead of moths and clothe him as he goes about naked for us and our salvation, so that having been deemed worthy to clothe him we may hear on that dread day, "I was naked and you clothed me."[35] His precepts aren't burdensome, are they? They are not excessive, are they? What is rotting away, he says, what is being consumed by moths, what is used up idly and to no purpose—this take pains to dispose of profitably, so that you may both escape the harm of the loss and also store up for your-

34. Cf. Luke 16.9.   35. Matt 25.36.

self the greatest advantage from them. It is, after all, a mark of excessive inhumanity after so much enjoyment to store up the surplus in chests and cupboards and not succeed in alleviating the neediness of our fellows but rather choose to have it destroyed by rust and moths and fall into the hands of robbers, and thus earn condemnation on this account rather than win a reward on their account by disposing of it properly. Let us not, indeed, I beseech you, deal so negligently with the salvation of our souls, but instead dispose of our surplus to those in need and so lay up for ourselves great confidence so that we may be found worthy to enjoy ineffable blessings, thanks to the grace and loving kindness of our Lord Jesus Christ, to whom with the Father and the Holy Spirit be glory, power and honor, now and forever, for ages of ages. Amen.

HOMILY 36

"Now, after these events Abram received an oracle from the Lord in a vision by night, with these words, 'Don't be afraid, Abram, I am your shield. Your reward will be exceedingly great.'"[1]

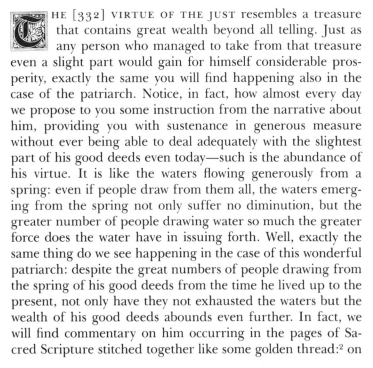HE [332] VIRTUE OF THE JUST resembles a treasure that contains great wealth beyond all telling. Just as any person who managed to take from that treasure even a slight part would gain for himself considerable prosperity, exactly the same you will find happening also in the case of the patriarch. Notice, in fact, how almost every day we propose to you some instruction from the narrative about him, providing you with sustenance in generous measure without ever being able to deal adequately with the slightest part of his good deeds even today—such is the abundance of his virtue. It is like the waters flowing generously from a spring: even if people draw from them all, the waters emerging from the spring not only suffer no diminution, but the greater number of people drawing water so much the greater force does the water have in issuing forth. Well, exactly the same thing do we see happening in the case of this wonderful patriarch: despite the great numbers of people drawing from the spring of his good deeds from the time he lived up to the present, not only have they not exhausted the waters but the wealth of his good deeds abounds even further. In fact, we will find commentary on him occurring in the pages of Sacred Scripture stitched together like some golden thread:[2] on

1. Gen 15.1, with the addition of the words "by night," perhaps by Chrysostom himself, since the words are not in Hebrew or the LXX generally, and yet Chrysostom makes some play on them.
2. This homily, like many others, eases the congregation into the subject matter through a series of figures to do with the rich fare being offered in a scriptural homily, as we noted in Introduction (12) in FOTC 74. This homily protracts the series more than most.

324

each occasion he is first observed giving evidence of his characteristic good sense, while immediately there follows reward from God.

(2) For you to learn that this is the case, we need to summarize for you his story from the beginning, [333] so that you may see both the extraordinary degree of the just man's faith shown in regard to God's promises and rewards provided generously by the loving God. In fact, this just man is capable of instructing us all to embrace with enthusiasm the struggles of virtue in our trust in rewards from above, to realize the generosity of our Lord and to accept with ease all the things considered difficult in this world's terms, nourished as we are by the hope of recompense. Pay close attention, I beseech you, how from the outset he brought to bear his own innate resources arising from the knowledge inherent in our nature and had no teacher from any external source; rather, he was raised by infidel parents and yet enjoyed the divine vision. You see, since, far from following in the erroneous footsteps of his father, from his earliest years he gave evidence instead of devotion to divine things, he soon had the good fortune to enjoy attention from above while still in Chaldea. This, remember, was what blessed Stephen explained clearly to us in these words, " 'The God of glory appeared to our father Abraham while he was in Mesopotamia before settling in Charran.' "[3] Do you see how the vision induced him to move from there? After all, it was to be expected that with his devotion to divine things he would have shown respect for his parents and won his father over to a loving frame of mind, and thus become the cause of his moving from there: on account of the son's love the father would have consented to abandon his own country and dwell in a foreign one. Consider, precisely, however, I ask you, how the attention given him by God on account of his anticipated virtue once more causes his virtue to be more patent: he chose to leave the paternal country and dwell in a foreign one so as to put into effect the command from God. In my opinion he was ready

3. Acts 7.2.

even without his relatives to make the move by himself; but, as I said before, the man's virtues and his great devotion to his parents brought it about that his father became a so-journer with him.

(3) Then, when he reached Charran, he pitched his tent there. At the death of Tharra—that was his father's name, remember—he is once more bidden by God to move from there. "'Go forth from your country,'" the text says, remember, "'and your kindred, onwards to the land that I will show you.'"[4] You see, since he had moved to Charran with his whole household, for that reason in giving him the command in this case to leave he added, "'from your country and your kindred,'" to show him that he wanted him to make the move by himself, alone, and not to drag his brother—I mean Nachor—or anybody else along with him. Now, he said "'from your own country'" since they had dwelt there no little time and by then had made their home in it as if in their own native land. Though admittedly his grief for his parents was still at its height, and there were many difficulties and obstacles involved in moving at that time, nevertheless he responded with great alacrity to the command from the Lord without knowing where an end would come to his journeying. "'Onward,'" the text says, remember, not to this land or that, but to "'the one I will show you.'" Despite the direction being so vague, he carried out the command without being concerned about it in any way; he did, however, take his nephew [334] with him, showing in this his characteristic virtue. I mean, since he had taken him into his company as a young man and gradually made him an imitator of his own virtue, he would not bear to leave him behind and instead took him as a companion on his journey. In other words he said to himself, If my father, infidel though he was, agreed through love of me to leave his ancestral home, where we were born and raised, and accompany me, and ended his life in a foreign land, surely much more unwilling would I be to allow

---

4. Gen 12.1. Having already spent 35 homilies on 14 chapters of Genesis and dealt with this incident adequately in Homily 31, Chrysostom can still halt further progress to return to it—doubtless for its moral value.

my brother's son, who from his earliest years has shown that he is gradually advancing in virtue, to be left here.

(4) Since he had shown his godliness in every way and had even made this transfer, accordingly when he reached Palestine and crossed the frontier of the Canaanites God appeared to him out of a wish to strengthen his resolve and offer him his hand. He said to him, "'I will give this land to your descendants.'"[5] What he really longed for—I mean posterity—this he immediately promises him, granting him recompense for such great labors. You see, though he had been deprived of natural progeny, and age by then had obliged him to give up hope of any, by his promise God restores his vigor and transforms him into a person of greater enthusiasm, making a new man of him and preparing him for the struggles ahead. Accordingly, notice the just man after this promise engaging in another contest: with the onset of famine and the presence of extreme hardship in Canaan he made tracks for Egypt, and in his desire to find relief from famine he involved himself in greater perils. Sarah's womanly beauty and charm almost brought him face to face with death. Hence when he was on the point of entering Egypt, he said to her, "'I know that you are very beautiful.'"[6] I recognize the bloom of your charm, and I am afraid of the Egyptians' lust. So if they see you and know that I have you always with me as my wife, perhaps they will spare your life so as to put into effect their passionate frenzy, whereas they will kill me so as to be able to perpetuate their crime without fear in the absence of anyone capable of bringing their turpitude to light. "'So say that I am your brother.'" See his spirit of steel, see his attitude firmer than iron; the dreaded outcome did not sway his thinking, nor did he think or say to himself, Is this the reason I left my own country and as index of my great obedience I went to another one, to fall victim to these scoundrels? Didn't he promise me just recently, "'I will give this land to your descendants'"? Lo, he strikes our soul with fear of dishonor and death. On the contrary, Abram allowed nothing of the

5. Gen 12.7.   6. Gen 12.11.

sort to affect his thinking; instead, his one concern was how to act in this evil scenario so as to succeed in escaping at least one of these two perils besetting him.

(5) He had brought all his resources to bear in making his plans with courage; his wife had acted with every sign of obedience and devotion to her husband and had put into effect his decisions. So when they completed what lay within their power, when things offered no hope by human reasoning and the criminal events had almost come to pass, then it was that the great providence of God in their regard was revealed. That is to say, not only did God snatch the woman from outrage in his anger vented on the king and all his household, but he also caused the patriarch to return with much acclaim from Egypt to Palestine. [335] Consider how in the midst of these trials the loving Lord made available his grace and caused him to be at the peak of his condition for facing the contests still ahead, not permitting him to be bereft of his assistance but arranging by every means to make perfectly clear to him that, trifling though his contribution might be, he was being accorded wonderfully abundant resources even surpassing human nature.

(6) So do you see the good man's endurance? Observe likewise after his return from there the extent of his humility and his great restraint. I mean, when he returned from Egypt after acquiring great affluence (not himself solely, however, but accompanied by his nephew), "the countryside could not manage to support their living together," (the text says) "since their company was numerous"[7]—whence even trouble broke out between the herdsmen of Lot and Abram. This just man, however, showed his mildness of spirit and the extraordinary degree of his good sense by calling Lot and saying to him, " 'Let there be no trouble between you and me, nor between my herdsmen and yours, for we are brothers' "[8]—as if to say to him, Nothing is so important as peace, nothing is more serious than strife; so to rid ourselves of every ground of contention, choose whatever territory you wish and leave

7. Gen 13.6.   8. Gen 13.8.

me the remainder for the sake of our remaining free from all rivalry and dispute. Do you see the man's virtue? He allowed his junior the choice of the best parts, and was content with the poorest land. See him, however, in another situation, enjoying great reward after giving evidence of effort on his part: as soon as the separation took place, God said to him after Lot's parting from him: "'Lift up your eyes and see all the land on either side: all the land you see I will give to you and your descendants forever.' "[9] Notice how much regard he was accorded for the humility he had displayed in regard to his nephew; whereas he made slight concessions and yet was granted far greater rewards, Lot on the contrary shortly afterwards fell into perils after taking pride of place, not only gaining no advantage from his choice but also suddenly falling captive and losing hearth and home, learning through the very turn of events the just man's exceeding virtue and gaining the lesson himself never to perpetuate anything like that in future. You recall that after Lot took up residence in Sodom, immediately a bitter war broke out: the kings of the neighboring peoples attacked with great force and completely devastated the whole country, slaying the giants, driving out the Amalekites, even forcing the king of Sodom and Gomorrah to take flight, occupying the whole mountain region, overwhelming the cavalry of the king of Sodom, capturing Lot with his women and all his possessions, and thus taking their leave.

(7) Notice, however, God's wonderful providence: out of a wish to free Lot from captivity and at the same time to shed notoriety on the patriarch, he prompts the just man to come to the assistance of his nephew. Learning of the event, he fell on those kings with his retainers, routed them with complete ease, and recovered Lot, his women and all the king's horses, taking splendid spoils and making quite clear to everyone God's favor in his regard and the fact that he inflicted such a great defeat not by his own power but under the protection

9. Gen 13.14–15, in a somewhat paraphrased form of those verses already commented on by Chrysostom in Homily 34.

of help from on high. Then he took pains by this turn of events to become an [336] instructor in religion to all the residents of Sodom through his converse with the king. The king met him, expressed his thanks for what he had done and said he would let him keep all the horses while retaining the people for himself. Notice in turn the just man's magnanimity in the lesson he gives of his own sound values, namely, that he is protected against gifts from the king, and in leading the king to the knowledge of religion. You see, he did not simply tell him, I decline to accept anything from you, or I don't need any reward. Instead, what? "'I will raise my hand to swear before God the most high,'"[10] (as if teaching him that those worshipped by you are not gods, but figures of stone and wood; one alone is God over all) "'who made heaven and earth, that I will not accept from you even string or shoelace,'"[11] lest you think we have taken vengeance for their sake and be in a position to say you were responsible for my prosperity. In fact, the one who provides the victory and guarantees my triumph is he who supplies also the source of my wealth. Notice how, if only he had wanted to, the king could have gained a lot from the patriarch's virtue in everything. In case he might think that it was through stupidity or arrogance that he spurned what he had offered, consequently he said to him, While I will accept nothing—after all, I don't need it, and I don't depend on others to add to my wealth— yet I will allow my associates in danger to take portions lest they seem to have cold comfort for their good offices.

(8) While this was the reply the good man made to the king of Sodom, on the contrary, when Melchisedek king of Salem in his turn offered him bread and wine ("He was," the text says, remember, "priest of God the most high"[12]), he accepted the offerings from him and rewarded him for the blessing bestowed on him and the praise of God (he said, remember, as the text tells us, "'Blessed be Abram by God the most high, and blessed be God, who delivered your enemies into your

10. Gen 14.22.
11. Gen 14.22–23, again paraphrased.
12. Gen 14.18.

hands' "[13]) by giving him a tenth of all the spoils he had taken. Do you see the just man's godfearing attitude shown in every circumstance and how, while declining to take from the king of Sodom even string or shoelace, he did, on the other hand, accept the offering of Melchisedek and even recompensed him for them with offerings of his own, giving us the lesson of exhibiting great discretion instead of simply and without question accepting gifts from everyone. You see, whereas the king of Sodom proved well-disposed in giving gifts, yet he was in fact faithless in other matters and stood in need of much instruction; hence, on the one hand, Abram spurned the gifts, and on the other he went to considerable trouble to encourage him to a sense of religion both through the gifts he declined to accept and the conversation he had with him. Quite rightly, on the contrary, did he accept them from Melchisedek; after all, Sacred Scripture gave indication of the man's virtue in saying, "Now, he was a priest of God the most high." In particular, these events were a type [337] of Christ, and the offerings themselves prefigured a kind of mystery[14]— hence Abram accepted them and in taking them he also taught us by the recompense given by him the greatness of his own virtue. He gave him a tithe, you remember, indicating by that his godly purpose.

(9) Perhaps our sermon has been drawn out to great length, but not idly or to no purpose.[15] We came to know, in brief, the just man's bravery right from the beginning up to the text proposed to us today, his magnanimity, the extraordinary degree of his faith, his sensible attitude, the extent of his humility, his exceeding scorn for wealth, the constant

13. Gen 14.19–20, also paraphrased.

14. It is rare to find Chrysostom the Antiochene recognizing a spiritual or typological sense in Scripture, and then only (as here) with encouragement from the New Testament. His school's interest in the literal sense did not allow such departures, and his audience did not expect it. See Introduction (21) in FOTC 74.

15. Well might Chrysostom advert to the length of this introduction, which has been little other than a summary of those chapters 12–14 of Genesis he had already commented on in similar vein in recent homilies. Did he suspect that some of his congregation had in fact not attended those homilies and needed a synopsis?

providence of God's favor in his regard, and how the support
given him each day rendered the good man in every instance
more conspicuous and admirable. If, however, you don't
mind and are not weary, let us also touch on the text read
just now and draw the sermon to a close by proposing a few
matters to you in order that you may learn how much reward
he was again granted for scorning the gifts offered him by
the king of Sodom. What in fact does it say? "Now, after these
events Abram received an oracle from the Lord." Why did it
begin, "Now, after these events"? What events, tell me? Is it
referring to his actions in regard to the king of Sodom? After
that rejection, is it saying, after declining what was offered by
him, after the lesson he gave by rejecting the gifts in leading
him to a sense of religion and knowledge of the Creator of
all—"now, after these events," after providing Melchisedek
with the tithe, when (in short) he had discharged all that lay
in his power, then "after these events Abram received an oracle from the Lord in a vision by night, with these words:
'Don't be afraid, Abram, I am your shield. Your reward will
be exceedingly great.'"

(10) See the loving kindness of the Lord in immediately
coming to his support by rewarding him with acts of kindness, anointing his athlete for the contest and bringing new
life to him. "He received an oracle from the Lord in a vision
by night." Why by night?[16] So that he might receive the oracle
in tranquility. God said to him, "'Don't be afraid, Abram.'"
Notice the extraordinary degree of his care. Why did he say,
Don't be afraid? Since he had scorned so much wealth by
giving little importance to the offerings of the king, God said
to him, Have no fear for despising gifts of such value, nor be
distressed on the score of your diminished prosperity. "'Don't
be afraid.'" Then to cheer his spirit further, he adds his name
to the encouragement by saying, "'Don't be afraid, Abram.'"

16. As we have remarked, neither the Hebrew nor LXX support Chrysostom in this reading. He is perhaps reasoning from v. 5 that it is night,
though v. 12 speaks of the day (as Chrysostom admits in Homily 37)—something that suggests to modern commentators (but not Chrysostom, of course)
diversity of tradition.

It proves to be no little help in encouraging a person to invoke the name of the person we are addressing. Then he said, "'I am your shield.'" This phrase is also rich in meaning: I summoned you from the Chaldeans, I led you hither, I rescued you from the perils of Egypt, I promised once and again to give this land to your descendants, I it is who will be your shield; after daily making you acclaimed by all, I will be your shield—that is, I will struggle in your stead, I will be your shield. "'Your reward will be [338] exceedingly great.'" You refused to accept reward for the troubles you suffered in exposing yourself to such risks; instead, you scorned both the king and what he offered you. I will provide you with a reward, not to the degree that you would have received, but wonderfully, exceedingly great: "'Your reward,'" the text says, remember, "'will be exceedingly great.'"

(11) Do you see the Lord's generosity? Do you see the force of his words? Do you see how he encouraged this champion of religion? Do you see how he invigorated his spirit? I mean, the one who knows the unspoken thoughts of our mind understood that the just man could do with comfort from his own words; after all, see what he said in deriving confidence from his words: "Abram said, however, 'Lord, what will you give me? I am to pass on without children.'"[17] Since God had promised him a reward, a wonderfully, exceedingly great reward, Abram revealed his grief of spirit and the disappointment affecting him constantly on account of his childless condition in saying, Lord, what sort of thing will you give me? After all, behold, I have reached the height of old age and am to pass on without children. See how from the outset the just man showed his sound thinking in calling his departure from here passing on. I mean, people who live an assiduous life of virtue really pass on from struggle, as it were, and are freed from their bonds when they transfer from this life. You see, for people living virtuously it is a kind of transfer from a worse situation to a better, from a temporary existence to an everlasting one that is protected from death and has no

17. Gen 15.2.

end. "'I am to pass on without children,'" he said. And to win the merciful Lord over, far from resting content with these words what did he say? "'Since you have given me no offspring, a son of my household slave Mazek will be my heir.'"[18] These words reveal the extreme degree of the pain in his soul, as if to say to God, Far from being granted what my slave was, I am to pass away without child or heir, whereas my slave will inherit the gifts granted me by you, despite the promise received from you more than once in the words, "To your descendants I will give this land.'" Consider, I ask you, the just man's virtue in this case also in the fact that while entertaining these thoughts in his mind he did not protest nor say any harsh words; instead, because driven on in this case by the words spoken to him, he spoke boldly to the Lord, revealed the tumult of his interior thoughts and made no secret of the wound to his spirit—hence in turn he received instant healing.

(12) "Immediately," the text goes on, "the voice of God came to him." See the precision of Scripture! "Immediately," the text says. He did not allow the just man to be distressed for a moment, but rather brought immediate comfort and assuaged the severity of the pain through his words to him. "Immediately," the text says, "the voice of God came to him saying, 'Not that child will be your heir, but the one who comes from your body—he will be your heir.'"[19] Is this what you are afraid of? he asks. Is this what upsets you, does this aggravate your discouragement? Well, learn that "'not that child will be your heir, but the one who comes from your body—he will be your heir.'" So look not to human nature, nor consider your old age, nor Sarah's sterility; instead, trust the power of my promise, leave aside your discouragement, and rather take sufficient heart and convince [339] yourself that you will have an heir that will be born from your own

18. Gen 15.2b–3, a passage that is corrupt in the Hebrew and rendered in a more complicated fashion in the LXX generally; in abbreviating it Chrysostom has probably represented the sense of Abram's complaint of lacking a true heir.
19. Gen 15.4.

body. Then, since the promise was beyond nature and surpassed human reasoning (the natural difficulties, after all,
caused considerable tumult within him—his old age, Sarah's
sterility and the barrenness of her womb), he magnifies the
extent of the promise so that the just man might be able to
take heart in considering the generosity of the one making
the promise. "He took him outside," the text goes on, "and
said to him: 'Look up at the sky and count the number of the
stars—if in fact you can number them.' He said, 'That will be
the number of your descendants.' Abram had faith in God,
and this was reckoned as righteousness in him."[20]

(13) Why did it inform us that "he took him outside"? Well,
since it had said previously that God appeared to him in a
vision by night and addressed those words to him, whereas
now, however, he wants to show him the innumerable stars in
the sky, the text says, "He took him outside and said, 'Look
up at the sky and count the number of stars—if in fact you
can number them.' He said, 'That will be the number of your
descendants.'" Wonderful the promise, marvelous the extent
of the pledge—yet if we consider the power of the one promising, nothing will seem extraordinary to us. I mean, the one
who formed the body from dust, brought it into being from
non-being and created all visible things can also lavish upon
us what is beyond the limits of nature.

(14) Do you see the Lord's generosity? After Abram said,
remember, "'I am to pass on without children'" as though
finding himself at the very gates of death and no longer in a
position to do anything about having children, he added
those further words by saying, "'The son of my household
slave Mazek will be my heir.'" Hence, out of a desire to lift
his spirits and cause his thoughts to be optimistic, he both
liberates him from the pressing anxiety and also sets his mind
at rights with his promise and the greatness of the gift, and
by showing him the multitude of stars and promising that his
offspring would be equal to them he led him to sound hope.
That is to say, when he saw the Lord's promise and discarded

20. Gen 15.5–6.

every human consideration, having regard neither for himself nor for Sarah's being beset by so many handicaps, but rather surpassing all human problems and realizing that God is capable also of granting favors beyond human limits, he took heart from God's words and entertained no doubts nor had any qualms about what had been said. After all, this is what faith really is, when we trust in the power of the one promising, not on the basis of human plausibility of the promise made. "Faith is," remember, as blessed Paul also says, "the substance of things hoped for, the guarantee of what is not seen,"[21] and again, "After all, if a person sees something, what need has he also to hope for it?"[22] Accordingly, that is faith, when we believe in those things that are not seen and keep our mind fixed on the trustworthiness of the one who has made the promise. This, in fact, is exactly what this just man did, giving evidence of much genuine faith in regard to the promises—hence he is acclaimed also by Sacred Scripture, for it added immediately, "Abram had faith in God, and this was reckoned as righteousness in him." Do you see how even before the outcome of the promises he received a commensurate reward for his very act of faith? It was reckoned as righteousness in him, remember, to have faith in the promise from God and not to delve into the words spoken by God by human reasoning.

(15) Accordingly, let us learn, [340] I beseech you, a lesson for ourselves as well from the patriarch, to believe in the words of God and trust in his promise, and not to apply the yardstick of our own reasoning but give evidence of deep gratitude. This, you see, will succeed in making us also be seen to be righteous and will quickly cause us to attain to the promise made by him. In Abraham's case, however, the promise was made that a complete multitude would develop from his descendants, and the effect of the promise was beyond the limits of nature and human logic—hence also faith in God won righteousness for him. In our case, on the other hand, if we are alert enough to see it, he promised much

21. Heb 11.1 in Chrysostom's text.   22. Rom 8.24.

more and we are able in great measure to transcend human reasoning, provided we believe in the power of the one who promises, in order that we may gain also righteousness from faith and attain to the good things promised. You see, all the things that are the particular object of his promise defy human reasoning and surpass all imagining—such is the extent of the promises. I mean, he did not only promise things in this world, the substance of material things, but also after our departure from here and the corruption of our bodies, when our bodies dissolve into dust and ashes—then it is that he promised to raise them up and transform them in greater glory. Blessed Paul says, remember, "The perishable must be clad in imperishability and the mortal be clad in immortality."[23] After the resurrection of our bodies he promised to grant us enjoyment of the kingdom, life with the saints, enjoyment for all eternity, and those ineffable good things "which eye has not seen nor ear heard, nor have they been imagined by human heart."[24] Do you see the extraordinary extent of his promise? do you see the greatness of his gifts?

(16) With this in mind and aware of the impossibility of deceit by the one who promises, let us with enthusiasm prepare ourselves for the struggles of virtue so that we may be in a position to enjoy the good things promised and not put present concerns ahead of our salvation and the enjoyment of such wonderful blessings, and instead of considering the effort virtue involves let us have regard for its recompense; when there is need to give money to the poor, let us consider not the expense but the advantage to us stemming from it. You see, the reason that Sacred Scripture compared almsgiving to sowing seed was that we might engage in it with relish and much enthusiasm. After all, if people plough seed into the soil, gather and scatter what they have stored, complete the process with joy and buoyed up with optimistic expectations already sketch in their imagination the sheaves and the brimming barns, much more should those who have been granted the favor of sowing this spiritual seed rejoice and

23. 1 Cor 15.53.   24. 1 Cor 2.9.

exult in the fact that while sowing on earth they are destined to reap in heaven, and while dispensing money they receive remission of sins and find grounds for confidence, procuring for themselves through almsgiving here everlasting repose and life with the saints. If we have a love for self control, let us not have regard for the fact that virtue involves effort, nor that virginity involves a keen struggle; rather, let us consider the end awaiting us, and with this ever in mind let us check evil desire, get the better of the promptings of the flesh and discount the difficulty of effort with [341] the thought of the rewards received in return.

(17) The hope of real gain, after all, is enough to prepare us to face even great risk with boldness, not to mention putting up nobly with the effort virtue involves. I mean, when you consider that after fighting the good fight for a brief period and keeping the lamp of virginity shining you will be accorded that blessed existence and be in a position to join the bridegroom, provided you have your lamps alight and keep enough oil[25]—that is, the doing of good deeds—how can you fail to survive all those difficulties with ease by keeping in mind that saying of blessed Paul, "Seek after peace with everyone and the holiness without which no one will see the Lord"?[26] Do you see how he linked peace with holiness? You see, for us to learn that he stipulates not only purity of body but peace as well, he makes timely mention of it out of a wish for us to be secure on both scores and at rest in our thinking, so that there be no alarm or tumult in ourselves but that we live in peace and tranquility, be peacably disposed to all, mild, gentle and restrained so that all the colors of virtue may blossom on our countenance. In this way, you see, we shall be able for the future to scorn even the glory of this present life by preferring true glory, giving much attention to humility and despising all the prosperity of this present life so as to enjoy true and lasting prosperity and be deemed worthy to see Christ. "Blessed are the pure in heart," Scripture says, remember, "because they will see God."[27] Accordingly, let us

25. Cf. Matt 25.1–13. 26. Heb 12.14.
27. Matt 5.8.

purify our conscience and conduct our life meticulously so that by passing the present life in all virtue we may be deemed worthy to receive in the world to come the reward of our labors here, thanks to the grace and loving kindness of our Lord Jesus Christ, to whom with the Father and the Holy Spirit be glory, power and honor, now and forever, for ages of ages. Amen.

HOMILY 37

"The Lord said to Abram: 'I am the God who has brought you out of the land of the Chaldeans to give you this land for your inheritance.' But Abram replied: 'My lord and master, how shall I know that I am to inherit it?'"[1]

ONDERFUL IS [341] THE POWER of Sacred Scripture, and immense the wealth of ideas concealed in its expressions. Hence it behooves us to attend precisely and give ourselves to close study so as to reap the lavish benefits it offers. You see, the reason Christ himself gave this command, "Search the Scriptures,"[2] was that, far from idly listening to the mere reading, we should rather descend to its very depths and be in a position to grasp the true sense of Scripture. This, after all, is the way with Scripture: in a few words it is often possible to find a great number of ideas. Its teachings, you see, are divine, not human, and consequently you can see it all composed in a manner opposite to human wisdom. What way that is, I will tell you: in the latter case— I mean human wisdom—people's whole interest is concentrated on the sequence of the words, whereas in this case it is completely different. No study of Scripture is about words, their beauty or sequence: it has of itself divine grace resplendent upon it and its sayings have their own beauty. With that other writing you can grasp the sense only after a great amount of unspeakable [342] nit-picking, whereas in this case, as you know, often a short phrase suffices for us to piece out the complete message.

---

1. Gen 15.7–8. Chrysostom follows the LXX in avoiding reference to Ur as the home of the patriarchs after Haran had earlier been given that designation, though mention of the Chaldeans is still an anachronism.
2. John 5.39.

(2) Consequently, then, yesterday also we proposed the reading to you and picked up the thread of our theme, but since we found such wealth of ideas we weren't able to press ahead further without swamping your recollection with the multitude of ideas and distorting it with the words already spoken.[3] Hence I want to pick up that very thread and link together what was said yesterday with what follows so that we may be able to make a complete commentary on the reading and then send you home from here. But pay precise attention, I beseech you, to what is said: if the labor is ours, the gain is yours, or rather it belongs to us both. But why do I say labor? Not at all; instead, it is the gift of God's grace. Accordingly, let us in our turn receive with attention what is granted us by God so that we may gain something for our soul's salvation and thus go off from here. You see, the reason that we lay out for you each day this spiritual table is that by the frequency of the exhortation and by constant attention to the holy Scriptures we may fend off all the evil demon's wiles. After all, when he sees us displaying much zeal for spiritual things, far from attacking us he doesn't even dare to cast a glance in our direction, knowing as he does that he will be making efforts in vain and bringing trouble on his own head.

(3) So, come now, let us pick up the thread of yesterday's remarks and comment on what remains. Well, what was it you were told yesterday? We gave an account of the promise made to Abram, where he directed him to look up at the sky and see the multitude of stars. "'Count the number of the stars,'" he said, remember, "'if in fact you can number them.' He said, 'That will be the number of your descendants.'"[4] Then, to show us the patriarch's godfearing attitude and the fact that he had faith in God's words through having regard for the one who made the promise and considering the power of the one who gave the guarantee, Sacred Scripture added, "Abram had faith in God, and this was reckoned as righ-

3. As we remarked at that point, Chrysostom spent much of Homily 36 rehearsing the matter of the previous few homilies—and now finds an excuse in the richness of Scripture.

4. Gen 15.5.

teousness in him." Our sermon reached that point yesterday, and we were unable to proceed further; hence it is necessary to propose what follows. "The Lord said to Abram: 'I am the God who has brought you out of the land of the Chaldeans to give you this land for your inheritance.'" See God's considerateness in wanting to strengthen his faith and persuade him to have complete certainty about what had been promised, as if to say, Remember that I took you from your home. Lo, what was said by God about the patriarch proves to be consistent with blessed Stephen's words, that the Lord's directions led to his transfer from his home and from Chaldea itself.[5] His father, too, responding to his attitude, as we said before, infidel though he was, yet having in his love for Abram a strong basis for attachment, followed him and left that country.

(4) Consequently, on the present occasion God reminds Abram of all the care he had shown him by revealing to him that it was due to his great plans for him and his wish to put into effect his promises in his regard and bring them to fulfillment that he caused him to make such a long journey. "'I am the one who has brought you out of the land of the Chaldeans to give you this land for your inheritance.'" It was not idly and in vain that I brought you from that place, was it? The reason [343] that I wanted you to settle in Palestine, to leave your ancestral home and come to this land was that you might inherit it. Accordingly, considering how much care you have enjoyed on my account from the time you left Chaldea up until the present and how famous you have become from day to day as you proved to be more conspicuous for my support and providence in your regard, have confidence also in my words. Do you see the extraordinary degree of his loving kindness? Do you see the extent of his considerateness in wanting to confirm Abram's spirit and make his faith stronger so that he might no longer be inclined to have regard for natural obstacles but rather consider the power of the one who had made the assurances, as if his promises had already taken effect, and thus be free to trust him?

5. Acts 7.2–4.

(5) Once more, however, notice the patriarch, when he had taken comfort in these words, how he looked for greater certitude. "He said," remember, "'My lord and master, how shall I know that I am able to inherit it?'" Even if Sacred Scripture had previously testified to his having faith in the words of God, for which reason it was reckoned as righteousness in him, nevertheless when he heard that the reason why "'I have brought you from the land of Chaldea is to give you this land for your inheritance,'" he said, While it is not possible for me to have no faith in the words you have spoken, still I would like to know as well the way I would come to inherit it. After all, I see that by now I have reached my old age and to the present time I have been going about like a vagrant, unable to discern the future by human reasoning—even though from the outset (he says) I had faith in your words as being a statement from you, the one able to bring things from non-being to being, to create and transform everything. So it is not out of unbelief that I am asking this; but since you mentioned once again the inheritance, I was wanting to receive as well some more concrete and visible sign, something capable of shoring up the limitations of my thinking. What, then, did the good Lord do? Showing considerateness for his own servant, and out of a wish to fortify his spirit, when he saw him admitting his own limitations and, while believing in the promise, yet wanting some confirmation, he said to him: "'Bring me a three-year-old heifer, a three-year-old goat, a ram, a turtledove and a pigeon.'"[6] Observe how he makes a covenant with him in human fashion: just as in the case of human beings, when they make a promise to someone and want to convince the recipient of the promise not to entertain doubts about what is promised, they supply some sign or pledge so that the recipient may have it before his eyes and thus be in a position to know that the promises will take effect in every detail, so too the good Lord, when Abram said, "'How shall I know?'" replied, Lo, this too I provide you with: "'Bring me a three-year-old heifer, a three-year-old

6. Gen 15.9, involving a slight abbreviation on Chrysostom's part.

goat, a ram, a turtledove and a pigeon.'" Notice, I ask you,
the degree of detail the good Lord deigns to go into for the
sake of the just man's certitude. Since in ancient times it was
the custom to make covenants in this way for people of that
time and by that means to endorse them, this was the way the
Lord himself followed.

(6) "He brought them," the text goes on, "and [344] cut
them in half." Observe carefully how it was not idly or to no
purpose that it indicated the age as well: he bade him bring
three-year-old animals, that is, mature, perfect. "He cut them
in half, and put the halves opposite each other, but the birds
he did not cut." He sat down to take care that birds on the
wing should do no damage to the divided animals, and he
kept that watch through the whole day. "Other birds, however, swooped down on the divided carcases, and Abram sat
with them. Now, at sunset Abram fell into a trance and, lo, a
terrible gloom came upon him."[7] Why at sunset, when already the day had reached evening? God wants to make him
more attentive in every way; a trance and terrible gloom fall
upon him for the reason that through what happens he may
gain some sense of seeing God—this, after all, being God's
way invariably. Later, remember, when God was on the point
of giving the Law and the Commandments to Moses on Mt.
Sinai, "there was darkness and a hurricane," the text says,
"and the mountain smoking."[8] Hence Scripture also says, "He
touches the mountains and they smoke."[9] You see, since it is
impossible to see anything incorporeal through these physical
eyes, he wants to convey to him his characteristic activity. Accordingly, when that just man was terrified and fear struck

7. Gen 15.11–12. The Greek version of v. 11 differs from the Hebrew
and represents Abram's reactions strangely. Chrysostom, of course, who had
made an individual point in the previous homily of the vision of 15.1 occurring at night, has now some explaining to do with reference to day in v. 10
and sunset in v. 12: unable to have recourse, like modern critics, to diversity
of sources and traditions, he dodges the issue with hardly a comment and a
tangential digression.
8. Apparently a composite text of Chrysostom's, recalling Exod 10.22,
19.18; Deut 4.11, 5.22.
9. Ps 104.32.

his mind as well as the trance that had developed, word came to him (the text says): You asked, God said, How shall I know? and you wanted to get a sign of the way you were destined to inherit the land. Behold, I am giving you a sign: you need great faith to learn that I can bring things from desperate straits to optimistic prospects. "Abram was told, 'You shall surely know that your descendants will be inhabitants of a land that is not theirs, and people will enslave them, maltreat and humiliate them for four hundred years. My judgment, however, will fall on whatever people they are enslaved by, and later they will depart from there with great possessions.' "[10]

(7) A wonderful statement, requiring a robust spirit capable of rising above every human consideration and leaving it behind. I mean, if the patriarch had not possessed a noble and manly spirit and good sense too, these words would have been sufficient even to alarm him. " 'You shall surely know,' " the text says, remember, " 'that your descendants will be inhabitants of a land that is not theirs, and people will enslave them, maltreat and humiliate them for four hundred years. My judgment, however, will fall on whatever people they are enslaved by, and later they will depart from there with great possessions.' " Do not be surprised, he says, as you have eyes for yourself, your old age, Sarah's sterility and the barrenness of her womb, nor think that I have said anything remarkable in the word, " 'I will give this land to your descendants.' " It is not only this that I foretell to you, but also the fact that your very descendants as well will be led off to a foreign land. He did not say, to Egypt, nor did he state the name of the land, but said, "a land that is not theirs' "; they would undergo slavery and hardship, and suffer, not for a short time nor a small number [345] of years, but for four hundred years. Certainly I will wreak vengeance on them, and my judgment will fall on that people that enslaves them, and thus I will cause them to return from there with great possessions—in the one word foretelling to him precisely the things due to

10. Gen 15.13–14.

happen afterwards and revealing the enslavement, the descent into Egypt, the wrath which the Egyptians were due to experience on their account, and their return in glory. He shows him that it is not only in his case that developments beyond the limits of nature will occur and despite such great obstacles the outcome promised by God will reach a conclusion, but in the case of all his descendants as well this will occur. These things, however, he says, I already told you so that before you end your life you might be in a position to know the things about to happen in turn to your descendants.

(8) " 'You, however,' " he says, " 'will go to your fathers after reaching a fine old age.' "[11] He did not say die but "go," as if he were due to travel on and move from one homeland to another. " 'You will go to your fathers,' " he says, not to fathers in the flesh; after all, how could he, since his own father was an infidel, and it wasn't possible that the patriarch, believer that he was, would go to the same place as he had gone. "There is a great gulf," Scripture says, remember, "between us and you."[12] So why had he said, " 'to your fathers' "? Referring to good men, like Abel, Noe, Enoch. " 'After reaching a fine old age' ": perhaps someone may say, What kind of a fine old age could he have had, spending a life full of troubles? But don't have regard for that, O man; instead, consider as well his notoriety on every occasion and the manner in which esteem came the way of this stranger, this refugee, bereft of hearth and home, and the degree of support he enjoyed from God at all times.

(9) Accordingly, don't judge affairs by current values, nor think a fine old age consists in living in luxury and gluttony, or gaining wealth and hordes of servants and crowds of slaves. I mean, far from constituting a fine old age, this would bring heavy condemnation on the person showing no self-

11. Gen 15.15 in a text that departs from Hebrew and LXX, not only in omitting "in peace," which would have been grist to Chrysostom's mill, but in making the gross copyist's/reader's error of reading Greek *tapheis* ("buried") as *trapheis* ("brought to," "nourished")—something Chrysostom perhaps suspects, as he uncharacteristically allows the word to pass without comment.
12. Luke 16.26.

control in old age or giving no heed to anything appropriate to a person at his last gasp but rather wolfing food day in day out, panting after drunken orgies, and doomed to give an account of it all not long after. Of course, the person who lives his life with such great virtue has truly reached a fine old age before ending his days, and for the troubles of this life will gain reward and recompense. Hence, Scripture says: While these things will happen to your descendants, you will pass on after reaching a fine old age. Consider further in this case how, unless the just man's valor had been considerable and his good sense extraordinary, these very events also would have been sufficient to derange his thinking. I mean, he would have said, [346] had he been an ordinary man: Why does he promise to cause so many descendants to issue forth from me if they were fated to be beset with so many troubles and to endure slavery for so great a number of years? What good is that to me? The just man, however, had no such thoughts; instead, like a grateful servant he submitted to everything coming from God and gave precedence to his judgments ahead of his own preferences.

(10) Then God also indicates to him the time of their return from slavery: after quoting the number of years as four hundred the text goes on, "'But in the fourth generation they shall return here.'"[13] At this point, however, someone may raise the difficulty of how he said they would be slaves for four hundred years whereas in fact they spent not even half that time in Egypt. The reason he did not say they would spend four hundred years in Egypt but "'in a land that is not theirs'" was that it might be possible to calculate the years they spent down in Egypt from the time the patriarch was ordered to leave Charran. Scripture, you recall, revealed to us also his age at that time in saying that he was seventy-five years old when he left Charran.[14] So from that time till the Exodus from Egypt, if you want to check it, you will find the

13. Gen 15.16. Editors of the Hebrew text warn us against as specific a translation as "generation," to avoid the complicated calculations that Chrysostom and his editors are obliged to go into at this point.
14. Gen 12.4.

number correct. Another equation is possible, however, that the Lord in his loving kindness always measures his punishments by our limitations, so when he saw them suffering and the Egyptians giving evidence of great cruelty to them, he inflicted his vengeance before the set time and led them to freedom. You see, that is the way with him: since in every way he devises our salvation, even if he threatens to punish us, yet if we resolve to give evidence of real conversion, he revokes his sentences. On the other hand, even if he promises to provide us with some benefit, he likewise does not put his promise into effect lest we prove to be the worse off on that score.

(11) All this you will find to be the case to the extent that you are devoted to the reading of the holy Scriptures. "'But in the fourth generation,'" the text says, remember, "'they shall return here, for the iniquities of the Amorites will not have run their course until then.'" That will be the moment, it means, for bringing them to freedom and for the enemy to be punished for the extent of their sins and to be driven from the land. So both events will occur at the appropriate time— their redemption and the expulsion of the enemy. In this way, you see, the text says, their iniquities will have run their course, as if someone were to say, To that point they had not committed sin to such an extent as to sustain such dreadful punishment. Being loving as he is, you see, far from imposing harsher penalties than their sins deserve, he imposes much less. The reason he gives evidence of longsuffering even in their regard is that they may bring punishment on themselves and thus have no excuse.

(12) Do you see how precisely he brought everything home to the patriarch so as to strengthen his faith in every way and enable him to have confidence from the words spoken to him that even the events affecting his descendants would take effect, and [347] from what was said previously he might likewise gain a solid faith that what had concerned himself as well had of necessity already been implemented. Then, when the prophecy had been fulfilled, he also received an adequate sign of the events that affected him. "After the sun had set,"

the text goes on, "flames appeared, and lo, there was a smoking oven and fiery torches that passed between the cut portions."[15] The flames, oven and torches revealed to the just man the stability of the covenant and the presence of God's activity. Then, when everything had been fulfilled and completed and the fire had consumed the offerings, "On that day," the text goes on, "the Lord made a covenant with Abraham, saying, 'To your descendants I will give this land from the river of Egypt to the great river Euphrates, the Kinites, the Kenezites, the Kedmonites, the Chettites, the Pherezites, the Raphaim, the Amorrites, the Canaanites, the Evites, the Gergesites and the Jebusites.'"[16] See how once more by the repetition he confirms his promise to Abram. "He made a covenant," the text says, "saying, 'To your descendants I will give this land.'" Then, so that the just man could realize from the extent of the land and the length of its boundaries how far his descendants would be distributed, he added, "From the river of Egypt to the river Euphrates"—such, he says, will be the extent of your descendants. Notice how by every means he wants to bring out to him the extraordinary size of the multitude: having previously said that he would cause it to be counted by the great number of the stars, in this instance too he made clear the length of the boundaries so that in this way as well Abram might learn the extent of the multitude there would eventually be. In addition to this he makes particular mention of those nations whose occupancy he was about to cede to Abram's descendants, so that in every way he might convey greater certitude to the good man. Though such wonderful promises had been made, Sarah still remained childless and old age pressed further upon them, so that in giving a remarkable sign of their faith they saw both the limitations of human nature and the greatness of God's power.

(13) Lest, however, we once more prolong the instruction to great length, let us call a halt to the development of our theme at this point and bring the sermon to a close by urging you to become imitators of the patriarch. Consider, dearly

15. Gen 15.17.   16. Gen 15.18–21.

beloved, in view of the words he addressed to the king of Sodom and more especially all the virtues he gave evidence of throughout his whole life how great a reward he was accorded and how much considerateness the Lord evinced in his regard, revealing through the events affecting the patriarch the extraordinary degree of his generosity to us all and the fact that, despite our only being able to anticipate him with the slightest display on our part, he rewards us with wonderful gifts without delaying at all, provided we show sincere faith in the manner of this just man and never vacillate in mind but rather maintain a steady disposition. On these grounds, after all, this man won a reputation: listen to Paul's eulogy of the faith he showed right from the outset. "At the call of faith," he says, remember, "Abraham obeyed the command to depart for the place he was due to occupy, and he set out without knowing where he was going,"[17] referring to that statement from God, " 'Go [348] forth from your country, onwards to a land that I will show you.' "[18] Do you see his unshakable faith? Do you see his steady disposition?

(14) Let us in turn imitate this and go forth from the affairs of the present life with enthusiasm and relish, and travel to heaven. It is possible, you see, if we are willing, to take the road for that goal while still living here when we perform deeds worthy of heaven, when we are not caught up in the affairs of the world, when instead of chasing after the empty glory of this life we rather scorn it and devote ourselves to longing after that true and everlasting glory, when instead of being captivated by extravagance in dress and being anxious to deck out the body we exchange all this external adornment for care of the soul and do not permit ourselves to let it go bare and bereft of the garments of this virtue, when we mock luxury, when we avoid gluttony, when far from looking for parties and banquets we are content with frugality in keeping with the apostolic exhortation that says, "having food and shelter we will be content with these."[19] What good, after all,

17. Heb 11.8.   18. Gen 12.1.
19. 1 Tim 6.8.

tell me, is overabundance, bursting the stomach with excessive eating, or impairing the sense of judgment from immoderate drinking? Isn't that the source of all the troubles of body and soul? Whence come those manifold ills and paralysis of limbs? Is it not from your going to excess in loading the stomach? Whence come acts of adultery, impurity, robbery, greed, murder, piracy and the complete ruination of the soul? Is it not from letting desire go beyond the bounds of moderation? You see, just as Paul called avarice the root of all evils,[20] so one would not be wide of the mark in naming as the source of all evils intemperance and our desire to go beyond the proper limit in everything. After all, if we were prepared in matters of diet, clothing, shelter and all our other bodily needs not to let our desires run riot but to look only for what was needed, the human race would be relieved of great harm.

(15) I am at a loss to know, however, how each of us according to his own ability welcomes this infection of greed and shows no anxiety to keep within the bounds of need; instead, quite at variance with the apostolic exhortation in the words, "Having food and shelter, we will be content with these,"[21] we do everything in this way without realizing that we will be held to account for all our excesses beyond limits of necessity on the score of abusing the things provided us by the Lord.[22] You see, it was not only for us to serve our own enjoyment that he provided us with these things but that we might alleviate the neediness of our fellows. So how could they deserve pardon who give evidence of vanity in their clothes and go to pains to dress in the threads of insects—a shocking thing that they pride themselves on whereas they ought be ashamed of it and fear and tremble on the score

---

20. 1 Tim 6.10.   21. 1 Tim 6.8.

22. Chrysostom's editor De Montfaucon chooses this point to vent his spleen on an admittedly disconcerting habit of the preacher, his syntactical inconsistency: "He begins with the first plural, then the third plural, then moves to second singular, and finally returns to third plural." Perhaps the point serves to document the thesis that the homilies betray signs of actual delivery rather than merely carefully written composition. See Introduction (7) and (12) in FOTC 74.

that while they get about like that for no good reason or subject to no need but merely out of vanity and show and the
desire to be the object of public attention, someone else who
is in fact of the same human nature goes about naked without
a respectable cloak to wear.

(16) Not even nature itself provokes you to sympathy, nor
does conscience stir you to assistance of your fellow, nor the
thought of that dread day, [349] nor the fear of hell, nor the
greatness of the promises, nor the fact that the common Lord
of us all takes as done to himself what is done to our fellows.
Instead, as if they had hearts of stone and were not part of
human nature, they think they are now superior to mankind
on account of the garments they wear, heedless of the great
guilt they thus incur by wrongly disposing of what has been
entrusted to them by the Lord; far from wanting to give some
portion to their fellow slaves, they are happy to have it consumed by moths and thus are already fuelling the fire of hell
in prodigal manner for themselves. After all, even if people
of wealth distributed to the needy all they had stored up, not
even in this way would they escape the punishment for continuing to live luxuriously in matters of clothing and diet. I
mean, how could those people not fail to deserve punishment
who go to all kinds of trouble to dress up in silken garments
and strut around in public decked out in clothes of gilt or
otherwise embroidered while despising the naked Christ and
declining to supply him with necessary sustenance?

(17) These words, I should remind you, are particularly
applicable to women: among them you would find a greater
degree of vanity and intemperance, and the habit of wearing
gold-encrusted dresses and golden adornments on the head,
around the throat and on other parts of the body, as well as
taking a lot of pride in all this. How many poor people's stom-
achs could have been filled and how many bodies reduced to
nakedness could have been covered merely with the proceeds
of what dangles idly and to no purpose from their ears, to no
one's advantage but only to the harm and damage of their
soul? Hence the world's teacher, too, after saying, "Having
food and shelter," then directs his remarks to women and

adds, "Let them not adorn themselves in braid or gold, in pearls or extravagant clothing."[23] See how he doesn't want them to be adorned in these things nor to wear gold adornments, pearls or extravagant dresses, but rather to apply real adornment to their souls and through the practice of good deeds to heighten the soul's beauty, and not to have to despise it as it hankers after these things for being defiled, squalid, clad in rags, wasted with hunger and frozen with cold. You see, the very anxiety about beautifying the body betrays its ugliness, luxurious diet makes clear its hunger, and extravagance in clothing shows up its nakedness.

(18) I mean, it is impossible for someone who cares for his soul and places great store by its loveliness and beauty to hanker after external adornment, just as, on the other hand, it is impossible for someone absorbed in external appearance, beauty of attire and adornments of gold to give much attention to the soul. After all, when will such a person manage to take account of anything that is proper or commence contemplating spiritual matters once he has given himself to earthly things and crawls on the ground, so to say, unable ever to draw breath, lying prone and weighed down with the burden of countless sins? In fact, it is impossible to bring home to you in words the number of maladies that spring from this behavior; instead, it suffices to leave to the conscience of the people absorbed in those things the thought of how many delusions they experience daily on that score. That is to say, either some of the gold crumbles, and a great storm and panic strikes the whole household; or a servant turns thief, and all are subjected [350] to stripes, torture and bonds; or some envious people hatch a plot and all at once relieve them of their possessions, to their great disappointment beyond all limits; or their business affairs take a turn for the worse and reduce them to extreme indigence, making their life more onerous than death; or something else befalls them and brings upon them deep gloom.[24] In short, it is not possible to

23. 1 Tim 2.9.
24. For all his exclusively scriptural interest as a preacher and his lack of reference to contemporary events, Chrysostom is nevertheless aware of his congregation's real life situation and capable of evoking it, as here.

find a soul absorbed in these things that is ever free from turmoil; instead, just as the waves of the sea can never be still or be counted owing to their great number, in just the same way you could not count the number of all the disturbances arising from that source.

(19) Hence, I beseech you, let us shun greed in all its forms and the tendency to exceed what is needful. True wealth, after all, real prosperity safe from default happens to be this: wanting what is necessary and disposing properly of what is over and above the necessary. Such a person, in fact, will never fear indigence nor endure insult nor be subjected to turmoil; rather, he will be beyond calumny, will be free from the plotting of conspirators and, in a word, will enjoy unbroken peace, tranquility and harmony. And what is greater than all these, the very pinnacle of good things, such a person will have God's favor and enjoy abundant grace from on high for being a faithful steward of the things of the Lord. "Blessed is that servant," Scripture says, remember, "whom the master at his coming finds behaving this way,"[25] dispensing his possessions to his fellow servants in this way, not locking them up behind doors and bars nor allowing them to become the food of worms, but assuaging the neediness of the poor and proving a good and faithful steward of the things bestowed by the Lord so as to gain as well the great reward for this excellent management and be judged worthy to attain the promised blessings, thanks to the grace and loving kindness of our Lord Jesus Christ, to whom with the Father and the Holy Spirit be glory, power and honor, now and forever, for ages of ages. Amen.

25. Luke 12.43.

HOMILY 38

"Now, Sarah, Abram's wife, had borne him no children. She had, however,
an Egyptian maidservant, whose name was Hagar."[1]

ODAY'S [350] READING AS WELL BIDS our tongue follow the theme of the patriarch. Don't be surprised if
after giving an exposition of this story on so many
days we haven't yet been able to bring it to a close. You see,
there is great richness in the just man's virtue, and the extent
of his good deeds taxes every human tongue. What human
being, after all, could worthily commend the man whom God
rewarded and eulogized from on high? Still, even if we fall
far short of doing him justice, at least we have dealt with him
to the level of our ability and would like to encourage you to
imitation and emulation of his virtue. The man's sound commonsense, remember, was sufficient to instruct the whole human race and to draw those willing to heed him to follow the
way of virtue. Pay attention, however, I beseech you, to what
is said so that we may come to learn the just man's commonsense from what was read just now. This passage, in fact, is
capable of instructing both men and women to give evidence
of harmony in relating to each other and to preserve inviolate
the bond of marriage, to teach the husband not to contend
against his wife but to make great allowance for her as being
the frailer vessel,[2] and the wife not to disagree with her hus-

---

1. Gen 16.1. Unless Migne's text is faulty, Chrysostom is inconsistent
throughout this chapter in aspiration in citing Hagar's name; we shall stay
with "Hagar."

2. De Montfaucon defends Chrysostom's use of this term of women by
commenting: "In the *Rule of Pachomius*, too, women are called 'frailer vessels'.
But in Livy and other historians they are called *impedimenta*, 'baggage'." See
Introduction (14) in FOTC 74. Cf. 1 Pet 3.7.

band, but to rival each other in carrying the other's burdens and to prize domestic peace [351] ahead of everything.

(2) It is necessary, however, to listen to the words themselves so that the teaching may become clearer to you. "Now, Sarah, Abram's wife, had borne him no children. She had, however, an Egyptian maidservant, whose name was Hagar." Consider in this passage, I ask you, dearly beloved, God's unspeakable longsuffering and the extraordinary degree of the just man's faith and gratitude of which he gave evidence with regard to the promises made to him. You see, though God had so often promised that he would give the land to his descendants, and that they would grow into such a great multitude as to be compared with the multitude of the stars, Abram saw that none of the promises had taken effect and that on the contrary the fulfillment of the promises was still at the level of words. Far from being disturbed in mind or shaken in his resolve he remained firm in his faith in the power of the one making the promises. Hence Sacred Scripture suggests as much in this passage too when it says, "Now, Sarah, Abram's wife, had borne him no children," as if to indicate to us that despite all these disappointments, despite the covenant made with him, despite the promise of an unnumbered multitude descending from him, he was not distressed, he held no doubts to see that none of the words had taken effect but quite the reverse. Hence it says despite all that, "Now, Sarah his wife had borne him no children," for you to learn that nothing further had happened to him despite the wonderful promises, and in fact Sarah's sterility and the infertility of her womb should have been enough to instill into him a deep sense of perplexity. The patriarch, however, far from regarding any longer the obstacles on the side of nature, realized instead the inventiveness of the Lord and the fact that, being creator of nature, he is able to find ways even where there are none, and so, like an obedient servant, he did not concern himself with the manner of fulfillment but left it to his inscrutable providence and had faith in his words.

(3) Hence it says, "Now, Sarah," despite such wonderful promises, "had borne him no children. She had, however, an

Egyptian maidservant, whose name was Hagar." It was not without purpose that Sacred Scripture even at this point made mention of the maidservant, but rather for us to learn from where she got her. The reason it added that she was Egyptian was that we might refer back to that incident and the fact that she was one of the things handed over by Pharaoh when he was the object of such awful vengeance from the God of all, and Sarah took her with her on her return; her name and race Sacred Scripture sedulously communicated to us. Notice, however, at this point Sarah's sensible attitude and the extraordinary degree of her self-control, as well as the patriarch's unspeakable faith and obedience. "Now, Sarah said to Abram in the land of Canaan," the text goes on, "'Lo, the Lord has stopped me from bearing children; so go into my maidservant so that you may have children by her.'"[3] Notice the woman's excellent attitude: she said nothing of the kind that Rachel later said to Jacob, "'Give me children—if not, I'll die.'"[4] Instead, what did she say? "'Lo, the Lord has stopped me from bearing children.'" Since the Creator of our nature has rendered me childless, she is saying, and has deprived me of progeny, accordingly, lest you remain without an heir on account of my sterility now that you have reached old age, "'go into my maidservant so that you may have children by her.'"[5] A remarkable degree of good sense in the woman, beyond all telling: what woman would ever have elected to do this, either to give her husband this advice, or to cede the marriage bed to her maidservant?

(4) [352] Do you see how independent they were of any emotional influence? They had but one end in view, not to die childless; they were concerned how they might salvage some comfort from the situation and preserve intact the bond of peace. Consider, I ask you, the patriarch's great self-

3. Gen 16.2, with the addition by Chrysostom of "in the land of Canaan."
4. Gen 30.1.
5. In the Hebrew it is Sarah whose posterity will thus be assured—albeit by an ambiguous expression; the LXX and Chrysostom cut the Gordian knot by assigning posterity to Abram.

control in this incident and the extraordinary degree of his restraint: he didn't rant and rave against his wife for her childless condition, as some mindless people do, nor diminish his love for her. You know, of course, you well know how this of all things proves for the majority of men a cause of scorn for their wives,[6] just as, on the other hand, they take the contrary as a basis for greater affection, quite stupidly and without reason attributing both sterility and fecundity to their wives without acknowledging that everything comes from nature's Creator and that neither intercourse nor anything else is capable of ensuring succession unless the hand from above intervenes and prompts nature to birth. Having a precise understanding of this, the just man did not attribute childlessness to his wife, and he continued to show her the proper regard. This was the reason, of course, that sensing his love she wanted to show how great was her affection for him, concerned not for herself but for a way in which she might devise some compensation for him for the lack of children; as though with her own hands, she took the Egyptian maidservant and led her to her own marriage bed, while showing by her words the reason she had in consenting to do it—namely, Since I appear to be useless and unsuited for childbearing, for "the Lord has stopped me from bearing children."

(5) See her wonderful disposition of spirit in uttering no cross word nor lamenting her sterility; instead, the intention was simply to indicate to us that by attributing this to nature's Creator she bore it meekly and nobly, giving prior regard to God's decision ahead of her own desire and considering how she might console her husband. Since, she said, therefore, "'the Lord has stopped me from bearing children.'" What tremendous import in these words of hers! how she demonstrates God's providence and ineffable power! She is saying, after all, just as we close and open our house, so too the Lord works on our nature, turning the key by his personal command and then opening it whenever he wishes and bidding

6. Chrysostom uses here as correlatives the generic *anthrōpos* (not *anēr*) and *gunē*. Cf. Introduction (14) in FOTC 74.

nature take its course. Since, then, she is saying, "'the Lord has stopped me from bearing children, go into my maidservant so that you may have children by her.'" I know that I am the cause of our childlessness; hence I don't want to deprive you of consolation on this account. Perhaps, on the other hand, Sarah even suspected that the cause of their childlessness lay not with her alone but also with the patriarch; hence out of a wish to determine it by the course of events she yields place to her maidservant and leads her to the very marriage bed so as to learn from developments whether she should attribute it all to herself. "Abram consented to Sarah's request." Remarkable the just man's commonsense: what I said before I say again, that he had not planned this previously despite being in advanced old age, and now being given this invitation by Sarah he readily consented to it, showing that it was not simply from desire nor in response to passion that he agreed to intercourse but so as to guarantee succession of his line.

(6) "Abram's wife Sarah, after ten years of living with her husband Abram in Canaan, brought her Egyptian maidservant and gave her as a wife to her husband Abram."[7] Consider [353] the precision of Scripture: for us to learn that Sarah did not show haste in execution of the deed even after the words she had addressed to him, it goes on to say, "His wife Sarah brought her Egyptian maidservant Hagar," as if Sacred Scripture wants to show us that it was to console his spouse and out of a wish to consent to her request that he agreed to the deed. I mean, so that you might learn with precision the patriarch's self-control and the extraordinary degree of his restraint, it added, "After ten years of living with her husband Abram in Canaan." It was not without purpose that even the time was conveyed to us, but for us to be in a position to know for how many years the good man showed his patience in nobly bearing his childlessness, prov-

7. Gen 16.3, where Chrysostom's reading differs from Hebrew, and LXX in speaking of ten years of life together rather than just ten years' residence in Canaan—an almost irrelevant comment Chrysostom has perhaps adjusted himself, though he later accepts and justifies it!

ing superior to all passion and giving evidence of great self-control.[8] And not merely this, but also for us to learn something else from the incident, it added, "After ten years of living with her husband Abram in Canaan." It did not at this point reveal to us the total period of their living together but the period spent by them in Canaan. What was the reason of this? Well, the loving Lord had promised him immediately on arrival in Canaan, "'To your descendants I will give this land,'" and again afterwards more than once he had made the promises to him so that you might know, dearly beloved, for how many years the Lord had postponed putting his promises into effect without the good man being disturbed in mind; rather, he had placed greater reliance on God's words than on his own thoughts. Hence it says, "After ten years of their living together in Canaan."[9]

(7) Do you see the valor of his soul, do you see his practice of commonsense, how the Lord wishes to make him more conspicuous and so defers the promise? You see, since he is concerned for his servants, he does not simply want to bestow kindnesses on them but also to bring them to public attention and cause their faith to be made obvious. In other words, if after promising to give the land to his descendants he had immediately opened Sarah's womb and granted him succession of his line, he would not in this manner have revealed an extraordinary marvel nor would the just man's faith have been rendered conspicuous to everyone. I mean, while on the other hand God's power would then have been manifested, since once again he had personally with his own power brought to life nature's work place that had been dead and had proved useless for childbearing, yet the patriarch would not have been crowned in the way he now was for the trial of his virtue for such a length of time and its daily becoming more resplendent.

8. Does Chrysostom portray Abram instead of Sarah as the object of Scripture's implied encomium here for altruism?

9. Now Chrysostom alters his text somewhat in the direction of Hebrew and LXX—to support the rather different point he has been making, Abram's virtue instead of Sarah's.

(8) For you to learn that it is not only his wish to bestow kindnesses and provide gifts at his hand, but it is his custom also to cause their recipients to be more conspicuous, see him practicing this also in the case of the Cananite woman, postponing and delaying, for the purpose not only of granting her request but also of bringing her to the attention of the whole world. When she approached him, remember, making her request in these words, "'Have pity on me, Lord, my daughter is possessed by an evil spirit,'"[10] merciful and loving though he is, always anticipating our requests, he did not vouchsafe her a reply. The disciples for their part did not realize what was going to happen, and that it was because of his concern for the woman and his wish that her treasure [354] not be hidden that he did not reply; so they approached him like people all the more moved, and besought him in these words, "'Grant her relief, because she comes shrieking after us,'"[11] as if to show that they still had no patience with her insistence. "'Grant her relief,'" they said, note, not because she was deserving of pity or because her request was eloquent, but "'because she comes shrieking after us.'" So what did the Lord do? Wishing to reveal little by little even this woman's treasure and to teach them how far they fell short of his loving kindness, he gave a reply which was capable of devastating her thinking, had her mind not been on the alert, her desire alive and her enthusiasm heightened, and capable also of causing them to desist from entreaty on her behalf. "'I was not sent,'" he said, remember, "'except to the lost sheep of the house of Israel.'"[12] While causing them to desist from entreaty on behalf of the woman, on the other hand, far from making her less insistent, he even made her become more demanding. This, you see, is what a suffering soul is like, making supplication with warmth of manner; it heeds nothing that is said, considering one thing alone—how to gain the object of its endeavors—as the woman did, too. Hearing this, the text repeats, "she fell at his feet and said,

10. Matt 15.22.   11. Matt 15.23.
12. Matt 15.24.

'Have pity on me, Lord.'"[13] She knew the Lord's pity, and for that reason she applied considerable pressure.

(9) Notice in turn, however, the wise and inventive Lord: far from acceding to her request at this point, he delivered an even more severe and abrasive reply. You see, he knew the woman's fortitude, and his intention was that she should not escape notice in receiving the favor but rather that the disciples as well should discover the reason for his reluctance and everybody else learn the power of entreaty and the woman's great virtue. He said, you recall, "'It's not right to take the children's bread and toss it to puppies.'"[14] Consider in this case, I ask you, the woman's perseverance in being fired with the ardor of enthusiasm, borne up by her faith in God, with her very entrails, so to say, torn asunder, and aching with concern for her daughter, far from being deterred by the haughtiness of the reply she is prepared to accept the remark about pups and confesses she is a pup so as to be acquitted of the ferocity of dogs and be admitted at once into the ranks of sons. Listen now to the woman's reply so as to learn how great an advantage came from God's reluctance: not only did the severity of his words to her not deter the poor creature, but it even prompted her to greater earnestness. When she heard those words, remember, she said, "'True, Lord; even the puppies eat some of the scraps that fall from their master's table.'"[15]

(10) Do you see why he gave evidence of reluctance to that point? So that we might learn from the woman's words the extraordinary degree of her faith. I mean, see how the Lord immediately sang her praises and rewarded her, saying, "'O woman, great is your faith.'"[16] With admiration and praise he sent on her way the woman who originally had not been vouchsafed a reply from him. "'Great is your faith,'" he says. Truly great it was, in fact, for being refused her request over and over again without losing heart or desisting but rather winning him over with the persistence of her supplication and

13. Matt 15.25 in a variant reading.
14. Matt 15.26.   15. Matt 15.27.
16. Matt 15.28.

causing him to put into effect her request. "'Let it be done to you,'" he said, remember, "'as you wish.'" Do you see how he, who previously had not even deigned to reply, now plies her with favors? Nor did he [355] simply grant her request but sang her praises and rewarded her, and by saying, "'O woman,'" he showed how he was struck by her faith, and by saying, "'Great is your faith,'" he made clear to us the woman's wealth. Then he said, "'Let it be done to you as you wish'": whatever you want, whatever you wish, this I grant you. In other words, such extraordinary supplication demonstrates your worthiness of the request. Do you see the woman's perseverance, do you see the reason for God's reluctance and the fact that out of his wish to make her more conspicuous he consequently kept putting her off?[17]

(11) Let us, however, if you don't mind, return to the story before us to learn that for so many years he did not put into effect the promises made to the patriarch for no other reason than that he might grant them to him with great publicity and draw to everyone's attention the just man's faith. Hence the text reads, "after ten years of their living together in Canaan," so that you may learn how much time passed from the time he received the promises. Immediately on arriving in Canaan, remember, he heard that "'to your descendants I will give this land,'" and for such a long period of time he had remained childless and Sarah's sterility was accentuated. "She gave Hagar as a wife to her husband Abram," the text reads. See how much commonsense was practiced by them in olden times, how men were continent and gave a great example of self-control, and women proved to be above jealousy. Of set purpose, you see, Scripture says, "Sarah brought her maidservant Hagar," and immediately goes on to say, "and gave her as a wife," so that you may learn how disinterested she was in putting the scheme into effect and how great was

17. De Montfaucon notes the resemblance of this treatment of the pericope of the Canaanite woman in Matt 15 to Chrysostom's commentary on the gospel (not to mention a recurrence in Homily 44)—a case that reminds us of the similarities between his Genesis homilies and sermons in places. See Introduction (7) in FOTC 74 for the likely explanation of such similarities.

the degree of their commonsense. "He went in to Hagar," the text goes on, "and she conceived."[18] See how Sarah obtains the proof that the cause of their childlessness lay not with the good man but with her own sterility, intercourse leading immediately to conception.

(12) Now, however, on the contrary, see the ingratitude of the maidservant and the frailty of woman's nature so that you may learn in this instance as well the patriarch's great restraint. "She saw that she was pregnant," the text goes on, "and her mistress was shown scant respect by her." This, you see, is the way with servants; if they happen to gain some slight advantage, they can't bear to stay within the limits of their station but immediately forget their place and fall into an ungrateful attitude. This is what happened to this maidservant, too: when she saw the change in her figure, she gave no thought either to her mistress's ineffable forbearance, nor her own lowly station, but became arrogant and self-important, scorning the mistress who had shown such great regard for her as even to bring her to her husband's very marriage bed. So what did Sarah do? "She said to Abram," the text goes on, " 'I am being wronged on your account. Lo, I gave my maidservant into your arms, but when she saw she was pregnant, I was shown scant respect by her. Let God judge between you and me.' "[19] In this case, I ask you, consider the just man's unspeakable longsuffering and the regard he shows for Sarah, begging pardon of her for this unreasonable accusation. I mean, it was she who gave her maidservant into her husband's arms, she who said, " 'Go in to my maidservant,' " she who of her own accord urged him to have intercourse, whereas now she changes her mind and says, " 'I am being wronged on your account.' " After all, O woman, he did not take the initiative in running off to have intercourse with your maidservant, did he? It wasn't at the spur of lust that he rushed into the affair, was it? He did it in response to you [356] and your direction—so why are you aggrieved with your husband? " 'Lo, I gave my maidservant into your arms.' "

18. Gen 16.4.   19. Gen 16.5.

Well, if you admit that you yourself gave her and he didn't take her on his own initiative, why do you claim injustice? All right, she says, if in fact I did give her, still once you saw her frowardness you should have corrected her insolent attitude; after all, "'once she saw she was pregnant, I was shown scant respect by her. Let God judge between you and me.'"

(13) Really, all these words were women's words, coming from the frailty of her nature, as if to say this to him: I for my part wanted to console you for your childlessness, so I demonstrated so much concern as to hand over to you my maidservant with my own hands and encourage you to have intercourse with her; whereas when you saw her becoming arrogant on account of the change in her figure and filled with self-importance, you should have corrected her and punished her for disrespect shown me, but instead of doing so you were prepared, as if forgetful of all that had happened before, to despise me, the one who had lived with you for so many years and am now being mocked by my Egyptian maidservant. "'Let God judge between you and me'": the cry of a tortured soul. Had the patriarch not been a man of good sense, and had he not shown great concern for Sarah, he would have been distressed by these words and have fallen into depression at her remarks. This remarkable man, however, had regard to the frailty of her nature and made complete allowance for her. "'Let God judge between you and me.'"[20] Consider, she is saying, what an awful exploit I deigned to be involved in for your comfort, in my wish for you to have the name of father at least in your old age, and so I elevated my maidservant to my own position, whereas you saw her behaving ungratefully but did not chide her, you did not reward me for the care I showed you. He who understands the secrets of each person's mind, she is saying, he will be judge between us and decide how I for my part proved superior to every passion in placing your comfort ahead of mine and bringing my maidservant into the marriage bed,

20. For a preacher who has only reached ch. 16 of Genesis after 38 homilies, Chrysostom is permitting himself the luxury of exploiting all the emotive potential of this incident.

whereas you took no account of what was happening to me and allowed her to take advantage of my restraint, you did not check her insolence or restrain her ingratitude.

(14) So what was the response of the man of steel, God's noble athlete, who won recognition for his deeds on all sides? See what he says to her to show his characteristic virtue in this as well: "'Lo, your maidservant is in your hands; treat her whatever way seems best to you.'"[21] Wonderful commonsense in the just man, extraordinary the degree of his longsuffering; not only did he not get upset by the words from Sarah but he even makes reply with extreme restraint, saying, You suspect me of being the cause of the insults shown you, and you think I take satisfaction in what was done by the maidservant because on one occasion she shared the marriage bed with me; accept the fact that in the first place, had I not been prepared to take your advice, I would never have agreed to take the maidservant into your marriage bed. As it is, to make quite sure through the facts themselves, lo, she is in your hands, "'treat her whatever way seems best to you.'" I mean, no one has undermined your authority, have they? No one has deprived you of your position, have they? After all, even if I consented to have intercourse with her, you still have your authority and she is in your hands: punish her, chide her, chastize her, wreak upon her whatever is your will and desire—only don't get upset, don't blame me for her fractious behavior. You see, it was not [357] under the impulse of my own desire that I consented to have intercourse with her with the result that I should accord her any unreasonable preference out of my passion for her from that incident. I know the respect due to you, I am not unaware of servants' ingratitude. She has no claim on me, she is not a concern of mine; one thing alone concerns me, to keep you undisturbed, without distress, free from any sorrow and enjoying the highest respect.

(15) This is a true relationship, this is the duty of a husband, while not taking too much notice of his wife's words

21. Gen 16.6.

but making allowance for natural frailty, to make it his one concern to keep her free from anguish and tighten the bonds of peace and harmony. Let husbands take heed and imitate the just man's restraint in according their wives such great respect and regard and making allowances for them as the frailer vessel so that the bonds of harmony may be tightened. This, you see, is real wealth, this is the greatest prosperity, when a husband is not at odds with his wife but rather they are joined together like one body—"'the two will come to be one flesh,'"[22] Scripture says. Such couples, be they even in poverty, be they in low estate, would be more blessed than all the rest, enjoying true delight and living in unbroken tranquility, just as those who don't enjoy this have to put up with jealousy and lose the advantage of peace. Even should they abound in wealth, have luxurious tables and happen to live in the glare of publicity, they still live a more miserable life than anyone, day in day out experiencing troubles and disturbances, suspecting one another, unable to have any joy as the conflict within them causes total confusion and creates complete disgust within them. In the present instance, however, there was nothing like that; instead, the patriarch both allayed the mistress's anger and by giving her complete authority over her maidservant he filled his house with unbroken peace.

(16) "Sarah maltreated her," the text goes on, "and she fled from her presence." That is to say, probably because she punished her insolence, the maidservant took to flight. That is the way with servants, after all: whenever they are not permitted to have their own way but rather their efforts at independence are thwarted, immediately they throw off the yoke of their masters and take to flight. See once more in this incident, however, how much favor from on high the maidservant also enjoyed on account of the esteem for the just man: since she carried with her the just man's seed, accordingly she was accorded also the vision of the angels. "An angel of the Lord," the text goes on, remember, "found her at the

22. Gen 2.24.

spring in the desert on the Sour road."[23] Consider the Lord's
loving kindness in overlooking no one; instead, even if she be
a servant or maidservant he personally gives evidence of his
characteristic providence for everyone, having regard not to
the difference in status but to the disposition of soul. In this
case, however, the angel appeared, not on account of the
maidservant's position, but out of regard for the just man: as
I said before, she was due to be shown great care for the
reason of her being worthy to receive the just man's seed.
"On discovering her," the text says, "the angel said to her,
'Hagar, maidservant of Sarah, where have you come from
and where are you going?'"[24] See how even the angel's words
made her mindful of her proper station: to make her more
attentive, he immediately brought her name to the fore by
saying, "'Hagar.'" We are accustomed, you see, to pay attention to people who call us by our name. Then he said, "'Maidservant of Sarah.'" He reminded her of her mistress, so that
she might know that even if she shared her mistress's marriage bed countless times, [358] she still ought acknowledge
Sarah as her mistress.

(17) Consequently, see the angel questioning her so as to
put her in a position of having to reply: from where have you
now arrived at this lonely spot, he says, and to what destination are you rushing off? The reason that the angel appeared
to her as she found herself in this lonely spot was in case she
should think it was just a chance traveler who was questioning
her; it was a desert, you see, and nobody else was present, so
for her to be in a position to know that it was not simply a
chance traveler who was conversing with her, he accordingly
appeared to her in the desert and questioned her. "She replied, 'I am running away from the presence of Sarah, my
mistress.'"[25] Do you see how she does not deny her authority,
but admits everything truthfully? It is not a human being who
is questioning me, she says, of the kind that I could mislead:
he forestalled me by mentioning my name and reminding me

23. Gen 16.7.
24. Gen 16.8, slightly altered to suit Chrysostom's running commentary.
25. Ibid.

of my mistress, so I for my part should speak the truth completely. "'I am running away from the presence of Sarah, my mistress,'" she says. See how she recalled the fact objectively: she didn't say, She gave me a hard time; she didn't say, She maltreated me, and through my inability to put up with the intense persecution I took to flight; far from making any complaint she only accused herself of running away. Do you see her good disposition? See in turn the angel's words to her: "The angel of the Lord said to her, however, 'Return to your mistress and submit yourself to her control.'"[26] In response to her admission, "'I am running away from the presence of my mistress,'" he says, "'Return,'" go back, don't be ungrateful to the one who has done you so many kindnesses. Then, since she had enraged her mistress from her superior airs and sense of importance, he says, "'and submit yourself to her control,'" be subject to her, as befits you, after all. Acknowledge your servitude, don't ignore her authority, don't get ideas above your station, entertain no high and mighty thoughts; "'submit yourself to her control,'" give evidence of your subjection.

(18) The angel's words adequately appeased her spirit, settled her thoughts, restrained her resentment and brought complete tranquility to her thinking. Then, in case you might think it was idly and to no purpose that she was accorded such wonderful care instead of learning that it was on account of the just man's seed that she enjoyed such great concern, see how he consoles her, restores her spirit and grants her abundant comfort in the following words: "The angel of the Lord said to her, 'I will greatly multiply your descendants, and there will be no numbering the multitude of them.'"[27] This I foretell to you, he says, that your descendants will be so numerous as to defy numbering. So do not lose heart or be dejected or get upset in your thinking; rather, let your complete obedience be evident. "'Lo, you are pregnant, remember, you will have a son and call him by the name Ishmael.'"[28] The reason, you see (he says), that I foretell the

26. Gen 16.9.   27. Gen 16.10.
28. Gen 16.11.

birth to you and already impose the name on the child to be
born is that you may gain greater certainty and thus make
your way back and soon put to rights your mistakes, "'because the Lord has paid heed to your abasement,'" he says.

(19) Let us learn from this incident how great an advantage
stems from adversities, how great the benefit of misfortune.
I mean, after she left home and pangs of distress grew
stronger and she felt the onset of great distress, living in solitude, isolation and deprivation after great prosperity and el-
evation to equality of status with her mistress, on that account
she enjoyed prompt assistance. What I promised, he said, remember, will happen to you; you will have a son, and [359]
your descendants will be beyond number, "'because the Lord
has paid heed to your abasement.'" So let us not on our part
be distressed when we are humbled by some onset of problems. Nothing, you see, is so advantageous to our nature as
humbling ourselves, having our self-importance lowered and
our frowardness of spirit checked. Then in particular, after
all, the Lord gives heed to us, when we listen to him with
sorrowing spirit and contrite heart, bringing fervent supplication to our entreaties. "'Because the Lord has paid heed to
your abasement,'" the text reads.

(20) Then he foretells the occupation of the child due to
be born: "'He will be a rough, uncultivated type,'" he went
on; "'his hand will be raised against everyone, and everyone's
hand will be raised against him; he will take up his abode in
opposition to all his brothers.'"[29] He predicts to her that he
will be bold, warlike, and will exert himself greatly in tending
the soil. Do you see in what happened to the maidservant the
regard for the patriarch? I mean, the care for her shows the
Lord's favor demonstrated towards the just man. After giving
counsel in this way and announcing good tidings to Hagar,
the angel departed. Notice again, however, the maidservant's
gratitude: "She invoked the name of the Lord as he spoke to
her, 'You are God, who watched over me,' or in other words,

29. Gen 16.12, where the Greek softens somewhat the unflattering reference to Ishmael.

'I saw him face to face as he appeared to me.' Hence she called the well 'Well Where I Saw Him Face to Face.' It is between Kadesh and Barach."[30] Consider how even she wants to leave a perpetual memorial to this place in its name: she called the place, the text says, "'Well Where I Saw Him Face to Face.'" Do you see the maidservant becoming gradually wiser from the hardship affecting her, giving evidence of deep gratitude for the kindness done her and acknowledging as far as in her lay the great care that had been accorded her. "Hagar bore Abram a son," Scripture goes on, "and to the child that Hagar bore him Abram gave the name Ishmael."[31]

(21) From this incident let us learn how great a good restraint is, how great an advantage we can gain even from afflictions. We see, on the one hand, restraint in the example of the patriarch appeasing Sarah's indignation, giving her authority over the maidservant and in this way filling the house with peace, while on the other hand we can see the advantage of afflictions in what happened to the maidservant. When she ran away, remember, after being maltreated by her mistress and putting up with great hardship, and after she called on the Lord in anguish of spirit, at once she was granted attention from on high. You see, for her to learn that she was accorded such wonderful care on account of her being humble and deferential, the angel said to her, "'You are pregnant, you will have a son and call him by the name Ishmael.'"

(22) Knowing, therefore, dearly beloved, that, if we are on the alert, afflictions rather recommend us to the Lord, and that then we will succeed in winning favor from him when we approach him with anguish of spirit and warm tears, let us not grieve in our afflictions but consider the advantage of afflictions and bear equally all occurrences; let us learn to be restrained and gentle with everyone, especially our wives, and take particular care not to be too demanding, even if they chide us, rightly or wrongly, but rather make it our sole concern to remove the cause of sadness and bring about a deep

30. Gen 16.13–14, where the Hebrew text is uncertain.
31. Gen 16.15.

sense of peace at home [360] so that the wife's attention may
be devoted to her husband[32] and he may be able to find refuge in a haven from external confusion and disturbance and
find there utter consolation. The wife, after all, is given by
way of assistance so that the husband, strengthened by her
support, may succeed in withstanding assaults against him.
You see, if she is discreet and restrained, not only will she
provide her husband with comfort from their association but
in all other respects as well she will give evidence of her great
usefulness, rendering everything light and easy for him, not
allowing him to find difficulty either in external matters or
indeed in the problems that daily arise at home; instead, like
a skilled pilot she will transform for him the storm of his
spirit into calm by means of her particular wisdom, and by
the understanding she shows she will provide him with deep
comfort. Nothing of the affairs of this life, in fact, will succeed any longer in worrying people bound together in this
manner, nor in undermining their contentment. You see,
wherever there is harmony and peace and a loving relationship between wife and husband, all good things come together there and the couple will be safe from any stratagem,
protected as they are by some wonderfully impregnable rampart, namely, their harmony in God's sight. This renders
them stronger than steel, this makes them firmer than iron,
this contributes to them more than all wealth and prosperity,
this conducts them to glory on high, this also wins for them
favor from God in generous measure.

(23) Accordingly, I beseech you, far from prizing anything
more highly than this, let us move might and main to have
peace and harmony in our family life. Then, you see, the
children born of such union will follow the virtue of their
parents, the servants will imitate them, in every respect the
householder will advance in virtue and there will be great
prosperity in our affairs. After all, when we give pride of
place to God's concerns, everything else will go without hindrance for us and we will experience no sense of difficulty,

32. Chrysostom's phrase employs the language of Gen 3.16.

since God's goodness is supplying us with everything in generous measure. In order, therefore, that we too may pass this present life free from distress and may win favor from the Lord to a greater degree, let us hold fast to virtue, make it our concern to introduce harmony and peace into our home, attend to the orderly behavior of our children and give thought to the conduct of the servants, so that after receiving rewards to an extent beyond all others we may also be found worthy of those promised good things, thanks to the grace and loving kindness of our Lord Jesus Christ, to whom with the Father and the Holy Spirit be glory, power and honor, now and forever, for ages of ages. Amen.

HOMILY 39

"Now, when Abram was ninety-nine years old, God appeared to him."[1]

O YOU SEE, [360] dearly beloved, how there is nothing idle in the contents of Sacred Scripture? Did you notice yesterday how in drawing to your attention the story of Hagar and her return home we gained considerable advantage from the exercise? We came to know, you recall, the patriarch's great restraint, the extraordinary degree of his self-control, the regard he showed for Sarah out of the value he placed on concord with her above all other things. We saw God's loving kindness beyond all telling, how on account of his regard for the good man he not only brought back [361] Hagar who had wandered in the desert and run away out of fear of her mistress, but also favored him with the birth of Ishmael, having in mind the great comfort this would bring to the just man and giving him a reward for his wonderful endurance. When Ishmael was born, Sacred Scripture, wanting to teach us the patriarch's age, indicated to us also the number of his years in saying that "when Ishmael was born, Abram was eighty-six years old."[2] At this point, however, let us look at the sequel, so that we may learn once again from what follows both the just man's great endurance and the Lord's ineffable and exceeding love.

(2) Now, we will know this precisely if we succeed once again in determining the years of the just man's life and the

1. Gen 17.1, a verse in which the Hebrew and LXX differ, and where Chrysostom differs slightly again.
2. Gen 16.6, reshaped somewhat by Chrysostom to make his point about the precision of Scripture. It is a pity Chrysostom's time could not provide him with the means to distinguish different narrative strands in the Genesis text and recognize the priestly contributor's fascination with chronology.

way the good God arranged the events that concerned him, testing his servant on each occasion and revealing the godliness of his attitude. Of course, he himself knew clearly ahead of time the sound dispositions of his servant, he appreciated the beauty of his spirit and recognized precisely the pearl that he was; yet since he also wanted to make him known to all the people of that time so that the just man's virtue might in future generations as well attract willing souls to emulation and imitation of him, accordingly he gradually unfolds the wealth of the just man's attitude so that we too may learn never to distrust God's promises, and instead of fretting at delay have confidence rather in what is not seen than in what is visible and before our eyes when the Lord of all makes the promise. We should also realize that it is not possible for what is promised by God ever to fall short of realization; rather, even if with the passage of a long period of time things contrary to God's promises transpire, our thinking should not be disturbed but we should consider the inventive and irresistible power of the one who promises and the fact that when he wishes to put his decisions into operation, everything yields and gives place. After all, since he is Lord of our nature and Creator, it is possible for him as well to bestow gifts surpassing nature.

(3) Consequently, let us not become curious about God's doings by having an eye to our own limitations, nor divide our mind in two by keeping in focus the natural way of doing things, but like dutiful servants recognizing the exceeding power of our Lord let us have faith in his promises and prove superior to natural limitations so that we may attain the promises, enjoy favor from on high and have reverence for God to the best of our ability. This, you see, is the greatest reverence for him on our part, to have confidence in his power even if to bodily eyes things are seen to be in opposition. Why are you surprised if in God's mind the greatest reverence is not to doubt? Even amongst our peers, when they promise something of this perishable and passing world, provided we don't doubt but rather have confidence in the one making the promise, all to a man consider the greatest sign

of respect the fact that we have obviously not wavered but
have trusted in their promises. So if this happens among people who frequently change or on account of their limitations
are incapable of translating decisions into action, how much
more in the case of God ought we trust in his promise, even
if a long period elapses in the meantime.

(4) These things, however, I remind you, were not idly said
on this occasion; instead, it was for us to be in a position to
know, when we came to the beginning of the text proposed
to us today, how the loving God wanted to make the patriarch
conspicuous to everyone, [362] and so gave evidence of a particular procrastination for such a great number of years without the just man getting upset, becoming fainthearted because of the length of time or giving up hope—rather, he was
buoyed up on sound hope and thus in every way demonstrated the godliness of his attitude. Now, we will know precisely all the patriarch's virtue if we learn how much time
elapsed in the meantime. You see, all this blessed Moses
teaches us under the inspiration of the Holy Spirit.[3] So what
does he say? When Abram obeyed God's direction, moved on
from Charran and took himself into Canaan, he was seventy-
five years old. As soon as he took possession of Canaan, God
promised him he would give all the land to his descendants
and would cause them to grow into such a great multitude as
to defy numbering, like the sand and the stars. After this
promise, many things befell the just man in the meantime,
the journey down into Egypt on account of the famine, the
abduction of Sarah and immediately God's providential inter-
vention; again, after the return from there the abuse of Sarah
at the hands of the king of Gerar[4] and the immediate assistance from God. Though he saw all this happening to him
after that promise, the just man was not upset in his thinking
nor did he worry within himself why the recipient of such a

3. One of Chrysostom's frequent unequivocal statements of biblical inspiration, asserting the role of the human and divine authors, and employing
Chrysostom's unusual term for inspiration, *enēchein*. See my "terminology."
4. Chrysostom is (consciously?) anticipating the events of ch. 20 to strengthen
his case.

great promise should encounter so many awful trials day in day out and continue for so long without children. Instead, being a godly man he could not bring himself to submit to the limitations of his own reasoning what was done by God, and so he was content and accepted willingly God's decisions.

(5) After the tenth year he took Ishmael, his child by the maidservant, and considered that the promises had been fulfilled for him in the child. The patriarch was, you remember, the text tells us, eighty-six years old when Ishmael was born. The loving God, however, exercised the virtue of the just man for a still further period of thirteen years: when God saw that he had been purified like gold in a furnace[5] for a long period of time, and had rendered the just man's virtue more conspicuous and resplendent, Scripture says, "when Abram was ninety-nine years old, God appeared to him again."[6] Why did God delay so long? Not simply that we should get to know the just man's endurance and his great virtue, but for us to see as well the extraordinary degree of his power. You see, when nature lost its potency and was now useless for childbearing, his body being wasted and chilled with old age, to show his peculiar power God put into effect the promise. We must listen, however, to the very words spoken to him by God. "God appeared to him when he had reached ninety-nine years," the text says, "and said to him."[7] But when you hear "appeared," don't suspect anything ordinary or think that divine, irresistible power was seen by bodily eyes, but rather imagine everything in a reverent manner.[8]

(6) So "God appeared to him," that is to say, of his own accord he granted him quite plainly a vision; considering him worthy of a providential gesture from himself and displaying

5. Cf. Wis 3.6.
6. This time the text of Gen 17.1 contains "again," not included previously by Chrysostom, nor by the LXX generally.
7. Again a different version of the text without foundation.
8. As we have had occasion to remark before, at Homily 17 n.2, anthropomorphisms in the scriptural text put Chrysostom at once on the alert in case his Antiochene congregation should fail to keep together those binomials—divine transcendence and considerateness for human limitations—which the Scriptures (as also that other Incarnation) eminently exemplify.

great considerateness, he addresses him in these words, "'I am your God: be pleasing in my sight and prove yourself blameless, and I will lay down my covenant between me and you, and I will make you exceedingly numerous.' Abraham fell on his face."[9] [363] Excellent the just man's disposition, exceeding the good God's loving kindness for him! "'I am your God,'" he says, as if to say, I am he who arranged things in your regard in various ways up to the present, who moved you on from your home and brought you here, who proved to be your champion each day, and rendered you superior to those plotting against you; he did not say, I am God, but "'I am your God.'" See his great goodness in revealing his love for the just man through the addition of the pronoun: the God of the whole world, the Creator of everything, the Maker of heaven and earth says, "'I am your God.'" Wonderful the manner of his esteem for the just man.

(7) This is the way the inspired authors are also accustomed to speak: just as on this occasion he deigned to be named after his slave, though being the common Lord of all, and we will find him later saying, "'I am the God of Abraham, Isaac and Jacob,'"[10] so too are the inspired authors accustomed to say, "O God, my God," not to restrict his dominion to them but by way of a personal declaration of uninhibited desire. For human beings to do this, however, is nothing remarkable; but when he does it in regard to human beings, that is novel and surprising. Still, let us not marvel, dearly beloved, but listen to the words of the inspired author, "Better one person doing the will of the Lord than countless numbers of lawless people,"[11] and again blessed Paul's words, "They went about in skins of sheep and goats, destitute, persecuted, mistreated;

9. Gen 17.2–3, where the Greek versions lose the force of the patriarchal title, El Shaddai.

10. Cf. Exod 3.6.

11. Sir 16.3, an uncertain text where Chrysostom follows a marginal correction to one LXX MSS. It is also noteworthy that this *prophētēs* that Chrysostom takes as typical is a Wisdom author, confirming the usual sense for Chrysostom of an "inspired author" and hence applicable to all kinds of Old Testament (only) composers from psalmist and sage to major prophet.

the world was not worthy of them."[12] While the inspired author of the Old Testament highlighted the one doing the
Lord's will as better than countless numbers of lawless people,
blessed Paul, on the other hand, the world's teacher, recalled
all those good people under persecution, existing in straitened circumstances, in the words, "The world was not worthy of them." By saying all the world, he contrasts it with
those who are persecuted, those who are distressed, so that
you may learn how great virtue is. Hence, too, the Creator of
all says to the patriarch, "'I am your God: be pleasing in my
sight and prove yourself blameless.'" That is to say, far from
overlooking the struggles of such marvelous virtue, "'I will
lay down my covenant between you and me, and I will make
you exceedingly numerous.'" I will not simply cause you to
grow into a multitude, but "'an exceedingly great one'" as
well, showing the great degree of development; and what he
said previously, like the sand and the stars, the same thing he
indicated in this instance by "'exceedingly.'"

(8) The dutiful and godly servant was amazed to see God's
wonderful considerateness and his care for his servant; being
mindful of his own nature, God's goodness and invincible
power, "he fell on his face," showing forth in this manner his
own prudence. Not only was he not rebellious, not being
high-minded on account of the favor which had been shown
him by God, but rather he humbled himself even further,
"And he fell," it says, "on his face." This is what the prudent
soul is like, since when it enjoys more confidence, it shows
even greater reverence to God. [364] "For he fell," it says, "on
his face." Despite such wonderful intimacy, the just man had
an eye to himself and the limitations of human nature, and
dared not look up, but by prostrating himself he gave evidence of greater reverence. So, see in response the ineffable
generosity of the good God: "God spoke to him," the text
goes on, "in the following terms: 'Lo, I am making this covenant with you. You will be the father of a host of nations; you

12. Heb 11.37–38.

will no longer be called by the name Abram—instead, your name will be Abraham, because I have appointed you father of many nations; I will make you numerous, I will make a nation of you, and kings will be descended from you.'"[13]

(9) Notice, dearly beloved, how he foretells everything clearly to the good man in this case, too, and, so as to give him greater certainty, he makes the addition of the syllable to his name in the words, "'You will be father of a host of nations; you will not be called by the name Abram but Abraham, since I have appointed you father of many nations.'" That is to say, just as the former name suggested a crossing over from the other side (Abram, after all, means "traveler" in Hebrew, as is known by those with a knowledge of that tongue),[14] so since he was destined to travel over from the other side into Canaan, consequently his parents gave him that name. Perhaps, however, someone may say, If in fact his parents were infidels, how did they come by this foreknowledge so as to give him a name suggesting something due to happen long after? This is an attribute of God's inventive wisdom, managing such things often through the agency of infidels, and you will find many such things happening in other cases.

(10) Immediately, in fact, there comes to mind the name of Noe: it was not idly or by chance that his parents gave him that name—rather, it was to foretell the deluge due to take place five hundred years later. You see, for proof that it was not on account of his virtuous lifestyle that his father gave this name to his child, heed the clear statement of Scripture that Noe alone was found upright, faultless by comparison with his contemporaries. Scripture would not have kept silence, nor would it have been said Noe alone was upright, if

13. Gen 17.4–6 in a somewhat more restrained version than the Hebrew and some Greek texts.

14. In translating Abraham's intriguing agnomen as "traveler" at Gen 14.13 (see note *ad loc.*), Chrysostom did not proceed as here to identify the two words on the basis of consonantal similarity—a move which attracts De Montfaucon's stern correction. Chrysostom's admission here that he is ignorant of Hebrew confirms a similar admission in Homily 4; see Introduction (3) and n. 6, in FOTC 74.

his father Lamech in turn was an imitator of the just man's virtue. Accordingly, when he was on the point of giving his child a name he said, "'He will be called Noe: he will surely bring us relief from our labors, the troubles of our hands, and from the curse the Lord God placed on the earth.'"[15] Where, tell me, did he get the knowledge of what would happen after so many generations? "'He will be called Noe,'" the text says, note, "'for he will bring us relief.'" The word Noe in the Hebrew language means "relief." So since he alone was destined to be preserved when that dreadful flood overwhelmed the world and to provide some new beginning to existence for a later generation, hence he said, "'He will give us relief,'" calling the deluge relief.[16] You see, just as the onset of the flood with its rush of water, in removing the evil of those wicked people, also cleansed the whole earth, affected as it was by the evil of its inhabitants, the victim of severe abuse and made unclean on account of the vices of its inhabitants, it also gave them relief in the form of punishment. "Death is relief for a man,"[17] Scripture says, remember.

(11) Do you see how even through infidels in many cases he causes future events to be foretold? Well, in just the same way the patriarch's [365] parents gave him his name, making clear from the very outset that there would be a move and he would cross the river and come to a foreign land. So God is saying, Since the imposition of that name by your parents foretold your crossing from one side to the other, accept also the addition of this syllable so as to learn that it reveals to you that you will be father of many nations.[18] See the precision of

15. Gen 5.29, with Chrysostom's own introductory clause.
16. De Montfaucon gives Chrysostom better marks for this essay into etymology; Speiser, who struggles to rescue the efforts of the LXX in the same direction, also warns that "biblical etymologies are not guided by linguistic considerations" (*Genesis* 41)—a view with which Chrysostom could sympathize from his tendency to approach them from his moral standpoint.
17. Job 3.23 in the LXX.
18. Again Chrysostom is wide of the mark with his etymologizing, though one could hardly fault him with his Antiochene interest in linguistic precision. As Von Rad, however, reminds us, "the name 'Abraham' is linguistically nothing else than a 'lengthening' of the simpler 'Abram,' which means 'my father (the god) is exalted'" (*Genesis*, p. 194).

the words: he did not say all nations but "'many nations.'" You see, since there were other nations as well that he intended to drive out from there so that the just man's descendants might succeed to the inheritance, hence he said, "'I have appointed you father of many nations.'" Knowing the greatness of your virtue, I will make you teacher of many nations, "'I will make you numerous, I will increase your numbers over and over, I will make a nation of you and kings will be descended from you.'"[19] Do not pass the expressions idly by, dearly beloved. I mean, if we consider the patriarch's age and the fact that he heard these words in extreme old age, we will be amazed both at the just man's faith and the extraordinary power of God's loving kindness in indicating that the descendants of a man now at death's door, so to speak, with limbs weakened and the prospect of death daily before him, would increase to such magnitude as to develop into many nations—and not only this, but "'kings will be descended from you,'" he says. Do you see the extent of the promise? "'I will increase your numbers over and over,'" he said: it was not without purpose that he inserted the duplication but to indicate to the just man the extraordinary size of the multitude.[20] You see, since by the addition of the syllable he had inscribed an indelible guarantee of the promise, as if on some monument, once more he says, "'I will establish my covenant between myself and you, and your descendants after you in their generations, as an eternal pact, to be God for you.'"[21] Not only in your regard, he says, will I give evidence of deep concern, but also for your descendants, even after your departure. See how he reinvigorates the just man's spirit by promising him that he will provide great care even for his descendants.

19. This time in quoting v. 6, Chrysostom goes from one extreme to the other: after the previously restrained form by comparison with the LXX, he now adopts the LXX and embellishes it to enhance the generosity of the promise. This has implications also, of course, for the provenance of the text of the homilies; see Introduction (7) in FOTC 74.

20. The double adverb *sphodra sphodra* found in most LXX texts, omitted originally by Chrysostom, is grist to his mill at this point, where he now omits the extra verb he employed before.

21. Gen 17.7.

(12) What is the force of this pact? "'To be God for you,'" he says, "'and for your descendants after you.'" This, in other words, will be the summit of good things, both for you and for your descendants. "'I will give to you and to your descendants after you the land you occupy, all the land of Canaan, as an everlasting possession; and I will be their God.'"[22] On account of your virtue your posterity as well will enjoy my care, I will give them the land of Canaan as an everlasting possession, "'and I will be their God.'" What is the meaning of "'I will be their God'"? It means I will give evidence of deep concern, of great care, I will provide them with assistance from me in all situations, only "'you must observe my covenant, you and your descendants after you in their generations.'"[23] I look for nothing else from you than obedience and gratitude, and I shall put into effect all that I promised.

(13) His intention then was to make his own those born of him and to turn them into his people so that in future the vast numbers that developed from them might not mingle with the nations whose lands they were meant to possess, especially since afterwards according to his prediction they were destined to undergo slavery in Egypt. So in case they should mix with [366] the races in Egypt even after falling into slavery, he imposed on the just man by way of a sign circumcision in these words, "'This is the covenant which you shall observe between myself, you and your descendants after you in their generations. Every male among you shall be circumcised. You shall circumcise the flesh of your foreskin.'"[24] Then to teach them, and also all of us, the reason why he gave that direction and the fact that he intended it to have no other purpose than to be a sign that the people had been dedicated to him, he said, "'It will act as a sign of the covenant between me and you.'" Then he also prescribes the time that this ought be done. "'Your child of eight days shall be circumcised, as also children born in the household or purchased for money—in short, all living among you, so to

22. Gen 17.8.   23. Gen 17.9.
24. Gen 17.10–11.

speak, shall receive this sign. Whoever is not circumcised on the prescribed day shall be rooted out for breaking my covenant' "[25]—for breaking the command, he means.

(14) See the Lord's wisdom in knowing how inobservant future generations are likely to be, and so, as though putting a bit in their mouths, he gave them this sign of circumcision, curbing their unrestrained urges in case they should mingle with other peoples. You see, since he was aware of their lustful tendencies in not practicing restraint, even though it had been drummed into them[26] countless times to refrain from their irrational impulses, consequently he gave them a perpetual reminder with this sign of circumcision, as though fastening them in a chain, and set limits and rules to prevent them overstepping the mark instead of staying within their own people and having no association with those other peoples but rather keeping the patriarch's line uncontaminated, so that in this way even the fulfillment of the promises could be achieved for their benefit. It is like a man of self-control and good sense having a froward child: he puts limits and rules on him not to show his face outside the front door nor to be seen by passers by, and in fact oftentimes ties him up by the feet so as to succeed in this way in getting the better of his extreme indiscipline. Well, in just the same way the loving Lord also placed this sign of circumcision in their flesh, like shackles on their feet, so that with this reminder at home they might have no further need of instruction from others.

(15) The ungrateful and unresponsive Jews, however, even now when the right time has passed, insist on keeping circumcision and betray their juvenile attitude. I mean, why is it, tell me, that they insist on being circumcised now? At that time, after all, in case they were contaminated by those other lawless peoples, they were given that command; now, on the other hand, thanks to God's grace they have all been led to the light of truth—so what value is there in circumcision? I

---

25. Gen 17.12–14, in an abbreviated form.
26. Interestingly, Chrysostom here employs the word that he normally uses for the inspiration of the biblical authors, *enēchein*.

mean, getting rid of skin contributes nothing to freedom of spirit, does it? Didn't they listen to God's wise words, "'It will act as a sign of covenant,'" as if to show that they had need of a sign on account of their deep ingratitude? This, you see, is what often happens in human affairs. Since we have no trust in some people, we are keen to get from them a sign by way of pledge; similarly, the God of all, realizing the instability of their attitude, deigned to request this sign of them, not that this sign should remain forever, but that after the conditions of that time had come to an end the use of the sign would be cancelled. You see, just as whenever people ask for a sign and want to get a pledge, [367] the sign is removed at the time when the occasion for the arrangement comes to an end, so too in this case, since this sign had been introduced among you[27] on account of the patriarch's people becoming well known, it was appropriate that, after some of the races for whose sake they had adopted the sign had been utterly destroyed while others after them had made their approach to the light of truth, the people should no longer carry about the proof of their own ingratitude but be freed from it and return to their pristine nobility.

(16) Consider, after all, I ask you, the fact that that remarkable man—I refer to the patriarch—before receiving the command about circumcision (he was, remember, ninety-nine years old when he was given this command) had proved pleasing to God and as well had been countless times commended by the Lord. Since at this point the fulfillment of the promise was about to take effect, Isaac was due to be born, the race to be multiplied and the patriarch, on the other hand, to be transferred from this life, it was then that he received the command in such extreme old age so that what happened to the patriarch might prove to be a kind of law and rule for all coming later.

(17) For you to learn precisely, dearly beloved, that this contributes nothing to virtue of spirit, you can come to an

27. A strange use of the second person, which gives Chrysostom's editors pause.

understanding from the events themselves. Why does Scripture say, remember, "'A child of eight days shall be circumcised'"? Now, I think this time was prescribed by the loving
God for the following two reasons: firstly, that at that tender
age the pain of circumcising flesh could be more easily borne;
and secondly, that they might be instructed by the very actions that the event contributes nothing to the soul but acts
as a sign. After all, a tender child, ignorant of what takes
place, lacking any appreciation—what benefit could it gain
for its soul from this? The good actions, you see, that belong
specifically to the soul are those that are done by choice.
Good behavior by the soul, after all, is to choose virtue and
to shun evil; good behavior by the soul is not only not han-
kering after greater wealth but passing on one's goods to the
needy; good behavior by the soul is not to cling to present
realities but to scorn them, on the one hand, and to contemplate future realities daily, on the other. Receiving a sign in
the flesh, on the contrary—what sort of good behavior is
that?

(18) The ungrateful and unresponsive Jews, however, despite the light of truth, are still seated in darkness and, despite the sun of justice shining and spreading its rays of light
in every direction, they are still attached to the light of a lantern and, despite the age for solid food, they are still depen-
dent upon milk, nor can they bring themselves to heed
blessed Paul shouting aloud about the patriarch, "He received the sign of circumcision, a seal of the righteousness of
the faith he showed while uncircumcised."[28] See how in this
respect he taught us both facts, that he received circumcision
as a sign and, while still uncircumcised, he gave evidence of
righteousness arising from faith. You see, in case the Jew
should shamelessly maintain, Did not circumcision win righteousness for him? Accordingly this blessed man, schooled at
the feet of Gamaliel, precise student of the Law, said, Don't
think, O shameless Jews, that circumcision was of any avail
for righteousness for him: having given evidence of faith

28. Rom 4.11.

[368] in the time when he was uncircumcised, he heard the words, "Now, Abraham had faith in God, and this was reckoned as righteousness in him."[29] So, being already in the condition of righteousness on account of faith in God, he then receives circumcision by way of sign; God firstly adds a syllable to his name, and afterwards orders circumcision so as to show that it was on account of his great virtue that he then admitted the good man to his friendship and for his sake those who would be descended from him. Just as when a person acquires a slave, he frequently changes his name and attire and makes every effort to render him obvious so that in every way he may proclaim his ownership, so too the God of all, as though wishing to mark him out now from other human beings, indicates through the addition of the syllable that he will be father of many nations, while through circumcision he indicates that they will be his chosen people, and the descendants due to be born from him have been marked out from the other nations.

(19) But they, for their part, in their characteristic blindness insist on still keeping circumcision of the flesh, not heeding Paul's words, "After all, if you undergo circumcision, Christ will be of no benefit to you."[30] The reason, you see, for the Lord's coming was to cancel all these things, and the reason for his fulfilling the entire Law was to replace the observance of the Law in future—hence blessed Paul's exclamation, "Whoever find their justification in the Law have fallen from grace."[31] We, on the contrary, believe blessed Paul and accept a circumcision not the work of human hands. "You have been circumcised in him with a circumcision not the work of human hands, by putting off the sins of the flesh, with the circumcision of Christ."[32] Then, to teach us more precisely what this kind of circumcision is, he added, "buried with him in baptism."[33] In other words, just as the sign of

29. Gen 15.6; cf. Rom 4.3.   30. Gal 5.2.
31. Gal 5.4.   32. Col 2.11.
33. Col 2.12. The length and intensity of this tirade against circumcision illustrate Chrysostom's feelings about the Judaism of his time. His principal biographer, Baur, accounts for it on the score of the Jews' influence in An-

circumcision distinguished them from the other peoples and showed their belonging to God, in just the same way in our case, too, circumcision by baptism achieved a more precise distinction and a separation of the believers from those who are not such. "In him," the text says, remember, "you have been circumcised with a circumcision not the work of human hands, by putting off the sins of the flesh." I mean, whatever in the former case circumcision achieved by way of putting off the flesh, in this case baptism achieves by way of putting off sins. That is to say, having once put off the sins of the flesh and put on clean apparel, let us remain in cleanliness, dearly beloved, and by being above the passions of the flesh let us attain to virtue.

(20) Let us who live by grace imitate him who lived by the Law, or rather before the Law, so that we may conduct our lives by following in his footsteps and thus be judged worthy of meeting him face to face and of gaining eternal blessings, thanks to the grace and loving kindness of our Lord Jesus Christ, to whom with the Father and the Holy Spirit be glory, power and honor, now and forever, for ages of ages. Amen.

---

tioch at this time (*John Chrysostom and His Time* 1, pp. 331–33); cf. also D. S. Wallace-Hadrill, *Christian Antioch* (Cambridge, 1982) and R. Wilken, *John Chrysostom and the Jews* (Berkeley, Calif., 1983). Yet it must be admitted such outbursts are infrequent in the Genesis homilies, despite the subject matter.

HOMILY 40

"God said to Abraham, 'Sarah your wife will not be called Sarah; instead, Sarrah will be her name.'"[1]

OME [368] NOW, let us spread before you the leftovers from yesterday's table and let us desire the goal of today's sermon—or, rather, the blessing and promise that the God of all made to the patriarch. But when you hear "table leftovers," don't form an impression of anything material; you see, the leftovers from food are not the same as spiritual [369] leftovers: while the former don't provide eaters with the same enjoyment once they have gone stale, but if left a day or two become completely useless, these other leftovers, on the contrary, provide equal benefit even if left not for a day or two, but for all time, without losing their taste. They are from God, after all, and spiritual, and far from risking any damage from the passage of time they show fresh attractiveness as each day passes and fill with great relish those wishing to enjoy them. So, since this is the efficacy of these leftovers, come now, be enthusiastic about satisfying your enjoyment of them, and let us have confidence in their efficacy as we set them before you, dearly beloved.

(2) In order, however, that the sermon may be clearer to you, we need to recall the close of yesterday's remarks so that by picking up the thread in this way we may link the instruction together. We brought to your attention the command about circumcision and God's words to the patriarch, "'Every male among you shall be circumcised, and it will act as a sign of the covenant between me and you. Your child of eight days shall be circumcised; whoever is not circumcised, that person

1. Gen 17.15.

389

shall be rooted out for breaking my covenant.'"[2] At this point
we terminated our teaching on the matter of circumcision
and, not to overwhelm your brain with a plethora of words
we couldn't bring ourselves to proceed further. You see, it is
not our sole concern to speak at great length and then take
our leave; rather, we want to gauge the instruction in the sermon by your ability so that you may reap some benefit from
what is said and then all go off home.[3]

(3) So, come now, let us add the remainder to what has
been said, and see what the loving God proceeded to address
to the patriarch after the command about circumcision. "God
said to Abraham," the text goes on, "'Sarah your wife will not
be called Sarah; instead, Sarrah will be her name.'" As in
your case, he is saying, I indicated by adding a syllable that
you would be father of many nations, so likewise also I am
adding a letter to Sarah, for you to learn that now the time
has come for the promises made of old by me to come into
effect.[4] "'Sarrah will be her name,'" the text says, remember.
"'Now, I shall bless her, and I shall give you a child by her;
he will become a nation, and kings of nations will spring from
him.'"[5] My reason for previously making the addition of a
syllable was for you to learn that my words would be completely realized. Instead of being despondent by having in
mind the limitations of nature, have regard for the greatness
of my power and trust in what has been said by me. "'I shall
bless her, and I shall give you a child by her; he will become

2. A précis of Gen 17.11–14, approximating more closely this time in one
detail to the LXX text.
3. As we have noted frequently before (see Introduction (11) and (12) in
FOTC 74), Chrysostom was often in danger of testing the patience of his
congregation, to judge from his own admissions and the increasing length
of the homilies. He preferred to have his congregation going home to discuss
and ruminate on the day's theme.
4. Once again Chrysostom's exegetical instincts lead him to see great significance in this morphological item—and again without sound linguistic
support. De Montfaucon notes that the change in the Hebrew feminine ending from *Sarai* to *Sarah* is represented by the Greek translators by a double
consonant in *Sarrah*—nothing more.
5. Gen 17.16. The Greek translators have applied the second half of this
verse to Isaac instead of Sarah.

several nations, and kings of nations will spring from him.'" The promises exceeded human nature; it was like promising to make people out of stones. After all, they were no different from stones as far as childbearing was concerned: the patriarch by this stage was impotent through old age and without the capacity to have children, and Sarrah in addition to her sterility had the extra handicap of extreme old age.[6]

(4) The just man, however, upon hearing this, thought that the promise made of old by God had been fulfilled in Ishmael. You see, when God said, "'To you and your descendants I will give this land,'" without making clear that it was about [370] the child born of Sarrah that he was speaking, Abraham thought within himself that the fulfillment of the promise had already occurred. But now, hearing the Lord God saying, "'I shall bless Sarrah, and I shall give you a child by her, and he will become several nations,'" and again, "'kings of nations will spring from him,'" he had nothing to say—after all, he couldn't fail to believe the words spoken by God, being the godly man he was. So, having regard to his own old age and Sarrah's sterility that had lasted to her old age, and being at a loss and in a quandary about God's promise, "he fell on his face and laughed,"[7] Scripture says.

(5) He saw the extraordinary scope of the promise, and considering the greatness of the power of the one making it "he fell on his face and laughed," that is, he was overjoyed. His mind was entertaining thoughts of how, by human logic, this could never happen, and whether a child could be born to a man of a hundred, and whether a sterile woman who had continued childless into her nineties could all of a sudden be awakened to fertility. Though entertaining these thoughts in his mind, he did not presume to utter the like in speech, but to show his gratitude he referred to the comfort found in Ishmael as if to say, Lord, you have sufficiently consoled me

6. De Montfaucon gravely remarks that Chrysostom is stretching the comparison with stones; he concedes Sarah's condition but points out that Abraham later had other children—which goes to show that later editors are not always more critically minded than early commentators.

7. Gen 17.17.

and changed into joy my disappointment at being childless by
the gift of Ishmael. I mean, once that child was born, I no
longer had any idea or ever imagined I would have a child by
Sarrah, nor did she expect it; that was the reason why she
gave Hagar into my arms, giving up all hope on her own
account. Consequently we both had sufficient consolation
with the birth of Ishmael. Let this child, therefore, given us
at your hands, live in your sight,[8] and we will have sufficient
comfort, and his life will console our old age.

(6) So what was the response of the loving Lord? Since he
had sufficiently tested the godliness of the just man's attitude
through the passage of time, and Sarrah's faith as well, and
saw that both had no expectations, the one on account of old
age and the other on account of sterility and advanced years,
he said, This now seems to you to be quite impossible. In fact,
my reason for being responsible for such a long delay was to
show you that the gift given by me is beyond the possibilities
of human nature, and for you and everyone else to learn
through the events themselves that I am the Lord of nature,
that it responds to my wishes and yields to my commands.
After all, if I created it from being nothing, much more, now
that it exists, can I correct its impediments. Accordingly, so
that you may be able to have confidence, listen, bestir yourself, banish the thought rising in your mind, receive sufficient
certitude from what I say. Behold, in fact, Sarrah your wife,
whom you judge incapable any longer of having children owing to both sterility and old age—she will bear you a son. For
you to have no doubt about this, lo, I foretell to you as well
the name of the child that will be born: you will call the child
Isaac. "'I will establish my covenant with him as an everlasting covenant and with his descendants after him.'"[9] You see,
he is the one I promised you from the very outset, and in
him the fulfillment of my promise will be achieved. Hence I
am foretelling everything to you, not only that she will have
a child, [371] but the name you will give him and the fact that
I will establish my covenant with him, and not only that, but
"'with his descendants after him.'"

8. Cf. Gen 17.18.   9. Gen 17.19.

(7) Then the Lord, ever generous with his gifts and surpassing by far our requests, since he had uplifted the just
man's spirits and had, you might say, turned an old man into
a young one by his promises, and had by his words breathed
new life into a corpse, so to speak, now lavished further blessings on him in these words: What I promised I will put into
effect, and I accept as well your prayer about Ishmael.[10] You
see, I have heeded your petition, " 'and I have blessed him. I
will make him numerous and increase his numbers over and
over. He will father twelve nations, and I will make him grow
into a mighty nation.' "[11] Since, you see (he is saying), he is
your offspring, I will make him numerous to that extent and
increase his numbers exceedingly so that twelve nations will
spring from him.

(8) " 'Nevertheless, my covenant I will establish with Isaac,
whom Sarrah will bear you by this time next year.' "[12] See in
this case, I ask you, dearly beloved, how in one brief moment
the just man gained the rewards of a lifetime, and that saying
of Christ to his disciples was fulfilled, "Whoever has left father or mother, house or brothers, for my name, will receive
a hundredfold here and will inherit eternal life."[13] Consider,
I ask you, this just man: he promptly obeyed the Lord's command, left his fatherland and preferred a foreign country to
his native country; he gradually gave evidence of sustained
endurance, and having reached the summit of virtue he became so conspicuously the object of attention of all eyes that
those born from him were compared with the multitude of
the stars.

(9) Perhaps if someone wanted to understand this in a
proper sense, what this just man received here would be
merely not a hundredfold, but even a thousandfold. If, however, he had been granted so much, what language could succeed in expressing his enjoyment in the next life? As far as
possible, however, our sermon will still manage to demon-

10. Chrysostom's editors find the text at this point, Chrysostom's paraphrase of v. 20a, uncertain.
11. Gen 17.20.   12. Gen 17.21.
13. Cf. Matt 19.29.

strate it. You see, when you hear that all the just from that time until now, and up to the very end, make it the object of their prayer to be carried into the bosom of the patriarch, what greater honor than this could you propose? Do you see what endurance means, how great a thing virtue is, and how great it is to love God and to give evidence of deep gratitude for the Lord's kindnesses? I mean, since he contributed what he could at the appropriate time and received everything gratefully, both favorable and unfavorable, accordingly the loving God granted him this also as the very summit of all good things and the particular object of the just man's virtue for twenty-four years: when he left Charran in response to the Lord's command he was seventy-five, Scripture says, whereas now when he heard this he was in his hundredth year.

(10) Hearing this, dearly beloved, let us learn to give evidence of great endurance and never grow uneasy or faint-hearted by the fact of the effort virtue involves, but rather realize that our Lord, generous and munificent as he is, returns us lavish rewards for meager efforts; he not only lays up imperishable blessings in the future but also supports the weakness of our nature in the present life by lavishing many gifts upon us. This can be seen to be true from the patriarch's enduring not a few [372] hardships lest our weakness give way to pressure, but rather he comes in person to offer ready support, strengthening our enthusiasm and enlivening our reason. Nor does he leave us in perpetual ease lest we become more indifferent and thus drift into wickedness. Human nature, after all, when it finds itself in complete relaxation, forgets its nobility and no longer respects its proper limits; consequently, like a loving father he sometimes gives respite, sometimes checks us, so as in this way to prescribe for our soul's health.

(11) A physician, too, in treating a patient does not invariably confine him to abstinence nor invariably allow him to enjoy food without a care in the world, in case gluttony gives rise to fever and aggravates the complaint or energy is exhausted by constant fasting and the patient is made weaker;

instead, by carefully estimating the patient's strength and carefully employing his skill he marshals his resources. In exactly the same way the loving God, when he sees what befalls each of us, sometimes permits us to enjoy ease, sometimes puts us through our paces by way of trials. If in fact some people are more virtuous and prove to be more conspicuous with the onset of trials, they will win greater favor from on high; if, like us, they are in fact sinners, and yet by thus welcoming the onset of trials, they gratefully lose the heavy load of sins, they too in turn will enjoy generous pardon.

(12) Hence I beg you, aware as we are of the inventive wisdom of the physician of our souls, let us never pry into his dealings. I mean, even if our mind does not succeed in grasping these things, let us on this account rather marvel at God's wise provisions and praise him above all for the fact that we have such a Lord whose designs neither our mind nor the reasoning of human nature can do justice to. After all, we do not know what is for our benefit as well as he understands it; we do not have as great a concern for ourselves as he cares for our salvation, moving might and main so as to lead us to virtue and snatch us from the hands of the devil. When he sees us unable to profit from good times, like a skillful physician noting his patients becoming obese through gluttony and bringing them to health through dieting, in exactly the same way the wonderful physician of our souls allows us gradually through the onset of trials to encounter a sense of the harm we sustained from prosperity. When he sees the complete restoration of health, then it is that through his own assistance he grants us release from trials and gives evidence of providence on his part in generous measure.

(13) If, therefore, on the one hand, people of virtue encounter trials, let them not panic but all the more on that account buoy themselves up in the sound hope that the onset of trials will prove for them grounds for reward and commendation. If, on the other hand, people living in sin fall into trouble, let them likewise not get upset, knowing as they do that the experience of this will in good time prove the purifying of their sins, when we accept all that befalls us with

gratitude. This, after all, is the mark of a grateful servant, not simply to be grateful to his master [373] when he enjoys peace, but also to give evidence of the same gratitude in difficult situations. This, you see, was the way the patriarch distinguished himself, finding much confidence with God, and by vanquishing human nature he was rewarded with gifts.

(14) It is necessary once more, however, to return to the theme of our sermon,[14] and to see the just man's obedience and the way he put into effect the directions from God without looking for an explanation or seeking reasons, unlike many silly people who pry into God's dealings, saying, What's the point of this? What's the point of that? What value comes from this or that? Not so the just man; instead, like a dutiful servant he made it his concern to put into effect without question whatever he was commanded. To learn this, listen to what follows: when the Lord had made the promise to him and finished his remarks, at once the just man carried out the order and marked on Ishmael the sign ordered by God— I mean circumcision—and all his household and acquired slaves,[15] as God had told him. Now, he too was circumcised; "He was ninety-nine when he was circumcised in the skin of his foreflesh, while Ishmael was thirteen."[16] Don't think it was without purpose that Scripture indicated to us his age; instead, it was for you to learn from the just man's obedience in meekly submitting to pain despite his extreme old age on account of God's command, and not only he but also Ishmael and all the servants—that was the reason for giving the ages.

(15) You see, dearly beloved, it is no slight thing to cut away healthy skin as though it were morbid. I know, of course, that surgeons amputate a gangrenous limb, but the pain in that case is not the same: then it's dead, so to speak, and they amputate something deprived of vital power. In our story, however, an old man advanced in years (he was, in fact, a

14. Chrysostom seems to get second wind here, after appearing to move to a conclusion beforehand by way of his normal moral exhortation. Evidently he has not yet said all he wants to say on the question of circumcision and its comparison with baptism, so a few more verses are commented on.

15. Cf. Gen 17.26–27.   16. Gen 17.24–25.

hundred, remember) meekly submitted to pain, at once being anxious to carry out God's command and also rendering his son and all his servants more zealous to avoid delay and with all haste to discharge the command from God. Do you see what a wonderful thing a man of virtue is, how he instructs all his servants as well to follow in his footsteps? In other words, what I said yesterday I repeat today, that the command came from God at that time so that the children would undergo this process in early years and so have no experience of pain from submitting to the removal of skin while yet insensitive.

(16) Consider, on the other hand, I ask you, dearly beloved, God's loving kindness and his unspeakable kindness to us. In that case pain and distress resulted from the action, and no benefit came from circumcision, except simply making people recognizable through this sign and separating them from the other peoples. Our circumcision, on the contrary—I mean the grace of baptism—involves a physic free from pain and is the means of countless good things for us, filling us with the grace of the Spirit; it has no limited span as in that other case, but rather in early years, in middle age and in the very height of old age can a person receive this circumcision not the work of human hands,[17] which involves not simply endurance but laying aside sin's burden and [374] finding pardon for the faults of all time. You see, when the loving God saw the extraordinary degree of our limitations and the fact that we are suffering from incurable diseases and need a lot of care as well as his ineffable love, he is in his provision for our salvation granted us the renewal that comes from the bath of rebirth, so that by setting aside the former person—that is, evil deeds—and putting on the new we may advance along the way of virtue.

(17) I beseech you, however, let us not be worse than the ungrateful, unresponsive Jews;[18] they, for their part, by receiving this sign of circumcision, had sufficient caution against

17. Cf. Col 2.11.
18. Cf. Homily 39, n. 33, on the degree of Chrysostom's antisemitism in the Genesis homilies.

mingling any further with other peoples on the basis of commerce, whereas, being the ungrateful lot they were, they even surpassed them in impiety. Let us, on the contrary, having once received circumcision through baptism, manage our own conduct with caution. I am not warning against our mingling with other peoples, but recommending that we adhere to our own ways of virtue and when mingling with them we attract them to religion, and through a life of good works we may become the occasion of instruction for them. The reason, after all, that the common Lord of all permitted good people and wicked to mingle together, the religious and the irreligious, was that the evil might profit from the good and those still imprisoned in impiety might be guided to religion. Nothing, you see, is so anxiously sought by God as the soul's salvation. Accordingly, let us not neglect it, I beseech you, neither our own nor our neighbors': our own, by managing our affairs in the way pleasing to God; our neighbors', by being so conspicuous that without our saying a word those espying us may have sufficient instruction.

(18) As, therefore, by being virtuous we both gain the greatest advantage ourselves and also benefit non-believers, likewise, should we be indifferent,[19] we will incur heavy punishment ourselves and prove a cause of scandal to others. I mean, just as those who practice virtue gain a double reward from God, for practicing it and also for attracting the neighbor to a like practice of it, in just the same way with evil we are punished not merely for what we have committed, but also for matters in which we have scandalized others. But God forbid that this sort of thing should happen to anyone attending here; let us all direct our own life to the edification of those who see us so that we may be able with confidence to stand before the judgment seat of Christ and be found worthy of those ineffable blessings which it may be the good for-

19. Again Chrysostom's frequent moral correlatives *rhathumia*, "indifference," "neglect," and careful attention. See Introduction (13) and (17) in FOTC 74.

tune of all of us to attain, thanks to the grace and loving kindness of our Lord Jesus Christ, to whom with the Father and the Holy Spirit be glory, power and honor, now and forever, for ages of ages. Amen.

HOMILY 41

"Now, God appeared to Abraham at the Oak of Mambre as he was sitting at the door of his tent at midday."[1]

ODAY [374] I SHRINK BACK in distaste from unfolding the teaching. I mean, I have in mind the fact that day in day out we are dinning in the message, exhorting you, laying before you this spiritual meal, while many of those who attend here and share in this spiritual teaching and awesome [375] repast waste their time at the races[2] and have profited nothing from our zeal. Instead, as though slaves to habit, at a mere nod from the devil they rush off in a trance to those illicit spectacles and fall willingly into the evil demon's snares, neither our urging nor the experience itself proving of any avail to instruct them. So what kind of enthusiasm can we now bring to the task of instructing men bent on gaining nothing from what we say? Don't be surprised at that: when a farmer likewise sees the soil unproductive despite great effort and hardship and yielding a reward not worth the effort, he becomes more reluctant about sowing and does not continue his farming with the same eagerness. A physician, too, when he sees the patient not following his directions and the ailment on the contrary growing worse day by day, frequently allows the patient to continue in the ailment so that the experience itself may prove a lesson for him of what is to his advantage. Likewise those who give lessons to children, when they see them rejecting the elements and discarding the memory of what has already been given them,

1. Gen 18.1.
2. This, of course, is not the first time that Chrysostom departs from his theme to scourge his congregation for attending the races—a practice that involved more than placing bets, it seems. See Homily 6, and my "horses."

frequently abandon the task of correcting their indifference and of leading them to greater zeal.

(2) In the case of the farmer, however, it is probable that he frequently becomes less enthusiastic on realizing that he sustains a loss when undergoing effort and expense while being deprived of a harvest. The physician not unreasonably abandons his patient in many cases; it is the body, after all, that is the object of care, and he leaves it alone so that the extremity of pain may cause the patient to arrive at some sense of the ailment and thus accept the cure. The teacher of children on account of their immaturity in many cases chastises the children to good purpose. Surpassing all those, however, we take steps to give evidence of fatherly affection towards the wayward and teach them that if they persist in the same indifference, this itself will prove grounds for heavier condemnation for them. You see, whereas the farmer sows the seed without the same enthusiasm when considering that expense has already been incurred idly and to no purpose, we, on the contrary, are free from this problem. I mean, we sow this spiritual seed, and even if we reap no harvest on account of the indifference of the listeners, our reward will be complete. You see, we have spent money that is borrowed, carrying out the command of the Lord; later an account is due from the listeners with him who will be looking for what has been spent plus interest. Our object, however, is not that we avoid loss and recover our investment; instead, we intend that you too make a great profit from what is invested and so avoid becoming liable to that awful punishment suffered by the man who buried the talent and, far from multiplying his master's money, even hid it in the ground.[3] This is what people are like who receive the word of our teaching (this, after all, being the meaning of the talent and money), without betraying a concern for showing any result or making a great profit. But perhaps someone may say this parable concerns the teachers. I agree. But if we approach it precisely, you will realize that whereas the teachers [376] are in fact responsible

3. Cf. Matt 25.14–30.

only for the expense, you on the contrary are responsible not only for what has been spent on you but also for the profit.

(3) To learn this, we must bring the parable to your attention. "A certain householder going abroad," the text says, "summoned his servants and gave them some talents, to one five talents, to another two, to another one. Now, after a while he returned and his servants came to him. The one who had received five talents approached him with the words, 'Master, you gave me five talents; but, behold, I have gained five talents in addition to them!'"[4] Deep the gratitude of the servant, lavish the loving kindness of the master. What in fact did he say? "'Well done, good and faithful servant; you have been faithful in a few things, I will put you in possession of many. Enter into the delights of your master.'"[5] Since you have shown deep gratitude, he is saying, in what has already been entrusted to you, you are deserving of even greater things being confided to you. "Now, the one who had received the two talents approached him in the words, 'Did you not hand over to me two talents? But, behold, I have gained two talents in addition to them.'"[6] Very proper this man's disposition, too, in regard to his master's money, and accordingly he is given the same reward as the previous man. Why is it that the man who produced two talents was accorded the same commendation as the one who delivered five? Rightly so; it was not the zeal of the latter nor the indifference of the former that caused the greater or less profit but the rates of the borrowers. Surely the display of zeal by the one and the other can be paralleled; consequently they enjoyed the same reward.

(4) The third servant, however, did not behave in the same way. Instead, what? He approached him with these words: "'I knew you are a demanding person, harvesting where you haven't sown, reaping where you haven't scattered; so taking fright I went off and hid the talent in the ground. Behold,

4. Matt 25.14–15, 19–20, slightly paraphrased.
5. Matt 25.21.
6. Matt 25.22, in a variant of Chrysostom's own.

you have back what is yours.'"⁷ O, what wickedness of a servant! O, what extreme ingratitude, not only in doing nothing with the talent given him, but also in laying charges in return for the talent! This, you see, is what evil is like: it dulls the intellect and causes the person who has once strayed from the straight and narrow to fall down the precipice. Now, all this is said with reference to teachers lest they hide what has been entrusted to them instead of passing it on with all zeal to their disciples. But take heed now, dearly beloved, from the anger directed at this servant how the disciples also become responsible: not only is the money outlaid due but they are subject as well to an accounting with interest. So what does the master say to him? "'Wicked servant.'" Fearful anger, threats sufficient to strike terror. "'If you knew,'" he says, "'that I harvest where I haven't sown and reap where I haven't scattered, you should have lent the money to the bankers, and on my return I could have looked for it with interest,'"⁸ meaning by money his precious words and calling you, the recipients, bankers. It was your task only to lend, he says, whereas it is for me to reclaim it from them, not simply what was lent but the interest on it as well. See, dearly beloved, how great a dread these words inspire. What then could they reply who had evinced neglect even in watching over what was lent them when they were required as well to declare interest on it?

(5) See the Lord's loving kindness. In the case of material wealth, on the one hand, he forbids our taking interest. Why, and for what reason? Because both parties suffer great harm from it. You see, whereas [377] the poverty of one party is aggravated, the creditor by contrast heaps up for himself a multitude of sins along with the surplus of his wealth. Hence from the very beginning he laid down this law on the Jews with their rather materialistic mentality, namely, "You shall not lend money with interest to your brother or your neighbor."⁹ So what sort of excuse could they claim who prove even more savage than the Jews, and who, despite the Lord's favor

---

7. Matt 25.24–25.   8. Matt 25.26–27.
9. Deut 23.19, with the addition of "neighbor" on Chrysostom's part, perhaps to strengthen his point.

and wonderful love, are found to be inferior to those under
the Law and in fact even worse? In spiritual things, to be
sure, he himself promises he will look for interest. Why? Because this spiritual interest is the opposite of material wealth.
You see, in the former case the debtor is brought suddenly to
extreme penury, whereas in this case, whenever the debtor
gives evidence of deep gratitude, he enjoys more generous
reward from above the more interest he pays. Accordingly let
each of you, dearly beloved, when we lend to you on credit,
feel the need to give evidence of double effort and vigilance,
for one thing guarding what has been lent so that it may
remain untouched, for another thing working to share it with
others and guide many along the path of virtue, so that your
profit in turn may be doubled to the advantage both of your
own salvation and of the salvation of those others. If in fact
you do this, you will render us happy ("Happy is he who
speaks to listening ears,"[10] Scripture says, remember), and
you will cause this spiritual banquet to be laid more generously for you.

(6) Do not neglect your brethren, therefore, nor consider
only your own concerns; instead, let each of you be anxious
to snatch your neighbor from the jaws of the devil and those
illicit spectacles, and lead him to church, showing him in all
restraint and gentleness both the extreme risk of harm and
also the extent of the good things to be gained here. Do this
not merely once or twice but ceaselessly. I mean, even if today
he doesn't heed your words, he will heed them in future; if
not in future, in due course seeing your insistence he will
perhaps feel ashamed, will come to respect your care for him
and desist from those harmful pursuits. Never say, Once,
twice, three times, again and again I told him and got nowhere. Don't stop telling him; the more you persist, the more
your reward will be increased as well. Don't you see how
much longsuffering we enjoy from the God of all, and how

10. This is proving a very lengthy introduction to the day's homily, including that lengthy elaboration of the parable of the talents, all to make the
point of responsive listening (perhaps, in the manner of preachers the world
over, berating those present for the sins of the absent).

day after day we fail to heed his commands without his desisting from caring for us but rather supplying us with everything, making the sun to rise, giving us rain from heaven and everything else? Let us, in exactly the same way, take great pains in regard to our brethren and take issue with that evil demon so as to render his wiles ineffectual. After all, if everyone attending here managed to gain one person, consider how much the Church would receive great satisfaction in the vast numbers of its children and the devil would be dismayed to see his net cast idly and to no purpose. If in fact you do this, you too will hear on that dread day, "'Well done, good and faithful servant; you have been faithful in a few things, I will put you in possession of many.'"

(7) We are quite convinced, however, that you will do this: I see your faces and presume that you receive advice from us with [378] pleasure, and hence I hope that you in turn will do what lies in you. Consequently, let us bring our exhortation on this matter to a close at this point; on the other hand, we will spread before you our poor and meager table so that you may enjoy the accustomed instruction and thus go off home. It is necessary today, too, you see, to draw to your attention the patriarch Abraham so that you may learn what reward he received from God for his hospitality. "Now, God appeared to him," the text goes on, "at the Oak of Mambre as he was sitting at the door of his tent at midday." Let us examine each of the words with precision,[11] open up the treasure and disclose all the wealth concealed there. "Now, God appeared to him," the text says. Why did it begin in that way, "Now, God appeared to him"? See the Lord's loving kindness and consider, I ask you, a servant's gratitude. I mean, when God appeared to him previously and gave him the command about circumcision along with all the others, this remarkable man without fail hastened to put the orders from God into effect and without hesitating in the slightest he himself was

11. Once again Chrysostom's typical concern for the precision of Scripture emerges, based on his Antiochene theology of the Word incarnate in the inspired text and leading him to seize on each of its elements. See Introduction (21) in FOTC 74, and my articles, "Incarnation" and "Akribeia."

circumcised to discharge God's command, he circumcised Ishmael and all the slaves, demonstrating his complete obedience. So God appeared to him again. This, you see, is what our Lord is like: when he sees people grateful in the first instance, he lavishes further kindnesses on them and never desists from rewarding the gratitude of those obedient to him.

(8) This, then, was the reason why he appeared to him again, Scripture says, because he was obedient. So on this account blessed Moses began in this way, in the words, "Now, God appeared to him at the Oak of Mambre as he was sitting at the door of his house at midday." Notice, I ask you, in this instance the just man's virtue: "As he was sitting," the text says, "at his tent." He was putting hospitality into practice to such a degree as to be unwilling to entrust to anyone else in the household the task of attending to guests; instead, although he had three hundred and eighteen servants,[12] and was himself an old man, having attained advanced years (after all, he was a hundred years old), he took his seat at the door. In his case he was practicing this virtue; old age was no problem for him, he was not concerned for his own repose, nor was he reclining inside on his bed but was seated at the door. Other people, by contrast, in many cases not only do not show such concern but just the opposite, trying to avoid meeting visitors as if they were forced to receive them against their will.

(9) The just man, on the other hand, was not like that: he was sitting at the door of his tent at midday. This, you see, was the great extent of the just man's hospitality and the extraordinary degree of his virtue, the fact that he behaved like this at midday. Very properly, too: since he realized that people obliged to travel are in need of much service at that time particularly, accordingly he chose that time as suitable, seated himself and kept an eye out for passers-by without caring whether they were known to him or not. You see, it is not part of hospitality to worry about such things: friendliness

12. Cf. Gen 14.14.

involves sharing one's possessions with all comers. Since he cast a wide net of hospitality, he in turn was judged worthy to welcome the Lord of all with his angels. Hence Paul too said, "Do not neglect hospitality, for through it some people have entertained angels all unawares,"[13] referring precisely to the patriarch. Hence Christ too said, "Whoever receives one of the least [379] of these in my name, receives me."[14]

(10) Let us take heed, dearly beloved, and when due to entertain visitors never be overly concerned as to who they are and where they come from. After all, had the patriarch been too concerned about this, he perhaps would have sinned. But he knew the dignity of the visitors, you say. Where does that emerge? On the contrary, had he known that, how would it have been a matter of remark? You see, his attention to hospitality would not have been so remarkable if he had been concerned about those things as in fact was the case when without knowing the identity of the visitors he approached them with such alacrity and respect, like a slave to his masters, as if ensnaring them with his words and entreating them not to decline and thus inflict on him the greatest loss. He knew, you see, what was to be done; hence it was with great ardor that he capitalized on the occasion.

(11) Let us listen, however, to the words of the writer himself,[15] so that you may see his rejuvenated enthusiasm in the depths of old age and the old man himself rejuvenated as if made glad and convinced he had found a treasure in the coming of the visitors. "Now, he raised his eyes," the text goes on, "and looked and, lo, three men were standing in front of him. On seeing them he ran forward from the door of his tent to meet them."[16] The old man runs and flies; you see, he

13. Heb 13.2.
14. Matt 18.5, with elements also of Matt 25.40, 45.
15. This is a unique reference by Chrysostom to Moses as "writer," *syngrapheus,* and almost without parallel in all his homilies on the Old Testament, where *prophētēs* is the usual term for the inspired authors from Moses to David. The distinction is significant for Chrysostom's theology of inspiration in that he clearly sees the Scriptures as God's inspired Word delivered primarily at the oral level. See my "terminology."
16. Gen 18.2.

had espied his prey, and making no account of his weakness he ran to snare it, not summoning his servants, not bidding a child, giving no evidence of indifference, but running of his own accord as if to say, Wonderful treasure, important business; by myself I should discharge this affair in case this advantage should pass me by. This is what the just man did, deciding to welcome these men, unknown travelers though they were.

(12) Let us discover and emulate the just man's virtue. If in fact we do so, it is likely that we, too, will have the good luck of such a wonderful catch; rather, we would always have that good luck if we wanted to. The loving Lord's intention, you see, was that we should not be indifferent about such friendship nor be too fastidious about our visitors—hence his words, "Whoever receives one of the least of these in my name receives me." So don't have regard to the station of the visitor nor despise him on the basis of what you can see, but consider that in him you are welcoming your Lord. You see, when in his name you give evidence of attention to the visitor, you will gain a reward just as if you welcomed him. So even if the person enjoying your friendliness is heedless and neglectful, make no account of it: you will receive a perfect reward for doing it out of regard for the Lord and imitating this particular virtue.

(13) "On seeing them," the text says, "he ran forward from the door of his tent to meet them." Very appropriately is the word "ran forward" used, so that you may learn that they arrived unknowing and did not come to the tent for a set purpose. Hence in case this spiritual advantage should escape him, this old man, this greybeard, this centenarian ran forward and by his running revealed his enthusiasm. "Espying them he bowed to the ground and said, 'Sir, if I have really found favor with you, do not pass by your servant. Let some water be brought, have your feet washed and rest under the tree; I will fetch some bread, you can eat and afterwards continue your journey when you have rested with your servant.'"[17] Extraordinary the just man's [380] words, not for

17. Gen 18.3–5.

welcoming them—a wonderful example of enthusiasm—but for acting with such earnestness, without regard for his own age or the condition of his visitors (perhaps, in fact, they appeared to him to be young people), nor thinking that an appeal in word alone would suffice; "he bowed to the ground," the text says, as if making supplication and addressing an earnest prayer to them lest it be thought his appeal was made merely perfunctorily. This is really the reason why Sacred Scripture reveals the just man's virtue beyond telling in the words, "He bowed to the ground," thus giving evidence by his posture and his words of his great ardor, his great humility, his intense spirit of hospitality, his ineffable care.

(14) "Bowing to the ground," the text goes on, "he said, 'Sir, if I have really found favor with you, do not pass by your servant.'" Who could do justice in words to this just man? How could anyone praise him even with countless lips? I mean, while the term "sir" is a customary one, on the other hand saying "'if I have really found favor with you'" is unusual. You are giving a favor, he says, not receiving one. You see, this is what hospitality really involves: the person exemplifying it with enthusiasm receives something rather than gives it. Let no one hearing this, however, disparage the just man's virtue nor think that he spoke these words in the knowledge of who the visitors were. It would have been, in fact, as has often been said, no great thing had he spoken these words from prior knowledge; but the really remarkable thing is that he spoke such words while approaching them as fellow human beings.

(15) Now, don't be surprised at the fact that, whereas there were three visitors being welcomed, the just man addressed his plea to one in the word, "'Sir.'" Perhaps in fact one of the visitors seemed the more logical one to whom the plea should be addressed. Then he went on and made his remarks applicable to them all: "'Let some water be brought and have your feet washed'"; and again, "'Rest under the tree, eat some bread, and afterwards continue your journey now that you have rested with your servant.'" Do you see how, without knowing who they were and speaking to the visitors as though

to fellow human beings, he makes his common plea to them all, calling himself more than once their servant? See how he suggests the poverty of his hospitality, instead of its extravagance. "'Let some water be brought,'" he says, "'have your feet washed, and rest under the tree.'" You see, since you are weary (he is saying) and have endured the burning heat, I beg you not to pass your servant by. After all, it is no great gesture being made by me, is it? I have only water to offer you for you to wash and rest from your great weariness under the tree. Then he mentions the kind of repast; Don't think I will offer you anything extravagant, a range of spices or variety of dishes; eat some bread, and then "'continue your journey now that you have rested with your servant.'"

(16) Do you see how he employs various stratagems in his wish to importune the visitors, endeavoring to win them over by his posture, his words, and every means possible? First, you see, the text says, he bowed low, he called them "sirs" and himself "servant"; then he told them the kind of service he would be rendering them, minimizing it and showing it was nothing extraordinary: Only water, he says, (something available to everyone) I have to offer you for your feet, bread, and the shade of the tree. Do not scorn my tent, [381] do not despise my old age, do not reject my plea. I know how much hardship you have endured, I can imagine the intensity of the heat, so I want to offer you some little relief in this way. Could any loving father have shown such great kindliness towards his child as this man showed to unknown strangers whose background was so far a mystery to him? Since, however, he made his approach with eagerness and great devotion, he attained his goal and succeeded in drawing the prey into his nets.

(17) "They said," the text goes on, "'We will do as you have said.'"[18] The old man found new life and vigor: I have the treasure in my hands, he said, I have won riches, I have forgotten my age. See him quite heartened by the affair: as if

18. Gen 18.5b, where Chrysostom supplies a first person plural for the imperative "Do."

jumping for joy and holding countless good things in his hands, he was so happy. "Abraham made all haste into the tent,"[19] the text goes on. Just as when he was pressing upon his quarry Sacred Scripture referred to his dedication and enthusiasm, so now that he saw the men and achieved the object of his desire his enthusiasm did not cease; instead, he then gave evidence of more ardent love and, though he had reached certainty, he did not then become less interested. That often happens with us: in the beginning we sometimes give evidence of great zeal but, once we make some progress in the affair, we don't bring the same enthusiasm to the task.

(18) Not so the just man, however; instead, what? Once more the old man sets to, presses on with the task and runs into the tent to Sarrah, "and says to her, 'Hurry, mix three measures of finest flour.'" Consider how he makes Sarrah as well a sharer in the quarry and how he taught her to imitate his virtue: he urges her on, too, to perform the task without indifference—rather, "'Hurry,'" he says.[20] What great good fortune has come our way, let us not lose the treasure; instead, "'Hurry, mix three measures of finest flour.'" You see, since he realized the importance of the action, he wanted to make the woman who shared his life a sharer also in receiving reward and recompense. Why, after all, tell me, did he give this direction to none of his servants but to his aged wife instead? Sarrah, far from declining the request, shows exactly the same enthusiasm. Let men take note, let women take note: men, on the one hand, to instruct their partners, when they have the prospect of some spiritual advantage, not to have the task carried out by servants but to see to it all personally; women, on the other hand, to be sharers with their husbands in such wonderful exploits and not to shrink from hospitality and attention to visitors but rather to imitate old Sarrah, who was prepared in old age to take pains and perform the tasks of menials.

19. Gen 18.6.

20. For Chrysostom, Abraham, like the other major characters of primeval and patriarchal history, is a moral figure conspicuous for that cardinal virtue, *prothumia*, "enthusiasm," as opposed to the capital sin of *rhathumia*, "indifference." See Introduction (17) in FOTC 74.

(19) I realize, however, that no one accepts what I am saying. These days, of course, everyone is anxious to take the opposite course to her: women are given to great decadence, interest in the condition of their clothes, gold ornaments, necklaces and cosmetics, with no attention given to their souls. Not even Paul's cries move them: "not in braided hair, gold, pearls or expensive clothing."[21] See this soul reaching up to heaven, how he thought it not shameful for him to take [382] his sermon to such a fine point as to preach about braided hair. And rightly so; after all, his complete attention was given to care for the soul. So since he realized that these things in particular contribute to the soul's ruin, he shirked nothing calculated to instruct people suffering from these vices; instead he said, If you insist on adorning yourself, adorn yourself with true adornment, the kind that befits religious women: adorn yourself with good works. This is the soul's adornment, this is subject to no condemnation by outsiders, no one will be able to rob you of it, it remains proof against theft forever. You see, from external adornment countless evils take their rise; I am not yet referring to damage to the soul, false airs stemming from that, scorn for one's neighbors, mental aberration, ruin of the soul, and a host of improper pleasures, but the fact that this sort of adornment is vulnerable to the mischief of servants, assault by robbers, wiles of flatterers, and you could list countless evils and persistent problems arising from it.

(20) Sarrah, however, was not like that; instead, she made use of true adornment. Hence she was worthy of the patriarch, and just as he made haste to run into the tent, she too carried out the direction with promptness and mixed three measures of finest flour. You see, since there were three visitors, he ordered three measures to be mixed so that the bread would be ready sooner. After giving this direction he in turn ran to the cattle. What youthful vigor in an old man! What devotion of soul! He runs to the cattle, not letting any of the servants go, showing the visitors in every way how much sat-

21. 1 Tim 2.9.

isfaction he enjoyed and how great an honor he considered their visit to be, as well as his judgment that the occasion was a treasure for him. "He took a fine tender heifer," the text says. He made the selection himself, choosing the best of them and giving it to his servant, and pressing him not to hesitate but to show all speed. Consider how everything is done with haste, with lively enthusiasm, with relish, with joy, with deep satisfaction. "The servant hastened to do it," the text adds. Nor did the old man rest at that, but once more pressed on with his role of service. "Taking curds and milk and the heifer he had prepared, he set it before them."[22] He personally saw to the preparation and the serving; and instead of judging himself fit to recline with them, he took his own position under the tree while they were eating.

(21) What a wonderful extent of hospitality! What an extraordinary degree of humility! What a remarkable example of godly attitude! This hundred year old person stands nearby while they are eating. In my opinion, under the impulse of keen desire and enthusiasm he had at that time been rendered safe from weakness and had gained some additional strength. You see, it often happens that when enthusiasm of spirit is heightened, it overcomes bodily weakness. Accordingly the patriarch stands like a servant nearby, considering it a great honor to be judged worthy to serve the visitors and give them relief from the weariness of their traveling. Do you see how great was the just man's hospitality? I mean, don't concentrate on the fact that he served them bread and meat, but consider with how much respect, how much humility he displayed his hospitality, unlike most people who, even should they do something similar, think themselves superior to the recipients and oftentimes despise them for the attention given them. This, however, is like the case of someone acquiring and amassing wealth and then throwing away all he has amassed. You see, the person who does something from a warped intention and acts as one giving rather than receiving does not know what he is doing; hence he loses the reward for it as well.

22. Gen 18.8.

(22) The just man, [383] on the contrary, knew what he was doing; through everything that happened, he revealed his enthusiasm of spirit. After he had with liberality and great cheerfulness sown the seed of hospitality, at once with generous hand he reaped the sheaves. You see, after he had done all that lay within him and, far from leaving anything undone, had brought the process of hospitality to completion, and thus the just man's virtue was made manifest, then it was that, with a view to the just man's knowing the extent of his good fortune and the number of good things of which his hospitality had proved the cause for him, the visitor revealed his identity and gradually made manifest to the just man the greatness of his power. Seeing him standing by the tree and betraying by his position his great respect and attention, the visitor said to him, "'Where is your wife Sarrah?'"[23] Immediately by this question he revealed to him that he was no casual visitor, since for one thing he knew his wife's name. He replied, "'See, in the tent there.'" Since, being God, he was now about to promise him something beyond the limits of nature, consequently by mentioning Sarrah's name he suggested that the one who had visited his tent was more than a human being.

(23) He said, in fact, "'When I return and visit you at this time next year, your wife Sarrah will have a son.'"[24] Behold the fruits of hospitality, behold the reward of heightened enthusiasm, behold the recompense of Sarrah's exertion. "Now, she was listening near the door of the tent, standing behind him. On hearing this, she laughed to herself and said, 'So far this hasn't yet happened to me, and my husband is an old man.'"[25] So as to offer an excuse for Sarrah, Sacred Scripture had previously indicated that "Abraham and Sarrah were advanced in years," and without stopping there it added further, "Now, Sarrah's periods had ceased to occur."[26] The spring had dried up, it is saying, the eye had lost its sight, the very workplace had been rendered useless. With this in mind,

23. Gen 18.9.
24. Gen 18.10.
25. Gen 18.12.
26. Gen 18.11.

therefore, Sarrah daily reflected on her own age and the patriarch's advanced years. But while she was thinking this in her tent, the one who understands the unspoken thoughts of the mind wished to show both the extraordinary degree of his power and the fact that none of our unspoken thoughts escapes his notice; so he said to Abraham, "'Why did Sarrah laugh and say to herself, Am I really to have a child, at my age?'"[27] This, in fact, was what she was thinking.

(24) "'Nothing is impossible for God, is it?'"[28] Lo, he revealed his identity openly! Do you know, he says, that being Lord of nature I can do everything I wish, bring life to an infertile womb and make it fit for childbearing? "Nothing is impossible for God, is it?'" Do I not make everything and transform everything? Have I not power over life and death? "'Nothing is impossible for God, is it?'" Did I in fact not make this promise before? My word will take effect, will it not? So take heed that "'I will return to you at this time next year and Sarrah will have a son.'" When I return at this time, he says, then Sarrah will know by the way things turn out that neither age nor sterility will prove a difficulty for her; instead, my word will be inescapable, and the birth will teach her the power of my words. Then, on hearing that not even the thoughts passing through her mind [384] escaped the notice of the visitor, "she denied it, saying, 'I didn't laugh.'"[29] Fear, you see, had shaken her mind. Hence Scripture attributed it all to her weakness in saying, "For she was frightened." But the patriarch said to her, "'Not so: you did laugh.'"[30] Don't think, he says, even if you were entertaining these thoughts in your mind and having a private laugh, that you could escape the power of the visitor. So don't deny what has happened nor compound your sin. After all, wonderful blessings have come our way today, thanks to our hospitality.

27. Gen 18.13, Chrysostom omitting from his text reference to the speaker as Yahweh, significant for other commentators on the Hebrew and Greek texts.

28. Gen 18.14.   29. Gen 18.15.

30. Against the flow of the dialogue Chrysostom attributes the corrective to Abraham, perhaps to allow for moral elaboration, or reluctant to see the Lord involved in a wrangle.

(25) Let us all imitate this and display much zeal in practicing hospitality, not merely to receive some recompense for these perishable and corruptible things but to lay up for ourselves as well the enjoyment of immortal blessings. You see, if we practice hospitality, we shall welcome Christ here and he will, in turn, welcome us in those mansions prepared for those who love him, and we shall hear from him, "'Come my Father's blessed ones, take possession of the kingdom prepared for you from the foundation of the world.'"[31] Why so? "'For I was hungry, and you gave me something to eat; I was thirsty, and you gave me something to drink; I was a stranger and you made me welcome; I was in custody and you came to see me.'"[32] What could be less troublesome than this? He didn't bid us scrutinize and investigate those about to be given hospitality by us, did he? You play your part, he says, even if the person is of lowly station and unprepossessing; I will take as done to myself what is done to them. Hence he added, "'Whatever you did to one of the least of my brethren you did to me.'"[33]

(26) So don't spurn such wonderful profit accruing to you from hospitality, but day in and day out exert yourself to gain this fine merchandise, in the knowledge that our Lord looks for generosity of spirit, not great amounts of food, not a rich table but a cheerful attitude, not simply attention in words alone but also love from the heart and sincere mind. Hence a certain sage also said, "Likewise a kind word is more acceptable than a gift."[34] In many cases, you see, attention in word has helped a needy person back on his feet more effectively than a gift. Aware of this, then, let us make no difficulty about meeting visitors; instead, if on the one hand we are in a position to alleviate their poverty, let us do so with love and cheerfulness, not as giving something but as gaining very great advantage. On the other hand, if we cannot do so, let us not be uncivil with them but at least offer them attention in word and respond to them with restraint. I mean, why

31. Matt 25.34.
33. Matt 25.40.
32. Matt 25.35.
34. Sir 18.16.

adopt an uncivil attitude towards him? He didn't pressure you, after all, did he? He didn't use force, did he? He asks, entreats, begs; but someone doing this doesn't deserve abuse. Why do I say asks and begs? He pours out countless requests, all for a single penny, and we slip him not even this much. What excuse would we have? What account could we give, we who each day spread a lavish table and often have more than we need, whereas with them we share not a scrap, even if by so doing we could win all these countless blessings?

(27) O, what awful indifference! I mean, what good comes from this? What great gain are we letting slip from our grasp? We are rejecting the basis of our salvation offered us by God, [385] without giving it so much as a thought or even considering the insignificance of our offering or the extraordinary degree of the wonderful rewards. Instead, we lock everything up in cupboards and allow the gold to be consumed by rust—or, rather, we thrust it into the hands of robbers. Our resplendent wardrobe, on the other hand, we allow to be eaten by moths, unable to bring ourselves to have the surplus properly disposed of so that it may be kept for us in the future and we may thus succeed in being accorded these ineffable blessings. May this be the good fortune of all of us, thanks to the grace and loving kindness of our Lord Jesus Christ, to whom with the Father and the Holy Spirit be glory, power and honor, now and forever, for ages of ages. Amen.

HOMILY 42

"Now, when the men rose, they looked directly at Sodom and Gomorrah."[1]

ROM [385] WHAT WAS READ YESTERDAY, dearly beloved, we learnt the extraordinary degree of the just
man's hospitality. Today, too, let us move to what follows and come to discover the patriarch's love and compassion. You see, this good man possessed each of the virtues to
an extraordinary degree: he was not only loving, hospitable
and compassionate, but he gave evidence as well of all the
other virtues in generous measure. If there is need for him
to display endurance, you will find him reaching the very
height of that virtue; if humility, you will see him in turn, far
from yielding place to anyone, surpassing them all; if there is
need for him to display faith, he will again be found in this
conspicuous above all others. His soul, in fact, is like an ani-
mated image, revealing in itself a range of colors of virtue.
So what excuse remains for us when, despite the example of
one human being adorned with every virtue, we prove to be
so bereft as to have no intention to practice any virtue? You
see, for proof that our being bereft of all goods is a matter
not of being unable, but of being unwilling, we have clear
indication in the fact that we find many of our peers conspicuous for virtue. The very fact that the patriarch, who lived
before the age of grace and before the Law, reached such a
degree of virtue of himself from the knowledge innate in his
nature is sufficient to deprive us of any excuse.

(2) Some people, however, will perhaps say that this man
had the advantage of great care from God, and the God of
all gave evidence of deep concern for him. Yes, I admit that;

1. Gen 18.16.

418

still, if he himself had not first given evidence of his own goodwill, he would not have enjoyed the Lord's help. So do not have eyes only for that, but each day study and learn how by first providing a sample of his own virtue in every circumstance, he was judged worthy of help.[2] More than once we pointed out to you, when he was making his move from his ancestral land how, far from receiving from his forebears the seeds of religion, he gave evidence from his very own disposition of his great godliness. Despite his being a recent refugee from Chaldea, he was suddenly called upon to choose a foreign land in exchange for his own, and without hesitation, without delay he immediately obeyed the command, and without knowing where his traveling would end he pressed on in haste in these uncertain matters as though they were clear, giving pride of place over everything else to the command from God.

(3) Do you see how from the very outset he exerted every effort of his own, and consequently he daily gained help from God as well, in very generous measure? In just the same way, let us, too, dearly beloved, if we want to enjoy favor from above, imitate the patriarch, and instead of drawing back from virtue let us embrace each and every virtue and practice it with such zeal as to win over that unsleeping eye to rewarding our effort. You see, he understands the unspoken thoughts of our mind, [386] and when he sees us giving evidence of a sound attitude and anxious to embrace the struggles of virtue, immediately he supplies us with assistance from himself, at the one time lightening our exertions, supporting the limitations of our nature and granting us generous rewards.

(4) At the Olympic Games you would not find anything like this happening. On the contrary, the trainer stands by, merely in the role of a spectator of the contestants, unable to contribute any help of his own, but merely waiting for victory to be declared. Our Lord, on the other hand, is not like that; instead, he becomes a contestant himself with us, offers us his

2. Had Chrysostom been living somewhat later in the West, statements such as these on the relation of human effort to divine grace might have earned him the charge of Semipelagianism.

hand, takes part in the struggle, and seemingly in every way hands over our adversary to us in defeat, striving might and main that we may prevail and wrest the victory, so that he may place on our head the unfading crown. Scripture says, remember, "You will receive a crown of graces upon your head."[3] Whereas in these Olympic Games the crown after victory is nothing more than a laurel wreath, or applause, or acclamation of the crowd, all of which disappears and is lost with the coming of evening, the crown for virtue and its struggles has nothing material about it, it is not subject to decay in this world but is everlasting, immortal, enduring for all ages. Whereas the effort lasts only a short time, the reward for the effort has no end, is not affected by time and does not fade. To grasp this, behold how many ages and how many generations have passed since this patriarch lived: as though it were yesterday or today, the crown for his virtue is still so resplendent, and until the end of time he proves an occasion of instruction for all rightminded people.

(5) Since this just man's virtue is so wonderful, therefore, let us bestir ourselves to imitation of him, and at least at this late stage let us acknowledge our own nobility, emulate the patriarch, show some consideration of our salvation and display considerable concern not only to keep the body healthy but also to cure the various ills of the soul. In fact, provided we are ready to be awake and on the alert, we will more easily heal the ills affecting the body's passions. You see, no matter what passion disturbs us, as long as we are prepared to keep in mind the Judgment on that dread day by pious thinking and have regard not for present delight but the pain afflicting us afterwards, immediately it will take flight and depart from our soul. Let us therefore not be indifferent, but in the knowledge that it is a contest and struggle and there is need to be ready for battle let us each day keep our mind fresh and strong so that we may enjoy help from on high and succeed in crushing the head of that evil beast [387]—I mean the one who plots against our salvation. After all, the Lord

3. Prov 1.9.

himself has made us this promise: "Behold, I have given you power to walk on snakes and scorpions, and power over all the enemy's might."[4]

(6) Let us, therefore, I beseech you, take care to follow in the footsteps of this patriarch by practicing virtue and so be in a position to be awarded the same crown as his, to be transported into his bosom, to escape punishment in hell and to be judged worthy of those good things beyond all telling. But for the purpose of promoting in you greater zeal and bestirring you to imitation of this just man, come now, once more let us recount his story to you, dearly beloved, by picking up the thread of what follows. After that generous hospitality of his, remember, judged not by the quality or quantity of food but by his enthusiasm, he was immediately granted reward for his hospitality. Learning who the visitor was and how great his power, the patriarch accompanied them, the text goes on to say, as they were about to proceed to the overthrow of Sodom. See the Lord's loving kindness in employing so much considerateness by showing regard for the good man and wishing at the same time to reveal the virtue that was concealed in his soul. "Now, when the sun arose," the text says, "they looked directly at Sodom and Gomorrah." It is referring to the angels: whereas here in Abraham's tent both the angels and their Lord were seen at the same time, now like ministers they were sent about the overthrow of those cities while he stayed behind as if communing with the just man, like one friend to another, about what he was going to do.[5]

(7) Accordingly, when they departed, the text goes on, "The Lord said, 'I shall not conceal from my servant Abraham what I am going to do.' "[6] Wonderful is God's considerateness and his regard for the good man surpassing all

4. Luke 10.19.
5. For some reason Chrysostom has omitted v. 16b in the Hebrew and LXX stating that, despite Chrysostom's picture of intimate colloquium, all three left the scene and even Abraham left with them.
6. Gen 18.17, as a statement, rather than the interrogative of the Hebrew and LXX.

reckoning. I mean, see how he converses with him, man to man, so to say, showing us how much regard the virtuous are accorded by God. Lest you think such great regard for the good man was a mark of God's goodness only, see how Sacred Scripture teaches us that he rendered himself deserving of such great regard for his obedience to God's commands with great responsiveness. You see, in saying, "'I shall not conceal from my servant Abraham what I am going to do,'" he does not immediately say what is about to happen: the sequel shows him adding the words that he was about to set Sodom on fire. But even that should not be passed over; no syllable or particle of the contents of Sacred Scripture ought be passed idly by.[7] How great a regard do you think that very remark is an index of, "'My servant Abraham'"? How much affection? How kind a disposition? In fact, it demonstrates in particular the regard for the just man and his remarkable character.

(8) Then, as I have remarked, after saying, "'I shall not conceal,'" he does not immediately go on to say what is happening—instead, what? For us to learn that it was not idly or to no purpose that he shows this care for him, he says, "'Now, Abraham will become a great and populous nation, and in him all the nations of the earth will be blessed. I am aware, of course, that he will instruct his sons and his household after him, and they will keep the ways of the Lord God in practicing righteousness and sound judgment, so that the Lord will bring Abraham all the things he has promised him.'"[8] Bless me, what a marvelous extent of the Lord's loving kindness! Since after this he was about to bring on the destruction [388] of Sodom, now in advance he encourages the patriarch by promising him the most marvelous blessing and the fact that he would become a great multitude, and at the same time teaching him that he would receive this reward

7. A classic statement of the position of Chrysostom and his school on the importance of the literal sense of Scripture and the *akribeia*, "precision," of the sacred text—all flowing from their conviction of biblical inspiration. See my *Inspiration*, pp. 128–49, and "*Akribeia*."
8. Gen 18.18–19.

for his godly attitude. I mean, consider how great was the patriarch's virtue when God says, "'I am aware, of course, that he will instruct his sons after him, and they will keep the ways of the Lord.'" Great the degree of his virtue: he does not only receive reward for his own practice of virtue, but he is awarded generous recompense for the instruction he gave his children. And rightly so; after all, from then on he proved an instructor of everyone. You see, having provided a basis at the outset, he would have been responsible as well for those coming later.

(9) See also the Lord's goodness: not only does he reward him for his virtue in the past but also for the future. "'I am aware,'" the text says, remember, "'that he will instruct his sons.'" Since I know in advance the good man's attitude, he is saying, accordingly in advance I offer reward. You see, he knows the unspoken thoughts of our mind, and when he notices us forming proper intentions and giving evidence of a sound attitude, he offers us his hand and rewards us for our efforts, making us thereby more zealous. This you would find to be the case with all good people. After all, knowing the limitations of human nature, he frequently intervenes in our struggles to provide us with assistance and reward from himself lest we despair in the face of difficulties, and thus he lightens the effort and intensifies our purpose.

(10) "'I am aware,'" he said, remember, "'that he will instruct his sons, and they will keep the ways of the Lord.'" In saying, "he will not instruct," he is making a prediction not only about him but also about his sons, that "'they will keep the ways of the Lord,'" referring to Isaac and Jacob. "'The ways of the Lord,'" that is, his orders, his commands. "'In practicing righteousness and sound judgment,'" he said, remember, to prefer nothing to goodness, to stay clear of all wrongdoing. This, you see, is the greatest virtue; this certainly was the reason that everything spoken of by the Lord to him would take effect. But I think he was referring to something else as well in saying, "'Now, Abraham will become a great and populous nation,'" meaning, You for your part have chosen the way of virtue, you obey my commands and

give evidence of virtue, and so you will become a great and populous nation, whereas these wicked people inhabiting the region of Sodom will all be destroyed. You see, just as virtue proves the basis of salvation for those practicing it, likewise wickedness becomes the cause of destruction.

(11) Then, after he had encouraged the good man to greater confidence through his praise and commendation, he turned to his theme in these words: "'The outcry of Sodom and Gomorrah,'" he says. Admittedly other cities as well would be destroyed along with them, but since they were the most notorious he made mention of them. "'It has come to me more and more, and their sins are exceedingly great.'"[9] See the intensity of their evil deeds: the clamor is deafening, not only from the outcry but from their wickedness as well. I am inclined to think the phrase, "'The outcry of Sodom and Gomorrah has come more and more,'" means that in addition to that unspeakable iniquity, beyond all pardoning, they were giving evidence also of many other offenses, the powerful oppressing the weak, the rich the poor.

(12) So, not only [389] is the outcry very distressing, he says, but their sins as well, far from being light, are great— in fact, exceedingly great. I mean, they had devised novel forms of sinfulness, they had invented monstrous and illicit norms for intercourse, the frenzy of their wickedness was so powerful that all were infected with total defilement, and far from giving evidence any longer of good behavior they called for utter destruction. After all, their maladies had reached the incurable stage and were now proof against treatment. Then, to teach the whole human race that, even if their sins are exceedingly great and confessed to be such, he does not pronounce sentence before proof is manifest, he says, "'I am going down to see if their deeds correspond to the outcry reaching me, so as to know if it is true or not.'" What is meant by the considerateness of the expression? "'I am going down to see if their deeds correspond to the outcry reaching me, so as to know if it is true or not.'" What is meant by the

9. Gen 18.20–21.

considerateness of the expression? "'I am going down to see.'" I mean, does the God of all move from place to place? No indeed! It doesn't mean this; instead, as I have often remarked, he wants to teach us by the concreteness of the expression that there is need to apply precision, and that sinners are not condemned on hearsay nor is sentence pronounced without proof.[10]

(13) Let us all take heed of this: it is not only those facing the tribunal who must respect the Law, but each of us ought never condemn our neighbor on mere slander. This is the reason, in fact, why later blessed Moses, inspired by the Spirit,[11] exhorts us in the words, "Don't accept an idle report."[12] And blessed Paul in his writings cries out, "But why do you judge your brother?"[13] Christ instructed his disciples and taught the Jewish populace, the Scribes and the Pharisees in these words, "Do not judge, lest you be judged:"[14] why are you, he asks, usurping the role of judge ahead of time? Why are you anticipating that dread day? Do you want to play the judge? Be one for yourself and your own faults—no one will stop you; in fact, in this way you will correct your own sins and sustain no harm from the exercise. But if you neglect your own case and sit in judgment on others, you will not be aware you are amassing a greater burden of sins for yourself.

(14) Hence, I beseech you, let us avoid altogether passing sentence on our neighbor. You see, even though you have no share in judicial authority and yet you still pass judgment in your mind, you have rendered yourself guilty of sin for ac-

10. As always, the anthropomorphisms of Scripture predictably—if we consider his first principles—concern Chrysostom and lead to a rehearsing of these principles. He wants his congregation to preserve that fine balance between divine transcendence and divine considerateness, of which latter the *pachutēs*, "concreteness," of scriptural expression in anthropormorphisms is an example.

11. A frequent phrase in Chrysostom's mouth, indicating his clear conviction of the inspiration of Scripture, even if his thinking on the manner in which the inspiration affects the biblical author is no more explicit than most other of the Fathers'. His term for "inspire" here, *enēchein*, obviously contains the elements of "echo"; it can mean "make resound." See my "terminology."

12. Exod 23.1 in the LXX.

13. Rom 14.10.   14. Matt 7.1.

cepting no proof and acting in many cases only on suspicion and mere slander. This, in fact, was the reason blessed David also cried out in the words, "The man who slanders his neighbor in secret I drove out."[15] Do you see the extraordinary degree of virtue? Not only did he not entertain what was said but he also gave short shrift to the person bent on slandering his brother. So if we, too, want to reduce our own faults, we should be on our guard about this most of all, not to condemn our brothers nor to encourage those anxious to slander them, but rather to rebuff them as the inspired author[16] recommended and utterly repel them. In fact, I am inclined to think this is what the inspired author Moses also was indicating in his words, "Don't accept an idle report."[17]

(15) Hence, of course, in the present case as well, the Lord of all employed such remarkable concreteness of expression with a view to the benefit of our souls in saying, "'I am going down to see.'" Why, in fact? Didn't he know? Wasn't he aware of the magnitude of their sins? Hadn't he learnt of their [390] incorrigibility? Still, as if to offer some excuse to the people intending later shamelessly to make accusations, and as if to show their unrestrained behavior and great lack of virtue, he shows this remarkable longsuffering. Perhaps, however, it was not solely for that purpose but to provide the good man with the occasion of showing the compassion and affection of his attitude. So when the angels went off to Sodom, as I remarked before, the patriarch stood before the Lord.[18] "Abraham approached him," the text goes on, "and said, 'Surely you won't destroy the good along with the impious, so that the good will be as the impious?'"[19]

(16) O, what great confidence on the just man's part—or, rather, his great compassion of spirit, overwhelmed as he was with a rush of compassion and not knowing what he was say-

15. Ps 101.5.
16. For Chrysostom, prophētēs can be applied to the Old Testament "inspired authors" David, Moses, the prophets—but not usually the historical writers (former prophets, in the terms of the Hebrew Bible).
17. Exod 23.1.
18. A paraphrase of Gen 18.22.
19. Gen 18.23.

ing. To show that he made this plea in great fear and trembling, Sacred Scripture says, "Abraham approached him and said, 'Surely you won't destroy the good along with the impious?'" What are you doing, blessed patriarch? Does the Lord require entreaty from you not to do this? Still, let us not think this way. You see, he doesn't say it to the Lord as if he were about to do it; instead, since he wasn't bold enough to speak directly on his nephew's behalf, he made a general entreaty for everyone out of a desire to save his life along with theirs and rescue them along with him.

(17) So he begins his entreaty in the words, "'Should there be fifty good people in the city, will you destroy them? Won't you spare the whole place on account of the fifty good people, should there be such there? Surely. You won't put this into effect, killing a good person along with an impious one, so that the good person will be the same as the impious. Surely not! Will not the one who sits in judgment on the whole world exercise judgment here?'"[20] See how even in his entreaty he betrays the godliness of his attitude in acknowledging God's judgment of the whole earth and imploring him not to destroy a good person along with an impious one. Then the gentle and loving God accedes to his request in the words, I will do as you say and heed your entreaty: "'If fifty good people can be found in the city, on their account I will spare the whole place.'"[21] To the fifty good people, he is saying, if they can be found, I will grant the favor of the salvation of the others, and I will put your petition into effect.

(18) Let us see, however, how the good man becomes confident and in the knowledge of God's loving kindness presents a second request in the words, "'Now I have presumed to speak to my Lord, dust and ashes though I am.'"[22] Don't think, Lord, he says, that I am unaware of my condition and am overstepping the mark in displaying such confidence: I know that I am dust and ashes, but in knowing that and realizing it clearly, I am also not unaware that the extent of your

20. Gen 18.24–25.   21. Gen 18.26.
22. Gen 18.27.

loving kindness is immense and that you are rich in goodness and wish all people to be saved. After all, how would the one who creates people from nothing ever destroy them once they are made unless the malice of their sins were great? Hence I must once more beg you, "'If fewer than fifty can be found, and there are forty-five good people in the city, will you not save the city?' He replied, 'If forty five can be found, I will not destroy it.'"[23]

(19) Who could worthily praise the God of all for his marvelous longsuffering and considerateness, or congratulate the good man for enjoying such great confidence? "He continued [391] to speak," the text goes on, "'But what if only forty can be found there?' He replied, 'For the sake of the forty I will not destroy it.'"[24] Then at that point the good man, while respecting God's ineffable longsuffering and being afraid of ever seeming to go too far and surpass the limit in his entreaty, said, "'Pardon me, Lord, if I continue to speak: if only thirty can be found there?'"[25] Since he saw he was disposed to kindness, he still did not proceed gradually with his compromise: he sought to rescue not merely five good people but ten in pursuing his request thus, "'If only thirty can be found there?' He replied, 'I will not destroy it if I find thirty there.'" Consider the degree of the good man's persistence: as though he personally were due to be liable for sentence, he takes great pains to snatch the people of Sodom from the impending punishment. "He said, 'Since I am able to speak to the Lord, what if there are only twenty there?' He replied, 'For the sake of the twenty I will not destroy it.'"[26] O, the goodness of the Lord beyond all telling and all imagining! I mean, which of us living in the midst of countless evils could ever choose to exercise such wonderful considerateness and loving kindness in executing a sentence against our peers?

(20) Nevertheless, the good man saw the wealth of God's loving kindness, and instead of stopping there he spoke on: "'Pardon me, Lord, if I speak once again.'"[27] You see, since

23. Gen 18.28.   24. Gen 18.29.
25. Gen 18.30.   26. Gen 18.31.
27. Gen 18.32.

God's loving kindness was beyond telling, he was afraid he might move the one he was petitioning to indignation at him, and so he said, "'Pardon me, Lord,'" surely, I'm not doing something rash? I'm not giving evidence of shamelessness, am I? I'm not committing a deed deserving of condemnation in speaking still again, am I? In that great goodness of yours accept from me one further petition. "'But what if ten can be found there?' He replied, 'For the sake of the ten I will not destroy it.'" And since he had previously said, "'I will speak once again,'" the text goes on, "The Lord departed after he ceased speaking to Abraham, and Abraham returned to his own place.'"[28]

(21) Do you see the Lord's considerateness? Do you see the good man's affection? Did you gain an insight into the great power of those who practice virtue? If ten good people can be found, he says, remember, for their sake I will grant everyone forgiveness of their sins. Wasn't I right in saying that all this happened so that no basis for excuse would be left for those who later show no sense of shame? I mean, there are a lot of people who lack balance, whose tongue is out of control, who insist on making accusations in these words: Why was Sodom overthrown? If they had had the advantage of tolerance, perhaps they would have repented. Hence it shows you the gravity of their wickedness, that in the midst of such a large population there was such a dearth of virtue as called for a further deluge of the proportions that previously overwhelmed the world. Since, however, it is God's promise that never again would such a punishment be inflicted,[29] accordingly he imposes a different kind of punishment by submitting them to punishment and at the same time providing a perpetual instruction for people coming later. That is to say, since they had overturned the laws of nature and had devised novel and illicit forms of intercourse, consequently he imposed a novel form of punishment, rendering sterile the womb of the earth on account of their lawlessness and leaving a perpetual reminder to later generations not to attempt the

28. Gen 18.33.   29. Cf. Gen 8.21.

same crimes in case they encounter the same punishment. [392] If you want to, you can visit those places and see the land screaming aloud, so to speak, and revealing the traces of punishment, even after such a number of years, as though inflicted yesterday or the day before—so vivid are the signs of God's wrath. Hence, I beseech you, let us profit from the example of others being punished.

(22) Perhaps, however, someone may say, Why so? Although they were punished that way, are there not today as well a lot of people who break the same laws as they did without being punished? Yes, but this will be the means of bringing greater punishment on those committing such offenses. You see, whenever we fail to learn from what happened to them and gain nothing from God's longsuffering, consider how we are fanning the inextinguishable fire more savagely for ourselves and preparing a more biting worm.[30] From another point of view, however, there are a lot of people even today who, thanks to God's grace, are virtuous and able to appeal to the Lord, like the patriarch of those times; and even if we ourselves from a consideration of our own affairs and having regard to our own indifference consider there is a great dearth of virtue, nevertheless God gives evidence of longsuffering for us on account of those others' virtue.

(23) For proof that such persons' good standing is a means of winning longsuffering for us, take heed in that very story to what he says to the patriarch: "'If I find ten good people, I will not destroy the city.'" Why do I say ten good people? No one was found there free from lawlessness, except alone the good man Lot and his two daughters. His wife, you remember, perhaps on his account escaped punishment in the city but paid later the penalty for her own indifference.[31] Now, however, since through God's ineffable love the growth of religion was taking place, there were many people unobtrusively in the heart of the cities capable of appealing to

30. Cf. Mark 9.48.
31. Again, as we have seen so often, *rhathumia*, "indifference," is for Chrysostom the universal cause of human failing, from the Fall to Lot's wife's misfortune in ch. 19.

God, others in hills and caves, and the virtue of these few succeeded in canceling out the wickedness of the majority.

(24) The Lord's goodness is immense, and frequently he finds his way to grant the salvation of the majority on account of a few just people. Why do I say on account of a few just people? Frequently, when a just person cannot be found in the present life, he takes pity on the living on account of the virtue of the departed, and cries aloud in the words, "I will protect this city for my own sake and the sake of my servant David."[32] Even if they do not deserve to be saved, he is saying, and have no claim on salvation, yet since showing love is habitual with me and I am prompt to have pity and rescue them from disaster, for my own sake and the sake of my servant David I will act as a shield; he who passed on from this life many years before will prove the salvation of those who have fallen victim to their own indifference.

(25) Do you see the Lord's loving kindness in having regard for those people conspicuous for virtue, giving them pride of place and showing esteem for them ahead of the whole multitude? Hence Paul too said, "They went about in skins of sheep and goats, destitute, distressed, ill treated, of whom the world was not worthy."[33] This whole universe, he is saying, this whole world could not be compared with those people living in distress, mistreated, poorly clothed, ever on the move, living in caves for the sake of God. [393] So, dearly beloved, whenever you see a man clad on the outside in shabby clothing but invested with virtue within, far from despising him for his appearance acknowledge the wealth of his soul and his splendor within, and then you will discover the virtue glowing in every part of him.

(26) The blessed Elias was like that; he had only a sheepskin, and Achaab, who was dressed in purple, had need of his sheepskin. Do you see Achaab's indigence, on the one hand, and on the other the wealth of Elias? See also how different they were in power. The latter's sheepskin shut off the heavens; it stopped the fall of rain, and the prophet's

---

32. 2 Kgs 19.34.   33. Heb 11.37–38.

tongue proved a brake on the heavens so that for three years and six months there was no rain. The man wearing purple and diadem went about seeking the prophet, powerless to gain any advantage from his royalty. But see the Lord's loving kindness. When he saw the prophet moved by zeal and great ardor and inflicting this terrible punishment on the whole earth, he said to him in case he too should incur punishment along with them and likewise be punished for their wickedness: "'Rise and set out for Sarpeta, a town of Sidon. You see, I will instruct a widow there to look after you.' He rose and set out."[34]

(27) See the grace of the Spirit, dearly beloved; yesterday, too, our whole sermon was devoted to hospitality and, lo, today this hospitable widow is about to cap off our sermon for us. "He paid a call on the widow," the text goes on, "and found her gathering wood; he said to her, 'Give me a little water to drink.'" She obeyed. "He said to her again, 'Make me a biscuit to eat.'"[35] Now, however, she reveals her extreme poverty, or rather her unspeakable wealth: the degree of her poverty betrays the extent of her wealth. She said: "'Your servant has only a handful of flour and a little oil in a jar for my children and me to eat and then die.'" Piteous words, enough to melt even a heart of stone. Now, she says, there is no hope of survival; death is at our door; all that is left for our life is this, hardly enough for me and my children. What lay within my power I have done: I have shared the water with you.

(28) But, for us to learn both the woman's hospitality and the good man's extreme readiness to make request, see what happens. When the prophet grasped everything precisely, in order to reveal to us the woman's virtue (God, after all, it was who said, "'I have instructed a woman to look after you,'" he being the one working through the prophet) he said to her,

34. 1 Kgs 17.9–10.
35. Chrysostom is roughly paraphrasing the text of this incident in 1 Kgs 17.8–16. De Montfaucon notes that Chrysostom cites the example of the widow of Zarephath on other occasions—a rare enough reference to the OT historical books. See Introduction (18) in FOTC 74.

"'First make something to eat for me, and then for your children.'" Take heed, ladies, you who are affluent and spend your substance on countless inanities, often unable to bring yourself to offer two pennies to the needy despite your own indulgence, nor to a poor man of virtue for God's sake.[36] This woman, on the contrary, had nothing more than a handful of flour and was shortly, as she imagined, to witness the death of her children; but hearing from the prophet, "'First make something for me, and then for you and your children,'" she offered no objection, she did not tarry. Instead, she carried out the command, instructing us all to prefer [394] God's servants to our own rest, and not to pass idly by such great advantage but rather to realize a great recompense will come to us on their account.

(29) See, at any rate, how this widow, in return for a handful of flour and a little oil, gained access to an eternal threshing floor. After her care of the prophet, remember, the handful of flour was not exhausted nor was the oil cruet, though the whole earth was being destroyed by famine. And the truly remarkable feature is that there was no longer any need of effort; instead, she always had plenty of flour and oil without having recourse to farming or the help of oxen or any other skills, but rather was able to see it all happening outside the natural processes. Whereas the king in his crown was at a loss and perishing with hunger, the needy widow, deprived of everything, found herself in enduring prosperity for welcoming the prophet. Hence Christ also said, "Whoever welcomes a prophet in the name of a prophet will receive a prophet's reward."[37] You saw yesterday how much the patriarch was granted for giving evidence of lavish hospitality with great ardor; see also the Sidonian woman suddenly enjoying untold wealth. You see, the prophet's tongue, which had held the heavens back with a bridle, caused the handful of flour and the cruet of oil to flow like a river.

36. Is it the life of Antioch at the same time or Chrysostom's own prejudices that lead him often to lecture the ladies on extravagance and neglect of the poor, while the men (*anēr* in this case) are generally the figures of virtue? See Introduction (14) in FOTC 74.
37. Matt 10.41.

(30) Let us all, men and women alike, imitate this woman.
I had in fact intended encouraging you to emulation of the
prophet and imitation of his virtue; but this seemed to be a
problem for you. Though he was a human being, clad in flesh
like us and sharing the same nature as ours, yet he exerted
himself in generous measure and chose virtue, and so he was
accorded grace from above. But at this point let us also imitate this woman, and then we will gradually come to imitate
the prophet as well. Accordingly, let us emulate her hospitality, and let no one in the future offer the pretext of poverty.
Poor though you may be, you would not be poorer than this
woman, who had food enough for one day only without being
unresponsive on that account to the good man's request; instead, by displaying great enthusiasm she won a swift recompense. This is the way, you see, things are with the Lord: he
is accustomed to bestow great gifts for small services. After
all, why was it, tell me, that he conferred all that she received?
Our Lord is not in the habit of attending to the amount but
to the generosity of attitude, and on that score little things
become great, and great things are often made paltry whenever deeds are performed without a cheerful enthusiasm.
Hence also that widow in the gospel, when many people were
putting much money in the treasury, surpassed them all by
putting in two small coins, not because she put in more than
the others but because she gave evidence of her generous attitude. Whereas the others, it says, remember, did this out of
their surplus, she on the contrary put in all she had.[38] She
put in her whole life, you see.

(31) Let us men imitate the women and not be seen to be
inferior to them, but be zealous not only to expend our substance on our own enjoyment but also to show great care for
the needy and do it with enthusiasm and joyfulness. The
farmer, you see, in sowing seed in the soil, far from working
at it gloomily, rejoices and exults already in his expectation,
thinking he sees the sheaves [395] fully grown, and in this
manner he casts the seed on the soil. In your case, therefore,

38. Luke 21.1–4.

dearly beloved, don't regard only the person receiving from you, nor the cost outlaid; consider instead that while the person who receives from you is before your eyes, another takes as done to himself the things done to the poor, and he is no casual observer but the Lord of all, the Ruler of all, Creator of heaven and earth, and that this outlay earns interest, not only not diminishing your capital but rather augmenting it, provided you do this with faith and cheerful enthusiasm. Let me nominate the chief of these benefits: along with the interest on this outlay you have also the advantage of pardon for sin—and what could compare with that?

(32) So if we want to know how to gain real wealth, and along with the wealth find pardon for sin as well, let us pour our possessions into the hands of the needy and thus send them ahead of us to heaven, where there is neither thief, nor robber, nor burglar, no plotting by servants nor anything else capable of impairing our wealth. That place, you see, is protection against such harm. Only, let us not do it from vainglory but in response to the laws given us by him so as to win the praise, not of human beings but of the common Lord of all, and thus we may not suffer the expense and yet lose the profit. I mean, as the wealth that is deposited there by the hand of the poor is proof against all other schemes, so it is at risk only to vainglory; and as here on earth worm and moth cause the ruin of clothing, so vainglory has this effect on the wealth amassed from almsgiving.

(33) Hence, I beseech you, let us not only practice almsgiving, but also do it carefully so that we may gain great blessings in return for small, incorruptible for those that are passing, and eternal for those that are temporary, and that with all these we may also succeed in attaining the forgiveness of sins and those ineffable good things. May this be the good fortune of all of us to arrive at, thanks to the grace and loving kindness of our Lord Jesus Christ, to whom with the Father and the holy and lifegiving Spirit,[39] be glory now and forever, for ages of ages. Amen.

39. An unusual variation of the customary doxology.

HOMILY 43

"Now, the two angels arrived at Sodom in the evening," the text
goes on.[1]

S A FLOWERY [395] MEADOW displays in itself different flowers of many hues, so Sacred Scripture displays to us the virtues of good people, not so that we
may enjoy only for a short time their fragrance as with the
flowers, but for us to gain from them a benefit that is lasting.
You see, in the former case we only picked flowers by hand,
and after a short time they faded and lost their particular
beauty. But in the present case it is different; instead, when
we come by the virtues of good people through hearing and
lay them up in the recesses of our mind, we are able to enjoy
their fragrance for all time, if we want.

(2) So, come now, since the fragrance of holy ones mentioned in Sacred Scripture is so great, today let us come to
know the fragrance of Lot so that we may learn precisely how
association with the patriarch led him to the very pinnacle of
virtue and how, by following in his footsteps, he, too, gave
evidence in practice of hospitality in his own right. For our
sermon to become clearer to you, however, it would be worth
listening to the very words of Scripture. "Now, the two angels
arrived at Sodom in the evening," the text says. Why did it
begin in this way, "Now, the two angels arrived at Sodom in
the [396] evening"? After the friendly interlude with the patriarch they made tracks from there, whereas the caring and
loving God, faithful to his characteristic goodness, under the
appearance of human form stayed conversing with the patriarch, as you heard yesterday. His intention was to teach us

1. Gen 19.1.

436

both the extraordinary degree of his own longsuffering and the patriarch's affection. The angels, on the other hand, made for Sodom. Following its sequence Sacred Scripture at this point tells us, "Now, the two angels arrived at Sodom in the evening" in discharge of their mission.

(3) See the precision and minute observation[2] of Sacred Scripture in indicating to us the time that they arrived; "in the evening," it says, remember. Why did it reveal the time? Why did they arrive in the evening?[3] To show us the great degree of Lot's hospitality. You see, just as the patriarch was seated at the hour of midday when he observed the visitors and set about snaring them by running to meet them and welcoming the travelers with joy, in just the same way this good man, too, though aware of the evil behavior of the inhabitants of Sodom, did not excuse himself from the task of remaining in wait even at evening time but remained at his post till then in case some treasure should come his way and he might be in a position to reap the fruit of hospitality. The extraordinary degree of this good man's virtue is really remarkable in that, though living in the midst of such villains, he not only had grown more indifferent but even gave evidence of much greater virtue; while all had tumbled into the abyss, so to say, he alone in all that multitude was treading the straight and narrow.

(4) Where now are those who say that it is not possible for someone growing up in the environment of the city to keep one's virtue, but for this is required retreat and a life in the mountains, and that it is not possible for the man of the house, with a wife and with children and servants to look after, to be virtuous? Accordingly, let them see this good man with a wife, children and servants, living in the city, passing his days amidst so many scoundrels and villains, and standing

2. Chrysostom's term for this, *paratērēsis,* which occurs a few times in the Genesis homilies (cf. Homily 36 [Migne col. 338], Homily 53 [467]), has much the same sense as the more frequent *akribeia.*

3. Chrysostom does not remark, as does the modern commentator Speiser, that following their late afternoon meal the travelers had a distance of forty miles to cover by evening (*Genesis,* 138). Precision is not always expedient, it seems.

out like some spark in the open sea, not only unquenched but emitting a resplendent light. I say this, not to oppose retreat from the cities nor to discourage life in the mountains and deserts,[4] but to show that for a person intent on remaining vigilant and alert none of these things proves an obstacle. So just as for the indifferent and faint of heart the desert is of no avail, since in fact it is not place that affects virtue but attitude and inclination, likewise, for a person that is vigilant and alert, living in the environment of the city cannot bring any harm.

(5) Hence I would prefer virtuous people in particular, like this blessed man, to be in the environment of cities so that they would be like yeast to the others and lead many to imitation of them. Since, however, this seems to be difficult to achieve, let the alternative happen. "The form of this world, after all, is now passing away,"[5] and the present life is brief; if now while we are still in the arena we do not engage in the struggle of virtue and escape the snares of wickedness, later on it will be futile for us to blame ourselves when repentance brings no benefit. You see, while we are in the present life it is possible for us to gain some advantage from repenting and by washing away our former sins to be found worthy of the Lord's loving kindness; but if we are suddenly snatched away while letting slip this present opportunity, we will then be sorry [397] but will gain no benefit from it.

(6) For proof of this, listen to the inspired author's words, "Now, who will express his faith in you in hell?"[6] and again, "Will a man be able to ransom himself or his brother?"[7] There will be no one then, the text is saying, able to rescue from there a victim of his own indifference, be he brother or father or mother. Why do I say brother or father or mother? Not even the just themselves, who have good grounds for confidence, will be of any assistance to us then if we have now been guilty of indifference. Scripture says, remember, "Even

4. His biographers tell us of Chrysostom's own early experience of such a situation.

5. 1 Cor 7.31.   6. Ps 6.5.

7. Ps 49.7 in the LXX.

if Noe and Job and Daniel were there, they would not rescue their own sons and daughters."[8] See the magnitude of the threat and the kind of just people he brought forward as examples. These men, you see, at a critical time proved a source of salvation even to others: Noe saved his wife and sons when that terrible deluge overwhelmed the world; Job likewise proved a source of salvation even to others; and Daniel rescued many from death when that awful barbarian in his quest for things beyond human nature wanted to do away with the Chaldeans, the Magi and Gazarenes.

(7) In case we should think that some such things will happen even in the future age and that virtuous people with grounds for confidence would be able to free from the punishment there their own friends who have lived a life of indifference here, accordingly he brought these good people forward as reminders to us, aggravating our dread and teaching us that our hope of salvation rests in our own good deeds following grace from on high, and that we should not place great importance on our forebears' virtue if we ourselves happen to be guilty of wickedness, nor on anything else. Rather, we should make this alone the object of attention: if we have virtuous forebears, to imitate their virtue; if the contrary is true and we come from disreputable forebears, not to think any handicap results from this but to fall to the labors virtue involves, no harm ensuing from this, to be sure. After all, each person will be either rewarded or condemned for the works performed, as blessed Paul also says, "So that each one may be rewarded by good or ill for what he has done in the body,"[9] and again, "He will reward everyone according to his works."[10]

(8) Aware of all this, let us shake off all indifference and set much store by virtue. While we are still in the arena and before the show is over, let us concentrate on our salvation so that by practicing virtue in this brief period we may gain a reward for it in the age that never ends. Just as this good

8. Ezek 14.20 in Chrysostom's own version.
9. 2 Cor 5.10.   10. Rom 2.6.

man, living among so many villains, with no one to imitate his virtue but everyone scoffing at him to his face and ridiculing him, did not only not become less vigilant but even proved so conspicuous as to be judged worthy of entertaining angels; when everyone else was completely destroyed, he alone with his daughters escaped the destruction inflicted on them.

(9) But let us take up the thread of our sermon. "Now, the two angels," the text says, "arrived at Sodom in the evening." The time in particular shows us this good man's extraordinary virtue in the fact that even despite the coming of evening he stayed at his post and did not leave it. That is to say, since he realized the advantage accruing to him from that, consequently he was anxious to attain the wealth and brought great vigilance to bear, not even desisting at the end of the day. This, you see, is what a fervent and vigilant soul [398] is like: far from being impeded by any obstacles from giving evidence of its virtue, it is spurred on to greater heights by the very impediments in particular and burns with a brighter flame of desire. "Now, on seeing them," the text goes on, "Lot rose to meet them." Let this be heeded by those who are given to repulsing people who call on them with requests to make and causes to plead, and who show them great inhumanity. I mean, see how this good man did not wait till the visitors reached him but like the patriarch, without knowing who the visitors were but presuming that they were travelers of some kind, well nigh jumped for joy on seeing them, as though falling upon his prey and not missing the object of his desire.

(10) "On seeing them," the text says, note, "he rose to meet them and prostrated himself on the ground." He gave thanks to God for being found worthy to welcome the visitors. Notice his virtue of soul: he considered it a great kindness on God's part to encounter these men and by welcoming them to fulfill his private longing. Now, don't tell me they were angels; remember, rather, that this good man did not realize that yet but behaved as though receiving unknown travelers. "He said, 'Lo, sirs, break off your journey at your servant's house,

rest and bathe your feet; then rise early and resume your journey.'"[11] These words are sufficient to reveal the virtue resid-
ing in the good man's soul: how could you help being amazed
at his exceeding humility and the fervor with which he displayed his hospitality? "'Lo, sirs,'" he said, "'break off your
journey at your servant's house.'" He addresses them as "sirs"
and calls himself their servant. Let us listen precisely, dearly
beloved, to these words and learn how we too can do likewise.
This man of good name and reputation, enjoying great prosperity, a householder, addresses as master these travelers,
these strangers, unknown, unprepossessing, wayfarers, no
connections of his, and says, "'Break off your journey at your
servant's house and rest.'" You see, evening has fallen, he
says; accede to my wish and assuage the day's hardship by
resting in the home of your servant. I mean, surely I'm not
offering you anything wonderful? "'Bathe your feet'" wea-
ried with traveling, "'and rise early and resume your journey.'" So do me this favor and don't refuse my entreaty.

(11) "They replied," the text goes on, "'No, instead, we
shall rest in the street.'" Seeing that despite his entreaty they
declined, he did not lose heart, he did not give up what he
was intent on, he did not have the kinds of feelings we often
do. If at any time we want to win someone over and then we
see them somewhat reluctant, we immediately desist; this is
due to our doing it without ardor and longing and especially
to our thinking that we have excuse enough to be able to say
that at any rate we did our best. What do you mean, you have
done your best? You have let slip the prey, you have missed
the treasure—is this doing your best? Then you would have
done your best if you hadn't let the treasure slip through
your fingers, if you hadn't bypassed the prey, if your display
of hospitality was limited to a perfunctory remark.

(12) Not so the just man; instead, what? When he saw [399]
them resisting and bent on resting in the street (the angels
did this out of a wish to reveal more clearly the just man's
virtue and to teach us all the extent of his hospitality), then

11. Gen 19.2.

he in turn did not stop at making entreaty in words but also applied force. Hence Christ also said, "Men of violence seize the kingdom of heaven."[12] In other words, where spiritual advantage is involved, pressure is in order and violence commendable. "He compelled them,"[13] the text says. It seems to me he drew them in against their will. Then when they saw the just man applying this effort and not desisting until he should achieve the object of his desire, "they turned aside to him and entered his house. He prepared a meal for them, cooking flat bread for them; they ate before lying down."[14] Do you see here as well hospitality manifested, not in richness of fare but in generosity of attitude? I mean, when he succeeded in bringing them into his house, at once he gave evidence of the signs of hospitality. He occupied himself in attending on them, providing something to eat and giving evidence of respect and attention to the visitors in his belief that they were only human beings, travelers of some kind.

(13) "The men of the town, however, the Sodomites surrounded the house, the whole population at once, from young to old, and called out to Lot, saying to him, 'Where are the men who are staying the night at your place? Bring them out to us so that we may have intercourse with them.'"[15] Let us not pass these words idly by, dearly beloved, nor see in them only their quite inexcusable frenzy, but consider rather how the just man, by living in the midst of such monstrous animals, was so conspicuous and gave evidence of such an extraordinary degree of virtue in being able to put up with their lawlessness, in not shifting from there, in bringing himself to have converse with them. How he managed, I will tell you. The Lord of all had foreknowledge of their excessive wickedness and arranged for this just man to dwell there so that like a skillful physician he might be able to get the better of their ailments. When, however, he saw that their illness was incurable and they had no intention of accepting any treatment, he still did not give up. A doctor is like that, after all;

12. Matt 11.12.
14. Gen 19.3-4.
13. Gen 19.3.
15. Gen 19.4-5.

if he sees the ailments proving too much for the treatment, he doesn't stop exerting all his energies, so that on the off-chance of being able to reclaim the patient in due time he may demonstrate the virtue of his treatment; if, on the other hand, he achieves nothing more, he has the most telling excuse in that he left nothing undone appropriate to the case.

(14) This, in fact, is what happened here: this good man was even reared amongst them, and by demonstrating his sound commonsense he remained good in this way, whereas the others were consequently left without any excuse on account of not only refusing to give up their evil ways but even taking them to further excess. Observe: "They surrounded the house," the text says, "from young to old, the whole population at once." Extraordinary their unity in evildoing, overwhelming the impetus of their wickedness, beyond all telling the excess of their lawlessness, without defense this endeavor of theirs. "From young to old," the text says. Not only was youth in search of these lawless pleasures, it is saying, but even the elderly, the whole population at once. They did not stop short of this reckless and shameless exploit, nor take heed of that unsleeping eye, nor blush at [400] the just man, nor spare the men thought to be strangers, resting there as guests of the just man; instead, brazenly and, so to say, with head bared they made their demands in those licentious terms, calling out to the good man, "'Where are the men who are staying at your place? Bring them out so that we may have intercourse with them.'"

(15) I think it was on account of their insolence and lawless behavior that the just man sat waiting until evening, so as not to allow any unsuspecting traveler to fall into their clutches. For his part the good man gave evidence of the extraordinary degree of his own probity along with his hospitality, taking pains to welcome all travelers and letting no one escape him, and thinking in the present case as well that they were not angels but human beings. Those lawless men, on the contrary, as well as giving no evidence of any such concern as the just man's, were intent only on committing crimes. So the reason why the angels intended to rest in the street was to provide

the just man with an opportunity of showing them hospitality
and to demonstrate to him in action how those guilty of lawlessness to such an extraordinary degree were about to incur
a fitting punishment.

(16) Let us now, however, see the extent of the good man's
virtue. "He went outside to them in the entrance," the text
goes on, "closed the door, and said to them."[16] See how the
just man was in fear and trembling for the safety of the
strangers; it wasn't without purpose that he closed the door
behind him:[17] he knew their frenzy and boldness and, suspecting rash behavior on their part, he then said to them,
"'By no means, brothers.'" O what longsuffering on the just
man's part, what extraordinary humility! This is true virtue,
to relate to such people with restraint. I mean, no one wanting to cure a sick person or bring a maniac to his senses goes
about it with roughness and bad temper. Consider, in fact,
how he calls these men brothers, despite their intent to commit such heinous crimes, wishing as he did to dissuade them,
appeal to their conscience and divert them from their dis-
gusting purpose.

(17) "'By no means, brothers,'" he says, "'don't be so depraved.'" Don't entertain such ideas, he is saying, don't think
of doing such awful things, don't be false to your very nature,
don't even imagine such illicit relations. But if you're bent on
satisfying the frenzy of your passion, I will supply the means
of rendering your exploit less serious. "'I have two daughters,
who have had no relations with men.'"[18] They are still without experience of marital intercourse, in fact they are virgins,
in their prime, with the bloom of youth upon them; I will
hand them over to you to be used as you wish. Take them, he
says, and on them spend your lust and discharge your evil
desires. "'Only don't do any wrong to these men, since they
have found protection under my roof.'" Since I obliged them,
he is saying, to come under my roof lest crimes committed

16. Gen 19.6–7.
17. The two words that Chrysostom's version of v. 6 omitted from the
LXX text.
18. Gen 19.8.

against them be attributed to me and I be held guilty of this insult to them, consequently I offer my two daughters for them to save them from your hands.

(18) What marvelous virtue in the just man! He surpassed all the standards of hospitality! I mean, how could anyone do justice to the good man's friendliness in not bringing himself to spare even his daughters so as to demonstrate his regard for the strangers and save them from the lawlessness of [401] the Sodomites?[19] Whereas this man hands over his own daughters so as to rescue from outrage by lawless men these strangers, these travelers (again I make the same point, notice) who were not known to him from any source, we, on the other hand, often are content to see our brothers brought to the very depths of impiety and, so to say, into the devil's jaws without troubling to share advice with them, counsel them, offer encouragement in word, snatch them from evil and guide them towards virtue.

(19) So what excuse would we have if, whereas the good man did not spare his daughters out of concern for the strangers, we on the contrary are so inclined to be heedless about our own brothers and often utter those frivolities and remarks full of inanity? After all, one says, what have I in common with him? He's no concern of mine, I have nothing to do with him. What are you saying, human being that you are? You have nothing in common with him? He is your brother, he shares the same nature as yours, you are both subject to the same Lord, in fact often you share the same table—I mean the awesome spiritual one—and yet you say, I have nothing in common with him, and you pass him by heedlessly, offering him no hand as he lies there. Whereas the Law bade the Jews not to ignore even enemies' animals that had fallen down, you on the contrary are often content

19. Chrysostom's congregation must have wondered if he spoke with tongue in cheek in commending Lot's behavior in this incident, driven as he is by the logic of his school to treat all elements in these patriarchal narratives without discrimination. Von Rad notes that "this procedure to which Lot resorted scarcely suited the sensibility of the ancient Israelite" (*Genesis*, 218), and Chrysostom would be aware of its impact on his listeners; so he quite quickly gives the sermon a moral twist.

to see your brother lying wounded in the devil's power, not on the ground but in the depths of sin, without lifting him up with your encouragement, offering him your advice or taking pains to bring others to his aid, if that is possible, so as to free a part of your own body from the jaws of the beast and return him to his pristine nobility, so that if—God forbid—you yourself should ever fall into the snares of that awful demon, you would be in a position to have friends to protect you and free you from the devil's hands.

(20) Paul also speaks to the same effect in his wish to prompt the Galatians to care of their own limbs, "Considering yourself in case you too should be tempted,"[20] as if to say, If you pass your brother by without sympathy or attention, perhaps someone else will pass you by, too, when you have fallen. So if you would prefer not to be ignored if ever you come to grief, don't ignore others yourself but give evidence of deep affection and consider it a wonderful boon to be in a position to rescue your brother. Nothing, in fact, would be on a par with this as far as virtue is concerned. I mean, if you only consider that this person whom you ignore and pass by is accorded such respect by the Lord that on his account he did not decline even to shed his own blood (as Paul also says, "Your weak brother will perish by your knowledge after Christ died for him"[21]), how will you not bury yourself in the earth for shame? Consequently, if for his sake Christ even shed his blood, what great gesture are you making if you show him affection, raise him from the ground with encouragement by word of mouth, lift from the depths of evil his spirit that has perhaps been immersed and overwhelmed, and cause him to see the light of virtue and not run back to the darkness of evil?

(21) Accordingly, let us imitate this just man, I beseech you, and if it is necessary to run some risk in being active for the salvation of our neighbor, let us not decline to do so. Such a risk, in fact, will prove an occasion of salvation for us and a cause of great confidence. Consider, I ask you, how this just

20. Gal 6.1.   21. 1 Cor 8.11.

man stood up to the whole population, evincing as they were
a common purpose for evil, and with great restraint [402]
gave evidence of unspeakable bravery in the hope of being
able in this way to deflect them from their unbridled passion.
Despite those words, you see, his exceeding restraint and his
apparent offer to give his daughter into their hands, what did
they say to him? "'Get out of the way.'"²² O what extraordinary sottishness, what extreme stupidity! This, in fact, is what
wicked and unrestrained lust is like: when it overpowers the
reason, it prevents it from recognizing anything that is needful, and in fact it does everything as if in darkness and some
nocturnal battle.

(22) "'Get out of the way,'" they said. "'You came here to
dwell as an alien; surely you're not making the decisions? All
right, now we'll treat you worse than them.'" See how,
whereas the just man spoke with restraint to them, they indulged in extreme audacity by contrast. As though now
brought to a pitch of frenzy by the devil and under his power,
they beset the good man in this fashion, saying, "'You came
here to dwell as an alien; surely you're not making the decisions?'" We accepted you as a visitor; surely you haven't
turned into our judge? O height of ingratitude! They should
have felt shame, they should have respected the just man's
advice, but on the contrary, like lunatics bent on assailing
their doctor, they spoke to him thus: "'We will treat you worse
than them.'" If you're not prepared to hold your peace, they
said, you will learn that your defense of them is of no avail
except to put you at risk while they escape it. "They set upon
Lot with a will," the text goes on. See this just man displaying
such bravery and endeavoring to oppose such a large mob.
"They pressed forward to break the door down." You see,
since he was about to come out and had closed the door behind him in view of their rage, these frantic and lawless people couldn't tolerate the just man's exhortation, and so they
laid hands on him and tried to break the door down.

(23) Since, however, the just man's virtue had been dem-

22. Gen 19.9.

onstrated in action, as well as his concern for those thought to be strangers and the concerted drive towards evil on the part of all that crowd, then at that point the visitors revealed their identity. On seeing the good man exerting himself in every way, they gave evidence of their special power by coming to the good man's aid as he was being overpowered by their frenzy. "The men put out their hands," the text goes on, remember, "pulled Lot in the house with them, and slammed the door of the house. But the men who were at the door of the house they struck with blindness, one and all, and they were paralyzed as they attempted to find the door."[23] Do you see this just man, too, immediately gains the reward for hospitality and those lawless people pay a fitting penalty? "They pulled Lot into the house," the text says, remember, "and slammed the door. But the men they struck with blindness, one and all, and they were paralyzed as they attempted to find the door." Since their mind's eye had been blinded, they suffered loss of sight as well for the reason that you might learn that bodily eyes were of no benefit to them if the eyes of their mind were blinded. Since they gave evidence of concert in evil, with neither young nor old desisting from their wicked exploit, consequently all were blinded, the text points out. Not only were they afflicted with blindness, but as well the strength of their body was undermined: since they had lost control of the soul, the superior part of their person, consequently they also lost the power of their body. Those who were previously trying to break the door down and belaboring the good man with threats suddenly found themselves paralyzed, unable to see the door in front of them.

(24) At that point the good man breathed freely, seeing the identity of the visitors and the greatness of their power. The text goes on: "The men said to him, [403] 'Is there anyone of yours here—sons-in-law, sons, daughters, or anyone else in the city?'"[24] See how they reward the good man for his hospital-

---

23. Gen 19.10–11.
24. Gen 19.12. Speiser notes the unusual insertion and positioning of "son-in-law," especially in the singular unlike the plural of the LXX, and

ity, and how they wish to grant him the salvation of all his
family. If there is anyone belonging to you in the city, it says,
if there is anyone you're close to, if you know anyone to be
unconnected with these people's lawlessness, "'take them out
of this place'" and this country, and take out all your relatives. "'For we are about to destroy this place.'"[25] Then they
gave the reason, teaching the just man everything with precision: "'Because the outcry against them,'" it says, "'has
risen up in the Lord's hearing, and the Lord has sent up to
wipe them out.'" This is what had been said to the patriarch,
namely, that "'the outcry of Sodom and Gomorrah has come
to me more and more.'"[26] "'The outcry against them has
risen up in the Lord's hearing,'" it says here.

(25) Extreme the extent of their lawlessness, and accordingly, since their disease was beyond cure and their wound
admitted of no treatment, the Lord sent them to destroy it.
This is what blessed David said: "He makes the winds his
messengers and the flame of fire his ministers."[27] Since we
have come, it says, to destroy the whole region (the country
suffered the punishment for the wickedness of its inhabitants,
you see), leave here. Hearing this, and realizing the reason
for the visit of these men, as it seemed, who were in reality
angels and ministers of the God of all, the good man "went
out and spoke to his sons-in-law who had taken his daughters
in marriage."[28] Actually, he said before to those villains, "'Lo,
I have two daughters, who have had no relations with men'";[29]
so how does the text say, "to his sons-in-law who had taken
his daughters in marriage"? Don't think this contradicts what
was said by the good man previously: it was customary with

---

concludes it is an intrusion from v. 14. Chrysostom, interestingly, retains the
singular against the LXX. For a discussion of Chrysostom's peculiar OT text,
see Introduction (15) in FOTC 74, and D. S. Wallace-Hadrill, *Christian Antioch*, p. 30.

25. Gen 19.13.   26. Gen 18.20.
27. Ps 104.4.
28. Gen 19.4, where the LXX takes an ambiguous Hebrew verb form to
mean the marriage had been finalized, thus posing a problem for Chrysostom.
29. Gen 19.8.

people in olden times to celebrate the betrothal ahead of time, and often for the betrothed to live together and at the same time to live with their parents, something which happens even today in many places. So since the ceremony of betrothal had already taken place, hence it calls them sons-in-law and says, "'those who had taken his daughters in marriage,'" having taken them in intention and by mutual consent.

(26) "He said, 'Away, leave the place, for the Lord is going to destroy the city.' But in the eyes of his sons-in-law he seemed to be joking." See how these men were affected by that evil influence. Hence, since God wanted to free the just man quickly from association with them, he did not allow the just man's daughters to mingle with them, but instead he carried these men off ahead of time with the evil ones so that the good man should leave with his daughters and avoid association with them. Accordingly, when they heard that dire prediction from the just man, they made as if to scoff at him, thinking what he said was a joke. Nevertheless the just man did what he could, and since he had once betrothed his daughters to them, he wanted to rescue them from punishment, but they wouldn't have it, and instead persisted in their evil way, and later came to know by the events themselves that it was to their loss that they had rejected the just man's advice.

(27) "At the crack of dawn, however, the angels urged Lot on: 'Away, take your wife and the two daughters you have and set out in case you are destroyed along with the villains of the city.' They were upset."[30] Don't delay, it is saying: already destruction must [404] fall on them. So save yourself, your wife and your two daughters. In fact, for being unwilling to respond to his advice, those men before long will share in the destruction with the rest. So don't delay, in case you yourself as well share in the destruction of the villains. "They were upset" to hear this, referring to Lot, his wife and daughters; "they were upset," it says, that is, they became fearful, they fell into an awful dread, they were distressed by the threat.

30. Gen 19.15–16.

Hence, out of care for the good man "the angels took his hand," the text adds. Scripture no longer talks of men; instead, since they were about to inflict punishment, it calls them angels in saying, "They took his hand, his wife's hand and his daughters' hands as the Lord spared him." They comforted them by taking their hand and strengthened their spirit lest fear should undermine their strength; hence the text added, "as the Lord spared him."

(28) You see, since the Lord judged him deserving of salvation (the text says), accordingly the angels also wished to strengthen their spirit and so took their hand, "led them out and said, 'Save yourself. Don't look back or stop anywhere in the district. Take refuge in the mountains lest at any time you be involved.'"[31] Since we have now freed you from these villains, it is saying, no longer look back or want to see what is about to happen to them; instead, make all speed and reach a distant place so as to escape the punishment being inflicted on them. Then the good man, being afraid that he might never succeed in reaching the place specified by them and arrive at the mountain, said, "'I beg you, sir, since your servant has found mercy in your sight and you have marvelously shown your goodness in my regard by saving my life: I could not reach the mountain in safety without danger overtaking me and I will die. See, this city is near enough for me to flee to; it is tiny, I will be safe there, my life will be spared thanks to you.'"[32] Although you once decided to grant me salvation, he is saying, yet reaching the top of the mountain is beyond my strength; so give evidence of further kindness to me by making the effort less demanding. In case, therefore, I be overtaken by the impending punishment and share in their fate, assign this town nearby for me. Even if in fact it is tiny and unprepossessing, yet I will be able to reach it in safety and then be secure there.

(29) "He said to him, 'Lo, I am impressed with your appearance and your request not to overwhelm the city you

31. Gen 19.17 with some departures from the LXX.
32. Gen 19.18–20.

have spoken of.'"[33] I have accepted your petition, he is saying, I will do as you say, I will concede your request, and for your sake I will even spare the city. "'So be quick, take refuge in the place and save yourself; I will do nothing in fact until you arrive there.'"[34] In fact, he is saying, I cannot execute the deed until you arrive there. Since I care for your salvation, I await your arrival there, and only then will I inflict the punishment on them. "The sun came out on the earth, and Lot entered Segor."[35] He reached the town at sunrise, and as soon as he was inside the city they were punished. "The Lord rained down fire and brimstone on Sodom and Gomorrah," the text goes on, remember, "from the Lord in heaven, and he overwhelmed these cities and the whole district, all the inhabitants of the cities and every plant on earth."[36]

(30) Don't be surprised, dearly beloved, at the expression: [405] it is characteristic of Scripture, which often employs words identically in that way, as you can now see in this case, too. "The Lord rained down fire and brimstone from the Lord in heaven," the text says, remember, intending to mean that the Lord inflicted the punishment, not only overwhelming the cities, the whole district and all the inhabitants but also wiping the plants off the face of the earth. You see, since the people inhabiting this region had given evidence of much fruit of wickedness, accordingly I am making the fruit of the earth useless, he is saying, so that with this destruction as well it may prove an everlasting reminder to later generations, teaching everyone through its peculiar barrenness the wickedness of its inhabitants. Do you see all that is involved in virtue, and in wickedness, how the just man was saved whereas the others received their just desserts? As the good man through his own virtue saved his daughters as well and averted the catastrophe from that city, likewise those others through the excess of their own evil were not only completely destroyed

33. Gen 19.21.
34. Gen 19.22 in an independent version.
35. Gen 19.23.
36. Gen 19.24–25.

themselves but were also responsible for the land being without fruit in the future.

(31) "His wife looked back," the text goes on, "and was turned into a pillar of salt."[37] You see, when she heard the angels bidding the good man not to cast a backward glance but to make his retreat with great haste, she disobeyed the command, did not keep their word, and accordingly paid the penalty for her indifference.

(32) Let us, on the contrary, heed it, take great care of our salvation and avoid imitating their lawlessness. Let us instead emulate the just man's hospitality and the rest of his virtue so as to avert as well the anger from on high. It is not possible, you see, it is not possible for the person who practices virtue zealously not to win great treasure thereby. After all, these just men, the patriarch and Lot, were in this way accorded grace from above; thinking they were welcoming human beings, they were even found worthy to welcome angels and the Lord of the angels. We too are permitted, if we wish, to welcome him now. He in fact it is who has said, "Whoever welcomes you welcomes me."[38] Accordingly, let us welcome strangers in this fashion and never have regard for their unprepossessing appearance. I mean, if on some occasions we give evidence of the practice of hospitality in such a spirit, we too will be found worthy to welcome such guests, thought to be men but in fact practicing the virtue of angels—provided we don't pry and become inquisitive at the risk of losing the treasure. Especially so, since blessed Paul also refers to them in these words to teach us how they were fortunate enough to receive such a welcome: "Do not neglect hospitality; after all, it was the cause of some people entertaining angels unawares."[39] This it was especially, in fact, that revealed their remarkable greatness, that unaware of their identity they still

37. Gen 19.26. Chrysostom has been conducting his commentary on these verses at an unusually rapid rate, and this verse, which would normally be such a fertile soil for him with its egregious example of *rhathumia*, "indifference," and in a woman to boot, he dispatches with utmost brevity.

38. Matt 10.40.   39. Heb 13.1.

showed them attention. So in faith and reverence let us discharge this duty so as to be able also to attain the treasure. May it be the good fortune of all of us to enjoy this, thanks to the grace and loving kindness of our Lord Jesus Christ, to whom with the Father and the Holy Spirit be glory, power and honor, now and forever, for ages of ages. Amen.

HOMILY 44

"Now, Abraham rose early in the morning and went to the place where he had stood before God."[1]

ESTERDAY'S [405] THEME of the Samaritan woman gave us adequate [406] instruction in the Lord's ineffable longsuffering and surpassing concern for her, as well as her gratitude.[2] You saw how she came to draw material water but in fact drew from divine streams coming from an invisible spring, and thus went off home, fulfilling the word of the Lord, "The water that I shall give will become a spring of water in him gushing forth to life everlasting."[3] Once she had drunk her fill of that divine and spiritual spring, remember, she did not keep the waters to herself but overflowed, so to say, and poured out on the inhabitants of the town as well the grace of the gift given her; the woman, the Samaritan, the foreigner, immediately turned preacher. You saw how important gratitude of soul is, you saw the Lord's loving kindness in not scorning anyone but immediately directing his grace to anyone, be it woman or pauper—wherever at all he finds a spirit watchful and alive.

(2) Accordingly, I beseech you, let us also imitate this woman and receive the teachings of the Spirit with close attention. They are not our words, you see, nor do we utter with our own tongue whatever we say; instead, we are guided by the Lord's loving kindness for the sake of your salvation and the building up of the Church of God. So do not have

1. Gen 19.27.
2. This, in fact, was not the theme of Homily 43; the reference is lost on us, and we are encouraged to think that particularly in this post-Easter period the Genesis homilies were not necessarily given on successive days without interruption. See n. 5, *infra*.
3. John 4.14.

regard to my person as a speaker, dearly beloved, nor my poverty of expression, but to the fact that I pass on what comes from the Lord; so keep your thoughts fixed on the one who has commissioned me and in this way receive my words with lively attention.

(3) This is true in human affairs, too. When the emperor wearing his crown dispatches letters, the bearer of them is in fact of no account in himself but only someone unimportant, often with no lineage to claim, an obscure son of obscure parents. Yet those due to receive them, while giving no heed to him personally, still pay him great respect also on account of the emperor's letters, and they receive the letters in great fear and complete silence. If, then, that person who brings the letters of a human being, and bears paper and nothing more, is given a welcome by everyone, much more would you be right in receiving with great attention the sayings of the Spirit sent to you by means of us, and thus win a great reward for your right attitude. You see, if the Lord of all sees your enthusiasm of spirit, he will also provide you with generous assistance with a view to your upbuilding and will grant you deeper understanding so as to grasp what is said. After all, the grace of the Spirit is abundant and, far from undergoing any diminution when poured out on everyone, it is rather increased by distribution, and the more numerous those who share in it, the more widely the effects of grace are felt.[4]

(4) So come now, if you don't mind, let us take up the thread of what we said the other day[5] and see where we closed the sermon and at what point we ought resume it today. Where, then, did we break our sermon and conclude our in-

4. This passage expresses in striking form Chrysostom's thinking on Scripture and his role as scriptural commentator; the simile of the emperor's letters is akin to that in Homily 2, of Moses delivering letters from God. He sees himself speaking under divine inspiration (some manuscripts employ in place of "guided" the word Chrysostom normally uses for "inspired," *enē-choumenos*, as applied to biblical authors): when he speaks, it is the Spirit speaking. He is commissioned to "pass on" what comes from the Lord, for the salvation of his listeners and the building up of the Church—all arising from God's loving kindness.

5. If *proēn* is to be taken to mean, as often, "the day before yesterday," we can understand how the sermon on the Samaritan woman intervened.

struction? We outlined to you the story of Lot [407] and the burning of Sodom, and we stopped our sermon at the point where the just man arrived safely at Segor. "The sun came out on the earth," the text said, remember, "and Lot entered Segor,"[6] and then that divinely inspired rage fell upon Sodom, causing the destruction of the earth; the just man's wife forgot the words of the angels, looked back, and was turned into a pillar of salt, providing later generations with an everlasting reminder of her indifference.

(5) Today, therefore, it is necessary to press on to the sequel and say something briefly so that once again you may realize the compassion and affection of the patriarch and God's favor towards him. At sunrise, remember, the good man Lot arrived safely at Segor whereas the inhabitants of Sodom met their just desserts; the patriarch both pitied them for the destruction they suffered on account of their own lawlessness and at the same time was very anxious about the good man, and so he rose early, the text says, to find out what had happened. "Abraham rose early in the morning," the text says, remember, "and went to the place where he had stood before God; he looked in the direction of the district of Sodom and Gomorrah, and, lo and behold, he saw flame rising up from the earth like steam from an oven."[7] Reaching that place, the text says, where he had held conversation with the Lord and made intercession for the Sodomites, he saw the traces of that fearful punishment and was anxious to find news of the good man. This, after all, is the way with holy people: to be caring and compassionate.

(6) To teach us that the grace of the Spirit imparted to him knowledge about him so as to relieve him of his anxiety about Lot at the same time, Sacred Scripture says, "When the Lord wiped out the cities of the district, God was mindful of Abraham and dispatched Lot from the midst of the destruction."[8] What is the meaning of "God was mindful of Abraham"? Of the petition he made, it means, in saying, "'Surely you won't

6. Gen 19.23.
7. Gen 19.27–28, briefer than the Hebrew or LXX.
8. Gen 19.29.

destroy the good along with the impious?' "⁹ So why, someone may ask, was the just man saved because of the patriarch's petition and not because of his own goodness? True, it was also because of the patriarch's petition; after all, when we do what lies in us, the intercession of the just also brings us the greatest benefit. If we are indifferent ourselves while placing the hope of our salvation in them alone, it is of no further benefit to us—not because the just are powerless but because we undermine them through our own indifference.

(7) For proof that whenever we are negligent, even if those interceding for us are just or even prophets, no benefit comes to us from it (they give evidence of their own virtue by those actions, you see, whereas no advantage will come to us from our behavior), listen to the God of all speaking to the prophet Jeremiah, who was sanctified in the womb: "Do not pray for this people, because I will not heed you."¹⁰ See the Lord's loving kindness: he makes the prediction to the prophet lest, when ignored after interceding, he should think it happened through fault of his. Hence he foretells the people's wickedness to him and bids him not to pray so that he too may be in a position to realize the extremity of their evil behavior and they may learn that the prophet is of no advantage to them if they themselves are not prepared to do what lies in them.

(8) Mindful of this, [408] dearly beloved, let us have recourse to the intercession of the saints and call on them to intercede for us, but let us not only have confidence in their prayers but let us also manage our affairs properly and undergo a change for the better so as to provide grounds for the intercession made on our behalf. This is what the Lord of all said to another prophet as well: "Don't you see what they are up to? They are heating fat and making offerings to the heavenly host,"¹¹ as if to say to him, Do you intercede for them with me even though they have not ceased their evil-

9. Gen 18.22.　　　　10. Jer 7.16, abbreviated.
11. Jer 7.17–18 abbreviated. De Montfaucon is quick to observe that Chrysostom is quoting not another but the same prophet, Jeremiah; it is also the same passage as before.

doing and have no sense of the ailment afflicting them but rather act as though they had nothing wrong with them? Don't you see their utter arrogance? Have you no eye for their extreme folly? How could they ever fail to have their fill of impiety, but instead, like a pig in the mire, wallow in their own transgressions? After all, surely if they were prepared to be converted they would not put off all appeals? Am I not the one who cries aloud through the prophets, "And I said after her profligacy, 'After this, return to me,' but she did not return"?[12]

(9) I mean, surely I seek nothing else than a mere cessation of their wickedness and a stop to their evil? Surely I look for no accounting of past deeds if I see them willing to change? Do I not cry aloud each day, "Surely I have no real wish for the death of the sinner as for his conversion and life"?[13] Do I not take every means to snatch from destruction those ensnared in deceit? Surely, after all, if I see them changing, I will not hesitate? Am I not the one who says, "While you are still speaking I will say, 'Lo, I am here'"?[14] Surely they themselves are not so anxious for their own salvation as all peoples being saved and coming to the knowledge of truth is an object of concern to me?[15] Surely I don't bring you from non-being for the purpose of destroying you? It is not in vain that I prepared the kingdom and the countless good things beyond description, was it? Did I not also make the threat of hell for the purpose of encouraging everyone by this means also to hasten towards the kingdom?

(10) Accordingly, O blessed prophet, do not exclude those people in addressing your petition to me; instead, let this be your one concern, to have their ailment cured, to bring them to a sense of their wickedness and lead them to health, and then my blessings will follow in every way. You see, I do not hesitate, I do not delay when I see a soul that is well disposed: I look for one thing alone, confession of sins, and no longer do I press charges on the sinners. Surely, after all, what is

12. Jer 3.7. 13. Ezek 18.23.
14. Is 58.9. 15. Cf. 1 Tim 2.4.

proposed by me is not heavy and burdensome, is it? If I did not know that they would become worse by not confessing their former sins, I would not even look for that. But as I know the human race lapses all the more into wickedness, I wish them to confess their former sins for this reason, that confession may prove an obstacle to their falling into the same sins.

(11) Taking all this into account, therefore, dearly beloved, and considering our Lord's loving kindness, let us not be negligent but first take great care of ourselves, cleanse the stain of our sins and thus hasten to take advantage of the intercession of the saints. You see, provided we are prepared to be vigilant and alert, even by our own appeals we will obtain the greatest benefit. After all, since our Lord is loving, he does not accede to requests on our behalf by others as readily as he does to our own. See the extraordinary degree of his goodness: [409] if he sees us giving offence, suffering dishonor, having no confidence, and then gradually rising from our depression and wishing to have recourse to the riches of his loving kindness, he immediately accedes to our requests, extends his hand to us in our abjection and raises us where we have fallen, crying aloud, "Surely the fallen will not fail to rise?"[16]

(12) For you to learn, however, even from experience that many people succeed in attaining what they seek by making entreaty on their own rather than by means of others, it is necessary to parade before you those who have so attained in order that we may emulate them and be prompted to imitation. Accordingly, let us hear how that Canaanite woman, foreigner though she was and sorrowful in spirit, when she saw the physician of souls and the Sun of justice arising on those sitting in darkness, made her approach with ardent and lively enthusiasm, not made more reluctant by her being a woman or a foreigner; rather, overcoming all obstacles she came forward and said, "Have pity on me, Lord, my daughter is sorely

16. Jer 8.4.

abused by a demon."[17] But he who understands the unspoken thoughts of the mind kept silence and did not reply, not sparing her a word nor showing pity for the woman on seeing her approach with such lamentation; instead, he put her off, wishing to make the treasure lying unnoticed in the woman obvious to everyone. You see, he recognized the hidden pearl that he did not want to escape us; his purpose in putting her off and not deigning to reply to her was that the woman's earnest intercession should prove a lesson for everyone in future.

(13) See God's ineffable goodness: whereas he did not reply, the text says, the disciples were inclined to be more compassionate and kind but did not dare to say openly, Grant her request, have mercy on her, take pity on her. Instead, what did they say? "Have done with her, she's calling out after us,"[18] as if to say, Free us from this nuisance, spare us the noise made by her. So what did the Lord do? Do you think there was no reason why I have kept silence, he said, and didn't grant her a reply? Listen: "I was sent only to the lost sheep of the house in Israel."[19] Don't you know, he says, that the woman is a foreigner? Don't you know that I have already bidden you not to take the gentile road? So why do you heedlessly make a display of compassion? Consider God's inventive wisdom in that, although he had decided to reply, he dealt with the woman more severely than by his silence, delivering, as it were, a final blow in his wish to provoke her gradually so that the disciples, who were unaware of the faith concealed within her, might come to realize it.

(14) She, on the contrary, did not lose heart or become less persistent through seeing that the disciples achieved nothing further, nor did she say to herself, If not even they have succeeded in the appeal that they have been making on my behalf, why should I make an idle and vain entreaty? Instead, as though set alight by fire, with mind ablaze and heart in

17. Matt 15.22. Chrysostom had adduced the example of the Canaanite woman also in Homily 38.
18. Matt 15.23.   19. Matt 15.24.

anguish, she falls at his feet and pleads, "Lord, help me."[20]
He still does not yield to the woman, but makes a severer
reply than before. "It is not proper to take the children's
bread and throw it to the dogs."[21] Consider, dearly beloved,
the remarkable desire of her soul in this case and her extraordinary faith: when she heard the word "dogs," far from being
distressed or retiring, she replied with great respect, [410]
"True, Lord; even the dogs eat scraps from their masters'
table."[22] I admit, she says, being a dog; so, as a dog grant me
to be worthy of scraps from the table. Do you see the woman's
faith and sincerity? She accepted his word, and immediately
attained the object of her efforts, and attained it with lavish
praise.

(15) What, in fact, did Christ say? "O woman, great is your
faith: let it be done to you as you wish."[23] "O woman"—wonderful word, a remark redolent of warm commendation. You
have given evidence of great faith, he says; consequently the
things you want will come your way. See the lavishness of his
generosity and the Lord's remarkable wisdom. Did we not
think at the outset that he was rather lacking in compassion
to repel her in that way and at first grant her not even a reply,
but later through his first reply and the second one more or
less rebuffing her and scaring away the woman approaching
him with such ardent desire? From the conclusion, however,
recognize God's goodness in employing such tardiness for the
reason of his wish to render her more conspicuous. I mean,
if he had acceded immediately, we would have been ignorant
of the woman's virtue; but when he put her off we could
understand his ineffable love and the extraordinary degree
of her faith.

(16) Now, we were obliged to bring all this story to your
notice so that we might learn that we get our way in prayer,
not so much by means of others as on our own, when we
make our petition with ardor and mind alert. Though she
had the disciples interceding for her, notice, she succeeded in

20. Matt 15.25.   21. Matt 15.26.
22. Matt 15.27.   23. Matt 15.28.

gaining nothing until she persisted on her own account and so won over the Lord's loving kindness. And that parable of the friend coming to the house at dead of night suggests the same thing. "Even if he will not respond to him on account of being his friend," remember, "at least because of his importunity he will get up and give him what he asks."[24] So knowing our Lord's unspeakable love let us approach him, revealing and, as it were, placing before our eyes our sins in all their various kinds, and beg pardon for those in the past so that by showing great care in the future we may win greater favor from him.

(17) If you don't mind, however, let us pick up the thread of the reading.[25] "Now, Lot went up to Segor and settled in the hill country with his two daughters, as they were afraid to live in Segor. He dwelt in a cave with his two daughters."[26] Still, having a lively fear of the punishment inflicted on Sodom, the just man traveled far and settled in the hill country with his daughters, the text says, and so it happened that he was dwelling in extreme isolation and solitude with his two daughters in the hill country. "Now, the elder said to the younger," the text goes on, "'Our father is rather old, and there is no one in the land who will come to us as is customary in all the land. Come, let us ply our father with wine and sleep with him, and let us raise up seed of our father.'"[27]

(18) Let us listen, dearly beloved, with caution and great fear to the contents of the divine Scriptures: there is nothing written there idly and to no purpose; instead, everything is said carefully and to our advantage, even if we don't understand parts of it. You see, we can't understand everything precisely; on the contrary, even if we try to assign causes [411] for some things to the extent possible to us, yet it still holds within it some treasure that is hidden and difficult to

24. Luke 11.8.
25. It has been, by any standards, a lengthy digression to establish the point that, valuable though intercession on the part of others is, one's own prayer and virtuous behavior is indispensable. One wonders how a preacher could think all this a relevant expansion of "God was mindful of Abraham"—unless some other purpose was served.
26. Gen 19.30.   27. Gen 19.31–32.

interpret.[28] So consider how Scripture narrated everything
clearly and made known to us the intent of the just man's
daughters, in one place making an adequate excuse for them,
in another for the just man, lest anyone should have regard
only to what took place and condemn either the good man or
his daughters on the score of the licentiousness of this union.

(19) The text says, "The older said to the younger, 'Our
father is rather old, and there is no one in the land who will
come to us as is customary in all the land.'" Scrutinize their
intent, and acquit them of any crime: they thought that total
destruction had taken place and no one was still left alive;
then they also saw their father's old age. So, in case the race
should disappear, the text says, and we should be left without
descendants (this, you see, was of particular concern to the
ancients, that their line should continue through succession
of offspring)—so in case we too should have to suffer complete annihilation as our father slips into old age and there is
no man to be found whom we can get to mate with us and
leave a succession of progeny, "'Come,'" she said, to avoid
this "'let us ply our father with wine.'" Since our father
would never have brought himself to countenance even a
word of this, let us put the stratagem into effect by means of
wine. "They plied their father with wine that night, and the
elder sister went in and slept with her father; he was unaware
of her sleeping with him or getting up."[29]

(20) Do you see how Sacred Scripture made excuses for the
just man not once but twice? I mean, firstly from what the
daughters did in practicing deceit with the aid of wine it
showed that they would otherwise have been unable to convince their father to be part of it, whereas in this latter case
I think what happened later took place because of design
from on high so that he was so far oblivious of it as to be

28. This is a fair statement of Chrysostom's hermeneutical stance, based
on his limited exegetical skills. For him, lacking critical awareness of the
complexity of the formation of the patriarchal narratives, rationalizing was
a much invoked rule of thumb, but, as he admits here, rationalizing can take
the commentator only so far.
29. Gen 19.33.

completely unaware and so proved to be guiltless of sin. You see, those sins utterly condemn us which we commit knowingly and willingly. On the contrary, do you see Scripture giving testimony to the just man that he was completely unaware of what happened? Still another question, however, arises in the case of intoxication. What I mean is that everything should be carefully studied so that no occasion should be left to those of bad will and no sense of shame. So what should we say about it? That the instance of drunkenness befell him not so much from incontinence as from depression.

(21) Accordingly, let no one ever presume to condemn the just man or his daughters. After all, how could it be other than a mark of extreme folly and stupidity on our part, laden as we are with such countless burdens of sin, to condemn those whom Sacred Scripture discharges of all sin and for whom it rather even supplies such a remarkable defense, instead of heeding the words of Paul, "With God as your champion, who can condemn you?"[30] For you to learn that it was not idly or to no purpose that this happened but rather that his excessive depression allowed him to have no sense of being plied with wine, listen to what it goes on to say. "Now, it happened that next day the elder daughter said to the younger, 'Lo, last night I slept with our father; so let us ply him [412] with wine tonight as well, and you go in and sleep with him, and let us raise up seed of our father.'"[31] Do you see how they did this from a right attitude?[32] I mean, she is saying, I was able to achieve the object of my desires, and you ought to do the same thing; after all, perhaps our hopes will come to be realized and our line will not go into oblivion.

(22) "They plied their father with wine that night, too, and the younger daughter went in and slept with her father; he

---

30. Rom 8.33–34.   31. Gen 19.34.

32. Chrysostom's defense of these two women runs counter to his usual pattern, and is all the more surprising considering the conduct involved. It is therefore ironical that this departure from practice on Chrysostom's part runs counter to modern critical comment on the significance of the Hebrew narrative, such as Von Rad's, "Without doubt the narrative now contains indirectly a severe judgment on the incest in Lot's house" (*Genesis*, p. 224).

was unaware of her sleeping with him or getting up."[33] Consider, dearly beloved, that the whole exploit was conducted by God's design as with the first formed human being: as in that case, while he was asleep God allowed him to have no sensation while he took a part of his rib, shaped that rib into a woman and presented her to Adam. Exactly the same thing happened here: if the removal of the rib happened without causing pain after God put him into a trance, much more so did that happen here. What Sacred Scripture said there, "He caused a drowsiness to come upon Adam and he fell asleep,"[34] it also indicated here by saying, "He was unaware of her sleeping with him or getting up. They both conceived children of their father," the text goes on. "The elder daughter bore a son, and called him Moab, meaning, of my father; he is the ancestor of the Moabites. The younger daughter also bore a son, and called him Amman, meaning, son of my race; he is the ancestor of the Ammanites."[35]

(23) Do you see how the exploit did not arise from incontinence for the reason that they immediately gave names to the children to commemorate the event and made a record of the exploit by the names of the children, as if by some commemorative column, so as to foretell that peoples would descend from them and the race of their offspring would develop into a huge number. One would, in fact, be the ancestor of the Moabites, Scripture says; the other, ancestor of the Ammanites. Now, in those times, since it was at the very origin of things and people wanted to leave a memorial of themselves through the continuation of the race, the just man's daughters demonstrated such anxiety in that regard. Today, on the contrary, since through the grace of God the practice of religion has spread and, according to blessed Paul, "the form of this world is now passing away,"[36] let us leave a memorial of ourselves through the practice of good works so that after our passing from here the propriety of our perfect lifestyle will prove a reminder and instruction to those reflect-

33. Gen 19.35.
35. Gen 19.36–38.
34. Gen 2.21.
36. 1 Cor 7.31.

ing on us. People who are virtuous and live a life of continence, you see, can be of greatest benefit to those who
observe them, not simply while they happen to be in this life,
but even after passing from this life.

(24) For proof of this, consider, I ask you, what a great
number of years has passed till today and how frequently we
would have wished to encourage some people to emulation of
this continence. We have brought to your attention Joseph,
that fine, comely young man in the very prime of life, giving
evidence of such fortitude in the cause of continence, and in
this way we have been anxious to stir the listeners to imitation
of the just man. After all, tell me, who could adequately marvel at this blessed man for the fact that, despite his finding
himself enslaved and being in the bloom of youth, a time
when the fire of passion is more ardently enkindled, he saw
his mistress frantic to get her hands on him and yet gave
evidence of such fortitude and so prepared himself for the
contest chastity involves, that, though bereft of garments in
fleeing [413] from that willful woman, he was nevertheless
clad in the vesture of continence? We can see in this a novel
and surprising example of a sheep falling into the clutches of
a wolf, or rather, of a lioness, and succeeding in being saved;
like a dove fleeing from attack by a hawk, so the good man
escapes that woman's clutches.

(25) In my view, not so remarkable was the case of those
three children who in the middle of that awful Babylonian
furnace remained safe from the fire, and whose bodies came
to no further harm, compared with the remarkable and surprising example of this just man falling into this furnace
more lethal than the Babylonian one—I mean the Egyptian
woman's incontinence—and remaining unharmed and emerging from it with the vesture of continence preserved un-
stained. Do you see how virtuous people prove an occasion
of benefit to us, both while present here on earth and after
passing from here? The reason, you see, that we drew this
just man to your attention at this time was that we might all
follow his example.

(26) Accordingly, let us all imitate him, prove superior to

pleasures, and in the knowledge "that our struggle is not with flesh and blood but with the powers, authorities, and rulers of the darkness of this age,"[37] let us so arm ourselves; mindful that we, who are clad in a body, are forced to do battle with incorporeal powers, let us bring to our defense the weapons of the Spirit. You see, since we in our fleshly condition have to do battle with the invisible powers, the loving Lord provided us also with invisible weapons for this purpose that we might prevail over the enemies of our nature through the power of these weapons. Trusting, then, in the power of these weapons let us contribute what lies within us, and under the protection of this spiritual armor we will manage to strike the very eyes of the devil. In fact, he cannot bear the light flashing from that source, but even if he tries to confront it his eyes will be immediately blinded. You see, whenever there is self-control, sobriety and a numerous concert of virtues, there, also, the grace of the Spirit wings its way in generous measure. Hence, Paul too said, "Make peace with everyone your object, as also your own sanctification."[38] So let us purify our conscience, I beseech you, and cleanse our thinking, so that, free from all uncleanness of mind, we may win the grace of the Spirit, prevail over the devil's wiles, and be found worthy of those ineffable blessings. May it be the good fortune of us all to enjoy them, thanks to the grace and loving kindness of our Lord Jesus Christ, to whom with the Father and the Holy Spirit be the glory, now and forever, for ages of ages. Amen.

37. Eph 6.12.   38. Heb 12.14.

HOMILY 45

*"Abraham moved from there to the southern land, and dwelt between
Kadesh and Sour, sojourning at Gerar."*[1]

 AM PLEASED [413] to see you hurrying to listen and
receiving our instruction with great relish. For this
reason I for my part make it my concern to set before
you this meager table, the little I have to offer, with greater
enthusiasm each day. [414] Your keen appetite disguises the
meager quality of the meal and makes the scraps appear lavish. You can observe this in the case of material food, too:
when someone has guests that are already satiated, even if
food of great variety and large amount is offered, the condition of the guests undercuts the richness of the food, and
wonderful dishes seem worthy of no consideration for the
reason that the guests set to without relish. Likewise when
one invites to supper guests that are hungry and have an
appetite, even if he lays a meager table it seems abundant
owing to the anticipation of the guests who fall upon the
dishes with great relish. In just the same way we too have
confidence in your spiritual appetite and do not hang back,
even if we have a poor and meager table, before laying it in
customary manner before your good selves. This is what a
certain sage also remarked: "Better a meal of vegetables with
love than a beast from the manger with enmity,"[2] suggesting
that love has a different view of what is set forth, and to its
eyes ordinary things appear rich and scraps seem generous.

(2) So what better fortune could anyone have than ourselves as we address so many listeners and meet such a warm

1. Gen 20.1.
2. Prov 15.17, where Chrysostom's version approximates more closely
than the LXX to the Hebrew.

and attentive response? The speaker, after all, requires nothing so urgently as approval of the listener. You see, when he sees the lively enthusiasm of the audience, he for his part is buoyed up and gains greater strength, as it were, in the knowledge that the more he spreads this spiritual table, so much the more his own well-being is enhanced. Spiritual things, after all, are opposite to material things; in the latter case generosity at table involves expense and reduces the substance of the host, whereas in the former it is directly opposite, the increase in our prosperity occurring to the extent of the numbers taking part. You see, they are not our words that we are speaking but whatever the grace of God in his characteristic love supplies for your upbuilding.[3] So come now, since you give yourselves to listening with such relish and enthusiasm, let us make a study of the words read by us just now and reap some benefit from them. I mean, since according to the wonderful directive in Christ's words, "Study the Scriptures,"[4] there is great treasure contained in the Scriptures and hidden in their depths, there is need of study for the purpose of discovering the power concealed in their depths so that we may succeed in finding great benefit there.

(3) The reason, in fact, that the grace of the Spirit arranged for the virtues of all good people to be handed down was that we might have a consistent instruction and might order our own life in the direction of zealous imitation of these good people.[5] So let us heed what Sacred Scripture wishes today also to outline to us about the patriarch. "Abraham moved from there to the southern land," the text goes

3. Again Chrysostom's conviction of inspiration, its extent and effects: it is not simply the Scriptures that are inspired but also the scriptural homilist, and the beneficiaries of inspiration are the listeners—all as a result of God's loving kindness.

4. John 5.39, a verse that Chrysostom cites frequently as the motto of the exegetical school of Antioch that, unlike its counterpart at Alexandria, saw the scriptural text not as a point of departure but as a challenge to deeper investigation.

5. For Chrysostom the Bible is a hagiographical text, a moral compendium useful for instructing in good behavior, rather than a dogmatic outline of divine purpose; he does not follow his model, Paul, in finding the mystery of Christ sketched out in its pages.

on, "and dwelt between Kadesh and Sour, sojourning at Gerar." Moved on from where? From the place where he was camped, where he was given the privilege of hosting the Lord of all with the angels.[6] Moving from there, the text says, "he sojourned in Gerar." Notice the life of these good people, how restrained and austere it was, how they shifted place with ease and conducted their life like pilgrims or nomads, pitching their tent at one time in this place, [415] at another in that, as though living in a strange land—unlike us, who live in a strange land as though in our home country, erecting extravagant mansions, porches and covered walks, possessing land, building baths and countless other luxuries.

(4) By contrast see the good man holding all his possessions in his household and flocks alone, and never staying in one place but at one time pitching his tent in Bethel, at another by the oak of Mambre, at another going down to Egypt, and now camping at Gerar, submitting to all this with ease and giving clear evidence in every way of gratitude to his own Lord. Despite such wonderful promises and guarantees given him by God, he saw himself beset by such imposing difficulties and encountering such varied and differing trials; yet he stood unshaken like some piece of steel, showing his godly attitude and proving no less resolute in any of the problems surrounding him. See in the present instance too, dearly beloved, the kind of trial that befell him at Gerar and the wonderful caliber of the just man's virtue, how what everyone else found unbearable and could not bring themselves to accept he put up with without complaint and without demanding from the Lord explanation of what happened, as many people do, even though weighed down with countless burdens of sin. When they encounter some difficulties they become meddlesome and inquisitive, saying, Why has this or that happened? The just man, on the contrary, didn't behave like

6. It is a sound exegetical question Chrysostom puts to the text: he realizes it is not speaking of Lot's location in the previous chapter; yet lacking awareness of the diversity of strands to the narrative he opts for the situation of ch. 18 rather than the preference of modern commentators in seeing the E document of ch. 15 now being resumed.

that; hence he enjoyed greater favor from on high. This, after all, is truly the mark of a dutiful servant, not to pry into reasons for what is done by the master but to accept everything in silence and with deep thanks.

(5) Consider how also through the very trials that ensued the just man's virtue became more resplendent, as God rendered him conspicuous in every way. You see, just as he was a stranger, unknown to anyone when he went down into Egypt, but suddenly returned from there with great notoriety, so in the present instance while sojourning at Gerar he relies on his own resources at the outset but later enjoys such wonderful assistance from God that the king and all the inhabitants of the place go to great pains to attend to the just man. "Now, Abraham said about his wife Sarrah," the text goes on, "'She is my sister.' For he was afraid to say, She is my wife, in case the men of the city should kill him on account of her."[7] See how the just man's spirit is beset with the most violent feelings, and fear overwhelms him. Yet while it is true that his former fear, the fear of losing his wife, was extremely distressing, the fear of death overcame it. For to dispel that fear, he was prepared to see with his own eyes the one who shared his very life fall into the hands of the king. Now, how unbearable this is, those who have wives know. Hence also a sage has said, "Rage comes to a man from jealousy; he will have no mercy on the day of revenge nor will his hatred be appeased by any offering."[8] But see how on account of the fear of death the just man nobly bore this heavy trial so intolerable to everyone.[9]

(6) This is the way things happen with bodily passions: when two of them at the one time affect our body, the intensity of the one cancels out the other so that we are completely preoccupied with its pain and often have [416] no sensation

7. Gen 20.2. The LXX adds the explanatory sentence not found in the Hebrew, perhaps under the influence of the similar incident in Egypt in ch. 12.

8. Prov 6.34–35.

9. Again, as in ch. 12, one wonders if Chrysostom has tongue in cheek in presenting cowardice in the guise of noble fortitude.

of the other, as the stronger pain overwhelms us and does not allow us to feel anything of the lesser one. In just the same way, too, this just man in the present instance saw the fear of death affecting him and considered all other things tolerable. But when you hear this, dearly beloved, don't judge the just man guilty of faintheartedness for fearing death; marvel instead at the surpassing love shown us by the Lord of all in the fact that Christ has now made an object of scorn that death which in those times was dreaded by those good and holy people, and what those virtuous people feared even while having a wonderful confidence in God is now despised by youths and tender maids. It is no longer death, you see, but a dream and departure, a change from a worse life to a better. The death of our Lord, in fact, has granted us freedom from death, and by descending into hell he has broken its bonds and crippled its force; what was fearful and cruel he has rendered so much an object of scorn that some people rush forward in haste to their departure from here. Hence Paul also shouts aloud, "To depart and to be with Christ is far better."[10]

(7) This, however, is the present situation, after the coming of Christ, after the breaking down of the iron doors, after the Sun of Justice has shone throughout the entire world. But in those days death still bore a terrible aspect and shook the resolve of those just men—hence they easily bore all other things, even if these happened to be unbearable. For this reason this just man was also afraid of the plotting of the inhabitants of Gerar, and in making his stay there he introduced Sarrah not as his wife but as his sister. As God allowed him to go down into Egypt in his wish for those unresponsive and unperceptive people to learn the just man's virtue, so in this case, too, the Lord gives evidence of his characteristic forbearance so that the just man's endurance as well may be conspicuous in every way and God's favor in his regard may be obvious to everyone.

(8) "But Abimelech, king of Gerar, sent someone to bring

10. Phil 1.23.

Sarrah to him." Consider, I ask you, the turmoil in his thinking suffered by the just man on seeing his wife being taken
off without being able to help in any way. In fact, he bore
everything in silence, knowing that the Lord was not ignoring
him but would provide prompt assistance. Sarrah's great affection is also to be marveled at in wishing that the good man
be rescued from danger of death; after all, she could have
revealed the subterfuge and escaped the outrage that was
being connived at. Instead, she endured everything in noble
fashion so as to secure the just man's welfare. She fulfilled
that prediction, "The two will become one flesh."[11] In other
words, being one flesh they cared for each other's welfare and
gave evidence of such harmony as to be one body and one
soul.

(9) Let husbands heed this, let wives heed it: wives, so as
to give evidence of such great affection for their husbands,
and put nothing ahead of their own welfare; and husbands,
that they might show their wives great regard and do everything as though having one soul and being one body. This,
after all, is true wedlock, when such harmony operates between them, when there is such close relationship, when they
are bound together in such love. You see, just as a body would
never be at odds with itself nor a soul at odds with itself, so
husband and wife should not [417] be at odds but united.
Then also, in fact, countless blessings will be able to overflow
for them. I mean, where there is such harmony, there is a
concert of all blessings, there is peace, there is love, there is
spiritual joy; no war, no fighting, no hostility or hatred—instead, all these are absent, all these are removed by the root
of those blessings, namely, harmony.

(10) "But Abimelech, king of Gerar, sent someone to bring
Sarrah to him. God came to Abimelech in a dream by night
and said, 'Lo, you are going to die on account of the woman
you have taken; she is a married woman.'"[12] See God's loving
kindness: when he saw the just man through fear of death
nobly bearing Sarrah's removal and the king thus regarding

11. Gen 2.24.   12. Gen 20.2–3.

her as the good man's sister, then he gives evidence of his characteristic providence in rendering the good man more conspicuous, freeing Sarrah from outrage and preventing the king's crime. "God came to Abimelech in a dream by night." Wishing to forestall his lawlessness he brought realization to his mind at that time, the time of dreaming, the text says, shed light on what had escaped his notice, and instilled into him a deep fear by threatening him with death. "'You are going to die,'" the text says, remember, "'on account of the woman you have taken; she is a married woman.' Now, Abimelech had not laid a hand on her."

(11) Now, all this happened so that God's promise to the patriarch might take effect. You see, a little earlier he had promised him the birth of Isaac, and now the time was near; so in case there should be any threat to the promise he instilled such fear into Abimelech that he was too frightened to dare to lay a hand on Sarrah. This is the reason, in fact, that Sacred Scripture added, "Abimelech had not laid a hand on her"; instead, he apologized for his rashness and said, "Will you destroy an innocent people for what they did not know?'"[13] I didn't do this, he is saying, in the knowledge that she was his wife, did I? I mean, I didn't intend to wrong the foreigner, did I? It was as his sister that I was about to take her and I did what I did, thinking that he would also be honored in her. So "'will you destroy an innocent people for what they did not know?'" Are you going to destroy me, he says, for having acted in good faith?

(12) Then, to make clearer what he said, he added, "'Was it not he that said to me, She is my sister, and did she not say to me, He is my brother?'"[14] Consider how they enjoyed harmony and consensus: he said this to me, he explained, and she agreed with what was said by him. "'I acted in good faith and with clean hands,'" he said, not as though on the point of committing some crime; rather, I did something sanctioned by law and in keeping with it, without any blame. So what was the response of the loving Lord? "But God spoke

13. Gen 20.4.   14. Gen 20.5.

to him in a dream."[15] See how much considerateness the Lord of all employs in giving evidence of his characteristic goodness in every way. "'I knew that you acted in good faith.'" I realize, he is saying, that they themselves brought on this situation and that you acted under a false impression created by what they said; in case you should sin as a result of their deceit, "'I prevented you from sinning against me.'"

(13) Wonderful the considerateness of the expression, extraordinary the Lord's loving kindness. The sin would have been directed against me, he says. You see, just as with human beings, when someone delivers an insult to one of the servants who enjoys [418] his master's great regard, the master takes the insult as done to himself and says, You committed an outrage against me by this ill treatment meted out to my servant, so in the same way the good Lord too said, "'I prevented you from sinning against me.'" They are in fact my servants, he says, and I take good care of them in this way by treating what is done to them as done to myself, be it good or ill. "'For this reason I didn't allow you to lay a hand on her.'" Since I care greatly for them, and I was aware that it was in ignorance that you were about to commit this outrage on them, I prevented you from sinning against me.'" Don't just pay attention to this man as any one of a number, but come to understand that he is one of those dear to my heart and particularly close to me.

(14) "'So restore the man's wife to him, because he is a prophet; he will pray for you, and you will live.'"[16] See how he reveals the good man's virtue; he calls him a prophet as though to make the king his suppliant: "'He will pray for you, and you will live,'" the text says. In other words, fearful of death at your hands, he planned this stratagem and more or less connived at the outrage against Sarrah; on the other hand, realize that his prayers will win you your life.

(15) Then, in case he should be inflamed with desire and overcome by Sarrah's beauty and should scorn the com-

15. Gen 20.6.
16. Gen 20.7. Chrysostom's LXX text employs *anthrōpos* as "man" in association with *gunē*, "woman," "wife," as correlatives.

mands, he aggravated his fear by promising to inflict worse
punishment. "'If in fact you do not restore her, realize that
death will come upon you and all that is yours,'" the text goes
on. Not only will you personally be punished for your disobedience, he is saying, but as well death will carry off on your
account all that is yours. Now, this was the reason that God
told him all this at night time, so that he might receive the
warning in peace and quiet and carry out the direction with
great fear. "First thing in the morning," the text goes on,
"Abimelech arose, summoned his attendants and reported to
them all these words."[17] See how the king now becomes a
herald of the just man's virtue, bringing him to the notice of
everyone. Summoning all his attendants, the text says, note,
he narrated to them everything revealed to him by God so
that all might know both God's favor towards him and the
providence accorded by the Lord on account of virtuous behavior.

(16) "But all the people were very frightened." Do you see
how it was not idly or to no purpose that the good man had
shifted place? I mean, had he remained at his former en-
campment, how would all the people of Gerar have been able
to realize the degree of favor he enjoyed from God? "But all
the people were very frightened." A great fear fell on them;
they worried about everything. Then "Abimelech summoned
Abraham," the text goes on. Consider, I ask you, the degree
of notoriety with which the just man is now brought into the
presence of the king after being treated a little before as beneath contempt, in the manner of a vagabond and stranger.
When everyone is assembled in haste, the patriarch is summoned, for the time being ignorant of all this, and he then
learns from the king in person what has happened to him on
his account at God's hands. "He said to him," remember,
"'Why did you do this to us? What offense did we give you
to cause you to bring such a great sin on me and my kingdom? You have done to us a deed no one else would do. What
did you have in mind in doing it?'"[18]

17. Gen 20.8.
18. Gen 20.9–10.

(17) What was the reason, he asked, that you wanted to embroil me in such a terrible sin? What on earth did you have in mind in doing it? See how he shows by his own words the threat delivered against him by God. You see, since God had said to him, "'If you do not restore her, death will come upon you and all that is yours,'" [419] Abimelech interprets this very thing in saying, "'What offense did I give you to cause you to bring such a great sin on me and my kingdom?'" I mean, surely the extent of the punishment did not stop at me? My whole kingdom was set to be utterly destroyed through the deception you contrived. "'So what did you have in mind in doing it?'"

(18) Notice at this point, dearly beloved, the just man's noble purpose in presenting them with a lesson in the knowledge of God under the guise of an explanation. "'I said to myself,'" the text goes on, remember, "'Surely there is no respect for God in this place, and they will kill me on account of my wife.'"[19] I was concerned, he is saying, that as a result of being still held in ignorance you would have no regard for justice, and so I made allowance for the fact that when you discovered she was my wife you would, out of lust, have wanted to kill me—that was the reason I did it. See how in a few words he both takes them to task and at the same time teaches them that the person who has God uppermost in mind ought commit no crime, but rather fear that unsleeping eye and in view of the heavy judgment impending from that source have regard for justice.

(19) Then, from a wish to make excuses for himself, he said, Don't think I lied to you in that way; "'She is my sister on my father's side, though not my mother's, and she became my wife all the same.'"[20] She claims the same father as I, he says, and hence I called her my sister. So don't condemn me:

19. Gen 20.11. De Montfaucon gravely condemns Chrysostom at this point for misrepresenting Abraham's view of Abimelech as irreligious whereas the text shows him otherwise. In so doing De Montfaucon seems to have succumbed to the temptation of editor turning textual commentator: it is the "misjudgment" not of Chrysostom but of the Abraham of the text.

20. Gen 20.12.

even if the fear of death brought me to this sorry pass and
the dread of your killing me but sparing her, still what was
said by me was not a lie in the way you imply. See what great
pains the good man takes to show that he had not told a lie
even in this matter. For you to learn everything precisely
from me (he is saying), listen also to the plan we formed between us "'when God led me out from my father's home.'"²¹
Observe in this case, I ask you, the good man's wisdom in
teaching them by way of story telling that from the very beginning he had a special relationship with God, and that God
had personally moved him from home and led him thither
so that the king might learn that he was one of those people
who had great confidence in God.

(20) "'When God led me out from my father's house,'" he
said, "'I said to her, Please do me this kindness: whatever
place we enter, say, He is my brother.'" You see, since he had
said previously, remember, "'I said to myself, Surely there is
no respect for God in this place,'" and decided to take them
severely to task, in his desire to mitigate the severity of his
remarks he then said, Don't think we came to this decision to
do this on your account only. In fact, "'as soon as God led
me out from my father's house I said to her, Please do me
this kindness in whatever place we enter.'" I gave this direction to her, he said, about all the people inhabiting this country; he taught them that the pretense was free from deceit.
It was the fear of death, after all, that drove us to it. With
such words the good man subdued their wrath, revealed his
own virtue and instilled into them adequate instruction in religion. So the king respected the just man's great restraint,
and he rewarded the patriarch with generosity on his part.
"Abimelech took a thousand didrachma," the text goes on,
remember, "sheep and cattle, male and female slaves, and
[420] restored to him his wife Sarrah as well."²²

(21) Do you see, dearly beloved, God's inventive wisdom? I
mean, the man who was fearful of death, and took every

21. Gen 20.13.
22. Gen 20.14. The Hebrew leaves until v. 16 mention of the money.

means to be able to avoid it, not only did avoid it but was granted as well great confidence and became immediately famous. This, you see, is the way things are with God: not only does he deliver from distress those who make every effort to strive boldly against the onset of temptation, but he also guarantees them such serenity in this very distress that we have complete tranquility and achieve great material prosperity. See now the attention of the king to the just man: not only does he show his regard with so many gifts but he also grants him the right to occupy the land. "'Behold,'" he said, "'my land is before you; settle wherever you please.'"[23] You see, once he had learned that it was on his account and through his prayers that his life had been spared, he was anxious now to shower attention in this way on him, as a benefactor and champion, the man who was a stranger, a vagabond, one completely unknown.

(22) The text goes on, "He said to Sarrah, on the other hand, 'Behold, I have given your brother a thousand didrachma.'"[24] See how, having received information from the just man and trusting in his words, he too calls him her brother. "'What I have given your brother,'" he says, "'will restore your reputation; tell the whole truth.'" What is the meaning of "'restore your reputation; tell the whole truth'"? For trying in ignorance to take you, the just man's wife, into my household, for this alone I have given a thousand didrachma for being guilty of offense, and I want to amend what I have done to you. But "'tell the whole truth'"—what is the meaning of "'tell the whole truth'"? Let everyone learn from you, he says, that nothing wrong was done by me, that you emerged untouched from my house. Instruct your husband, he says, that I am guiltless of sin; let him learn from you that nothing was done by me. Now, why did he say this? So that the good man, on learning it from her, might be quite satisfied and so ply the Lord with prayers on his behalf.

23. Gen 20.15.
24. Gen 20.16. The text of the remainder of the verse differs in the Hebrew and LXX, as also in Chrysostom, who struggles (of course) to rationalize it.

(23) In fact, when he said, "'Tell the whole truth,'" that is to say, Instruct your husband as to what happened, Scripture immediately added, "Abraham prayed to God. God gave Abimelech the gift of full health for his wife and maidservants so that they gave birth; he had completely closed every womb in the house of Abimelech on account of Sarrah, Abraham's wife."[25] See how the Lord wishes in every way to render the just man conspicuous, and so he answers the patriarch's prayers by granting him the welfare of the king and all in his house. "Abraham prayed to God," the text says, remember. "God gave Abimelech the gift of full health for his wife and maidservants so that they gave birth; the Lord had completely closed every womb in the house of Abimelech." The reason why the good Lord inflicted this penalty on the king, guiltless though he was of sin, was that he might accede to the just man's prayers and thus resolve the problem, thereby rendering the just man more famous and well known. You see, all his planning and each arrangement he makes have the purpose of rendering conspicuous those who serve him, just like lamps, and making their virtue obvious in every way.

(24) See now, I ask you, dearly beloved, [421] how after his release from trouble the consummation of good things falls to the lot of the just man, the pledge of the promise, and there now takes effect the guarantee made to him in past times. "The Lord had regard for Sarrah," the text goes on, "just as he had promised, and he did the favor for Sarrah that he had said. Sarrah conceived and bore a son to Abraham in his old age at the time the Lord had told him."[26] What is the meaning of "as he had promised" and "as he had said"? Just as he pledged, it means, when he was shown hospitality with the angels at the oak of Mambre, and he said, "'I will come to you at this time, and Sarrah will have a son.'"[27] So this came to pass, and what was beyond hope by natural processes they saw came to be, not by human processes but by

---

25. Gen 20.17–18. The final clause requires a subject, not supplied by Chrysostom at this point; the Hebrew reads "Yahweh," LXX "God," and Chrysostom follows the former at his next quotation of the verse.

26. Gen 21.1–2.   27. Cf. Gen 18.14.

divine grace. "He called the son that Sarrah had borne him Isaac."[28] It was not idly that Scripture mentioned the words, "the son that Sarrah had borne him"; it did not say, "He called his son," but it added, "that Sarrah had borne him," that is, this woman who was sterile, childless, aged. The text goes on, "He circumcised him on the eighth day as the Lord commanded."[29] You see, the command was that newly born children should now be circumcised on the eighth day.

(25) Then, for us to learn at this point God's ineffable power in that things impossible for human beings are possible for him, Sacred Scripture once more mentions the time to us and teaches us in these words after the birth: "Now, Abraham was a hundred when his son Isaac was born to him. Now, Sarrah said, 'The Lord has brought laughter to me: whoever hears it will rejoice with me.'"[30] What is the meaning of "'The Lord has brought laughter to me'"? The birth is a source of joy to me. What is so remarkable about my joy? I will have everyone who hears it rejoicing with me, not because I gave birth but because it was in these circumstances that I gave birth. The unusual character of the birth amazed everyone and gave everyone particular joy on learning that, after being no better than a corpse, I suddenly became a mother, I bore a child from a frozen womb, and was actually able to suckle it and release a flow of milk after having thus far no prospects of childbearing.

(26) "She said, 'Who will let Abraham know that Sarrah is suckling her child?'"[31] You see, the reason that the flow of milk was also granted was to give credence to the birth and to prevent anyone's presuming the child belonged to somebody else;[32] after all, the flow of milk proclaims to all and sundry that the birth surpassed human expectations. "'Who will let Abraham know that Sarrah is suckling a child, that I

28. Gen 21.3.   29. Gen 21.4.
30. Gen 21.5–6. The word plays in the Hebrew text on Isaac's name do not survive into the Greek, and Chrysostom is probably unaware of them, grist though they would be to his mill.
31. Gen 21.7.
32. No detail of the text can be left unaccounted for.

have borne a son in my old age,'" that I have been able to have children despite my old age, and at such a time of life can feed it? "The child grew," the text goes on, "and was weaned. Abraham held a big celebration on the day his son was weaned."[33]

(27) Do you see God's ineffable wisdom in putting to the test the good man's endurance when he and all those who observed him had seemed to have given up hope, guided as they were by human nature, and then bringing to pass his own promise? Let us too, dearly beloved, consequently give evidence of the same endurance as the just man's and, far from ever losing heart, let us be buoyed up with sound hope in the knowledge that neither problems of daily life nor any other human factor proves a real obstacle for us when God's grace intends to give evidence of his characteristic generosity. I mean, whenever he manifests his will, everything yields place [422] and gives way, difficult things become easy and what is impossible proves possible, provided we only give evidence of deep faith in him and prove superior to all human considerations by keeping our gaze fixed on his greatness.

(28) You see, he has promised those future blessings beyond description to those who live out their lives here with virtue, so will he not all the more provide as well the present good things provided we press ahead to those future ones by looking beyond the here and now? We shall in fact enjoy them in generous measure at that time most of all when we are prepared to look beyond them. So with this knowledge let us hanker after those blessings that are enduring and secure and know no end, so that we may live out this present life free from distress and succeed in attaining them. May it be the good fortune of us all to enjoy them, thanks to the grace and loving kindness of our Lord Jesus Christ, to whom with the Father and the Holy Spirit be the glory, now and forever, for ages of ages. Amen.

33. Gen 21.8.